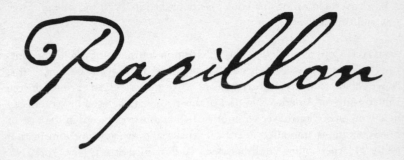

HENRI CHARRIÈRE

WITH AN INTRODUCTION BY
JEAN-PIERRE CASTELNAU

TRANSLATED BY JUNE P. WILSON
AND WALTER B. MICHAELS

Perennial
An Imprint of HarperCollinsPublishers

PAPILLON. Copyright © 1970 for U.S. edition translation by William Morrow and Company. French edition published by Robert Laffont, Paris, copyright © 1969 by Robert Laffont. All rights reserved. Printed in the United States of America. No part of this book may be used or reproduced in any manner whatsoever without written permission except in the case of brief quotations embodied in critical articles and reviews. For information address HarperCollins Publishers Inc., 10 East 53rd Street, New York, NY 10022.

HarperCollins books may be purchased for educational, business, or sales promotional use. For information please write: Special Markets Department, HarperCollins Publishers Inc., 10 East 53rd Street, New York, NY 10022.

First Perennial edition published 2001.

Designed by The Book Design Group

Library of Congress Cataloging-in-Publication Data
Charrière, Henri.
    [Papillon. English]
    Papillon / Henri Charrière ; with an introduction by Jean-Pierre Castelnau ; translated by June P. Wilson and Walter B. Michaels. — 1st Perennial ed.
        p. cm.
    Originally published: New York: W. Morrow, 1970.
    ISBN 0-06-093479-4
    1. Charrière, Henri, 1906–1973. 2. Prisoners—French Guiana—Biography. I. Title.

HV8956.G8 C513 2001
356'.6'092—dc21
[B]

2001016751

03 04 05 WB/RRD 10 9 8 7 6 5

To the Venezuelan people,
to the humble fishermen in the Gulf of Paria,
to everybody—the intellectuals, the military
and all the others—who gave me the chance
to live again,

and to Rita, my wife and dearest friend.

GLOSSARY

Bagnard: A convict serving out his sentence in a *bagne*.

Bagne: A penal colony, from the Italian *bagno* because Italian convicts were kept in cellars below sea level. When sails superseded galleys, convicts were given other forms of hard labor instead. Starting in 1854, all French convicts were deported to French Guiana. The penal colonies were suppressed during World War II. All prison sentences are now served in metropolitan France.

Camelote: Junk or shoddy goods, from the old French *coesmelot*, meaning a dealer in odds and ends.

Cavale: From *cavaler*, to beat it, or scram, especially from the police. Derived from the Latin *cabalus*, meaning horse. First used by Victor Hugo.

Gourbi: An Arabic word for primitive shelter. In military usage, a temporary shelter for soldiers in the trenches, dating from

1841. Now used to describe any kind of abode from a hole-in-the-wall to an apartment.

Libéré: A liberated convict serving out his *doublage* (the supplementary sentence, equal in length to his *bagne* sentence, which the convict had to serve in French Guiana before he could move on).

Mec: Originally meaning *pimp,* it has been rubbed down to signify *man, guy, pal, buddy* and the like (except among the "better class" of Frenchmen).

Plan: A metal cylinder for holding money which the convict carries in his lower intestine to safeguard it from frisking or theft. Probably from *plan* as in *plan d'évasion,* meaning plan of escape. By inference, the basic ingredients needed to realize such a plan.

Relégué: A chronic repeater of petty crimes, i.e., a small-time criminal.

INTRODUCTION

THIS BOOK WOULD PROBABLY NEVER have been written if, in July 1967—one year after the earthquake there—a young man of sixty had not read about Albertine Sarrazin in the Caracas newspapers. This small black diamond of a woman who had been all sparkle, laughter and courage, had just died. She was known all over the world for three books she had written in just over a year, two of them about her *cavales* and her life in prison.

The man's name was Henri Charrière and he had come a long way. From the *bagne* in Cayenne, to be precise, where he'd been sent in 1933. He had lived outside the law, to be sure, but he had been sentenced to life imprisonment for a murder he hadn't committed.

Henri Charrière—called Papillon in the underworld—was born to a family of teachers in Ardèche in 1906. French by birth, he is now Venezuelan. For the people of Venezuela chose to be impressed by his manner and his word rather than by his criminal record, and judged that the thirteen years he had spent struggling to escape from the horrors of the *bagne* were more eloquent of his future than of his past.

In July 1967, Charrière went to the French bookshop in Caracas and bought *L'Astragale*. Until then it had never occurred to him to write a line about his own adventures. He was a man of action who loved life. He had great warmth, a sharp eye and the rich and somewhat gravelly voice of a man from the Midi. You can listen to him for hours because he tells stories like—well, like all the great storytellers. Thus the miracle happened: following the example of Albertine Sarrazin, with no contacts and free of any literary ambition (in his letter to me he said, "Here are my adventures: have a professional write them up"), he wrote the way you tell a story. You see him, you feel him, you live his life, and if it's your bad luck to have to stop at the bottom of a page just when he's telling you that he's about to go to the toilets (a place that has a multiple and important function in the *bagne*), you find yourself forced to turn the page because it's no longer Charrière who is going there, but you yourself.

Three days after he had finished reading *L'Astragale,* he wrote at one sitting the first two sections in a student's spiral notebook. He stopped long enough to get some advice about this new adventure—probably more astonishing to him than all the others that had come before; then at the start of 1968 launched into the rest. In two months he had finished all thirteen notebooks.

As with Albertine, his manuscript arrived by mail, in September. Charrière was in Paris three weeks later. I had published Albertine with Jean-Jacques Pauvert, and that is why Charrière entrusted his book to me.

The book was written in the white heat of recollection, then typed by enthusiastic amateurs not too familiar with French, but I altered virtually nothing. I corrected the punctuation here and there, amended a few Spanishisms that were too obscure, and corrected some confusions of meaning and an occasional inversion that stemmed from the fact that the everyday language of Caracas comprises three or four dialects that can only be learned by ear.

As for its authenticity, I can vouch for it. Obviously, after thirty years, some of the details had become blurred and modified by memory. As for the background facts, you need only read Professor Devèze's book entitled *Cayenne* (Juilliard's Collected Archives, 1965) to be convinced that Charrière did not exaggerate either the way of life in the *bagne* or its horror. Quite the opposite.

As a matter of principle, we changed the names of all the *bagnards,* guards and wardens in the penal colonies. The purpose of the book was not to attack individuals but to describe particular types in a particular society. The same holds true for dates: some are precise, others approximate. That seemed enough. It was not Charrière's intention to write a history but to tell a story as he had lived it, to the full, with no holds barred and with complete faith in himself. The result is the extraordinary epic of a man who would not accept the disparity between society's understandable need to protect itself from its criminals, and a system of repression unworthy of a civilized nation.*

JEAN-PIERRE CASTELNAU

---

* I wrote this introduction in May 1969. The book was published in France in June of that same year. By April of 1970 it had sold one million copies there. As is perhaps inevitable when a writer has sold so phenomenally and has been so lionized as M. Charrière, the authenticity of his work has recently been questioned in some quarters. On March 17, 1970, a press conference was held in Paris by Editions Laffont and the author for the purpose of answering such charges. Charrière reaffirmed, allowing for lapses of memory in some instances as to dates and minor facts, that the book was as accurate and true as he could make it. After all, as he said, he did not go into "that hell" with a typewriter.

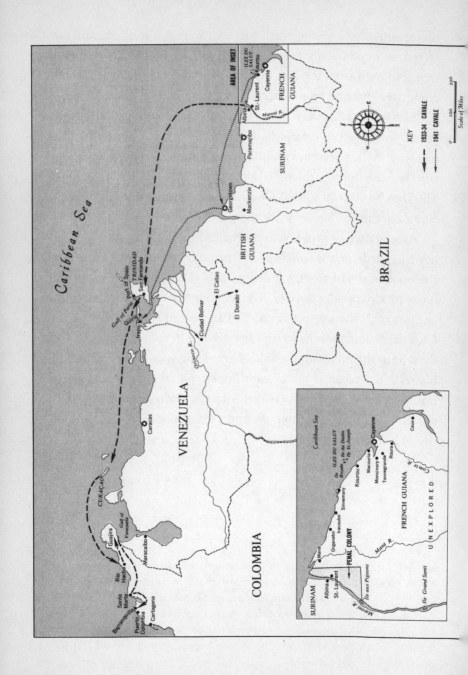

Caribbean Sea

COLOMBIA

Cartagena
Puerto
Colombia
Barranquilla
Santa Marta
Río Hacha
Maracaibo
Guajira
Gulf of
Venezuela

CURAÇAO

VENEZUELA

Caracas

Orinoco R.

Gulf of Paria
Güiria
Irapa
San Fernando
Port of Spain
TRINIDAD

Ciudad Bolívar
El Callao
El Dorado

BRITISH
GUIANA

Georgetown
Mackenzie

Paramaribo

SURINAM

Albina
St-Laurent
Maroni R.

ÎLES DU
SALUT
Kourou
Cayenne
FRENCH
GUIANA

AREA OF INSET

BRAZIL

KEY
1933-34 CAVALE
1941 CAVALE

Scale of Miles
0   100   200

Caribbean Sea

SURINAM

Maroni R.
St-Laurent
Albina
Mana
Organabo
Iracoubo
PENAL COLONY
Île aux Pigeons
Or Île Grand Santi

Mana R.

Île ÎLES DU SALUT
Royale Île du Diable
Île St-Joseph
Sinnemary
Kourou
Macouria
Monsinery
Tonnegrande
Roura

Cayenne

Cau

FRENCH GUIANA

Comté R.

UNEXPLORED

Papillon

FIRST NOTEBOOK

THE DESCENT
INTO HELL

THE ASSIZES

IT WAS A KNOCKOUT BLOW—a punch so overwhelming that I didn't get back on my feet for fourteen years. And to deliver a blow like that, they went to a lot of trouble.

It was the twenty-sixth of October, 1931. At eight o'clock in the morning they let me out of the cell I'd been occupying in the Conciergerie for a year. I was freshly shaved and carefully dressed. My suit was from a good tailor and gave me an air of elegance. A white shirt and pale-blue bow tie added the final touches.

I was twenty-five but looked twenty. The police were a little awed by my gentlemanly appearance and treated me with courtesy. They had even taken off my handcuffs. All six of us, the five policemen and I, were seated on two benches in a bare anteroom of the Palais de Justice de la Seine in Paris. The doors facing us led to the courtroom. Outside the weather was gray.

I was about to be tried for murder. My lawyer, Raymond

Hubert, came over to greet me. "They have no real proof," he said. "I'm confident we'll be acquitted." I smiled at that we. He wasn't the defendant. I was. And if anybody went to jail, it wouldn't be him.

A guard appeared and motioned us in. The double doors swung wide and, flanked by four policemen and a sergeant, I entered the enormous room. To soften me up for the blow, everything was blood red: the rugs, the draperies over the big windows, even the robes of the judges who would soon sit in judgment over me.

"Gentlemen, the court!"

From a door on the right six men filed in, one after the other: the President, then the five magistrates, their caps on their heads. The President stopped in front of the middle chair, the magistrates took their places on either side.

An impressive silence filled the room. Everyone remained standing, myself included. Then the Bench sat down and the rest of us followed suit.

The President was a chubby man with pink cheeks and a cold eye. His name was Bevin. He looked at me without a trace of emotion. Later on, he would conduct the proceedings with strict impartiality, and his attitude would lead everyone to understand that, as a career judge, he wasn't entirely convinced of the sincerity of either the witnesses or the police. No, he would take no responsibility for the blow; he would only announce the verdict.

The prosecutor was Magistrate Pradel. He had the grim reputation of being the "number one" supplier to the guillotine and to the domestic and colonial prisons as well.

Pradel was the personification of public vengeance: the official accuser, without a shred of humanity. He represented law and justice, and he would do everything in his power to bend them to his will. His vulture's eyes gazed intently down at me—down because he sat above me, and down also because of his great height. He was at least six foot three—and he carried it with arrogance. He kept on his red cloak but placed his cap in front of him and braced himself with hands as big as paddles. A gold band indicated he was married, and on his little finger he wore a ring made from a highly polished horseshoe nail.

Leaning forward a little, the better to dominate me, he seemed to be saying, "Look, my fun-loving friend, if you think you can get away from me, you're much mistaken. You don't know it, but my hands are really talons and they're about to tear you to pieces. And if I'm feared by the lawyers, it's because I never allow my prey to escape.

"It's none of my business whether you're guilty or innocent; my job is to use everything that's available against you: your bohemian life in Montmartre, the testimony extorted from the witnesses by the police, the testimony of the police themselves. With the disgusting swill the investigator has collected, I must make you seem so repulsive that the jury will cast you out of the society of men."

Was I dreaming or was he really speaking to me? Either way I was deeply impressed by this "devourer of men."

"Don't try to resist, prisoner. Above all, don't try to defend yourself. I'm going to send you down the road of the condemned anyway. And I trust you have no faith in the jury. Have no illusions in that quarter. Those twelve know nothing of life.

"Look at them, there in front of you. Can you see them clearly, those dozen cheeseheads brought to Paris from some distant village? They're only *petits bourgeois*, some retired, others small businessmen. Not worth talking about. You can't expect them to understand your twenty-five years and the life you've led in Montmartre. To them, Pigalle and the Place Blanche are hell itself, and anybody who stays up half the night is an enemy of society. They like to serve on this jury, are extremely proud of it, in fact.

Moreover, I can assure you, they're all acutely aware of their own mean little lives.

"And here you are, young and handsome. Surely you realize I'm going to hold nothing back when I describe you as a Don Juan of Montmartre? I'll make them your enemies straight off. You're too well dressed. You should have worn more humble garments. Ah, that was a major tactical error. Don't you see they envy you your clothes? They buy theirs at Samaritaine. Never have they gone to a tailor, even in their dreams."

It was now ten o'clock, and we were ready to start. Before me were six magistrates, one of whom was an aggressive attorney who was going to use all his Machiavellian power and intelligence to convince these twelve shopkeepers that I was guilty, and that the only proper sentence was prison or the guillotine.

I was going to be judged for the murder of a pimp and stool pigeon who operated in Montmartre. There was no proof, but the cops—they got a promotion each time they brought in a law-breaker—were going to insist I was guilty. For lack of proof, they would say they had "confidential" information that put it beyond the shadow of a doubt. They had primed a witness—a walking tape recorder at Police Headquarters by the name of Polein—and he would be the most effective element in the prosecution. Since I maintained that I didn't know him, in due course the President would say to me with a fine show of impartiality: "You say this witness lies. All right. But why should he lie?"

"Your Honor, if I've been staying awake nights since my arrest, it wasn't because I was sorry I killed Roland le Petit—I didn't kill him. It was because I kept trying to figure out this witness's motive, why he was determined to harm me as much as possible, and why, each time the prosecution threatened to collapse, he found something new to prop it up with. I've reached the conclusion, your Honor, that the police caught him committing a crime and made a deal with him: 'We'll look the other way if you testify against Papillon.' "

I didn't know then how close to the truth I was. Polein was presented to the court as an honest man with a clean record; a few years later he was arrested and found guilty for trafficking in cocaine.

Hubert tried to defend me, but he couldn't compete with the prosecutor. Only one witness, Bouffray, boiling with indignation, gave him even a few moments' trouble. Pradel's cleverness won the duel. As if that weren't enough, he flattered the jury and they swelled with pride at being treated as collaborators and equals by this impressive character.

By eleven that night the game was over. Check and mate. I, who was innocent, was found guilty.

French society in the person of Prosecutor Pradel had succeeded in eliminating for life a young man of twenty-five. And no reduced sentences, if you please! This heaping platter was served to me with the toneless voice of President Bevin.

"Will the prisoner please stand."

I stood. The room was silent, everyone held his breath, my heart beat a little faster. The jury looked at me or bowed their heads; they seemed ashamed.

"The jury having answered 'Yes' to all the questions except one—that of premeditation—you are condemned to hard labor for life. Have you anything to say?"

I didn't move; I just clutched the railing of the prisoner's box a little harder. "Your Honor, yes, I want to say I am truly innocent, that I'm a victim of a police frame-up."

A murmur rose from a group of specially invited ladies sitting behind the Bench.

Without raising my voice, I said to them, "Silence, you women in pearls who come here to indulge your sick emotions. The farce is played out. A murder has been solved by your police and your justice; you should be content."

"Will a guard please remove the prisoner," said the President.

Before I was led away, I heard a voice cry out, "Don't worry, baby, I'll follow you there." It was my good and true Nénette shouting her love. And those of my underworld friends who were in the courtroom applauded. They knew the truth about this murder and this was their way of showing they were proud of me for not squealing.

We went back to the small room where we had waited before the trial. There the police handcuffed me, and then I was chained to one of them, my right wrist to his left. No one spoke. I asked for a cigarette. The guard gave me one and lit it. Each time I lifted it to my mouth or took it away, the policeman had to raise or lower his arm to follow my motions. I finished about three-quarters of the cigarette. Still not a word. Finally I looked at the guard and said, "Let's go."

I went down the stairs escorted by a dozen policemen and came out into the inner courtyard of the Palais. The paddy wagon was waiting for us. We all found places on the benches. The sergeant said: "Conciergerie."

THE CONCIERGERIE

When we arrived at Marie Antoinette's last château, the police turned me over to the head warden, who signed a paper. They left without a word, but just before leaving—surprise—the sergeant shook my handcuffed hand.

The head warden asked me, "What'd they give you?"

"Life."

"I can't believe it." But he took another look at the police and saw it was so. Then this fifty-year-old jailer who had seen everything and knew my own case very well had these kind words for me:

"Those bastards! They must be crazy!"

Gently he removed my handcuffs and accompanied me to the padded cell specially designed for those condemned to death, madmen, the very dangerous and those sentenced to hard labor.

"Chin up, Papillon," he said as he shut the door. "They'll be sending you your things and the same food you had in the other cell. Chin up!"

"Thanks, chief. Believe me, my chin is up and I hope they choke on their 'for life.' "

A few minutes later I heard a scratching on my door. "What is it?"

A voice answered, "Nothing. It's only me. I'm hanging up a sign."

"Why? What does it say?"

" 'Hard labor for life.' Watch closely."

They really are crazy, I thought. Do they actually think the blow that just hit me could make me want to commit suicide? My chin's up and I'm going to keep it that way. I'm going to fight them all. Starting tomorrow, I go into action.

As I was drinking my coffee the next morning, I asked myself, Should I appeal? Would I have better luck in another court? And how much time would I lose doing it? One year, maybe eighteen months . . . and what for? To get twenty years instead of life?

Since I had decided to escape at all cost, the number of years didn't matter. I recalled the question another convict had addressed to the presiding judge: "Your Honor, how long does hard labor for life last in France?"

I paced back and forth in my cell. I had sent a consoling wire to my wife and another to my sister, who, alone against the world, had tried to defend her brother.

It was over. The curtain was down. My people would suffer more than I, and my poor father far away in the provinces would have a hard time carrying this heavy cross.

With a start I came to my senses. You're innocent, sure, but who believes you? I asked myself. Stop going around claiming your innocence; they'll just laugh at you. Getting life for a pimp, and on top of that saying it was somebody else who did it—that's too thick. Better keep your trap shut.

So much for that. The first thing to do was to make contact with another con who wanted to break out.

I thought of a man from Marseilles called Dega. I'd probably see him at the barber's. He went every day for a shave. I asked to go too. When I arrived, there he was with his nose to the wall. I noticed him just as he was surreptitiously letting another man go ahead of him so that he would have longer to wait his turn. I took a place directly next to him, forcing another man to step aside. I spoke very fast, under my breath.

"Well, Dega, how's it going?"

"O.K., Papi. I got fifteen years. What about you? I heard they really screwed you."

"Yes. I got life."

"Are you going to appeal?"

"No. I'm going to eat and keep in shape. You've got to be strong, Dega. Someday we're going to need strong muscles. Got any money?"

"Yes. Ten thousand francs in pounds sterling.* What about you?"

"Not a sou."

"Want a piece of advice? Get some and get it fast. Hubert's

---

* Worth about $1250 in 1970.

your lawyer? He's a bastard, he'll never lift a finger. Send your wife to Dante with a loaded *plan*. Tell her to give it to Dominique-le-Riche and I guarantee you'll get it."

"Ssh. The guard's looking at us."

"So you're having a little chat?"

"Oh, nothing interesting," Dega answered. "He says he's feeling sick."

"What's he got? Courtroom indigestion?" The slob burst out laughing.

So this was it. I was on the road of the condemned already. A man makes jokes and laughs like crazy at the expense of a kid of twenty-five who's in for life.

I got my *plan*. It was a highly polished aluminum tube, that unscrewed right in the middle. It had a male half and a female half. It contained 5600 francs in new bills. When I got it, I kissed it. Yes, I kissed that little tube, two and a half inches long and as thick as your thumb, before shoving it into my anus. I took a deep breath so that it would lodge in the colon. It was my strongbox. They could make me take off all my clothes, spread my legs apart, make me cough or bend over double, for all the good it would do them. The *plan* was high up in the large intestine. It was a part of me. Inside me I carried my life, my freedom . . . my road to revenge. For that's what was on my mind. Revenge. That's all that was, in fact.

It was dark outside. I was alone in my cell. A bright light shone from the ceiling so that the guard could see me through a little hole in the door. The powerful light blinded me. I placed a folded handkerchief over my sore eyes. I stretched out on the mattress on my iron bed and, lying there without a pillow, went over and over the details of that terrible trial.

To make you understand this long story as it unfolds and what sustained me in my struggle, I may have to be a little long-winded just now. I must tell you everything that happened and what I saw in my mind's eye during those first days after I was buried alive.

What would I do after I escaped? For now that I had my *plan* I never doubted for a moment that I would.

Well, I'd make it back to Paris as fast as possible. And the first man I'd kill would be that stool pigeon, Polein. Then the two informers. But two informers weren't enough, I had to kill *all* informers. Or at least as many as possible. I'd fill a trunk with all the explosives it would hold. I didn't know exactly how much that would be: twenty, thirty, forty pounds? I tried to figure what I'd need for lots of victims.

I kept my eyes closed, the handkerchief over them for protection, and I could see the trunk very clearly, looking very innocent but crammed with explosives, the trigger carefully primed to set them off. Wait a minute . . . It must explode at exactly ten in the morning, in the dispatch room on the second floor at Police Headquarters, 36 Quai des Orfèvres. At that hour there would be at least one hundred and fifty cops in the room, receiving their orders for the day and listening to reports. How many steps were there to climb? I had to get it right.

I must figure exactly the time it would take to get the trunk from the street to its destination at the very second it was to explode. And who would carry the trunk? All right; be bold. I'd arrive in a taxi immediately in front of the entrance, and with an authoritative voice I'd tell the two guards: "Take this trunk up to the dispatch room. I'll be right up. Tell Commissioner Dupont that Chief Inspector Dubois sent it and that I'll be along in a minute."

But would they obey? What if it was my luck that, out of all those idiots, I picked the only two intelligent men in the force? Then I'd be finished. I must think of something else. And I thought and thought. I would not admit that nothing would ever be 100 percent sure.

I got up for a drink of water. So much thinking had given me a headache.

I lay down again without the blindfold. The minutes dragged. And that light, that goddamned light! I wet the handkerchief and put it back on. The cold water felt good and its weight made the cloth stick to my eyes. From then on I always did this.

The long hours I spent piecing together my future revenge were so intense that I began to feel as if the project were already under way. Every night, and even parts of the day, I wandered through Paris as if my escape were already a fact: I *would* escape and I would return to Paris. And, naturally, I'd present my bill to Polein first, then to the informers. But what about the jury? Were those bastards to go on leading peaceful lives? Those old crocks must have gone home, smug and satisfied at having done their duty with a capital D—full of importance, puffed up with pride in front of their neighbors, and the wives waiting, hair uncombed, to guzzle soup with them.

All right now. What should I do with the jury? Nothing—that was the answer. They were a pitiful bunch, really not responsible. I'd leave them alone.

As I write down these thoughts I had so many years ago, thoughts that come back now to assail me with such terrible clarity, I am struck by how absolute silence and total isolation were able to lead a young man shut up in a cell into a true life of the imagination. He literally lived two lives. He took flight and wandered wherever he liked: to his home, his father, his mother, his family, his childhood, all the different stages of his life. And more important still, the castles in Spain that his fertile brain invented induced a kind of schizophrenia, and he began to believe he was living what he dreamed.

Thirty-six years have passed and yet it taxes my memory scarcely at all to write what I actually thought at that point in my life.

No, I wouldn't harm the jurors. But what about the prosecutor? Ah, I wouldn't botch that one! Moreover, thanks to Alexandre Dumas, I had just the right recipe. I'd do exactly as they did in *The Count of Monte Cristo* with that poor bugger they put in the cellar and left to die of hunger.

Oh, that vulture decked out in red—he'd done everything to deserve the most horrible possible end. Yes, that was it. After Polein and the police, I'd concentrate exclusively on him. I'd rent a villa, one with a very deep cellar and thick walls and a very heavy door. If the door wasn't thick enough, I'd pad it myself with a mattress and cotton batting. Once I had the villa, I'd find Master Pradel and kidnap him. I'd chain him to the rings in the wall as soon as we arrived. Then my turn would begin. . . .

I am face to face with him; I see him with extraordinary clarity beneath my closed eyelids. I look at him the same way he looked at me in court. I feel the warmth of his breath on my face.

The powerful spotlight I've aimed at him blinds his vulture's eyes; they are wild with terror. Huge drops of sweat run down his apopleptic face. Yes, I hear my questions; I listen to his replies. I live the moment intensely.

"You miserable clod, do you recognize me? It's me, Papillon. Papillon you so blithely consigned to hard labor for life. Do you think now it was worth all those plodding years to educate yourself, spending all those nights on Roman codes, learning Greek and Latin, sacrificing your youth? To get you where, you bastard? Where you could create a better social code? Convince the mob that peace is the most important thing in the world? Preach a saving new religion? Or simply influence others to become better men, or at least stop being bad? Tell me, did you use your knowledge to save men?

"You did none of that. Only one ambition moved you. To climb, climb. Climb the ladder of your wretched career. To you, glory was being the best caterer to the *bagne*, the most generous provider to the hangman and the guillotine.

"If Deibler* felt a shred of gratitude, he would send you a case of the best champagne at the end of each year. Isn't it thanks to you, you pig, that he was able to cut off five or six extra heads this year? In any event, I've got you now, chained tight to this wall.

"How well I remember your smile when you heard the verdict, your look of triumph! Well now, my friend, I'm going to change all that. You have one advantage I didn't have, of course. I couldn't scream; you can. So go ahead. Scream, scream as much as you like, as loud as you like. What am I going to do with you? Let you starve to death? No, not good enough. First, I'll gouge out your eyes. No, that comes later. First I'll cut out your tongue, that terrible tongue, as sharp as a knife—no, sharper than a knife, more like a razor. That tongue you prostituted to your glorious career!"

I walked and I walked, my head spun, but I stayed face to face with him . . . until all of a sudden the lamp went out and the pale light of day crept into my cell through the bars of the window.

How come? Was it morning already? Did I spend the whole night avenging myself? What beautiful hours those were! How fast it went, this long, long night!

I listened as I sat on my bed. Nothing. Absolute silence. From time to time, a small "tic" on my door. It was the guard in noiseless slippers raising the small iron slide so that he could fasten his eye to the tiny hole and watch me without my seeing him.

---

*Chief Executioner in 1932.

The machinery conceived by the French Republic was now in its second phase. It functioned wonderfully well; the first phase had eliminated a troublesome man. But that wasn't enough. The man must neither die too quickly, nor must he escape by committing suicide. They needed him. What would the Penal Administration do if there were no prisoners? So he must be watched, and he must go to the *bagne* in order to justify the lives of other bureaucrats.

Hearing the "tic" again, I had to smile. Relax, I told them silently, you're wasting your time. I won't escape you. At least, not the way you fear—by suicide. I ask only one thing: that I stay as healthy as possible and leave soon for French Guiana.

Heh, my old prison guard who makes that "tic" all the time, I know your colleagues are no choir boys. You're a kind papa compared to them. I've known this a long time, because when Napoleon III created the *bagnes* and was asked: "But who will guard these bandits?" he answered: "Worse bandits." Later on, I was able to confirm the fact that the founding father of the *bagnes* had not been lying.

Clack, clack, a wicket eight inches square opened in the middle of my door. I was handed coffee and a piece of bread weighing almost two pounds. As a convict, I no longer had the right to eat in the restaurant, but so long as I had money, I could buy cigarettes and a little food at the modest canteen. A few days more and I'd have nothing. The Conciergerie was the waiting room for solitary confinement. I smoked a Lucky Strike with delight, six francs sixty the pack. I bought two. I was spending my odd change because they'd be taking it all anyway to pay the costs of "justice."

I found a small note slipped inside the bread. It was from Dega, instructing me to go to the delousing room. "You'll find three lice in the matchbox." I took out the matches and there they were, three fat and healthy lice. I knew what I was to do. I must show them to the guard and tomorrow he'd send me and all my belongings, including my mattress, to the steam room to kill all the parasites—except me, of course. And so the next day I met Dega there. No guards. We were alone.

"Thanks, Dega. Thanks to you I got my *plan*."

"Does it bother you?"

"No."

"When you go to the toilet, wash it well before you put it back."

"Right. I think it's good and tight because the bills are still in perfect condition. And I've been carrying it for seven days."

"I'm glad it's working."

"What are you planning to do, Dega?"

"I'm going to play crazy. I don't want to go to the *bagne*. Here in France I'll do maybe eight or ten years. I have connections and might get five years off."

"How old are you?"

"Forty-two."

"You are crazy! If you lose ten or fifteen years, you'll be an old man when you get out. Does hard labor scare you?"

"Yes, and I'm not ashamed to say I'm scared of the *bagne*. It's terrible in Guiana, you know. Every year they lose eighty percent of the men. Each convoy replaces another and the convoys carry between eighteen hundred and two thousand men. If you don't catch leprosy, you get yellow fever, or dysentery, which can finish you off, or tuberculosis, or malaria. If you escape these, you stand a good chance of being assassinated for your *plan* or dying in a break. Believe me, Papillon, I'm not saying this to discourage you, but I know what I'm talking about. I've known several cons who returned to France after even short terms—five to seven years. They were human dregs. They spent nine months of the year in the hospital. As for escaping, it's not as easy as you think."

"I believe you, Dega, but I have confidence in myself, and I'm not going to hang around there, that's for sure. I'm a good sailor, I know the sea, and I'm going to waste no time making a break. Can you see yourself doing ten years in solitary? Even if they take away five—and there's no guarantee they will—do you think you can stand complete isolation without going nuts? Look at me now, alone in my cell twenty-four hours a day, with no books, no way to get out, nobody to speak to. Those hours aren't sixty minutes long, but six hundred. And that's not the whole story either."

"Maybe so, but you're young and I'm forty-two."

"Listen, Dega, what are you really afraid of? Is it the other cons?"

"If you want the truth, Papi, yes. Everybody knows I was a millionaire. And from there to killing me because they think I'm carrying fifty or a hundred thousand francs around isn't a very long step."

"Listen, do you want to make a deal? Promise me you won't go to the nut house, and I promise I'll always stick by you. We'll help each other out. I'm strong and quick, I learned to fight early, and I'm good with a knife. So don't worry. The other cons won't just respect us; they'll be afraid of us. For a *cavale*, we need nobody. You've got dough, I've got dough. I know how to use a compass and sail a boat. What more do you want?"

He looked me straight in the eye. . . . We embraced. The pact was sealed.

A few moments later the door opened. He went his way and I went mine. Our cells weren't very far apart, and we could see each other from time to time in the barbershop, at the doctor's, or at chapel on Sundays.

Dega had been caught in the scandal of the counterfeit National Defense bonds. A forger had made them in a very original way. He bleached five-hundred-franc bonds and reprinted them with the number 10,000. It was a beautiful job. Since the paper was the same, the banks accepted them without question. This had been going on for some years, and the Treasury had just about given up when one day they caught a man named Brioulet red-handed. Louis Dega was quietly minding his bar in Marseilles, where the flower of the Midi underworld gathered every night along with the world's biggest traveling crooks.

By 1929 he was already a millionaire. One night a pretty, well-dressed girl came up to the bar. She asked for Monsieur Louis Dega.

"That's me, madame. What can I do for you? Would you step into the next room?"

"I am Brioulet's wife. He's in prison in Paris for selling counterfeit bonds. I saw him in the visitors' room at the Santé. He gave me the address of your bar and told me to come and ask you for twenty thousand francs to pay the lawyer."

So Dega, one of the biggest crooks in France, faced with the danger of a woman's knowing his part in the affair, said the one thing he shouldn't have said:

"Madame, I know nothing about your husband, and if it's money you want, go walk the streets. You'll earn more than you need for you are very pretty."

This was too much for the poor woman; she ran out in tears. Then she went back to Paris and told her husband. Brioulet was furious. The next day he spilled everything to the examining judge and formally accused Dega of being the man who had furnished the counterfeit bonds. A team of France's smartest cops went after Dega. A month later Dega, the forger, the printer and eleven accomplices were arrested at the same time in different places and put behind bars. They appeared before the Assizes of the Seine and the trial lasted fourteen days. Each prisoner was defended by a top lawyer. Brioulet never retracted. The upshot was that for twenty thousand miserable francs and an idiot remark, the biggest crook in France was ruined and stuck with fifteen years at hard labor. This was the man with whom I had just signed a life-and-death pact.

. . . One, two, three, four, five and turn. . . . One, two, three, four, five and turn. For several hours I'd been pacing back and forth between the window and the door of my cell. I smoked, I was alert, my morale was good and I felt ready for anything. I promised myself not to think about revenge for the moment.

Let's leave the prosecutor where I left him, chained to the rings, facing me, but with no decision yet on just how I would finish him off.

Suddenly a cry, a horrible anguished cry of despair, penetrated the door of my cell. What was it? It sounded like a man being tortured. But this was no police station. No way of finding out. They shattered me, those screams in the night. What force they must have had to penetrate my padded door! No doubt someone had gone mad. It was so easy in these cells where nothing ever happened. Out loud I asked myself, "What the hell does it matter to you? Think of yourself, only of yourself and your new partner, Dega." I bent down, straightened up, then gave myself a sharp whack on the chest. It really hurt, so everything was all right: the muscles of my arms were in good shape. What about my legs? I should congratulate them, for I'd been walking over sixteen hours and wasn't the least bit tired.

The Chinese invented the drop of water falling on the head. The French invented silence. They suppressed every possible distraction. No books, no paper, no pencil, the window with its thick bars completely covered with planks of wood, although a few holes let a little light through.

That harrowing cry left me deeply troubled. I charged around the cell like a beast in a cage. I felt I'd been abandoned, literally buried alive. I was really alone; nothing would ever reach me but screams.

The door opened. It was an old priest. You're not alone after all. A priest is standing there, right in front of you.

"Good evening, my son. Forgive me for not coming sooner, but I was on holiday. How are you?" With no further ceremony, the kind old man came into my cell and sat down on my cot.

"What did you do?" he asked.

I saw how ridiculous it was to insist on my innocence, so I answered promptly, "The police say I killed a man, and if that's what they say, it must be so."

"Who was it?"

"A pimp."

"And for an underworld killing, they gave you hard labor for life? I don't understand. Was it premeditated?"

"No."

"I can't believe it, my poor child. What can I do for you? Do you want to pray with me?"

"Father, forgive me, but I never had religious instruction. I don't know how to pray."

"It makes no difference, my child. I'll pray for you. The Blessed Lord loves all his children, baptized or not. Will you please repeat each word I say?"

His eyes were so gentle and his wide face glowed with such kindness that I was ashamed to refuse him. He was kneeling; I did the same. "Our Father who art in Heaven . . ." Tears came into my eyes, and when the good father saw them, he put his pudgy finger to my cheek, caught a large tear, brought it to his lips and licked it.

"Your tears, my son, are the greatest reward that God could give me. Thank you." He got up and kissed me on the forehead.

We sat down on the bed again, side by side.

"How long has it been since you last cried?"

"Fourteen years."

"Fourteen. Why?"

"My mother died."

He took my hand in his and said, "Forgive those who have made you suffer."

I tore my hand away and, without knowing what I was doing, leaped off the bed and stood in the middle of the room. "Oh no! Not that. I'll never forgive. You want me to tell you something, Father? I spend all day, all night, every hour, every minute, plotting how and when I'll kill the people who sent me here."

"That's what you think and say now, my son. You're young, very young. When you're older, you'll give up the idea of punishment and revenge."

Thirty-four years later I agreed with him.

"What can I do for you?" the priest repeated.

"Break a rule."

"What rule?"

"Go to cell number thirty-seven and tell Dega to ask his lawyer to get him sent to the jail in Caen; tell him I did it today. That's the jail where they make up the convoys for Guiana, and we must get there as fast as possible. If we miss the first boat, we have to wait two more years in solitary before there's another. Come back here when you've seen him, Father."

"What shall I use for an excuse?"

"That you forgot your breviary. I'll be waiting for the answer."

"Why are you in such a hurry to go to the dreadful *bagne*?"

I looked at this traveling salesman of the Lord and, convinced he wouldn't give me away, I said, "So that I can escape sooner, Father."

"God will help you, my child, I'm certain. And you will make your life over, I feel it. You have the eyes of a good boy and you have a noble soul. I'll go to thirty-seven and bring you back the answer."

He returned in no time. Dega had agreed.

One week later, at four in the morning, seven of us were lined up in the corridor of the Conciergerie. The guards were there in full strength.

"Strip!"

We undressed slowly. It was cold. I had gooseflesh.

"Put your clothes in front of you. Turn around, take one step back!" We each found ourselves in front of a package.

"Get dressed!"

The cotton undershirt I was wearing a moment before was replaced by a heavy stiff shirt of unbleached cloth, and my handsome suit by a jacket and pants of coarse sackcloth. My shoes vanished and I shoved my feet into a pair of sabots. Until that day we had looked like normal men. I glanced at the other six: what a horror! Our individuality was gone; in two minutes we had been transformed into convicts.

"Right turn, single file! Ready, march!"

With our escort of twenty guards we came to the courtyard, where, each in turn, we were wedged into the narrow cells of a police van. We were off to Beaulieu, the jail in Caen.

THE JAIL IN CAEN

We were led into the director's office as soon as we arrived. He sat enthroned behind an Empire desk on a platform three feet high.

"Attention! The director will now address you."

"Prisoners, this is a way station while you wait to leave for the *bagne*. It's a prison. Silence is required at all times. You'll have no visitors, no letters. Bend or you'll break. There are two doors available to you: one, if you behave, leads to the *bagne*, the other to the cemetery. Bad behavior, even the smallest infraction, is punished by sixty days in the dungeon with only bread and water. No one has survived two consecutive sentences there. You've been warned!"

He addressed Pierrot le Fou, who had been extradited from Spain. "What was your profession?"

"Toreador, sir."

Infuriated by the answer, the director shouted, "Take this man away!" Immediately the toreador was knocked down, bludgeoned by four or five guards and carried out. We could hear him shout, "You shitheads! You're five against one and you have to use clubs, you dirty bastards!" We heard then the "Ah!" of a mortally wounded beast; after that, nothing. Only the sound of something being dragged along the cement floor.

By a stroke of luck, Dega was put in the cell next to me. But first we were introduced to a one-eyed, red-headed monster at least six foot five who held a brand-new bullwhip in his right hand. He was the trusty, a prisoner who served the guards as official torturer. With him around, the guards could beat the men without exerting themselves, and if someone died in the process, they were guiltless in the eyes of the Administration.

Later on, during a short stay in the infirmary, I learned all about this human beast. The director deserved congratulations for having chosen his executioner so well. He had been a quarryman by profession. One day, in the small northern town where he lived, he had the idea of committing suicide and killing his wife at the same time. For this purpose he used a good-sized stick of dynamite. He lay down next to his sleeping wife (there were six tenants in the house), lit a cigarette and held it to the wick of the dynamite, which was in his left hand between his head and his wife's. Ghastly explosion. Result: his wife literally had to be gathered up in spoonfuls, part of the house collapsed, three children were crushed to death under the debris, together with a woman of seventy. Others were injured in varying degrees.

As for Tribouillard, he lost part of his left hand—only his little finger and part of his thumb remained—and his left eye and ear. He also had a head wound that required surgery. But now, since his conviction, he was in charge of the jail's disciplinary cells, a maniac free to do what he pleased with the unfortunates who ran afoul of him.

One, two, three, four, five, and turn . . . one, two, three, four, five, and turn. . . . So began again the interminable shuttle between the wall and the door of the cell.

You were not allowed to lie down during the day. At five in the morning a strident whistle woke you up. You had to get up, make your bed, wash, and either walk or sit on a stool attached to the wall. You were not allowed to lie down! Crowning refinement of the penal system: the bed folded against the wall, and there it remained. This way the prisoner couldn't lie down and he could be watched more easily.

. . . One, two, three, four, five. . . . Fourteen hours of walking. To master the art of performing this continuous movement automatically, you had to learn to keep your head down, hands behind your back, walk neither too fast nor too slow, keep your steps the same length and turn automatically on the left foot at one end of the cell, on the right at the other.

One, two, three, four, five. . . . The cells were better lighted than those at the Conciergerie and you could hear noises from the outside, some from the disciplinary section, but also a few from the countryside beyond. At night you could catch the sounds of laborers whistling or singing on their way home from work, happy on a good cup of cider.

I had a Christmas present: through a crack in the planks that covered my window, I could see the countryside all covered with snow and a few big trees picked out by the full moon. Just like a Christmas card. Shaken by the wind, the trees had dropped their mantles of snow, black silhouettes against the white. It was Christmas; it was even Christmas in part of the prison. The Administration had made an effort for the convicts in transit: we were allowed to buy two squares of chocolate. I said two squares, not two bars. Those two squares of Aiguebelle chocolate were my New Year's Eve for 1931.

One, two, three, four, five. . . . The restrictions of justice had turned me into a pendulum. This shuttle back and forth in my cell made up my entire universe. It had been mathematically worked out. Nothing, absolutely nothing was to be left in the cell. The prisoner must have no distractions. Had I been caught looking through the crack in my window, I would have been severely punished. Actually they were right, since to them I was only a living corpse. By what right did I permit myself to enjoy a glimpse of nature?

A butterfly flew past, light blue with a thin black stripe, and a bee bumbled not far from the window. What were these little beasts looking for? Drunk with the winter sun, perhaps, unless they were cold and wanted to get into prison. A butterfly in winter is like life after death. Why wasn't it dead? And why had the bee left its hive? How foolishly bold of them to come here!

Tribouillard was a true sadist. I had a feeling something would happen between us and unfortunately I was right. The day after the visit of my charming insects, I got sick. I couldn't take it any more. I was suffocating with loneliness. I needed to see a face, hear a voice, even an angry one, but at least a voice. I had to hear something.

Standing naked in the glacial cold of the corridor, facing the wall with my nose almost against it, I was the next to the last in a row of eight men waiting their turn to see the doctor. I wanted to see people . . . and I succeeded too well. The trusty came upon us at the moment I was talking under my breath to Julot, "the man with the hammer." One whack of his fist against the back of my head and I was almost done for. I hadn't seen it coming and I banged my nose against the wall as I fell. The blood spurted out, and, as I picked myself up, I made a tentative gesture of protest. That was all the giant needed. He gave me a sharp kick in the gut which flattened me again, then he went on to flog me with his bull-whip. That was too much for Julot. He jumped on him; there was a wild struggle. Since Julot was getting the worst of it, the guards stood by impassive. No one took any notice of me. I looked around for some kind of weapon. Suddenly I saw the doctor leaning forward in his office chair to see what was going on in the corridor, and at the same time I noticed a lid bobbing over some boiling water. The big enamel pot sat on the coal stove that warmed the doctor's office. The steam probably served to purify the air.

I quickly picked up the pot by its handles—they burned me, but I didn't let go—and in the same motion I threw the boiling water in the trusty's face. He hadn't seen me because he was too busy with Julot. He let out a terrible scream. I'd really got him. He rolled around on the floor trying to peel off his three woolen sweaters. When he got to the third, his skin came off with it. The neck of the sweater was tight, and in his effort to get it over his head, the skin of his chest, his cheeks and part of his neck came too, stuck to the wool. His only eye was scalded, so he was blind as well. He finally got to his feet, hideous, bloodied, his flesh raw, and Julot took the opportunity to give him a violent kick in the groin. The giant collapsed and started to vomit and froth at the mouth. He had got his. As for us, we didn't have long to wait.

The two guards who had watched the scene were too cowed to

attack. They called for help. It came from all sides and the clubs rained down on us like hail. I was lucky enough to be struck unconscious at the start so I didn't feel the blows.

When I came to, I was two floors below, completely naked in a dungeon flooded with water. I slowly came to my senses and felt my bruises. They hurt. There were at least a dozen bumps on my head. What time was it? I couldn't tell. In this place there was neither day nor night. Then I heard a knocking on the wall. It came from far away.

Pang, pang, pang, pang, pang, pang. The knocks were the ringing of the "telephone." I had to knock twice if I wanted to get on the line. Knock, yes, but with what? In the dark I couldn't see a thing. Fists weren't enough; the sound wouldn't get through. I moved closer to where I thought the door must be; it was a little lighter there. I banged into the grill. Feeling around, I figured that the door to the dungeon must be about three feet beyond and that the grill prevented me from reaching it. This was designed so that if anyone entered a dangerous prisoner's cell, the prisoner couldn't get at him because he was in fact in a cage. You could talk to him, throw water on him, throw food at him, insult him, all with impunity. On the other hand, you couldn't strike him without exposing yourself to danger, for to get at him, you had to open the grill.

The knocking resumed. Who was trying to get in touch with me? The guy certainly deserved a reply—he was taking a big chance. As I walked around in the dark, my foot slipped on something round and hard, and I almost fell flat on my face. It was a wooden spoon. I grabbed it and got ready to reply. Ear to the wall, I waited. Pang, pang, pang, pang, pang. Stop. Pang, pang. I answered: pang, pang. Those two taps meant, "Go ahead, I'm listening." The taps began: pang, pang, pang—the letters of the alphabet rolled by quickly—*a b c d e f g h i j k l m n o p*, stop. It stopped at the letter *p*. I tapped a hard pang. This was to tell him I had registered the letter *p*, then came an *a*, a *p*, an *i*, etc. He was saying: "Papi, how's it going? You really got it. I have a broken arm." It was Julot.

We telephoned for over two hours, oblivious to the danger. We were carried away. I told him that I had broken nothing, that my head was covered with bumps, but that I had no open wounds.

He had seen me being pulled down the stairs by the foot and told me that at each step my head had banged against the one above. He had never lost consciousness. He thought that Tribouillard had been badly burned and because of the wool was in serious condition. He was through for a while, at least.

Three quick taps warned me that there was trouble coming. I stopped. A few moments later the door opened. I heard someone shout:

"Get back, you bastard! Get to the back of the cell and come to attention!" It was the new trusty. "My name is Batton and my name suits my profession." He trained a big ship's lantern on the dungeon and my naked body.

"Here's something to put on. But don't you move. Here's bread and water. Don't eat it all at once; it's all you'll get for the next twenty-four hours."

He let out a savage yell, then put the lantern up to his face. I saw that he was smiling, and not unkindly. He placed a finger to his lips and pointed to the things he was leaving me. There must have been a guard in the corridor, yet he wanted me to know that he was not my enemy.

And he wasn't. In the bread I found a big piece of boiled meat and, in the pocket of the pants—oh riches!—a package of cigarettes and a lighter. Here such presents were worth a million. Two shirts instead of one, and woolen underwear that reached to my ankles. I'll never forget Batton. What it meant was that he was rewarding me for getting rid of Tribouillard. Before the incident he had been only an assistant trusty. Now, thanks to me, he had the full title.

Since it required the patience of an Indian to locate the source of the "telephone" taps and only the trusty could do it, the guards being too lazy, Julot and I went at it to our hearts' content. We spent the entire day sending messages back and forth. From him I learned that our departure was imminent: in three or four months.

Two days later we were led out of the dungeon and, each of us flanked by two guards, were taken to the office of the director. Three men sat behind a table facing the door. It was a kind of tribunal. The director acted as president, and the assistant director and the head warden were the associate judges.

"Ah, my fine fellows, so you're here! What have you to say for yourselves?"

Julot was very pale, his eyes were swollen, and he probably had a fever. His arm had been broken for three days now; he must be in great pain. He answered very quietly, "I have a broken arm."

"Well, you asked for it. That should teach you not to attack people. You'll see the doctor when he gets here. I hope it will be within the week. The wait will be good for you; perhaps the pain will teach you something. You don't expect me to have a doctor come specially for a choice character like you, do you? So you wait until the doctor has the time to come, then he'll take care of you. Which doesn't prevent me from sentencing both of you to the dungeon until further notice."

Julot's eyes met mine. He seemed to be saying: "That elegant gentleman has a nice way of disposing of other people's lives."

I turned back to the director and looked at him. Thinking I wanted to speak, he said, "You don't care for my decision? You take exception to it?"

I replied, "No, sir. It's just that I feel an acute need to spit in your face. But I won't because I'm afraid to soil my saliva."

He was so surprised that he blushed, uncertain how to react. But the head warden knew. He called to the guards:

"Haul him away and take good care of him! I expect to see him groveling in an hour. We'll break him in! I'll make him clean my shoes with his tongue, both tops and bottoms. Give him the works. He's all yours."

Two guards grabbed my left arm, two others my right. I was forced to the ground, face down, arms behind my back, hands touching my shoulder blades. Handcuffs were put on me and a thumb-screw joining the index finger of my left hand to the thumb of my right. Then the warden pulled me up by the hair like an animal.

No need to go into further details. All you need to know is that I wore the handcuffs behind my back for eleven days. I owe my life to Batton. Each day he threw me the regulation piece of bread, but without the use of my hands I couldn't eat it. Even when I pushed it against the bars with my head it was no use. But in addition Batton threw in bite-size pieces of bread—enough to keep me alive. I made little piles with my feet; then, flat on my stomach, I ate them like a dog. I chewed each piece thoroughly so as to get the full value.

On the twelfth day they took off my handcuffs. The metal had cut into my flesh and it was covered in spots with rotten meat. This scared the warden, especially when I fainted from the pain. When I came to, I was taken to the infirmary and washed with sterilized water. The attendant insisted they give me an anti-tetanus injection. My arms were paralyzed; I couldn't get them back to their normal position. Only after a half hour's massage with camphorated oil was I able to bring them down to my sides.

I went back to my cell, and when the warden noticed the eleven pieces of bread, he said, "You're going to have a feast! It's funny, but you don't seem very thin after eleven days' fasting . . ."

"I drank a lot of water, chief."

"Oh, so that's it! I get it. Better eat a lot now so you'll get your strength back." And he left.

The idiot. He thought I hadn't eaten anything for eleven days and that if I ate it all in one gulp, I'd die of indigestion.

Toward evening Batton slipped me some tobacco and cigarette papers. I smoked and I smoked, blowing the smoke into the heating duct, which of course didn't work. I was at least putting it to some purpose.

A little later I called Julot. He also thought I hadn't eaten for eleven days and advised me to go slow. I was afraid to tell him the truth for fear some bastard might decipher the message. His arm was in a cast, he was in good spirits, and he congratulated me for holding out.

According to him, the convoy would be leaving soon. The orderly had told him that the vaccine for the departing convicts had arrived. It usually came a month before the departure. Foolishly, Julot also asked me if I'd held on to my *plan*.

Yes, I'd held on to it, but I won't describe what I went through to do it. My anus was painfully sore.

Three weeks later we were taken out of our cells. What was up? We were given sensational showers with soap and hot water. I felt myself come back to life. Julot laughed like a kid, and Pierrot le Fou was radiant with joy.

As this was our first time out of the dungeon, we had no way of knowing what was going on. The barber wouldn't answer the brief questions I whispered to him.

An unfamiliar prisoner with an ugly face said, "I think we're out of the dungeon. Maybe they're scared of an inspection. The important thing is to keep us alive."

We were each led into a normal cell. At noon, in my first hot soup in forty-three days, I found a small piece of wood. On the bottom side I read: "Departure in eight days. Tomorrow vaccination."

Who had sent me this? It must be some prisoner kind enough to give us the news. He was aware that if one of us knew, all would know. It was surely pure chance that the message had come to me.

I quickly notified Julot by telephone. "Pass the word along."

All night long I heard the telephone going. Once I'd given the message, I stopped. I was too comfortable in my bed and I didn't want to get into trouble. And I wanted no part of a return trip to the dungeon—that day least of all.

SECOND NOTEBOOK

EN ROUTE TO THE *BAGNE*

SAINT-MARTIN-DE-RÉ

DURING THE EVENING BATTON SLIPPED me three Gauloises and a piece of paper on which I read: "Papillon, I know you're leaving with a pleasant memory of me. I may be a trusty, but I try to do the prisoners as little harm as possible. I took the job because I have nine children and I'm in a hurry to get out. I'm going to try to win my pardon without doing too much harm. Good-by. Good luck. The convoy leaves the day after tomorrow."

The next day we were assembled in groups of thirty in the corridor of the disciplinary section. Medics had come from Caen to vaccinate us against tropical diseases. Each of us got three inoculations and two quarts of milk. Dega stood near me. We were no longer observing the rules of silence for we knew we couldn't be put back in the dungeon once we'd been inoculated. We talked in low voices under the guards' noses; they didn't dare say anything in front of the medics from town.

Dega was troubled. "Are they going to have enough paddy wagons to take us all at one time?" he asked me.

"I don't see how."

"Saint-Martin-de-Ré is pretty far, and if they take sixty a day it'll take ten days. There're almost six hundred of us here alone."

"The main thing is that we've been inoculated. That means we're on the list and we'll soon be in the *bagne*. Cheer up, Dega, we're on a new lap. You can count on me; I'm counting on you."

He looked at me and his eyes gleamed with satisfaction. He placed his hand on my arm and said, "In life or death, Papi."

The convoy was not worth describing except that we suffocated in our little closets in the van. The guards refused to let in any air, even to leave the doors ajar. When we reached La Rochelle, two men were dead of asphyxiation.

The people strolling on the quay—for Saint-Martin-de-Ré was an island and we had to take a boat to cross the channel—witnessed the discovery of the poor devils. They showed us no ill will. The police put the corpses on board with us, for they were supposed to deliver us at the other end dead or alive.

The crossing didn't take long, but it gave us a chance to take in some good gulps of sea air. I said to Dega, "It smells of *cavale*." He smiled. And Julot, who stood next to us, said:

"Yes, it sure does smell of *cavale*. Let's try to stick together. At Saint-Martin they pick ten people at random for each cell."

Julot was wrong. When we arrived, he and two others were summoned and placed apart. They were all escaped prisoners from the *bagne*; they'd been picked up in France and were going back for the second time.

In our cells, in groups of ten, we began a life of waiting. We were allowed to talk, to smoke, and they fed us well. The only danger was to the *plan*. For no reason you might suddenly be told to undress, then you were closely examined. First, every inch of your body down to the soles of your feet, then your clothes. Finally, "Get dressed!" then back to the cell.

That was our life: the cell, the mess hall, the yard where we spent long hours marching in line. One, two! One, two! One, two! . . . We marched in groups of one hundred and fifty. The queue was long, our wooden shoes clattered. Silence was obligatory. Then, "Break ranks!" Everybody sat on the ground; groups formed according to social categories. First, the men of the real underworld from all over—Corsica, Marseilles, Toulouse, Brittany, Paris, etc. There was even one man from Ardèche—me. And I must say in Ardèche's favor that there were only two in that convoy of nineteen hundred men: a policeman who had killed his wife, and me. Conclusion: men from Ardèche are good men. The other groups just happened, for there were more amateurs going to the *bagne* than members of the underworld. Those days of waiting were called "observation" days. And they were; we were watched all the time.

One afternoon I was sitting in the sun when a man came up to me. He was small and thin and wore glasses. I tried to place him, but in our uniforms it was hard.

"Are you Papillon?"

"Yes, that's me. What do you want?"

"Come to the toilets," he said and left.

"That's some Corsican square," Dega said. "Most likely a mountain bandit. What does he want?"

"That's what I'm going to find out."

I went to the toilets in the middle of the yard and pretended to urinate. The man stood next to me, in the same position. Without looking at me he said, "I'm Pascal Matra's brother-in-law. When he came to visit me, he told me that if I needed help, I was to come to you and use his name."

"Yes, Pascal is a friend of mine. What do you want?"

"I can't carry my *plan* any more. I've got dysentery. I don't know who to trust and I'm scared someone will steal it or the guards will find it. Please, Papillon, carry it for me for a few days." And he showed me a *plan* much bigger than mine. I was afraid it was a trap, that he was asking me this to find out if I had one. If I told him I wasn't sure I could carry two, he'd know. So I asked him coldly, "How much is in it?"

"Twenty-five thousand francs."

Without another word I took his *plan*. Very clean it was, too, and right there in front of him I pushed it up my anus, wondering if it was possible for a man to carry two. I had no idea. I stood up, put my pants back on. . . . It was all right. It didn't bother me.

"My name is Ignace Galgani," he said before leaving. "Thanks, Papillon."

I went back to Dega and told him the story.

"It's not too heavy?"

"No."

"O.K. then."

We tried to get in touch with the men who had escaped before, if possible with Julot or Le Guittou. We were hungry for information: what it was like over there, how they treated you, how to keep your *plan*, etc. As luck would have it, we fell in with a very unusual character. He was a Corsican who had been born in the *bagne*. His father was a guard and lived with his wife on the Iles du Salut. He had been born on the Ile Royale, one of the three islands, the others being Saint-Joseph and Diable (Devil's Island), and—oh destiny!—he was going back not as a guard's son but as a convict.

He had been given twelve years at hard labor for burglary with forced entry. He was nineteen, open-faced, with clear bright eyes. We could tell right away that he was a victim of circumstance. He knew very little about the underworld, but he would be useful in giving us information on what lay ahead. He told us about life on the islands where he had lived for fourteen years. We learned, for example, that his nurse on the islands had been a convict, a famous gangster who got his on the Butte in a duel with knives over the beautiful eyes of Casque d'Or.

He gave us some invaluable advice: we must plan our escape from Grande Terre; from the islands it would be impossible. Then, we mustn't get listed as dangerous, for with this label we'd no sooner land at Saint-Laurent-du-Maroni, our destination, than we'd be interned for years or for life, depending on how dangerous they thought we were. In general, fewer than 5 percent were interned on the islands. The others stayed on Grande Terre. The islands were healthy, but Grande Terre—as Dega had already told us—was a real bitch of a place: all sorts of diseases gradually drained a con, or he met with various forms of sudden death.

We hoped we wouldn't be interned on the islands. But I felt a knot in my throat: what if I had already been labeled dangerous? With my life sentence, the business with Tribouillard and the director, I was not in good shape.

Saint-Martin-de-Ré was bursting at the seams with prisoners. There were two categories: between eight hundred and a thousand convicts, and nine hundred *relégués*. To be a convict, you had to have done something serious or, at least, been accused of having done something serious. The sentences ranged from seven years of hard labor to life. A convict granted a reprieve from the death penalty automatically got life. With the *relégués* it was different. A man became a *relégué* after three to five convictions. It's true they were incorrigible thieves and you could understand why society had to protect itself. On the other hand, it was shameful for a civilized people to employ this extra form of punishment. The *relégués* were small-time thieves—and clumsy ones, since they were caught so often—and being a *relégué* in my time came to the same thing as a life sentence. No nation has the right to revenge itself or rush to eliminate people just because they cause society anxiety. They should be healed instead of given such inhuman punishment.

We had now been on Saint-Martin-de-Ré seventeen days. We knew that the name of the ship taking us to the *bagne* was *La Martinière*. It was to carry eighteen hundred convicts. Eight or nine hundred of us were gathered in the courtyard of the fortress. We had been standing in rows of ten for about an hour, filling the courtyard. A door opened and out came a group of men dressed very differently from the guards we had known. They wore sky-blue suits of a military cut and looked well dressed. They weren't police and they weren't soldiers. They all wore wide belts with holsters hanging from them; we could see the handles of their guns. There were about eighty of them. Some wore stripes on their sleeves. All were sunburned and looked to be between thirty-five and fifty. The older men seemed sympathetic; the young ones stuck out their chests with an air of importance. The commanding officer of the group was accompanied by the director of Saint-Martin-de-Ré, a police colonel, three or four army doctors in colonial dress and two priests in white cassocks. The police colonel put a loudspeaker to his mouth. We expected an "Attention!" but not at all.

"Listen carefully," the colonel said. "From here on you are under the jurisdiction of the officials of the Ministry of Justice representing the Penal Administration of French Guiana, whose administrative center is the city of Cayenne. Warden Barrot, I transfer to you the eight hundred prisoners present and listed here. Will you certify that they are all present."

The roll call began: "So and so, present; so and so, present, etc." It took two hours; everything was in order. Then we watched the exchange of signatures by the two administrations on a small table provided for the occasion.

Warden Barrot (he had as many stripes as the colonel, though his were colored instead of silver) took his turn at the loudspeaker. "Transportees, from here on that's what you'll be called—Transportee so and so, or Transportee such and such a number, whichever you are given. From this moment on you are under the special laws of the *bagne*, its regulations, its internal tribunals which, when called upon, will make the decisions they think necessary. These autonomous tribunals can punish you, depending on the offense you commit in the *bagne*, with anything from a simple prison sentence to the death penalty. These disciplinary sentences, whether for prison or solitary confinement, may be carried out in any one of the places that belong to the Administration. The police you see before you are called wardens. When you address them, you must call them 'Mister Warden.' After supper each of you will receive a navy pack with your clothing for the *bagne*. Everything has been anticipated; these are all you'll need. Tomorrow you will board *La Martinière*. We will make the trip together. Don't feel sorry to leave; you'll be better off at the *bagne* than in a penitentiary in France. You can talk, play cards, sing, smoke. Don't worry about being mistreated so long as you behave. I ask that you wait until you're in the *bagne* to settle any personal differences you may have. Discipline during the trip must be very severe and I trust you understand why. If there are any of you who don't feel well enough to undertake the trip, go to the infirmary, where you'll be examined by the medical captains who are accompanying the convoy. I wish you 'bon voyage.' " The ceremony was over.

"So, Dega, what do you think?"

"Papillon, old man, I see I was right when I told you the biggest danger was the other cons. That thing he said about 'wait until you're in the *bagne* to settle any personal differences' spoke volumes. There must be a lot of killings!"

"Don't worry about it. Just trust me."

I sought out François la Passe and asked, "Is your brother still an orderly?"

"Yes, he's a *relégué*."

"Go see him as soon as you can and ask him to give you a lancet. If he wants money, tell me how much and I'll pay him."

Two hours later I was the owner of a lancet with a very strong steel handle. Its only drawback was that it was a little too long, but it was a fearsome weapon.

I sat down near the toilets in the middle of the courtyard and sent for Galgani so that I could give him back his *plan*, but it must have been hard to find him in the shifting mob of eight hundred men filling the enormous yard. We hadn't seen Julot, Le Guittou or Santini since we'd arrived.

The advantage of communal life was that we lived, talked and belonged to a new society, if you could call it a society. There was so much to say, to listen to, to do that there was no time to think. When I realized how much the past had blurred and been relegated to second place in relation to my present life, I figured that once you arrived at the *bagne*, you probably forgot who you were and why you were there because you concentrated on only one thing— escape. But I was wrong. By far the most absorbing thing was to stay alive. Where were the cops, the jury, the court, the judges, my wife, my father, my friends? They were back there, very much alive, and each one had a place in my heart, but because of the excitement of departure, the great leap into the unknown, the new friends and acquaintances, they didn't have the same importance as before. But it only seemed that way. Once I willed it, when my brain was ready to open the drawer where each of them belonged, they'd all be there again.

They were leading Galgani to me, for even with his thick glasses he could barcly see. He seemed in better health. He came up and without speaking squeezed my hand.

"I want to give you back your *plan*," I said. "Now that you're well, you can carry it yourself. It's too much responsibility for me during the trip, and who knows if we'll be anywhere near each other or even if we'll see each other at the *bagne*. So it's better if you take it."

Galgani looked unhappy.

"Come on. Come to the toilets and let me give you your *plan*."

"No, I don't want it. You keep it. I give it to you as a present. It's all yours."

"Why do you say that?"

"I don't want to be killed for my *plan*. I'd rather live without money than be killed because of it. I give it to you because, after all, there's no sense in you risking your life to keep my money. This way, if you risk your life, it's for your own benefit."

"You're scared, Galgani. Have you been threatened?"

"Yes. Three Arabs are on my tail all the time. I haven't come to see you because I don't want them to suspect we're in this together. Every time I go to the toilet, day or night, one of those spooks comes and stands near me. I've tried to make it clear I don't have a *plan*—without making a big deal of it—but they keep watching me. I'm sure they think somebody else has it. They don't know who, but they follow me around to see if I get it back."

I looked at Galgani and realized that he was terrified. I asked, "What part of the yard do they hang around?"

"Near the kitchen and laundry."

"All right. You stay here and I'll go over. . . . No, you come with me." I took the lancet out of my cap and held the blade up my right sleeve, the handle in my hand. We spotted them right away. There were four of them, three Arabs and a Corsican named Girando. I understood right away: the Corsican had been snubbed by the underworld guys and had spilled to the Arabs. He must have known that Galgani was Pascal Matra's brother-in-law and therefore had to have a *plan*.

"How are things, Mokrane?"

"O.K., Papillon. How are things with you?"

"Not so good. I came over to tell you that Galgani is my friend. If anything happens to him, the first one to get it is you, Girando. The rest will follow. Take it any way you like."

Mokrane stood up. He was as tall as I—about six feet—and just as broad. He was ready for a fight, but then I pulled out the lancet, all shiny and new. I held it in the palm of my hand and said, "If you move, I'll kill you like a dog."

Clearly bewildered because I had a weapon, for we were constantly searched, and impressed by my air of assurance, not to mention the length of the lancet, he said, "I was only getting up to talk, not to fight."

I knew this wasn't true, but since it was in my interest to help him save face in front of his friends, I offered him an easy exit.

"O.K., since you were only getting up to talk . . ."

"I didn't know Galgani was your friend. I thought he was an amateur. You know how it is, Papillon, everybody steals from you here and you have to have money for the *cavale*."

"O.K., fair enough. You have every right to fight for your life, Mokrane. Only remember, this is forbidden territory. Look somewhere else."

He held out his hand and I shook it. Jesus, that was a close one. If I had actually killed the guy, I sure wouldn't have sailed the next day.

Galgani walked back with me. I said to him, "Don't tell anyone about this. I don't want to get in dutch with Papa Dega." I tried to persuade Galgani to take back his *plan* and he said, "Tomorrow, before we leave." But the next day he hid himself so well I had to set off for the *bagne* with both *plans*.

That night in our cell no one spoke. We were all thinking that it was our last day on French soil. Each of us felt at least a little nostalgic about leaving France forever, for an unknown land and an unknown way of life.

Ten of the eleven men in our cell were from the underworld, all but the little Corsican who had been born in the *bagne*. All these men were in a state of suspension, reduced to silence by the gravity and importance of the moment. The cigarette smoke billowed out of the cell into the corridor, and you had to sit below the clouds of smoke to keep your eyes from smarting.

The movie of my life unwound before me: my childhood in a family full of love—educated, mannerly, noble; the flowers in the fields, the murmuring of the streams, the taste of the nuts, peaches and plums that our garden produced in quantity; the perfume of the mimosa which bloomed by our front door each spring; the outside of our house, and the inside, filled with my family's special movements—all of it filed through my mind. It was a sound movie: I heard the voice of my poor mother who loved me so much, and then my father's—always tender and caressing; Clara's barking (she was my father's pointer) calling me from the garden to come out and play; the girls and boys I played with during the happiest days of my life. I had not asked to see this movie. It was the projection of a magic lantern brought to life by my subconscious, filling with emotion this night of waiting for the leap into the great unknown.

It was time to take stock. I was twenty-six years old, in good health, and in my gut I had five thousand six hundred francs of my own and twenty-five thousand francs belonging to Galgani. Dega, next to me, had ten thousand. I figured I could count on forty thousand francs, for if Galgani wasn't able to defend his money here, it would be even more difficult on the boat and in Guiana. And he knew it, which is why he hadn't come to claim his *plan*. So

I could count on this money, granted it meant taking Galgani with me. It was his money; he must reap the benefit. I'd use it for his good, although indirectly I'd benefit too. Forty thousand francs was a lot; it would make it easy to buy accomplices—cons, escaped prisoners, guards.

As soon as I arrived, then, I would escape with Dega and Galgani. I would concentrate on that and that alone. I touched the lancet, pleased to feel the cold steel. To have such a formidable weapon gave me a feeling of confidence. I had already proved its usefulness in the incident with the Arabs.

About three in the morning, eleven bulging navy packs were lined up outside our cell, each with a large label. One of them read: "C—, Pierre, thirty years old, five feet nine, size forty-two, shoe size eight, identification number X . . ." That Pierre C—was Pierrot le Fou, the man from Bordeaux convicted for murder in Paris with a sentence of twenty years at hard labor. He was a good guy, a straight and dependable member of the underworld whom I knew well.

I tried deliberately to make my brain conjure up a picture of the courtroom, the jury, the prosecutor and all the rest. It refused outright; all I got were vague outlines. I understood then that if I were to relive those scenes in the Conciergerie and Beaulieu as intensely as I had felt them when they occurred, I would have to be alone, completely alone. It was a relief to know this, and I realized that the communal life that lay in store would produce new needs, new responses, new projects.

Pierrot le Fou came up to the grill and asked, "How goes it, Papi?"

"How about you?"

"You know, I always dreamed of going to America, but being a gambler, I never managed to save enough money for the trip. The pigs decided to offer me the trip free of charge. No question, it's a good thing, eh, Papi?" He was talking naturally, not putting it on, seeming very sure of himself. "This free trip to America has definite advantages. I'd rather go to the *bagne* than spend fifteen years in solitary in France."

"I suppose we should wait until the returns are in, but I think I agree with you. Look, Pierrot, that's your tag."

He bent down to read it and said, "I can't wait to put that outfit on. How about those red stripes? I'd like to open the pack and do it right now. Nobody'll say anything. After all, they're mine."

"Don't. Wait until we're told. This is no time to make trouble, Pierre. I need peace." He understood and moved away.

Dega looked at me and said, "Young feller, it's our last night. Tomorrow we leave our beautiful country."

"Our beautiful country doesn't have a beautiful sense of justice, Dega. Maybe we'll get to know other countries, not so beautiful, perhaps, but with a more humane way of treating offenders."

I didn't know how close to the truth I was. The future would teach me.

DEPARTURE FOR THE *BAGNE*

At six o'clock, reveille. Some cons brought us coffee, then four guards came. Today they wore white, their revolvers still on their hips. Their gilt buttons glistened. One of them had three gold stripes in a V on his left sleeve, though nothing on the shoulders.

"Transportees, go into the corridor by twos. Each of you, find your pack—your name is on the label. Take your pack, stand against the wall and face the corridor with the pack in front of you."

When we had done this, he said, "Strip, make a bundle of your clothes, put it in your jacket and tie it by the sleeves. . . . Good. You there, pick up the bundles and put them in the cell . . . Now, put your new clothes on: underpants, undershirts, your striped pants, the shirt, shoes and socks. . . . Everybody ready?"

"Yes, sir."

"Good. Keep your sweaters out of the pack in case it rains or gets cold. Packs on your left shoulders! . . . Line up in twos and follow me."

With the man with the stripes in front, a guard on either side and the fourth bringing up the rear, our little column marched into the yard. In less than two hours they had eight hundred cons lined up. Then they called out forty men, among them me, Dega and the three who had escaped: Julot, Le Guittou and Santini. We stood in rows of ten; each row had a guard at its side. No chains, no hand-cuffs. Three yards in front of us were ten policemen. They faced us, rifles in hand, and walked backward all the way, each one guided by another policeman pulling him by the belt.

The great gates of the Citadel opened and the column slowly moved forward. As we emerged from the fortress, policemen—submachine guns in hand—came alongside the convoy and accompanied it to its destination. They held back the curious who had gathered to watch our departure. About halfway I heard a soft whistle. I looked up and there was my wife Nénette and Antoine D—, an old friend, leaning out of a window. Paula, Dega's wife, and his friend, Antoine Giletti, were at another window of the house. Dega spotted them too, and we walked with our eyes riveted to the windows as long as we could. I never saw my wife again, nor my friend Antoine, who died later in the bombing of Marseilles. No one spoke; the silence was complete. Neither prisoners, guards, police, nor public broke in on this poignant moment; everyone understood that these eight hundred men were leaving normal life behind forever.

We went aboard. We, the first forty, were led to the bottom of the hold into a cage made of thick bars. A sign hung from one of them: "Room No. 1, 40 men in special category. Constant surveillance." We each received a rolled-up hammock. There were lots of rings to hang them on.

Suddenly somebody grabbed me. It was Julot. He knew the ropes; he had made the same trip ten years ago. "Quick, come here," he said. "Hang your pack on the hook where you're going to put your hammock. Here we're near two portholes. They're closed now, but when we're out to sea they'll be opened. We'll have more fresh air than anywhere else in the cage."

I introduced him to Dega. We were talking when a man came over to us. Julot put out his arm to stop him. "You better stay away from here if you want to reach the *bagne* alive. Understand?" The other man said, "Yes." "You know why?" "Yes." "O.K. Beat it." The guy moved off. Dega was delighted with this demonstration of power. "With you two, I'll be able to sleep." Julot replied, "With us, you're safer than by an open window in a villa overlooking the sea."

The trip lasted eighteen days, with only one incident worth mentioning. One night a piercing scream woke us. A man was found dead, a knife deep between his shoulders. The knife, a fearsome weapon more than eight inches long, had penetrated up through his hammock.

Immediately twenty-five or thirty guards aimed their guns at us and shouted, "Everybody strip, and make it fast!"

We all undressed. I assumed we were going to be searched. I put my lancet under my bare right foot and bore my weight on my left. The steel cut into me, but the weapon was well hidden. Four guards came into the cage and began to search our shoes and clothing. Before entering, they had left their weapons outside, and the door of the cage closed behind them. However, outside the cage the rest of the guards kept their guns trained on us. "The first man who moves is dead," said the chief warden.

The search turned up three knives, two sharpened nails, a corkscrew and a gold *plan*. Six men, still naked, were called out on the deck. The head of the convoy, Warden Barrot, arrived with two doctors and the ship's captain. When the guards left the cage, everybody dressed again without waiting for orders. I retrieved my lancet.

The guards withdrew to the rear of the deck. Barrot stood in the middle, the others near the stairs. Facing them in a straight line, the six naked men stood at attention.

"This one belongs to him," said a guard who had made the search. He took one of the knives and pointed to its owner.

"That's right. It's mine."

"Fine," Barrot said. "He'll finish the trip in the cell over the engines."

The owners of the weapons—nails, corkscrew and knives—were identified and each admitted his ownership. Still naked, each of them climbed the stairs accompanied by two guards. Two things remained—a knife and the gold *plan*, but only one man. He was a young man, about twenty-four, well built, at least six feet tall, with blue eyes and an athlete's body.

"This is yours, isn't it?" said the guard, indicating the gold *plan*.

"Yes, it's mine."

"How much is in it?" asked Warden Barrot as he picked it up off the floor.

"Three hundred English pounds, two hundred dollars and two five-carat diamonds."

"O.K. Let's have a look." He opened it. We couldn't see anything, but we heard him say, "That's correct. Your name?"

"Salvidia, Roméo."

"You're Italian?"

"Yes, sir."

"You won't be punished for the *plan*, but for the knife, yes."

"Excuse me, sir, but the knife isn't mine."

"Don't give me that. Look, I found it in your shoes," the guard said.

"I repeat. The knife is not mine."

"So I'm a liar?"

"No, you're mistaken."

"Well, then, whose knife is it?" Warden Barrot asked. "If it isn't yours, whose is it?"

"It isn't mine, that's all I know."

"If you don't want to cook over the boilers, tell us who the knife belongs to."

"I don't know."

"Don't try to bullshit me. We find a knife in your shoes and you don't know who it belongs to? You think I'm stupid? Either it's yours or you know who put it there. Which?"

"It's not mine, and it's not for me to say whose it is. I'm no stoolie. Do I look like one of your bunch?"

"Guard, put him in handcuffs. You're going to pay for your insolence."

The two officers exchanged words. The ship's captain gave an order to a petty officer who then left. A few moments later a Breton sailor appeared, a giant with a wooden bucket full of sea water and a heavy rope as thick as your wrist. Roméo was tied kneeling to the lowest step. The sailor soaked the rope in the bucket and then, with all his strength, he slowly struck the poor bastard across the buttocks and back. Not a sound came from his lips, but the blood began to run from his buttocks and his sides. In the tomb-like silence a single cry of protest rose from our cage:

"You bastards!"

That was all we needed to set us off. "Murderers! Sons of

bitches! Assholes!" The more they threatened us, the more we yelled.

Then suddenly the warden shouted: "Turn on the steam!"

Wheels were turned and bursts of steam gushed against our chests with such force we were thrown to the floor. We panicked. The men who were scalded didn't dare to cry out. It lasted less than a minute, but everyone was terrified.

"I hope you troublemakers got the point. Anything happens and I turn on the steam. Is that clear? Now get up!"

Three men, seriously burned, were taken to the infirmary. The boy they had whipped was returned to our cell. He was to die six years later, in a *cavale* with me.

During the eighteen days we had plenty of time to pick up information about the *bagne*. Nothing turned out as Julot predicted, but he did his best.

He explained, for example, that Saint-Laurent-du-Maroni was a village about seventy-five miles from the sea on a river called the Maroni. "The penitentiary is in this village. It's the headquarters of the *bagne*. That's where they divide us up by categories. The *relégués* go directly to a penitentiary ninety-five miles from there called Saint-Jean. The rest are classified in three groups. The most dangerous will be called up as soon as we arrive and put in cells in the disciplinary section while they wait to be transferred to the Iles du Salut. They're interned there for the duration of their sentences. The islands are three hundred miles from Saint-Laurent and sixty miles from Cayenne. Cons hardly ever go to Diable. Those who go there are political prisoners.

"The second group of dangerous prisoners stay at Saint-Laurent and are put to work in the gardens and fields. If necessary, they're sent on to the toughest camps: Forestier, Charvin, Cascade, Crique Rouge and Forty Kilometers—which is called the death camp.

"Then there's the so-called normal category. They work in the Administration, the kitchens, cleaning the village or the camp, or working at different things in the workshops, carpentry, painting, ironwork, electricity, mattress making, tailoring, the laundry, etc.

"So the hour of truth is the hour of arrival. If you're called up and taken to a cell, it means you're going to be interned on the islands. That means you give up all hope of escape. The only way out is to get hurt fast—cut your knee or your gut so they'll send you to the hospital. You can escape from there. But don't go to the islands, no matter what. Another hope is, if the boat to the islands isn't ready for the trip, to offer money to the infirmary orderly. He'll give you a shot of turpentine or stick a piece of hair soaked in urine into your flesh to make it fester. Or he'll give you some sulphur to breathe, then tell the doctor you have a fever of a hundred and four. While you wait these few days, get to the hospital, no matter what.

"If you're not called up and you're left behind in the camp barracks, you have time to do something. In that case, try not to get a job inside the camp. Pay the man in charge so that you can work in the village as a cesspool cleaner or a sweeper, or get a job in a sawmill run by civilians. On your way back and forth to work you'll have a chance to make contact with liberated cons living in the village, or the Chinese, so they can start preparing your escape. Stay away from the camps around the village. Everybody there dies fast. There are camps where nobody lasts three months. They make you cut a quarter of a cord of wood a day in the middle of the bush."

Julot kept feeding us these precious bits of information all through the trip. He was prepared himself. He knew that, as a returned escapee, he'd be going directly into a dungeon. He also had a very small, very sharp knife, really a penknife, in his *plan*. As we docked, he planned to cut his knee open. Then, as he was leaving the boat, he would fall off the ladder in front of everybody. He hoped he'd be carried from the wharf directly to the hospital. And he was.

SAINT-LAURENT-DU-MARONI

Some of the guards went off duty so that they could change their clothes. They came back dressed in white, wearing the colonial cap instead of the kepi. Julot said, "We must be almost there." The heat was intense because they had closed the portholes. Through them we could see the bush. So we were on the Maroni! The water was muddy, the virgin forest vividly green. Birds flew off, disturbed by the ship's siren. We were going very slowly now, which allowed us plenty of time to examine the lush, dense, deep-green vegetation. Then came the first houses—wooden, with zinc roofs. Black men and women stood in front of their doors watching the ship go by. They were used to seeing it unload its human cargo and stood impassive. Three wails of the siren and the noise of the screws told us we were about to dock, then all sounds stopped. Silence. You could have heard the buzzing of a fly.

No one spoke. Julot had his knife out and was cutting his pants at the knees and roughing up the edges. He would cut himself only when he reached the bridge so that there would be no tell-tale trail of blood. The guards opened the cage door and lined us up in threes. We were in the fourth row, Julot between Dega and me. We climbed up to the bridge. It was two in the afternoon and a fiery sun beat down on my eyes and sheared pate. We were lined up on the bridge, then marched toward the gangplank. As the first man reached it, there was a general hesitation. I held Julot's pack to his shoulder; with his two hands he tore at the skin of his knees, dug the knife in and sliced off three or four inches of flesh. Then he slipped me the knife and resumed holding his pack. As we stepped on the gangplank, he fell and rolled to the bottom. He was picked up, and when they saw he was hurt, they summoned two stretcher-bearers. The scenario had been played out exactly as planned.

A motley crowd was on hand to watch us. Blacks, mulattoes, Indians, Chinese, dregs of whites (probably liberated convicts) examined each of us as we stepped on land and lined up with the rest. Behind the guards stood well-dressed civilians, women in summer dresses, children wearing the colonial cap. They were watching the new arrivals too. When there were two hundred of us, the convoy set off. We walked about ten minutes until we arrived in front of a building. On its thick wooden gate was writ-ten: "Penitencier, Saint-Laurent-du-Maroni. Capacité, 3000 hommes." The gate opened and we entered in rows of ten. "One, two, one, two, march!" A number of cons were watching us arrive. They leaned out of windows and stood on rocks.

When we reached the center of the yard, a guard shouted, "Stop! Put your packs down in front of you. You over there, pass out the hats!" Each of us was given a straw hat. We needed it, all right; two or three men had already fainted from sunstroke. A guard with stripes held a list in his hands. Dega and I looked at each other; we were thinking of what Julot had said. They called to Le Guittou: "This way!" Two guards flanked him and they left. Same thing with Santini. Girasole, ditto.

"Jules Pignard!"

"Jules Pignard [that was Julot] was hurt. He's in the hospital."

"O.K. Now listen carefully. When I call your name, step out of ranks with your pack on your shoulder and go stand in front of the yellow barracks. It's Number One."

So and so, present, etc. Dega, Carrier and I found ourselves among those lined up in front of the barracks. The door opened and we entered a hall about seventy feet long. Down the middle, a passage seven feet wide; to the right and left, iron bars that ran the length of the hall. Canvas hammocks stretched from the bars to the wall, and each hammock had a blanket. You could go where you liked. Dega, Pierrot le Fou, Santori, Grandet and I moved in next to each other and immediately set up housekeeping. I walked to the end of the hall: showers to the right, toilets to the left; no running water. We clung to the bars of the windows and watched the next arrivals. Our relief was intense; obviously we weren't going to be interned because we were here together in a barracks. If we were, we'd already be in cells, as Julot had said.

In the tropics there is no dusk or dawn. You pass from day to night just like that, at the same time, during the whole year. Night falls abruptly at six-thirty. And at six-thirty two old cons brought in two oil lamps which they hung from a hook in the ceiling. They gave only the faintest light. Three-fourths of the barracks was in total darkness. By nine o'clock everyone was asleep. The excitement of arrival had passed and we were overcome with the heat. There was not a breath of air; everyone was down to his undershirt. I was between Dega and Pierrot le Fou. We whispered for a while, then fell asleep.

The next morning it was still dark when reveille sounded. Everybody got up, washed and dressed. We were given some coffee and a piece of bread. A plank attached to the wall served as a table for our food and a shelf for the rest of our belongings. At nine o'clock two guards entered together with a young con dressed in white without stripes. The two guards were Corsicans and talked Corsican with their countrymen.

While this was going on, the infirmary orderly made a tour of the hall. When he reached me, he said, "How goes it, Papi? You don't recognize me?"

"No."

"I'm Sierra, the Algerian; I knew you at Dante's in Paris."

"Ah, yes, now I recognize you. But you came over in 'twenty-nine. This is 'thirty-three and you're still here?"

"Yes, it's not all that easy to get out of this place. Why don't you report sick? What about him? Who is he?"

"Dega. He's a friend of mine."

"I'll put him down for a visit too. You, Papi, have dysentery. And you, old man, you have attacks of asthma. I'll see you at eleven. I want to talk to you." He continued on his rounds, calling out in a loud voice, "Anyone sick here?" If a man raised a finger, he went over and put him on his list. The next time he passed us, he was accompanied by a very old and weathered guard.

"Papillon, I want you to meet my boss, Bartiloni, the infirmary guard. Mr. Bartiloni, this man and that one there are the friends I told you about."

"O.K., Sierra. We can fix it up during the visit. You can count on me."

They came for us at eleven. We were nine. We crossed the camp between barracks until we came to a newer one painted white with a red cross. We went in and found ourselves in a waiting room with about sixty other men. Two guards stood in each corner. Sierra appeared, dressed in an immaculate white smock. He said, "You, and you and you, go in." We went into what was obviously a doctor's office. Sierra spoke to three old men in Spanish. I recognized one of the Spaniards right away. It was Fernandez, the man who had killed three Argentinians at the Café de Madrid in Paris. They exchanged a few words and Sierra led him to a bathroom that opened into the main hall. Then he came back to me and said, "Papi, let me embrace you. I'm so happy I can do something for you and your friend. You are both internees. . . . Wait, let me speak! You, Papillon, are in for life, and you, Dega, for five years. Have you got any money?"

"Yes."

"You give me five hundred francs each and I'll see that you're hospitalized tomorrow morning, you, Papi, for dysentery. You, Dega, you knock on the door, or better still, one of you call the guard and ask for the orderly, saying Dega is suffocating. I'll take care of the rest. Papillon, I ask only one thing: if you make a break, warn me ahead of time and I'll be there. For one hundred francs each, they'll keep you in the hospital for a week. So you have to move fast."

Fernandez came out of the bathroom and handed Sierra five hundred francs. I went in, and when I emerged, I gave him not one thousand but fifteen hundred francs. He refused the extra five hundred. I didn't insist. He said, "This money is for the guard. I don't want anything for myself. We're friends, aren't we?"

The next day Dega, Fernandez and I found ourselves in a huge cell in the hospital. Dega had been hospitalized in the middle of the night. The orderly was a man of thirty-five named Chatal. Sierra had given him all the dope on us. When the doctor passed through, he was to show him the report of a stool examination that made it appear that I was riddled with amoebae. For Dega, ten minutes before the doctor's visit, he burned a little sulphur and made him breathe the fumes with a towel over his head. Fernandez' cheek was tremendously swollen; he had pricked the skin inside and had panted so hard and conscientiously for an hour that the swelling had closed his eye. The cell was on the second floor of the building; there were almost seventy sick, many with dysentery. I asked the orderly where Julot was.

"In the building across the way. Do you want me to give him a message?"

"Yes. Tell him that Papillon and Dega are here and that he should get to a window."

The orderly was able to come and go as he liked. He had only to knock on the door and an Arab opened it. The Arab was the turnkey, a convict serving as an assistant to the guards. On either side of the door sat three guards, their rifles across their laps. The bars of the windows were rails, and I wondered how we would ever manage to cut through them.

Between our building and Julot's was a garden full of beautiful flowers. Julot appeared at a window with a slate in his hand on which he had chalked "Bravo." An hour later the orderly brought me a letter from him. It said: "I'm trying to get to your room. If it doesn't work, you try to come to mine. Say that you have enemies in your room. So you're interned? Chin up, we'll get them yet." The incident in the Beaulieu jail where we had suffered together had created a great bond between us. Julot was an expert with the wooden mallet; that's why he was nicknamed "the man with the hammer." He would drive up to a jewelry shop in broad daylight when the best jewels were displayed in their cases in the shopwindow. The car, an accomplice at the wheel, would stop with the motor running. Julot would get out with his large mallet, smash the window with a single blow, grab all the jewel cases he could scoop up and leap back into the car, which would tear off at full speed. He had met with success in Lyon, Angers, Tours, Le Havre. Then he took on an important jeweler in Paris at three in the afternoon and carried off almost a million francs' worth of jewels. He never told me why or how he was identified. He was condemned to twenty years and escaped at the end of four.

We had now been in the hospital a week. Yesterday I gave Chatal two hundred francs, the payment for another week. To win friends, we gave everybody tobacco. A sixty-year-old con from Marseilles called Carora made friends with Dega. He acted as his adviser. He kept telling him that if he had a lot of money and people in the village found out about it (thanks to the French newspapers, everyone was up on the news), it would be better if he didn't try to escape because the liberated convicts would kill him for his *plan*. Dega made me privy to his conversations with Carora. I told Dega that the old man was obviously a waste of time since he'd been stuck here for twenty years, but he wouldn't listen to me. Dega was much impressed by the old man's prattle, and I had a hard time keeping up my side of the argument.

I passed Sierra a note asking him to send Galgani to me. It didn't take long. The next day Galgani was in the hospital but in another room. How to give him back his *plan*? I told Chatal that I needed desperately to speak to Galgani, letting him think it concerned plans for an escape. He said he could bring him to me at exactly five minutes to noon when the guards were changing shifts. Chatal would have him climb to a porch and talk to me through the window, and for free. Galgani appeared at the window at noon and I put his *plan* directly into his hands. He stood there and cried. Two days later he sent me a magazine stuffed with five thousand-franc bills and the one word: "Thanks."

Chatal, who brought me the magazine, saw the money. He said nothing, but I tried to offer him some. He refused.

"We want to get moving," I said. "Do you want to come with us?"

"No, Papillon. I'm involved in another one. I don't want to try an escape until five months from now when my friend is free. Our *cavale* will be better prepared and a surer thing. I can see why you're in a hurry—you're an internee. But here, with these bars, it's going to be hard. I'm afraid I won't be able to help you. I don't want to risk my job. I just want to wait here quietly until my friend is ready."

"Very good, Chatal. In this kind of life we have to be frank with each other. I won't mention it again."

"But I'll still carry your messages and do errands for you."

"Thanks, Chatal."

That night we heard a burst of machine-gun fire. We learned the next morning that Julot had escaped. May God go with him; he was a good friend. He must have seen an opening and made the most of it.

Fifteen years later, in 1948, I happened to be in Haiti, where I'd come with a Venezuelan millionaire to make a deal with the president of the Casino to run his gambling tables. One night, as we came out of a night club where we'd been drinking champagne, one of the girls with us—as black as coal and as well educated as any daughter of a good French provincial family—said to me:

"My grandmother is a voodoo priestess and lives with an old Frenchman. He escaped from Cayenne and he's been with her a long, long time. He's drunk all the time. His name is Jules Marteau."

I sobered up immediately. "Girl, let me see your grandmother right away."

She spoke to the taxi driver in Haitian dialect and off we went at top speed. We passed a brightly lighted night club. "Stop." I went up to the bar, bought a bottle of Pernod, two bottles of champagne and two bottles of the local rum. "Let's go." We stopped by the edge of the sea in front of a cozy little white house with a red slate roof. The sea came up almost to the steps. The girl knocked and the door was opened by a large black woman with white hair. She was wearing a shift that reached to her ankles. The two women talked in dialect. Then the old woman said, "Come in, the house is yours."

An oil lamp illuminated a tidy room full of birds and fish.

"You want to see Julot? Wait, he's coming. Jules! Jules! Some-body's here to see you."

An old man appeared, barefoot and dressed in blue-striped pajamas that reminded me of our uniform in the *bagne*.

"Who wants to see me at this hour of the night, Boule de Neige? Papillon! It can't be!" He took me in his arms and said, "Bring the lamp closer, Boule de Neige. I want to see my old pal's face. Yes, it's you, you old bastard! It's really you! Welcome! The house, the little money I have, my wife's granddaughter—it's all yours. Just say the word."

We drank the Pernod, the champagne, the rum, and from time to time Julot broke into song.

"What times we had, eh, old pal? There's nothing like a little adventure. I went through Colombia, Panama, Costa Rica, Jamaica. Since then I've been here with Boule de Neige, the best woman a man ever had. When do you leave? Are you here for long?"

"No, just a week."

"What are you doing here?"

"I'm trying to arrange with the president of the Casino to get the contract for his gambling tables."

"I'd like nothing better, pal, than to have you around for the rest of your life. But don't have anything to do with that son of a bitch. He'll have you murdered the minute he sees you're doing good business."

"Thanks for the advice."

"As for you, Boule de Neige, get your voodoo show ready, the one 'not for tourists.' I want the real thing for my friend."

So Julot made his escape, but Dega, Fernandez and I were still waiting. From time to time I casually examined the bars over the windows. They were real railroad tracks, so nothing doing there.

But there was still the door. Day and night, three guards were stationed there. Since Julot's escape the surveillance had tightened. The rounds were made at shorter intervals and the doctor was less friendly. Chatal came into the room only twice a day, to give injections and to take temperatures. A second week went by; again I paid two hundred francs.

Dega talked of everything but escape. Yesterday he saw my lancet and said, "You still have it? Why?"

I answered angrily, "To save my skin and yours, if I have to."

Fernandez was not a Spaniard but an Argentinian. He was a good man, a real adventurer, but he, too, was impressed by old Carora's nonsense. One day I heard him tell Dega, "They say the islands are very healthy places, not like here, and it's not so hot. Here you pick up germs and get dysentery just from going to the toilets." Every day one or two of the seventy men in our room died of dysentery. And strangely, they all died when it was low tide in the afternoon or evening. No one ever died in the morning. Why? A mystery of nature.

That night I had a talk with Dega and Fernandez. I told them that the Arab turnkey sometimes came into the room during the night to pull back the sheets and examine the very sick. It would be easy to knock him out and put on his uniform (we all wore only smocks and sandals). Once dressed, I'd go out, grab a rifle from one of the guards, aim it at them, force them into the cell and close the door. Then we'd jump over the hospital wall on the river side, dive into the water and drift with the current. After that we'd see. Since we had money, we could buy a boat and food and set out to sea. They both categorically rejected the project. I sensed they'd grown apathetic; I was very disappointed. And so the days passed.

We'd now been in the hospital three weeks less two days. We had only ten to fifteen days maximum to try for a break. Today, a memorable day—the twenty-first of November, 1933—Joanes

Clousiot came into the room. Someone had tried to kill him at the barber's on Saint-Martin. He was almost blind; his eyes were shut tight and were full of pus. Once Chatal had left, I went over to him. He told me that the other internees had left for the islands more than two weeks before but that he'd managed to get left behind. An official warned him three days before they were to leave. He had put castor oil grains in his eyes, they abscessed, and the infection had got him into the hospital. He was game for anything and crazy to get going, even if he had to kill to do it. He had three thousand francs. Once his eyes were bathed with warm water, he would be able to see fine. I explained my escape plan. He liked it, but he said that if we were going to take the guards by surprise, there would have to be three of us. We could remove the legs of the beds, and armed with an iron leg each, we could knock them all out. According to him, even if we had their rifles, they wouldn't believe we'd really shoot and they'd go alert the guards in the building Julot has escaped from, which was at least twenty yards away.

THIRD NOTEBOOK

THE FIRST
CAVALE

ESCAPE FROM THE HOSPITAL

TONIGHT I BUTTONHOLED DEGA, THEN Fernandez. Dega said he had no confidence in the plan but that he would pay any amount of money to get his internment lifted. He asked me to write Sierra, tell him that it had been suggested to him and was it at all possible? On the same day Chatal brought back the answer: "Don't pay anybody to lift your internment. It has to come from France, and no one, not even the director of the penitentiary, can do it. If you're desperate, you can try to get out, but only the day after the boat—the *Mana*—leaves for the islands."

We had eight days left before we were to leave for the islands, and I began to think it might be better to escape from there rather than from our room in the hospital. In the same note Sierra had said that if I wanted to, he would send a liberated convict to talk to me and help me prepare a boat behind the hospital. He was from Toulouse, his name was Jésus, and he had prepared Dr. Bougrat's escape two years earlier. In order to see him, I'd have to go for X-rays in another building. This place was built into the hospital wall; the *libérés* were provided access with fake passes. He warned me that before being X-rayed I should remove my *plan*, for the doctor might notice it if he took a picture of me below my lungs. I sent Sierra a note telling him to send Jésus to X-ray and to get together with Chatal to have me sent too. That same night Sierra told me it would be the day after tomorrow at nine.

The next day Dega and Fernandez both asked to leave the hospital. The *Mana* had left that morning. They hoped to escape from their cells in the camp. I wished them good luck; my plans were unchanged.

I met Jésus. He was an old *libéré*, as dry as smoked fish, with two ugly scars across his weathered face. One eye wept all the time. Ugly face, ugly expression. He didn't give me confidence, and the future proved me right. We spoke quickly.

"I can fix you up a boat for four or at most five men. A barrel of water, food, coffee and tobacco. Three paddles, empty flour sacks, needle and thread to make the mainsail and a jib. A compass, a hatchet, a knife, five quarts of rum. All for twenty-five hundred francs. There'll be no moon in three days. Starting on the fourth, if you agree, I'll wait for you in the boat every night for eight days from eleven to three in the morning. Once the moon shows the first quarter, I'll stop waiting. The boat will be exactly opposite the corner of the hospital wall. Guide yourself by feeling the wall, for you won't be able to see it even from six feet away."

I didn't trust him, but I still said yes.

"What about the money?" Jésus asked.

"I'll send it through Sierra."

We parted without shaking hands. Not a good start.

At three o'clock Chatal went to the camp to give Sierra the money: two thousand five hundred francs. It's thanks to Galgani I have this money to gamble, I reflected, and it's risky. Just so long as he doesn't spend it all on rum!

Clousiot was ecstatic; he was full of confidence—in himself, in me and in the project. Only one thing bothered him: the Arab didn't come every night, and when he did come it was usually too early. Then there was another problem: who to pick for a third. There was a Corsican from the Nice underworld named Biaggi. He'd been in the *bagne* since 1929 and was now in the maximum-security ward under suspicion of having killed a man. Clousiot and I discussed whether we should speak to him and when. While we were talking, a boy of about eighteen came up to us. He was as pretty as a girl. His name was Maturette and he had been condemned to death for the murder of a taxi driver, then given a reprieve because of his age—at the time, seventeen. There had been two of them, a sixteen- and a seventeen-year-old, and when they appeared in court, each declared he'd killed the taxi driver. But the driver had been hit by only one bullet. Their behavior in court aroused all the cons' sympathies.

Maturette approached us and, in his girlish voice, asked us for a light. We gave it to him and I threw in a present of four cigarettes and a box of matches. He thanked me with a seductive smile and we let him go.

Suddenly Clousiot said, "Papi, we're saved. I know how we can get that Arab in here as often and any time we like. It's in the bag."

"How do you figure?"

"It's easy. We'll tell that kid, Maturette, to make the Arab fall in love with him. Arabs like boys, you know. It's a cinch he'll want to screw him. All the kid has to do is put on an act, saying he's afraid of being seen, and we've got the Arab coming in exactly when we want him."

"Let's give it a try."

I went over to Maturette; he received me with another seductive smile. He thought he'd aroused me with the first one. I said straight off, "I just want to talk to you. Come into the toilets." We went in and I began, "If you repeat one word of what I'm about to say, you're a dead man. Here it is." I told him our plan and asked him how much money he wanted, or did he want to escape with us?

"I want to escape with you."

Agreed. We shook on it.

He went off to sleep and, after a few words with Clousiot, I did too. The next night, at eight o'clock, Maturette sat down next to the window. The Arab didn't need to be called. He came by himself and they talked in low voices. At ten o'clock Maturette went to bed. We had been in bed with one eye open since nine. The Arab came into the room, made the rounds twice, found one man dead. He knocked on the door, and soon afterward two stretcher-bearers came and took the corpse away. Corpses turned out to be useful for they justified frequent visits by the Arab at any hour of the night. Following our advice, Maturette made an assignation the next night for eleven o'clock. The turnkey arrived on time, passed by the boy's bed, pulled his feet to wake him up, then went on to the toilets. Maturette followed. Fifteen minutes later the turnkey came out, went straight to the door and left. At the same time Maturette went back to his bed without speaking. The next night the same thing, but at midnight. Everything was working like a dream. The Arab came whenever the boy asked him to.

At four in the afternoon on November 27, 1933, with two legs of the bed ready as bludgeons, I waited for word from Sierra. Chatal, the orderly, arrived but without a note. All he said was, "François Sierra told me to tell you that Jésus is waiting at the stated place. Good luck."

At eight in the evening Maturette said to the Arab, "Come after midnight. That way we can be together longer."

The Arab said he would. On the stroke of midnight we were ready. The Arab came in at quarter past twelve, went straight to Maturette's bed, pulled his feet and continued toward the toilets. Maturette followed him. I yanked the leg off my bed; it made a noise as it fell. Clousiot's made no sound. I was to stand behind the door and Clousiot was to walk up to the Arab to attract his attention. After a twenty-minute wait everything went very fast. The Arab came out of the toilets and, surprised at seeing Clousiot, said:

"What are you doing in the middle of the room at this hour of the night? Get back into bed."

Then I whacked him on the head and he fell without a sound. Quickly I put on his clothes and shoes. We dragged him under the bed and, just before we pushed him completely under, I gave him another crack on the back of the neck. Now he was really out.

Not one of the men in the room budged. I went straight to the door, followed by Clousiot and Maturette, who were both in their smocks. I knocked, the guard opened up, and I swung my iron leg, whack! right on his head. The other guard facing us dropped his carbine; he must have been asleep. Before he could react, I smacked him. None of mine made a sound; Clousiot's said "Ah!" before collapsing on the floor. My two guards were still on their chairs, the third was stretched out stiff. We held our breaths. To us, that "Ah!" had been heard by the entire world. It was certainly loud enough, yet no one moved. We left them where they lay and took off with their three carbines, Clousiot first, the kid in the middle and me last. We ran down the dimly lit stairs. Clousiot had left his bed leg behind; I kept mine in my left hand, the rifle in my right. Downstairs, nothing. Around us the night was as dark as ink. We had to look hard to find the wall next to the river. We went as fast as we could. Once at the wall, I made a footrest with my hands. Clousiot climbed up, straddled the wall, pulled Maturette up, then me. We slid down the other side. Clousiot fell into a hole and hurt his foot. Maturette and I made it without trouble. We both got up; we had abandoned the rifles before jumping. But when Clousiot tried to get up, he couldn't. He said he had broken his leg. I left Maturette with Clousiot and ran toward the corner of the wall, feeling along with my hand. It was so dark that I didn't see when I came to the end of the wall, and when my hand kept on going, I fell flat on my face. Down by the river, I heard a voice:

"Is that you?"

"Yes. Jésus?"

"Yes."

He lit a match. I stepped into the water and waded over to him. There were two men.

"You get in first. Who are you?"

"Papillon."

"O.K."

"Jésus, we have to go back up. My friend broke his leg jumping off the wall."

"Then take this paddle and row."

The three paddles dipped into the water and the boat quickly made the hundred yards between us and the place where I thought they were—for we could see nothing. I called, "Clousiot!"

"For Christ's sake, don't talk. L'Enflé, use your lighter." A few sparks flew off; they saw them. Clousiot gave a whistle between his teeth—a Lyon whistle; it makes no noise, but you can hear it clearly, like the hiss of a snake. He kept whistling until we came abreast. L'Enflé got out, picked Clousiot up in his arms and placed him in the boat. Then Maturette climbed in and finally L'Enflé. We were five, and the water came to within two fingers of the gunwales.

"Nobody move without a warning," Jésus said. "Papillon, stop paddling; put your paddle across your knees. Let's go, L'Enflé!"

Helped by the current, the boat plunged into the night. A third of a mile downstream, we passed the penitentiary. We were in the middle of the river and the current was carrying us at an incredible speed. L'Enflé was feathering his paddle. Jésus kept the boat steady, the handle of his paddle tight against his thigh—not paddling, just steering.

Then Jésus said, "Now we can smoke. It went all right, I think. You're sure you didn't kill anybody?"

"I don't think so."

"Goddammit! You double-crossed me, Jésus?" L'Enflé said. "You said it was a simple *cavale*. Now it seems it's a *cavale* of internees."

"That's right, they're internees. I didn't tell you, L'Enflé, because you wouldn't have helped me and I had to have another man. Relax. If we're caught, I'll take all the blame."

"You'd better, Jésus. For the hundred francs you paid me, I don't want to risk my neck if somebody got killed or wounded."

I said, "L'Enflé, I'll make you a present of a thousand francs for the two of you."

"All right then, *mec*. That's fair enough. Thanks. We're dying of hunger in the village. It's worse being liberated than in prison. In prison you at least get food every day, and clothes."

"*Mec*," Jésus asked Clousiot, "does it hurt a lot?"

"Not too bad," Clousiot said. "But how are we going to make it with my leg broken, Papillon?"

"We'll see. Where are we going, Jésus?"

"I'm going to hide you up a creek about twelve miles from the mouth of the river. You stay there eight days until the guards and the man hunters give up looking. You want them to think you went down the Maroni and into the sea on the same night. The man hunters use boats without engines. A fire, talking, coughing could be fatal if they're anywhere near. The guards use motor-boats; they're too big to go up the creek—they'd run aground."

The night grew lighter. It was nearly four in the morning when, after a long search, we finally came to the hiding place known only to Jésus. We were literally in the bush. The boat flattened the short brush, but once we had passed over it, it straightened up again, providing a thick protective screen. It would take a sorcerer to know that there was enough water here to float a boat. We entered the creek, then spent over an hour penetrating the brush and separating the branches that barred our passage. Suddenly we found ourselves in a kind of canal and we stopped. The bank was neat and green and the trees huge, their foliage so thick that daylight—it was now six o'clock—couldn't get through. Thousands of beasts we had never heard of lived under this impressive canopy. Jésus said, "This is where you stay for eight days. On the seventh I'll come and bring you supplies." He untangled the thick vegetation and pulled out a tiny dugout six feet long. Inside were two paddles. This was the boat to take him back to Saint-Laurent on the rising tide.

It was now time to do something about Clousiot, who was stretched out on the bank. He was still wearing only his smock, so his legs were bare. With our hatchet we split some dried branches to serve as splints. L'Enflé pulled on his foot and Clousiot broke into a heavy sweat. Suddenly he said, "Stop! It hurts less like that. The bone must be in place." We arranged the splints and tied them with a new hemp rope we found in the boat. The pain eased. Jésus had brought four pairs of pants, four shirts and four wool sweaters originally intended for *relégués*. Maturette and Clousiot put them on; I stayed in the Arab's clothes. We drank some rum. It was the second bottle since our departure. It warmed us. Mosquitoes attacked without mercy, forcing us to sacrifice a packet of tobacco. We put it to soak in a water bottle and spread the nicotine juice on our faces, hands and feet. The wool sweaters kept us warm in the penetrating damp.

L'Enflé said, "We're off. What about the thousand francs you promised?" I went off for a moment and returned with a brand-new thousand-franc bill.

"So long. Don't move from here for eight days," Jésus said. "We'll be back on the seventh. On the eighth you go out to sea. While you're waiting, make your sail, your jib, and get the boat ready. Put everything in its place, fix the pins in the rudder and mount it on the rear. If we haven't come after ten days, we've been arrested. There'll be bloody hell to pay because you attacked those guards."

Then Clousiot told us that he hadn't left his carbine at the base of the wall. He had thrown it over the wall and the river was so near—which he didn't know then—that it must have fallen into the water. Jésus said that was a good thing, for if it weren't found, the man hunters would think we were armed. Now we could relax a little: they were armed only with revolvers and machetes, and if they thought we had a carbine, they wouldn't go out of their way to find us. Well, so long. If we were discovered and had to abandon the boat, we were to follow the creek upstream until we hit dry land. Then, with the compass, we should keep going north. There was a good chance that after two or three days we'd come to the death camp called Charvein. Once there, we'd have to bribe someone to tell Jésus where we were.

The two old cons left. A few minutes later their dugout had disappeared. We could hear nothing, see nothing.

Daylight penetrated the brush in a very peculiar way. It was as if we were in an arcade where the sun reached the top but allowed no rays to filter down. It began to get hot. And there we were, alone: Maturette, Clousiot and me. Our first reflex was to laugh—

it had gone like clockwork. The only inconvenience was Clousiot's leg. But he said that with the strips of wood around it he was okay. He would like it if we made some coffee. It was quickly done. We made a fire and each drank a mug of black coffee sweetened with brown sugar. It was delicious. We had spent so much energy since the night before that I didn't have the strength to examine our equipment or inspect the boat. That could come later. We were free, free, free. We had arrived at the *bagne* exactly thirty-seven days before. If the *cavale* succeeded, my life sentence would not have been very long. I said, "Mr. President, how long does hard labor for life last in France?" and I burst out laughing. Maturette, who also had a life sentence, did too. Clousiot said, "Don't crow yet. Colombia is still far away, and this boat doesn't look all that seaworthy to me."

I didn't answer because up to the last minute I had thought this boat was only to bring us to where the real one was. When I discovered that I was wrong, I didn't dare say anything for fear of upsetting my friends. And also, since Jésus seemed to think it was perfectly normal, I didn't want to give the impression that I didn't know the kind of boats normally used for escapes.

We spent the first day talking and getting acquainted with this new unknown, the bush. Monkeys and a small species of squirrel made terrifying somersaults over our heads. A troop of small wild pigs came to drink and bathe in the creek. There must have been at least two thousand of them. They came down to the creek and swam, tearing at the hanging roots. An alligator emerged from God knows where and caught one of them by the foot. The pig started to squeal like a lost soul, and the other pigs attacked the alligator, climbing on top of him and trying to bite him at the corners of his enormous mouth. With each whack of his tail the alligator sent a pig flying. One of them was killed and floated on the surface with its belly in the air. His companions immediately set to eating him. The creek was full of blood. The spectacle lasted twenty minutes, until the alligator took off through the water. We never saw him again.

We slept soundly and in the morning made some coffee. I took off my sweater and washed with a big cake of Marseilles soap I found in the boat. Maturette gave me a rough shave with my lancet, then shaved Clousiot. Maturette himself had no beard. When I picked up my sweater to put it back on, an enormous violet-black spider fell from it. It was covered with very long hair which had tiny platinum-like balls at the ends. It must have weighed at least a pound; I crushed it in disgust.

We emptied everything out of the boat, including the barrel of water. The water was purple; Jésus must have put too much permanganate in it to keep it from going bad. We found matches and a striking pad in tightly closed bottles. The compass was no better than a child's; it showed only north, south, east and west, with nothing in between. Since the mast was only two and a half yards high, we sewed the flour sacks into a trapeze shape with a rope around the edges for reinforcement. I made a small jib shaped like an isosceles triangle. It would help to keep us pointed into the wind.

When we were ready to mount the mast, I saw that the bottom of the boat wasn't solid: the hole for the mast was completely eaten away. When I inserted the screws for the pin that was to support the rudder, they went right through—the wood was like butter. The boat was rotten. That son of a bitch, Jésus, was sending us to our deaths. Reluctantly I asked the others to take a look; I had no right to hide it from them. What should we do? When Jésus returned, we'd make him find us a better boat. We would disarm him; then I, armed with the knife and the hatchet, would go with him to the village to find another boat. It was taking a big risk, but it wasn't as bad as putting to sea in this coffin. At least we had enough food: a large bottle of oil and boxes of flour and tapioca. With that we could go a long way.

This morning we watched a strange spectacle: a band of gray-faced monkeys staged a battle with some hairy black-faced monkeys. While the fight was raging, Maturette was hit on the head with a piece of branch and got a bump as big as a nut.

We had now been here five days and four nights. Tonight it rained in torrents. We made a shelter of wild banana leaves. The water rolled right off their varnished surface and we stayed dry except for our feet. This morning, as I drank my coffee, I thought about Jésus and what a crook he was. To take advantage of our innocence by giving us this punky boat! For five hundred or a thousand francs, he would send three men to certain death. I wondered if, after I'd made him give us another boat, I shouldn't kill him.

The cry of jays startled our small world—such sharp, blood-curdling cries that I told Maturette to take the machete and find out what was going on. He returned after five minutes and beckoned me to follow. We came to a place about a hundred and fifty yards away, and there, suspended in the air, was an extraordinary pheasant or waterfowl twice as big as a large rooster. It was caught in a lasso and hung by its claws from a branch. With one whack of the machete I cut its neck to stop the ghastly noise. I felt its weight and guessed it to be at least fourteen pounds. We decided to eat it, but then it occurred to us that the snare had been put there by somebody and there might be more than one of him. We went to see and found a curious thing: a barrier twelve inches high made of leaves and creepers woven together, about thirty feet from the creek and running parallel to it. Here and there was a door, and at the door, camouflaged by twigs, a lasso made of brass thread, attached at the other end to the branch of a bush bent double. I figured that the animal would run into the barrier, then walk along it, looking for an opening. When he found the door, he'd start through, but his claw would catch in the thread which would spring the branch back. The animal would then hang in the air until the owner of the traps came to get it.

This discovery was very disturbing. The barrier looked well maintained and quite new; we were in danger of being discovered. We should make no fires during the day, only at night when the hunter would surely not be attending his traps. We decided to mount a guard to watch them. We hid the boat under some branches and secreted our provisions in the brush.

I was on duty the next day at ten. We had eaten the pheasant, or whatever it was, the night before. The bouillon had tasted marvelous and the meat, even though boiled, was delicious. We each ate two bowlfuls. So there I was, supposed to be on watch, but I became fascinated by some very large black tapioca ants, each one carrying a large piece of leaf to an enormous anthill. The ants were over a quarter of an inch long and stood very high on their legs. I followed them to the plant they were defoliating and I saw a vast organization at work. First there were the cutters, who did nothing but cut up the pieces. With great speed they sheared through the enormous leaves, which were similar to those of a banana tree, cut them with amazing dexterity into pieces of the exact same size, then let them fall to earth. Below them was a line of ants of the same general species but a little different. They had a gray line running down the sides of their jaws. These ants formed a semicircle and observed the carriers. The carriers approached in a line from the right, then headed left toward the anthill. First they loaded up, then they got in line, but from time to time, in their hurry to claim their burden and get back into line, there was a traffic jam. This brought on the police ants, who shoved the worker ants into their proper places. It wasn't clear to me what grave error one of the worker ants had committed, but it was pulled from the ranks and two police ants took over, one cutting off its head, the other slicing its body in two at the waist. The police then stopped two worker ants, who dropped their bits of leaf and made a hole with their feet. Then the ant's three sections—head, chest and the rest—were buried and covered with earth.

I was so absorbed in watching this small world and waiting to see whether the police carried their surveillance as far as the anthill that I was completely taken by surprise when I heard a voice say:

"Don't move or you're dead. Turn around."

There stood a man naked from the waist up, wearing khaki shorts and red leather boots, and carrying a double-barreled shotgun. He was bald, sunburned, of medium height, thickset, and his eyes and nose were masked by a bright blue tattoo. A cockroach was tattooed in the middle of his forehead.

"Are you armed?"

"No."

"Are you alone?"

"No."

"How many are you?"

"Three."

"Take me to your friends."

"I can't, because one of them has a carbine and I don't want you killed before I know your intentions."

"Ah! Then don't move and talk quietly. Are you the three who escaped from the hospital?"

"Yes."

"Which one is Papillon?"

"I am."

"Well, your escape sure caused a revolution in the village! Half the *libérés* are under arrest at the police station." He came nearer and, pointing the barrel of his gun to the ground, held out his hand. "I'm the Masked Breton," he said. "You've heard of me?"

"No. But I can see you don't belong to the manhunt."

"Right. I set traps here to catch *hoccos*. A cat must have finished one off, unless it was you people."

"It was us."

"Want some coffee?" He took a thermos from a pack on his back, gave me a swallow and drank some himself.

I said, "Come meet my friends."

He followed me and sat down with us. He laughed over the scare I'd given him with the carbine. He said, "I believed you because the manhunt wouldn't go after you when they learned you'd left with a carbine."

He explained that he had been in Guiana for twenty years and liberated for five. He was forty-five. Stupidly he had had the mask tattooed on his face, so he had been forced to give up any idea of returning to France. He loved the bush and his whole life centered around it: snake and jaguar skins, collecting butterflies and, most of all, catching *hoccos* alive—the bird we had eaten. He sold them for two hundred to two hundred and fifty francs. I offered to pay him, but he refused indignantly. Then he told us about the *hoccos*: "This wild bird is a cock of the bush. Naturally he's never seen a hen, rooster, or man. So I catch one, take him to the village and sell him to someone who has a chicken coop. They're in great demand. O.K. You don't clip his wings, you don't do anything to him, you just put him in a coop at the end of the day and in the morning, when you open the door, there he is right in front, looking as if he were counting the hens and roosters as they file out. He follows them, and as he pecks along with them, he watches them high, low and in the surrounding brush. He's the best watchdog there is. In the evening he stations himself by the coop door, and how he knows that one or two of the chickens are missing is a mystery, but he knows it and he goes looking for them. And, hen or rooster, he drives them back with sharp pecks of his beak to teach them that it's time to go home. He kills rats, snakes, shrews, spiders, centipedes, and the moment a bird of prey is sighted in the sky, he sends everyone scurrying into the grass while he stares it down. And furthermore, he never runs away."

And we had eaten this remarkable bird as if it were a common rooster.

The Breton told us that Jésus, L'Enflé and about thirty *libérés* were in prison at the police station in Saint-Laurent, where they were being questioned about our escape. The Arab was in a cell, too, under suspicion of being an accomplice. The two blows that put him out had done no damage, but the guards had slight swellings on their heads. "Nobody bothered me because everybody knows I never get involved in *cavales*." He told us that Jésus was a bastard. When I told him about the boat, he asked if he could have a look at it.

When he saw it, he cried out, "He was sending you to your deaths, that son of a bitch! At sea, this tub wouldn't last an hour. The first big wave would break it in two. Whatever you do, don't leave in that thing; it would be suicide."

"So what do we do?"

"You have money?"

"Yes."

"I'll tell you what you do; better still, I'll help you. You certainly deserve it. And I'll do it for nothing because I want to see you and your friends succeed. First, don't go near the village, no matter what. To get a good boat, you'll have to go to the Ile aux Pigeons. About two hundred lepers live on the island. There are no guards there and no healthy person ever goes ashore, not even a doctor. Every morning at eight a boat brings them a twenty-four-hour supply of food. The orderly at the hospital gives a case of medication to their two orderlies—they're lepers too. They alone take care of the islanders. Nobody—no guards, no manhunts, no priests—ever goes to the island. The lepers live in little straw huts they make themselves and they have a common room where they get together. They raise chickens and ducks to supplement their ordinary diet. Officially they can't sell anything off the island, but they have a black-market trade with Saint-Laurent and Saint-Jean and with the Chinese at Albina in Dutch Guiana. They're all murderers. They don't often kill each other, but they commit lots of crimes when they're off the island, then they return to take cover. For these expeditions they have a few boats stolen from a neighboring village. The worst offense they can commit is to have a boat. The guards fire on anything they see going or coming from the Ile aux Pigeons. What the lepers do is they sink their boats by filling them with rocks; when they need them again, they dive down, take out the rocks, and the boats float up to the surface. There are all kinds of people on the island, all races, and from every part of France. This boat of yours is good only for the Maroni, and lightly loaded at that! To go out to sea, you'll have to find another, and the best place is the Ile aux Pigeons."

"How do we get there?"

"Like this: I'll go with you up the river until we come in sight of the island. Alone you'd never find it, or you might make a mistake. It's about sixty miles from the mouth of the river, so you'll have to backtrack. It's about twenty miles beyond Saint-Laurent. We'll attach my boat to yours. I'll bring you as close as possible and, after that, I'll get back into my own boat. Then you head for the island."

"Why can't you come to the island with us?"

"Oh, God," the Breton said, "all I needed was to put one foot on the wharf where the Administration boat docks. It was in full daylight, but what I saw was enough. Forgive me, Papi, but I will never set foot on that island again. I wouldn't be able to hide how I felt. I'd do you more harm than good."

"When do we leave?"

"At nightfall."

"What time is it now, Breton?"

"Three o'clock."

"O.K. I'll sleep for a little while."

"No, you don't. You've got to load the boat."

"No, I'm going with the boat empty. Then I'll come back for Clousiot, who'll stay and watch over our things."

"Impossible. You'll never find this place again, not even in broad daylight. And don't ever be on the river during the day. They're still looking for you. The river is still plenty dangerous."

Evening came. He went to find his boat and we attached it to ours. Clousiot sat next to the Breton, who took the tiller. Maturette sat in the middle. I went up front. We had trouble getting out of the creek and by the time we reached the river, night was falling. An enormous reddish-brown sun was ablaze on the horizon across the sea. We could see clearly, twelve miles ahead, the estuary of the majestic river as it threw off pink and silver sequins in its rush to meet the sea.

The Breton said, "The tide is out. In an hour it will begin to rise. We'll use it to go back up the Maroni. That way we'll reach the island with the least effort." Night fell suddenly.

"Push off," said the Breton. "Paddle hard to get into the middle of the river. And no smoking."

The paddles sliced the water and we sped across the current. The Breton and I pulled in rhythm and Maturette did his best. The farther we got into the middle of the river, the more we felt the rising tide push us. We were skimming along fast now. The tide grew stronger and pushed us even faster. Six hours later we were very close to the island and heading straight for it: a black spot, almost in the middle of the river, slightly to the right. "That's it," the Breton said in a low voice. Although it wasn't a very dark night, it would be hard to see us from that distance because of the mist on the water's surface. We came nearer. When the outline of the rocks was clear, the Breton got into his boat, untied it quickly and whispered, "Good luck, boys!"

"Thanks."

"Don't mention it."

THE ILE AUX PIGEONS

With the Breton no longer at the tiller, the boat made for the island broadside. I tried to bring it around but couldn't, and with the current pushing us, we went sideways into the vegetation that hung down into the water. For all my frantic back-paddling, we struck with such force that, had we landed against rock instead of leaves and branches, we would surely have cracked up and lost everything. Maturette jumped into the water, pulled the boat under a thicket and tied her up. We shared a cup of rum and I climbed the bank alone, leaving my two friends in the boat.

I walked compass in hand, cutting back the brush and attaching strips of flour sacking to branches along the way. I saw a faint light ahead, suddenly heard voices and made out three straw huts. I moved forward, and since I didn't know how I should present myself, I decided to let them discover me. I lit a cigarette. As the light flared, a small dog came barking at me and nipped at my legs. Just so long as he isn't a leper, I thought. Then: Idiot, dogs don't get leprosy.

"Who's there? Who is it? Is that you, Marcel?"

"It's an escaped prisoner."

"What are you doing here? You want to rob us? You think we're too well off?"

"No, I need help."

"For free or for pay?"

"Oh, shut up, La Chouette!"

Four shadows emerged from the hut.

"Approach gently, friend. I bet you're the man with the carbine. If you've got it with you, put it on the ground; you have
nothing to fear from us."

"Yes, that's me. But I don't have the carbine now."

I inched forward. I was close now, but it was dark and I
couldn't make out their features. Stupidly I put out my hand. No
one took it. I understood too late that such a gesture was not made
here: they didn't want to contaminate me.

"Let's go back to the hut," La Chouette said.

The little cabin was lit by an oil lamp on a table. "Have a seat."

I sat down on a stool. La Chouette lit three more lamps and
placed one of them on a table directly in front of me. The smoke of
the coconut oil had a sickening smell. The five of them stood, so
that I couldn't make out their faces. Mine was well lighted because
I was at the same height as the lamp, which is what they had
intended.

The voice which had told La Chouette to shut up now said,
"L'Anguille, go ask at the main house if they want us to bring him
over. Come back with the answer right away. And make sure it's
all right with Toussaint. We can't offer you anything to drink here,
friend, unless you don't mind swallowing eggs." He placed a basket full of eggs in front of me.

"No, thank you."

Then one of them sat down near me and that's when I saw my
first leper. It was horrible. I had to make an effort not to look away
or otherwise show my feelings. His nose was completely eaten
away, flesh and bone; there was only a hole in the middle of his
face. I mean what I say: not two holes, but a single hole, as big as
a silver dollar. The right side of the lower lip was also eaten away
and exposed three long yellow teeth that jutted out of the bone of
the upper jaw. He had only one ear. He was resting a bandaged

hand on the table. It was his right hand. With the two fingers remaining on his left hand he held a long, fat cigar. He had probably made it from a half-ripe tobacco leaf, for it was greenish in color. Only his left eye had an eyelid; the lid of his right eye was gone and a deep scar stretched from the eye to the top of his forehead, where it disappeared into his shaggy gray hair.

In a hoarse voice he said, "We'll help you, *mec*. I don't want you to stay around here and become like me."

"Thank you."

"My name is Jean sans Peur. I was handsomer, healthier and stronger than you when I first came to the *bagne*. Look at what ten years have done to me."

"Doesn't anybody take care of you?"

"Sure. I'm much better since I started giving myself injections of chauhnoogra oil. Look." He turned his head and showed me his left side. "It's drying up there."

Feeling an immense pity for this man, I made a motion to touch his cheek as a sign of friendship. He threw himself back and said, "Thank you for wanting to touch me, but you must never touch a leper, nor eat or drink from his bowl." Of all the lepers, his is the face I remember, this man who had the courage to make me look.

"Where's the *mec*?" In the doorway I saw the shadow of a very small man not much bigger than a dwarf. "Toussaint and the others want to see him. Bring him to the center."

Jean sans Peur got up and said, "Follow me." We all set off into the night, four or five in front, me next to Jean sans Peur, more behind. After three minutes we arrived at a clearing faintly lit by the moon. It was the flat summit of the island. In the middle was a house. Light came from two windows. In front about twenty men waited for us. As we arrived at the door, they stood back to let us through. I found myself in a room thirty feet long and twelve feet wide with a kind of fireplace in which wood was burning, surrounded by four huge stones of the same height. The room was lighted by two large hurricane lanterns. On one of the stone stools sat an ageless man with black eyes set in a white face. Behind him on a bench were five or six others.

"I'm Toussaint, the Corsican; you must be Papillon."

"I am."

"News travels fast in the *bagne*. Almost as fast as you do. Where is your carbine?"

"We threw it in the river."

"Where?"

"Opposite the hospital wall, exactly where we jumped."

"So it would be possible to recover it?"

"I suppose so. The water isn't very deep there."

"How do you know?"

"We had to wade through it to carry my injured friend to the boat."

"What's the matter with him?"

"He broke his leg."

"What have you done for him?"

"I split some branches and made him splints."

"Is he in pain?"

"Yes."

"Where is he?"

"In the boat."

"You said you came for help. What kind of help?"

"A better boat."

"You want us to give you a boat?"

"Yes. I have money to buy it with."

"Good. I'll sell you mine; it's a great boat and brand-new. I stole it last week in Albina. It's not a boat; it's a transatlantic steamer. There's only one thing missing: a keel. But in two hours we can fix it up with a good one. It has everything else you could want: a rudder, a thirteen-foot mast of ironwood and a brand-new heavy linen sail. What will you give me for it?"

"Tell me what you want. I don't know what things are worth here."

"Three thousand francs if you have it. If you don't, go find the carbine tomorrow night and I'll give you the boat in exchange."

"No, I'd rather pay."

"O.K. It's a sale. La Puce, let's have some coffee!"

La Puce, the near-dwarf who had first come for me, went over to a board fixed to the wall above the fire, took down a bowl, shining new and clean, poured in some coffee from a bottle and put it on the fire. After a moment he took the bowl and poured the coffee in some mugs. Toussaint leaned down and passed the mugs to the men behind him. La Puce handed me the bowl, saying, "Don't worry. This bowl is only for visitors. No lepers drink from it."

I took the bowl and drank, then rested it on my knee. It was then that I noticed a finger stuck to the bowl. I was just taking this in when La Puce said:

"Damn, I've lost another finger. Where the devil is it?"

"It's there," I said, showing him the bowl.

He pulled it off, threw it in the fire and said, "You can go on drinking. I have dry leprosy. I'm disintegrating piece by piece, but I'm not rotting. I'm not contagious." The smell of grilled meat reached me. It must be his finger.

Toussaint said, "You'll have to stay through the day until low tide. Go tell your friends. Bring the man with the broken leg into one of the huts. Take everything you have from the boat and sink it. Nobody here can help you. You understand why."

I returned to my companions and we carried Clousiot to the hut. One hour later everything was out of the boat and carefully stowed away. La Puce asked if we'd make him a present of it and also a paddle. I gave it to him and he took it away to sink it in a special place he knew. The night went fast. All three of us were in the hut, lying on new blankets sent over by Toussaint. They were delivered in the heavy paper they'd been shipped in. As we lay there, I brought Clousiot and Maturette up to date on what had happened since our arrival on the island, and the bargain I had struck with Toussaint. Clousiot said without thinking, "Then this *cavale* is really costing six thousand francs. I'll pay half, Papillon, or the three thousand I have."

"We're not here to haggle like a bunch of Armenians. As long as I have money, I'll pay. After that we'll see."

During the night we were left to ourselves. When day broke, Toussaint was there. "Good morning. Don't be afraid to come out. Nobody can bother you here. There's a man watching for police boats on the river from a cocoa tree on top of the island. We haven't seen any so far. As long as the white rag is up, there's nothing in sight. If he sees anything, he'll come down and tell us. Pick yourselves some papayas if you like."

I said, "Toussaint, what about the keel?"

"We're going to make it from the infirmary door. It's made of heavy snakewood. The keel will need two planks. We brought the boat up while it was dark. Come see it."

We went. It was a magnificent boat sixteen feet long, brand-new, with two benches, one with a hole for the mast. It was heavy, and Maturette and I had trouble turning it over. The sail and the ropes were also new. There were rings on the sides for hanging a barrel of water. We went to work. By noon a keel, tapered from front to back, was solidly in place with long screws and four angle irons.

The lepers formed a circle around us, watching in silence. Toussaint told us what to do and we obeyed. There wasn't a sign of a sore on Toussaint's face; he looked perfectly normal, but when he talked you noticed that only one side of his face moved, the left side. He told me that he, too, had dry leprosy. His torso and right arm were paralyzed and he expected his right leg to go before long. His right eye was fixed, like a glass eye; he could see with it, but he couldn't move it.

I only hoped that no one who ever loved these lepers knew their terrible fate.

As I worked, I talked to Toussaint. No one else spoke. Just once, when I was about to pick up one of the angle irons, one of them said: "Don't touch them yet. I cut myself when I was removing one of them from a piece of furniture, and there's still blood on it even though I tried to wipe it off." One of the lepers poured rum on it and set it on fire, then repeated the operation. "Now you can use it," the man said. While we were working, Toussaint said to one of the men, "You've left the island several times. Papillon and his friends haven't, so tell them how to do it."

"Low tide is early tonight. The tide will start to ebb at three o'clock. When night falls, around six, you'll have a very strong current which in three hours will take you about sixty miles toward the mouth of the river. At nine o'clock you must stop. Get a good grip on an overhanging tree and wait out the six hours of the rising tide—that is, until three in the morning. But don't leave then; the current isn't moving fast enough yet. At four-thirty beat it into the middle of the river. You have an hour and a half before daybreak to do your thirty miles. This is your last chance. When the sun rises at six, you make for the sea. Even if the guards spot you, they won't be able to catch you because they'll be arriving at the bar just as the tide turns. They won't be able to get over it and you'll have made it. Your life depends on this half-mile headstart. This boat has only one sail. What did you have on your boat?"

"A mainsail and a jib."

"This is a heavy boat; it can take two more sails—a spinnaker from the bow to the mast, and a jib that will help keep the nose pointing into the wind. Use all your sails and go straight into the waves; the sea is always heavy at the mouth of the estuary. Get your friends to lie flat in the bottom of the boat to stabilize it, and you hold the tiller tight in your hand. Don't tie the sheet to your leg, but put it through the ring and hold it with a single turn around your wrist. If you see that the force of the wind plus the size of the waves is about to capsize you, let everything go—the boat will immediately find its own equilibrium. Don't stop; let the mainsail luff and keep going with your spinnaker and the jib. When the sea calms down, you'll have time to take down your sail, bring it in and move on after hoisting it again. Do you know the route?"

"No. All I know is that Venezuela and Colombia are north-west."

"Right. But be careful you're not driven back to the coast. Dutch Guiana, opposite us, turns in all escaped cons; so does British Guiana. Trinidad doesn't turn them in, but you can only stay two weeks. Venezuela will turn you in after making you work on a road gang for a year or two."

I listened closely. He told me that he left the island from time to time, but since he was a leper, he was always sent back in short order. He admitted that he had never been farther than George-town in British Guiana. He wasn't an obvious leper, having lost only his toes, as I could see since he was barefoot. Toussaint made me repeat my instructions and I did so without making a mistake.

At that point Jean sans Peur said, "How much time should he spend on the open sea?"

I answered straight off, "I'll do three days north northeast. With the drift, that makes due north. On the fourth day I'll head northwest, which comes out to due west."

"Bravo," said the leper. "The last time I did it, I spent only two days going northeast and I hit British Guiana. If you take three days going north, you'll pass north of Trinidad or Barbados, you'll bypass Venezuela, and before you know it you'll find yourself in Colombia or Curaçao."

Jean sans Peur asked, "Toussaint, how much did you sell your boat for?"

"Three thousand. Is that too much?"

"No, that isn't why I asked. I just wanted to know. Have you got the money, Papillon?"

"Yes."

"Will you have any left?"

"No, it's all we have, exactly three thousand francs belonging to my friend, Clousiot."

"Toussaint, will you buy my revolver?" said Jean sans Peur. "I'd like to help these *mecs*. How much will you give me for it?"

"A thousand francs," Toussaint said. "I'd like to help them too."

"Thanks for everything," Maturette said, looking at Jean sans Peur.

"Thanks," said Clousiot.

I began to feel ashamed of my lie, so I said, "No, I can't accept it. There's no reason for it."

Jean looked at me and said, "Sure there's a reason. Three thousand francs is a lot of money, but even at that price Toussaint is losing at least two thousand, for that's a great boat he's giving you. So there's no reason why I can't give you something too."

Then a very moving thing happened. La Chouette placed a hat on the ground and all the lepers came and threw in bills and silver. They came from everywhere and every last one put in something. Now I was really ashamed. How could I tell them that I still had some money? God, what a fix! It was despicable to let this go on in the face of such generosity. Then a mutilated black from Timbuktu—his hands were stumps, he hadn't a single finger—said to us, "Money doesn't help us live. Don't be ashamed to accept it. All we use it for is gambling or screwing the girl lepers who come here sometimes from Albina." This relieved my guilt and I never did admit I still had money.

The lepers supplied us with two hundred hard-boiled eggs in a crate marked with a red cross. It was the same crate that had arrived that morning with the day's medicine. They also brought two live turtles weighing at least sixty pounds each, some leaf tobacco, two bottles of matches and a striking pad, a sack of rice weighing at least a hundred pounds, two bags of charcoal, a primus stove taken from the infirmary and a demijohn of fuel. Everybody in this miserable community was touched by our predicament and wanted to help. It was almost as if our *cavale* were theirs. The boat was pulled to where we had made our original landing. They counted the money in the hat: eight hundred and ten francs. I owed Toussaint only twelve hundred. Clousiot handed me his *plan* and I opened it before everybody. It contained a thousand-franc bill and four bills of five hundred each. I gave Toussaint fifteen hundred francs and he gave me back three hundred, saying:

"Here, take the revolver. It's a present. This is your only chance; you don't want to fail at the last moment for lack of a weapon. But I hope you won't have to use it."

I didn't know how to thank them, him first, then all the others. The orderly prepared a small box with cotton, alcohol, aspirin, bandages, iodine, a pair of scissors and some adhesive tape. A leper produced two small, carefully planed planks and two Ace bandages still in their original wrappings so that we could replace Clousiot's splints.

Toward five o'clock it began to rain. Jean sans Peur said, "You're in luck. This will keep them from seeing you. You can leave now and it will give you a good half hour's headstart. You'll be that much nearer the mouth of the river by four-thirty tomorrow morning."

"How will I know the time?"

"You'll know by the tide, by whether it's rising or falling."

The boat was put in the water. It was a far cry from our old one. This boat floated more than sixteen inches above the water line, fully loaded, us included. The mast was rolled up in the sail in the bottom of the boat since we weren't to use it until we were out of the river. We put the rudder and tiller in place and found a grass cushion for me to sit on. With the blankets, we fixed up a corner for Clousiot in the bottom of the boat, between me and the water barrel. Maturette sat on the bottom in the bow. Right away I had a feeling of security I had never had in the other one.

It was still raining, and I was to go down the middle of the river but a little to the left, toward the Dutch side. Jean sans Peur said, "Good-by. And get moving!"

"Good luck!" said Toussaint, and gave the boat a strong shove with his foot.

"Thanks, Toussaint, thanks, Jean, everybody, thanks a million!" We were off and away fast, for the ebb tide had started two and a half hours before and was now moving with incredible speed.

It continued to rain and we couldn't see thirty feet in front of us. There were two small islands lower down, and Maturette was leaning over the bow, his eyes straining for any sign of rocks. Night came. A large tree was going down the river with us—happily at a slower pace. For a moment we were entangled in its branches, but we freed ourselves quickly and resumed our lightning speed. We smoked, we drank some rum. The lepers had given us six straw-covered Chianti bottles filled with it. It was odd, but not one of us mentioned the lepers' terrible deformities. We talked only of their kindness, their generosity and honesty, and our luck in meeting the Masked Breton. It was raining harder and harder. I was soaked to the bone, but our woolen sweaters were so good that, even soaking wet, they kept us warm. Only my hand on the tiller was stiff with cold.

"We're going more than twenty-five miles an hour now," Maturette said. "How long do you think we've been gone?"

"I'll tell you in a minute," Clousiot said. "Wait—three hours and fifteen minutes."

"You're joking. How do you know?"

"I've been counting in groups of three hundred seconds since we left. At the end of each one I cut a piece of cardboard. I have thirty-nine pieces. Since each one represents five minutes, that means three hours and a quarter since we started. And unless I'm wrong, in the next fifteen or twenty minutes we won't be going down any more; we'll be going back up where we came from."

I pushed the tiller to the right in order to cut across the river and get closer to the Dutch coast. The current stopped just as we were about to crash into the brush. We didn't move, either up or down. It was still raining. We stopped smoking, we stopped talking. I whispered, "Take a paddle and pull." I paddled, holding the tiller under my right thigh. We grazed the brush, pulled on the branches and hid underneath. It was completely dark inside the vegetation. The river was gray and covered with a heavy mist. Without the evidence of the tide's ebb and flow, it would be impossible to tell where the river ended and the sea began.

THE GREAT DEPARTURE

The rising tide was to last six hours. Then we were to wait an hour and a half after the turn of the tide. That meant I had seven hours to sleep, if only I could calm down. I had to sleep now, for when would I have time at sea? I stretched out between the barrel and the mast, Maturette used a blanket to make a tent between the barrel and the bench, and thus well protected, I slept and I slept. Nothing disturbed me, not dreams, rain, or my uncomfortable position. I slept, I slept—until Maturette woke me and said:

"Papi, we think it's almost time. It's a long time since the ebb tide started."

The boat was heading downstream. I felt the current with my fingers; it was moving very fast. The rain had stopped and the light of a quarter moon clearly revealed the river three hundred feet ahead with its floating burden of grass, trees and unidentifiable black shapes. I tried to make out the demarcation between river and sea. Where we were, there was no wind. Was there any in the middle of the river? Was it strong? We emerged from under the brush, the boat still attached to a big branch by a slipknot. It was only by looking at the sky that I could make out the coast, the end of the river and the beginning of the sea. We had come down much farther than we thought and it seemed to me we couldn't be more than six miles from the mouth. We drank a good snort of rum. I felt around in the boat for where the mast should go. We lifted it and it fitted nicely through the hole in the bench into its socket. I hoisted the sail but kept it wrapped around the mast. The spinnaker and jib were ready for Maturette when we needed them. For the sail to open, I had only to let go the rope that held it to the mast. I could do that from where I was sitting. Maturette was in front with one paddle, I in the rear with another. We must work fast to get away from the bank which the current was pushing us against.

"Careful. Now let her go and God help us!"

"God help us," Clousiot repeated.

"We are in Your hands," Maturette said.

We cast off. Together we pulled on our paddles. I dipped and pulled, Maturette did the same. It was easy. By the time we were sixty feet from the bank, the current had taken us down three hundred. The wind hit us all at once and pushed us to the middle of the river.

"Raise the jibs and make sure they're both tied fast!"

The wind filled them and, like a horse, the boat reared and was off. It was later than we had figured for the river was suddenly bathed in broad daylight. We could easily make out the French coast about a mile and a quarter to our right and the Dutch coast about half a mile to our left. Before us and very clear were the white caps of the breaking waves.

"Christ! We were wrong about the time," Clousiot said. "Do you think we can make it?"

"I don't know."

"Look how high those waves are! Has the tide turned?"

"Impossible. I see things floating down."

Maturette said, "We're not going to make it. We don't have time."

"Shut up and hold the jibs tight. You shut up too, Clousiot."

Pan-ingh . . . pan-ingh. . . . We were being shot at. On the second round I could fix where the shots were coming from. It wasn't the guards. The shots were coming from the Dutch side. I put up the mainsail and it filled so fast that a little more and it would have taken my wrist with it. The boat was heeling over at a forty-five-degree angle. I took all the wind I could, which was much too easy. Pan-ingh, pan-ingh; then nothing. We were being carried nearer the French coast—that must be why the shooting had stopped.

We moved ahead with dizzying speed, going so fast that I saw ourselves driven into the middle of the estuary and smack into the French bank. We could see men running toward it. I came about gently, as gently as possible, pulling on the sheet with all my strength. The mainsail was now straight out in front of me; the jib came by itself and so did the spinnaker. The boat made a three-quarter turn. I let out the sail and we left the estuary running before the wind. Jesus! We had made it! Ten minutes later the first wave barred our passage, but we climbed over it with ease, and the shuit-schuit of the boat on the river changed to a tac-y-tac-y-tac. We went over the high waves with the agility of a boy playing leapfrog. Tac-y-tac, the boat rose and fell with no vibration, no shaking—only the tac when it hit the sea after coming off a wave.

"Hurrah! Hurrah! We made it!" Clousiot shouted at the top of his lungs.

And to help celebrate our victory over the elements, the good Lord sent us a breathtaking sunrise. The waves kept up a continuous rhythm. The farther we got out, the smoother they became. The water was very muddy. Ahead of us to the north the sea was black; later it would change to blue. I didn't need to look at the compass: the sun was over my right shoulder. I was running before the wind in a straight line and the boat was heeling less, for I had let out the sail and it was now half full. Our great adventure was under way.

Clousiot sat up. He wanted to see what was going on. Maturette helped him sit facing me, his back against the water barrel. He rolled me a cigarette, lit it, passed it to me, and all three of us smoked it.

"Pass the rum around. Let's drink to our victory," Clousiot said. Maturette poured a generous ration in three metal mugs and we toasted our success. Maturette was sitting next to me on my left and we looked at each other. Their faces were bright with happiness. Mine must have been the same. Then Clousiot asked, "Captain, where are you going, please?"

"To Colombia, God willing."

"God better be willing, for God's sake!" Clousiot said.

The sun rose quickly and we dried out in no time. We converted our hospital smocks into Arab-style burnouses. When dampened, they were cool and stuck to the head, which prevented sunstroke. The sea was opal blue and the waves were wide and long, making sailing comfortable. The wind kept up its force and we moved away from the coast at great speed. The farther we got from the green fastness, the more mysterious it became until it was only a blur on the horizon. I had turned around to look at it when a wave caught us, reminding me of my responsibilities.

"I'm going to cook some rice," Maturette said.

"I'll hold the stove while you hold the pot," said Clousiot.

The demijohn of fuel was stashed up in the bow where no one was allowed to smoke. They cooked the rice in fat and it smelled good. We ate it hot, mixed with two cans of sardines. To top it off, a good cup of coffee. "A shot of rum?" I said no. It was too hot. Clousiot kept making me cigarettes and lighting them for me. From the sun's position, we guessed it was about ten in the morning. We'd been at sea only five hours, yet we had the impression that the water below us was very deep. The waves were flatter and we sliced through them noiselessly. It was a beautiful day.

I realized that we would have no need for the compass during the day. From time to time I would position the sun in relation to the needle and guide myself that way. But the sun's reflection hurt my eyes. I was sorry I hadn't thought of getting myself some dark glasses.

Suddenly Clousiot blurted out, "Man, I was lucky to meet up with you at the hospital!"

"You weren't the only one. I'm lucky to have you along." I thought of Dega, of Fernandez. . . . Had they said yes, they'd be here with us too.

"It wasn't only me," Clousiot said. "Without Maturette you would have had trouble getting the Arab into the room when you needed him."

"Yes, Maturette was certainly useful. I'm glad you came; you're a brave and clever kid."

"Thank you," Maturette said. "Thank you both for having confidence in me in spite of my age and the way I am. I'll try to live up to it."

Then I said, "And François Sierra—I wish he could have been with us. And Galgani . . ."

"As things turned out, Papillon, it couldn't have been done. If Jésus had been straight with us and given us a good boat, we could have waited for them in our hiding place. Jésus could have helped them escape, we would have done the rest. At least they know you and realize that if you didn't try, it was because it was impossible."

"While we're on the subject, Maturette, why were you in the maximum-security room in the hospital?"

"I didn't know I'd been interned. I went to the doctor's because I had a sore throat and also I wanted to take a look around. When the doctor saw me, he said, 'It says here on your form that you're to be interned on the islands. Why?' 'I don't know why, Doctor. What does interned mean?' 'Never mind, it doesn't mean anything. Go to the hospital.' And so I ended up in the hospital."

"He was doing you a favor," Clousiot said.

"You figure out his motives. But he must be saying to himself now, 'My little friend with the choirboy's face wasn't such a loser after all. He had the guts to leave *en cavale*.' "

We talked a lot of nonsense. I said, "Who knows, we may run into Julot. He must be a long way away, unless he's still hiding in the bush." Clousiot said, "When I left, I put a note under my pillow: 'Moved, leaving no forwarding address.' " We burst out laughing.

We sailed without incident for five days. During the day we took our position from the sun. At night we used the compass. On the morning of the sixth day a brilliant sun greeted us, the sea suddenly grew calm and flying fish passed near us. I was exhausted. That night, to keep me from falling asleep, Maturette wet my face with a cloth soaked in sea water, but I fell asleep all the same. Then Clousiot burned me with a cigarette. Now, since we were in a dead calm, I decided I could really sleep. We let down the sail and the jib, leaving only the spinnaker up. I slept like a rock in the bottom of the boat, protected from the sun by the sail which was stretched above me. Maturette shook me awake. "It's only around noon, but I'm waking you because the wind is picking up. And on the horizon where it's coming from, everything's black." I got up and took the tiller. The lone spinnaker carried us rapidly over the flat sea. Behind me in the east it was black, and the wind was picking up force. The two jibs were enough to maintain speed. I rolled the sail around the mast.

"Hold tight. A storm's coming."

Big drops of rain began to fall. An ugly black mass was surging toward us; in less than fifteen minutes it had caught up with us. A violent wind beat down on us. As if mesmerized, the waves responded, their crests exploding with spray. The sun disappeared, it rained torrents, we couldn't see a thing; and as the waves hit the boat, the stinging spray peppered my face. It was a hurricane, my first hurricane, with all the forces of nature unleashed: thunder, lightning, rain, waves, and the wind howling around us.

Like a piece of straw, the boat was tossed about from great heights into chasms so deep I thought we'd never climb out. And yet, in spite of the fantastic plunges, we climbed up and over each new crest. I was holding the tiller with both hands, and, thinking I should try to resist a deep swell that was on the point of breaking, I aimed the boat to cut through it. I had probably maneuvered too fast because I took in a huge amount of water. The entire boat was flooded. We must have taken in thirty inches. My nerves were on edge and, without meaning to, I courted disaster by taking the next wave broadside. The boat tipped so far over that it spilled most of the water we had taken in.

"Bravo!" Clousiot shouted. "You really know the ropes, Papillon! You made short work of emptying the boat."

"Didn't I, though!" I answered.

If he'd only known that my lack of experience had almost drowned us! I decided to stop fighting the waves or trying to maintain a direction; I would concentrate on keeping the boat as steady as possible. I took the waves at a slight angle, letting the boat go to the bottom of the trough and then climb up. I quickly realized that I'd made an important discovery and that 90 percent of the danger had been eliminated. The rain stopped although the wind continued to blow with fury, but I could now see clearly in front and in back. Behind it was clear, in front it was black; we were between the two extremes.

By five o'clock it was over. The sun was shining again, the wind was back to normal, the waves had calmed down. I put up the sail and we set off once more, very pleased with ourselves. What water remained in the boat we bailed out with our cooking pot. We hung the blankets to the mast, where the wind soon dried them. Then we made a meal of rice, flour, oil, some strong coffee and a good swallow of rum. The sun, about to set, spread a fiery light over the blue sea. It was beautiful: the sky a reddish brown, the sun half sunk into the sea, licking with great yellow tongues at the sky, the few white clouds and the sea itself. The waves were blue at the bottom, then green and red, pink or yellow on the crests, depending on the color of the sun's ray that touched them.

I felt an uncommon peace and with this peace, self-confidence. I had managed things well and the brief storm had taught me a lot. All by myself I had learned how to maneuver in a rough sea. I could greet the night with serenity.

"So, Clousiot, you liked the way I emptied the boat?"

"Pal, if you hadn't done it and a new wave had hit us broadside, we would have been finished. You're a champ."

"Did you learn that in the navy?" Maturette asked.

"Yes. The navy's good for something after all."

We must have been driven far off course. It wasn't surprising after four hours in that wind and those waves. I had to correct it by going northwest. Night swept down on us as the sun disappeared into the sea, leaving a last few violet sparks in farewell.

We sailed for six more days without incident: only a few gusts of wind and rain that never lasted more than three hours and certainly never approached the eternity of the first storm.

It was now ten o'clock in the morning. Not a breath of wind; the sea was like glass. I slept almost four hours. When I woke up, my face was burning. The skin was gone from my lips and nose. My right hand was raw. It was the same with Maturette and Clousiot. We spread oil on our hands and faces twice a day, but it wasn't enough: the tropical sun dried it up in no time.

From the sun's position, it was now two in the afternoon. I had something to eat and then, since the sea was a millpond, we arranged the sail to give us some shade. Fish came alongside where Maturette had washed the dishes. I took out our machete and told Maturette to throw them a few grains of rice. The rice had got wet in the storm and had begun to ferment. The fish gathered where the rice fell and, as one of them stuck its head almost out of water, I gave it a great whack with the machete. Immediately it turned its belly in the air. That fish must have weighed twenty-five pounds. We cleaned it and cooked it in salted water, and ate it that night with tapioca flour.

We had now been at sea for eleven days. During the entire time we had seen only one boat, far off on the horizon. I was beginning to ask myself where the hell we were. That we were on the high seas was obvious, but in what relation to Trinidad or the other

British islands? Speak of the devil . . . There straight ahead of us was a black dot that was growing bigger and bigger. Was it a small boat or a big steamer? It was a boat, but it wasn't coming toward us. We could see it clearly now, moving across our path. Actually it was coming nearer, but at an angle. Its route would not bring it close. Since there was no wind, our sails hung limp, so they must not have seen us. Then suddenly we heard the wail of a siren, followed by three more. The boat changed its course and came straight for us.

"So long as we don't collide," said Clousiot.

"There's no danger. The sea is as smooth as glass."

It was an oil tanker. As it came nearer, we could see the crowd on the bridge. They must be wondering what these madmen were doing in their cockleshell in the middle of the ocean. They approached us cautiously and we could make out the ship's officers, some members of the crew, then women in print dresses and men in colored shirts arriving on the bridge. Obviously they were passengers. Passengers on an oil tanker? That seemed odd. The tanker was now very close and the captain called out in English:

"Where are you from?"

"French Guiana."

"Do you speak French?" asked a woman.

"Yes, madame."

"What are you doing in the middle of the sea?"

"The Lord knows . . ."

The woman spoke to the captain and said, "The captain invites you to come aboard. He'll pull your boat up on deck."

"Tell him thanks, but we're very comfortable on our boat."

"Why don't you want help?"

"Because we're escaped convicts and we're not going in your direction."

"Where are you going?"

"To Martinique and beyond. We have no idea where we are. Can you tell us what direction to take for the Antilles?"

"Can you read an English nautical map?"

"Yes."

A few moments later they let down an English map, cartons of cigarettes, some bread and a roast of lamb.

"Look at the map." I looked, then said, "I have to make a quarter turn west for the British Antilles, is that right?"

"Yes."

"About how many miles is it?"

"You'll make it in two days," the captain said.

"Good-by, and thanks for everything!"

"The captain congratulates you on your sailor's courage!"

"Thank you again. Good-by!" And the tanker moved off gently, almost grazing us. I steered us as far away as I could to avoid the backwash. Just then a sailor threw his cap overboard—it fell right in the middle of the boat. I was wearing this cap with its gold braid and anchor when we arrived in Trinidad two days later.

TRINIDAD

Long before we could see it, a flight of birds announced our landfall. It was seven-thirty in the morning when they came wheeling over us. "We've made it! *Mecs*, we've made it! The first part of the *cavale* is over. The hardest part. *Vive la liberté*!" In our joy we behaved like children. Our faces were covered with the cocoa butter which the tanker people had given us to soothe our sunburn. Toward nine o'clock we sighted land. A fresh wind pushed us along at a good clip on a gently rolling sea. But not until four in the afternoon were we close enough to make out the details: clusters of white houses studded the shore of the long island and coconut trees crowned its summit. We couldn't yet see whether it was really an island or a peninsula, or whether the houses were inhabited. It was another hour before we could distinguish people running toward the beach where we were heading. In less than twenty minutes a crowd had assembled. The little village had spilled over onto the edge of the sea to receive us. We learned later that the place was called San Fernando.

Three hundred yards from shore I dropped anchor; it caught immediately. I did this partly to watch the people's reaction, partly to keep from scraping the boat if the bottom turned out to be coral. We let down the sails and waited. A small canoe came toward us. In it were two blacks paddling a white man in a colonial cap.

"Welcome to Trinidad," the white man said in pure French. The blacks laughed, showing pearly white teeth.

"Thank you, sir. Is the bottom here coral or sand?"

"It's sand. You can go up on the beach without danger."

We pulled up the anchor and the waves pushed us gently to the beach. We had barely touched when ten men ran into the water and, with one heave, pulled the canoe up on land. They looked us over, they caressed us, and the women—black, Chinese and Hindu—made appreciative gestures. The white man explained that everybody wanted us to stay with them. Maturette picked up a handful of sand and made as if to kiss it. This enthralled our audience. I explained Clousiot's condition to the white man, and he had him carried to his house near the beach. He told us that we could leave everything in the boat until morning, that no one would touch a thing. Everyone called me "captain" and this sudden baptism made me laugh. They said in English, "Good captain, long ride on small boat!"

Night came. I asked if our boat could be pushed up a little farther and tied to a bigger boat for safety. Then I followed the Englishman to his house. It was a bungalow, like those you see everywhere on English soil: a few wooden steps and a screen door. I entered after the Englishman with Maturette behind me. As I came in, there was Clousiot sitting in an armchair, his leg resting on another, basking in the attentions of two women.

"My wife and daughter," the Englishman said. "I have a son in school in England."

"Welcome to our house," his wife said in French.

"Please sit down, sir," the girl said as she brought up two rattan chairs.

"Thank you. Please don't put yourselves out for us."

"Why not? Don't worry, we know where you've come from, and I repeat: Welcome to our house."

The man was a lawyer and his name was Bowen. He had his office in Port of Spain, the capital of Trinidad, about twenty-five miles away. They served us tea with milk, toast, butter and jam. It was our first evening as free men and I shall never forget it. Not a word about our past, no indiscreet questions: only how many days we had been at sea and how the trip had gone; if Clousiot was in pain, and did we want to advise the police of our arrival tomorrow or wait another day; had we parents, wives, or children. If we wanted to write to them, they would mail the letters. How shall I say it—it was an extraordinary reception for three fugitives, both on the part of the people on the beach and this English family.

Mr. Bowen telephoned a doctor who told him to bring Clousiot to his clinic the next afternoon for X-rays and to see what needed to be done. Mr. Bowen then telephoned the head of the Salvation Army in Port of Spain. The captain said he would prepare a room at the Salvation Army hostel, that we could come when it suited us, that we should keep our boat if it was a good one because we would need it when we were ready to leave. He asked whether we were *bagnards* or *relégués*, and we answered *bagnards*, which seemed to please the lawyer.

"Would you like to have a bath and shave?" the girl asked me. "Please don't say no; it's no trouble at all. You'll find everything you need in the bathroom, I hope."

I went into the bathroom, took a bath and shaved, and emerged in gray pants, white shirt, tennis shoes and white socks.

A Hindu knocked on the door. He had a package for Maturette and told him that the doctor had noticed that I was about the same size as he and therefore would be easy to fit, but that little Maturette would find it difficult because no one at the lawyer's was that small. He bowed as Hindus do and left. Faced with so much kindness, what could we say? The emotion that filled my heart was beyond description. Clousiot went to bed early; then the five of us exchanged many thoughts on a variety of subjects. What intrigued the charming ladies most was how we planned to remake our lives. Nothing about the past; only the present and the future. Mr. Bowen was sorry that Trinidad didn't permit escaped prisoners to stay. He told me that he had asked for permission several times before, but it had never been granted.

The girl talked in very pure French, like her father, without accent and with perfect pronunciation. She was blond, covered with freckles, and somewhere between seventeen and twenty. I didn't dare ask her exact age.

She said, "You're all still young and have your lives before you. I don't know what you did to be imprisoned and I don't want to know. But to have had the courage to go to sea in such a tiny boat and make such a long and dangerous voyage shows you're willing to gamble a great deal to be free. And I think that is admirable."

We slept until eight the next morning. The table was already set. The ladies told us that Mr. Bowen had left for Port of Spain and wouldn't be back until afternoon, when he would have all the necessary information concerning our fate.

The fact that this man could go away leaving three escaped convicts in his house was a priceless lesson to us. He seemed to be saying: I consider you perfectly normal men; I have known you only twelve hours, but I have enough confidence in you to leave you in my home alone with my wife and daughter. After talking to you, I cannot believe you are capable of behaving badly in my home, and so I am leaving you there just as if you were old friends. This demonstration of faith moved us a great deal.

I am not a good enough writer to convey the intense emotion I felt over my newfound self-respect. It was a rehabilitation, if not yet a new life. This imaginary baptism, the immersion in purity, the elevation of my being above the filth in which I'd been mired and, overnight, this sense of responsibility, made me into a different man. The convict's complexes that make him hear his chains and suspect he's being watched even after he's freed, everything I'd seen, gone through, suffered, everything that was making me tarnished, rotten and dangerous, passively obedient on the surface but terribly dangerous in rebellion, all that had disappeared as if by a miracle. Thank you, Mr. Bowen, barrister in His Majesty's service, thank you for making a new man of me in so short a time!

The blond girl, her eyes as blue as the sea around us, was sitting with me under the coconut palm next to her father's house. Red, yellow and mauve bougainvillea in full bloom gave the garden a suitably poetic touch.

"Mr. Henri [she called me Mister. How long had it been since anyone had called me Mister!], as Daddy told you yesterday, because of the stupid and unfair attitude of the British authorities, you unfortunately won't be able to stay here. They give you just two weeks to rest over, then you have to go to sea again. I've been to look at your boat; it's very small and very light for the long trip you have ahead of you. Let's hope you land in a more hospitable and understanding country than ours. All the English islands are the same in this respect. I beg you—if your next trip brings you suffering—do not hold it against the people of these islands. They aren't responsible. The orders come from England, from people who don't know you. My father's address is 101 Queen Street, Port of Spain, Trinidad. Please, God willing, write us a few words and let us know how you fare."

Again, I was so touched I didn't know what to say. Mrs. Bowen came over to us. She was a very handsome woman of about forty with light chestnut hair and green eyes. She was wearing a simple white dress with a white cord around her waist and light-green sandals.

"My husband won't be back until five. He is trying to get permission for you to drive to the capital without a police escort. He also wants to prevent your having to spend your first night in the Port of Spain police station. Your friend with the broken leg will go directly to the clinic of a doctor friend of ours, and you two are to go to the Salvation Army hostel."

Maturette joined us in the garden. He told us that he had gone to look at the boat and reported that it was surrounded by curious natives. Nothing had been touched. But in the course of their examination the natives had found a bullet lodged under the rudder and one of them had asked if he could take it as a souvenir. Maturette had said, "Captain, captain." The native had understood that Maturette would have to ask his captain's permission. He also asked why we didn't set the turtles free.

"You have turtles?" the girl asked. "Let's go see them!"

We went to the boat. On our way there, a beautiful little Hindu girl stopped me to shake my hand as if it were the most natural thing in the world. "Good afternoon," she said in English. The entire motley crowd said, "Good afternoon." I took out the two turtles and asked the girl, "What should we do? Throw them back into the sea? Or would you like them in your garden?"

"The little pool at the back is sea water. We could put them in the pool and then we'd have a souvenir of your visit."

"Fine, that's what we'll do." I distributed everything I could find in the boat to the people standing around, keeping only the compass, some tobacco, the water barrel, the knife, the machete, the hatchet, the blankets and the revolver, which I quickly hid under the blankets—no one saw it.

Mr. Bowen arrived at five o'clock. "Gentlemen, everything is arranged. I'll drive you to the capital myself. We'll drop Mr. Clousiot off first, then go on to the hostel."

We placed Clousiot on the back seat of the car. I was saying good-by to the girl when her mother arrived with a suitcase and said, "Please take these things of my husband's. They carry our best wishes." What could you say to so much kindness? "Thank you, thank you so much." And the car drove off.

We reached the clinic at quarter to six. It was called St. George's. Orderlies lifted Clousiot onto a stretcher and placed him in a room where there was already a Hindu sitting on a bed. The doctor came in, shook hands with Bowen, then with the rest of us; he spoke no French, but told us through an interpreter that Clousiot would be well cared for and that we could come to see him as often as we liked. Back in Bowen's car, we crossed the city. We were amazed by the lights, the cars, the bicycles. Whites, blacks, Hindus, Chinese crowded the sidewalks of this city built of wood. The Salvation Army hostel was in a brightly lit square near a store on which I read *Fish Market*. The ground floor of the building was of stone, the rest wood. The captain of the Salvation Army received us with his entire "general staff," women as well as men. He spoke a little French, but everybody else spoke to us in English, which we didn't understand. From their smiling faces and the welcome in their eyes, however, we knew they must be saying kind things.

They led us to a room on the third floor in which there were three beds—the third was for Clousiot, should he be able to join us. There was a connecting bathroom with soap and towels. After showing us our room, the captain said, "We all have dinner together at seven, a half-hour from now."

"Thank you, but we're not hungry."

"If you would like to take a walk around the town, here are two Antilles dollars so that you can buy a cup of coffee or tea, or some ice cream. But don't get lost. When you're ready to come home, all you need to say is 'Salvation Army, please.' "

Ten minutes later we were in the street. We walked on sidewalks, elbowing other people; nobody looked at us, no one paid us any attention. We breathed deeply, absorbing the wonder of our first free steps in a city. This continued confidence in us, letting us walk freely in a good-sized town, was very gratifying; it gave us not only confidence in ourselves but also the certainty that we would never betray their faith in us. Maturette and I walked slowly through the crowd. We needed to be close to people, to jostle them, become part of them. We went into a bar and asked for two beers. It doesn't seem like much to say, "Two beers, please." It came so naturally, and yet it seemed fantastic that a Hindu girl with a gold shell in her nose should say after serving us, "Half a dollar, sir." Her pearly teeth when she smiled, her large violet-black eyes slanted up at the corners, her jet-black hair falling to her shoulders, her half-open blouse showing just enough of her breasts to suggest their beauty, all these little things that appeared so natural to everybody else seemed to us fantastic and magical. Come on, Papi! It's not true; you must be kidding! You were so recently a member of the living dead, a con condemned for life, and here you are in the process of becoming a free man!

Maturette paid. He had only a half-dollar left. The beer was deliciously cold. He asked me, "Shall we have another?"

A second round didn't seem wise. "Look here, you've been free less than an hour and already you want to get drunk?"

"Come on, Papi, don't exaggerate! Having a couple of beers is not exactly getting drunk."

"Maybe not, but I don't think it would be right for us to gobble up all the pleasures all at once. We should taste each one a little at a time and not be gluttons. Besides, the money isn't ours."

"O.K. You're right. Eyedroppers is what we should use. It's more fitting."

We left the bar and walked down Watters Street, the big main street that goes from one end of the city to the other. We were so amazed at the streetcars, the mules pulling their little carts, the cars, the flashing signs over the movie houses and night clubs, the eyes of the laughing young blacks and Hindus that suddenly we found ourselves at the port. In front of us were boats all lighted up, cruise ships bearing the magical names of ports like Panama, Los Angeles, Boston, Quebec; freighters from Hamburg, Amsterdam, London; and cheek by jowl the length of the quay, bars, cabarets and restaurants full of men and women drinking, singing and arguing noisily. I suddenly felt an irresistible need to join this crowd; vulgar it might be, but it was so bursting with life. Outside one of the bars, set out on beds of ice, was a display of oysters, sea urchins, shrimp, razor clams, mussels, an encyclopedia of seafood to tempt the passerby. Tables with red-and-white-checked tablecloths, most of them occupied, seemed to invite us to sit down. Girls with light-brown skins and fine profiles wore revealing, brightly colored blouses that invited you to extend the enjoyment further. I went up to one of them and asked, "French money good?" and handed her a thousand-franc bill. "Yes, I change for you." "O.K." She took the bill and disappeared into the noisy room. Then she returned. "Come here." And she took me to the cashier, a Chinese.

"You French?"

"Yes."

"Change thousand francs?"

"Yes."

"All for Antilles dollars?"

"Yes."

"Passport?"

"Don't have one."

"Sailor's identification?"

"Don't have one."

"Immigration papers?"

"Don't have one."

"All right." He spoke a couple of words to the girl; she looked around the room, went up to what looked like a sailor in a cap like mine—gold braid and anchor—and brought him over to the cashier.

The Chinese said, "Your identification?"

"Here."

And coldly the Chinese made out a conversion voucher in his name and had him sign it. Then the girl took him by the arm and led him back to his seat. He was past knowing what was going on, and I had two hundred and fifty Antilles dollars, with fifty dollars in one- and two-dollar bills. I gave one dollar to the girl. We went out and sat down at one of the tables and treated ourselves to an orgy of seafood washed down with a delicious dry white wine.

FOURTH NOTEBOOK

THE FIRST *CAVALE*
(CONTINUED)

TRINIDAD

I CAN RECALL, AS IF it were yesterday, that first night of freedom in the English town. We went everywhere, drunk with the lights and the warmth in our hearts, feeling at one with the happy, laughing crowd. The bars were full of sailors and girls waiting to fleece them. But these weren't like the sordid women of the underworld in Paris, Le Havre, or Marseilles, with their crudely made-up faces, and eyes bright with greed and cunning. The girls of Trinidad were of every color: yellow Chinese, black African, light chocolate with glossy hair; there were Hindu and Javanese women whose parents had been imported to cultivate the cocoa and sugar cane— "coolies," who were a mixture of Chinese and Hindu and wore a gold shell in their noses. Then there were the Llapanes with their Roman profiles and bronzed faces illumined by enormous, brilliant black eyes, their breasts exposed as if to say: "See how perfect they are." All these girls with flowers of different colors in their hair stimulated desire without making it dirty or commercial. They gave the impression that it wasn't work, that they really enjoyed it, and you felt that money was not the main thing in their lives.

Like a pair of June bugs bumping against a light, Maturette and I zigzagged from bar to bar. As we emerged into a small, brightly lighted square, I saw the clock on a church. Two o'clock. It was two o'clock in the morning! We had to get back. We'd carried things a little too far. I hailed a taxi which took us to the hostel for two dollars. Feeling very ashamed of ourselves, we entered and were greeted by a woman officer of the Salvation Army—a blonde somewhere between twenty-five and thirty. She spoke a few words in English which sounded pleasant and welcoming, then gave us the key to our room and wished us good night. We got into bed. In my suitcase I had found a pair of pajamas. I was about to turn off the light when Maturette said, "Don't you think we should thank the Lord for giving us so much so soon? What do you say, Papi?"

"You thank your Lord for me. He's a great *mec* all right. And it's true he's been damn good to us. Good night." And I put out the light.

This resurrection, this escape from the cemetery where I'd been buried and tonight's immersion in the world of people had left me so excited I couldn't get to sleep. In the kaleidoscope that passed before my eyes, I saw disconnected pictures and felt a confusion of sensations that were extraordinarily precise in outline: the Assizes, the Conciergerie, the lepers, Saint-Martin-de-Ré, Tribouillard, Jésus, the storm. . . . It was like a fantasmagoric ballet in which everything I had been through in the past year was trying to elbow its way into my mind. I tried to chase the images away, but they wouldn't go. And the strangest part was that they were all mixed in with the squeals of pigs, the cackle of *hoccos*, the roar of the wind, the sound of the waves and the music of the Hindu violins in the bars we had just left.

I fell asleep as day was breaking.

At ten o'clock there was a knock on the door. It was Mr. Bowen. He said, smiling, "Good morning. Still in bed? You must have come in late. Did you have a good time?"

"Good morning. Yes, we did come in late. Please forgive us."

"What on earth for? It's perfectly natural after what you've been through. You had to take advantage of your first night as free men. I've come to take you over to the police station. You have to go there to make the official declaration that you entered the country illegally. When that formality is over, we'll go see your friend. They took X-rays of him early this morning. We'll know the results soon."

We got dressed and went to the room downstairs where Bowen and the captain were waiting for us.

"Good morning, my friends," the captain said in his bad French.

"Good morning, everybody. How are things with you?" a lady officer of the Salvation Army asked. "Did you find Port of Spain to your liking?"

"Oh, yes! We had a very good time."

We had some coffee and walked to the police station, which was only two hundred yards from the hostel. The police saluted us without any particular interest. We passed between two black guards in khaki uniforms and were led into a severe and imposing office. An officer rose to his feet; he was about fifty and dressed in shorts and a khaki shirt covered with medals. He addressed us in French: "Good morning. Please sit down. Before we get to your official declaration, I'd like to ask you a few questions. How old are you?"

"We're twenty-six and nineteen."

"What was your crime?"

"Murder."

"What's your sentence?"

"Hard labor for life."

"So it was first-degree murder?"

"No, sir, mine was second degree."

"Mine was first degree," Maturette said, "but I was only seventeen."

"At seventeen you know what you're doing," the officer said. "In England you would have been hanged. However, it's not for British authorities to judge French justice. What we don't approve of is the way they send their convicts to French Guiana. It's inhuman and unworthy of a civilized nation like France. But unfortunately you cannot stay in Trinidad or any of the British islands. And I must ask you to be straight with us and not try to find some way to get around it, an illness or some other pretext to put off your departure. You are free to stay in Port of Spain for eighteen days. Apparently you have a good boat. I'm going to have it moved here to the port. If it needs repairs, Royal Navy workmen will make them. You'll be given all the food you need for your trip, as well as a good compass and a marine map. I hope some South American country will accept you. Don't go to Venezuela for you'll be arrested and put on a road gang until they decide to turn you over to the French authorities. Your offense may have been serious, but that still doesn't mean your lives should be ruined forever. You're young and healthy, you look like decent boys, so I hope that after what you've been through, you won't accept permanent defeat. The fact that you made it here suggests you won't. I'm happy I can have a hand in helping you become responsible members of society. Good luck. If you have any problems, telephone this number and there'll be somebody you can speak French to."

He rang a bell and a civilian came for us. We were taken to a room where several policemen and civilians were typing, and one of them took down our declaration.

"Why did you come to Trinidad?"

"It was a stopover."

"Where did you come from?"

"French Guiana."

"When you made your escape, did you commit any offense, did you injure or kill anyone?"

"No one was seriously hurt."

"How do you know?"

"We knew it before we left."

We gave him our ages, our penal situation as regards the French, and all the rest of it. Then he said, "You can stay here for up to eighteen days. During that time you are free to do whatever you like. If you change hostels, let us know. I am Sergeant Willy. Here's my card with two telephone numbers: one is my official police number, the other, my private number. If anything should happen to you, if you need help, call me immediately. We know you're worthy of our confidence. I'm sure you'll behave."

A little later Mr. Bowen accompanied us to the clinic. Clousiot was happy to see us. We didn't say anything about our night on the town. All we told him was that we were free to come and go as we pleased.

That surprised him and he asked, "With no escort?"

"Yes, with no escort."

"These 'roast-beefs' are a funny people."

Bowen had gone to find the doctor and now returned with him. He asked Clousiot, "Who set the fracture?"

"Me and another man who isn't here."

"You did it so well we won't need to reset the leg. The broken fibula is right back in place. We'll just make you a cast with an iron peg so that you can walk around a bit. Do you want to stay here or would you rather go with your friends?"

"Go with them."

"All right. You can leave tomorrow morning."

We thanked him profusely. The doctor and Mr. Bowen went their way and we spent the rest of the morning and a part of the afternoon with Clousiot. We were overjoyed when we found ourselves together again the next morning in our hostel room with the window wide open and the fans cooling the air. We congratulated ourselves on how healthy we looked and what fine figures we cut in our new clothes. But when the conversation started to turn to the past, I said:

"We must forget the past and think only about the present and future. Where we should go, for example. To Colombia? Panama? Costa Rica? We ought to ask Bowen what countries are most likely to admit us."

I called Bowen at his office; he wasn't there. I called him at home in San Fernando; his daughter answered. We talked for a while, and then she said, "Mr. Henri, there are buses to San Fernando that leave from the French market right near your hostel. Why don't you come and spend the afternoon here? Please do. I'll be expecting you." So all three of us set off for San Fernando, Clousiot magnificent in his new slightly military-looking brown suit.

It touched us to return to the house that had given us such a warm welcome. The two women must have understood our feelings, for they said, "You're back in your own home, dear friends." And they now addressed us by our first names: "Henri, may I have the sugar?" or "André [that was Maturette's name], would you like something more?"

Dear Mrs. and Miss Bowen, I hope God has repaid you for all

your kindness and that your generous souls have known only perfect happiness since that day.

We spread a map on the table and made our plans. The distances were long: seven hundred and twenty miles to the first
Colombian port of Santa Marta; twelve hundred miles to Panama;
fifteen hundred to Costa Rica.

Mr. Bowen returned. "I telephoned all the consulates and I
have good news," he said. "You can stay over a few days in
Curaçao to rest up. And Colombia has no established procedures
for escaped convicts. So far as the consul knows, no convict has
ever arrived in Colombia by sea, or in Panama, or anywhere else."

"I have an idea," Margaret, Mr. Bowen's daughter, said. "But
it's terribly far—eighteen hundred miles at least."

"Where's that?" her father asked.

"British Honduras. You might find help there because the governor is my godfather."

I looked at my friends and said, "Destination British Honduras." It's a British possession bordering Mexico to the north and
Guatemala on the west and south.

With the help of Margaret and her mother, we spent the afternoon mapping our route. First lap—Curaçao, six hundred miles.
Second lap—Curaçao to whatever island crossed our path. Third
lap—British Honduras.

Since you never knew what to expect at sea, it was decided that
we should have a special case of canned foods—meats, vegetables,
jams, fish, etc.—to supplement the provisions given us by the
police. Margaret thought Salvattori's Supermarket would be glad
to give us our supplies as a present. "But if they won't," she added,
"Mummy and I will buy them for you."

"No, indeed."

"Be quiet, Henri."

"No, I won't let you. We have money of our own; it would be wrong of us to take advantage of your kindness when we can easily pay for the things ourselves."

We parted with the promise that we would make one last visit before the big departure.

Every evening we went on the town at eleven o'clock. Clousiot sat on a bench in the square where there was the most activity, and Maturette and I took turns keeping him company while the other roamed the town. We had now been here ten days. Clousiot walked with little difficulty, thanks to the iron peg on his cast. We learned how to get to the port by streetcar and were considered regulars in several of the bars. The police saluted us; everybody knew who we were and where we'd come from, but nobody ever mentioned it. We did notice that the bars where we were known charged us less for food and drink than they did the sailors. So did the girls. Usually, when the girls sat with sailors, officers or tourists, they drank all the time and tried to make them spend as much as possible. In the bars where there was dancing, they never danced with a man unless he had bought them several drinks first. But with us it was different. They sat with us for long periods and wouldn't have a drink unless we insisted. And when they did accept one, it wasn't one of their famous tiny drinks but a beer or a real whiskey and soda. This pleased us, for it was their way of saying that they knew our situation and sympathized.

The boat was in Port of Spain in the Royal Navy Yard. It had been repainted, an additional six inches added to the gunwales and the keel strengthened. It looked in good shape. They replaced the mast with a higher and lighter one, and the flour sacks we had had for jib and spinnaker were replaced with a strong, ocher-colored sailcloth. A navy captain presented me with a proper compass and showed me how to use it with the map to determine our position. Our route to Curaçao would be one point north of due west.

The captain introduced me to a naval officer who was the commander of a school ship called the *Tarpon*. He asked me if I would please sail out of the port the following morning about eight o'clock. I was mystified, but agreed. The next morning Maturette and I went to the naval base. A sailor joined us and we put out in a good wind. Two hours later, as we were tacking in and out of the port, a warship suddenly appeared. The entire crew and all the officers were lined up on the deck in full dress. As they passed us, they yelled "Hurrah!" and dipped their colors twice. It was some kind of official salute, but I didn't have the faintest idea what it meant. We returned to the base, where the warship was already tied up. We moored, too, and the sailor made us a sign to follow him. We went aboard and the commander received us on the bridge. A blast of the whistle announced our arrival, and after we were introduced to the officers, they had us pass in front of the students and petty officers who were standing at attention. The commander spoke a few words in English and then everybody broke ranks. A young officer explained to us that the commander had told the students that we deserved their respect for having made such a long trip in such a small boat and that we were about to set off on a still longer and more dangerous voyage. We thanked the officer for the honor. He made us a present of three oilskins and, as it turned out, they served us well. They were black, with hoods and heavy zippers.

Two days before we were to leave, Mr. Bowen came to ask if, as a favor to the chief of police, we would take with us three *relégués* arrested the week before. They had been left on the island by their companions who had gone on to Venezuela, or so they said. I didn't like the idea, but we'd been too well treated to say no. I asked if I could meet these cons before giving my final answer. A police car came for me and I went in to speak to the chief. He turned out to be the officer who had interrogated us at the time of our arrival. Sergeant Willy acted as interpreter.

"We wonder if you would do us a favor."

"If it's at all possible, with pleasure."

"We have three French *relégués* in prison here. They claim that their companions abandoned them here and left. We think they sank their boat, but they say they don't even know how to sail. We think they're trying to put something over on us so that we'll give them a new boat. They have to go, but I don't want to have to turn them over to the first French ship that comes along."

"Chief, I'll do it, but I want to speak to them first. You must realize that it's dangerous to take on three total strangers."

"I understand. Willy, bring the three Frenchmen into the prison yard."

I wanted to see them alone, so I asked the sergeant to leave.

"You're *relégués*?"

"No, we're *bagnards*."

"Why did you say you were *relégués*?"

"We hoped we'd get better treatment if they thought we'd committed several small crimes instead of one big one. I guess we were wrong. What are you?"

"A *bagnard*."

"I don't recognize you."

"I came on the last convoy. Look, the chief of police called me to ask if I'd take you three on our boat. There are three of us already. He said that if I wouldn't take you, he'd have to put you on the first French boat that came along. What do you say?"

"We have reasons for not wanting to go to sea again. Couldn't we pretend to leave with you, then you leave us off on the end of the island and go on your way?"

"No, I can't do that."

"Why not?"

"Because that's a stinking way to pay back their kindness."

"You should think of us cons before you think of the 'roast-beefs.' "

"Why?"

"Because you're a con yourself."

"That may be, but there are a lot of different kinds of cons and maybe there's more difference between you and me than between me and the 'roast-beefs.' It depends on how you look at it."

"So you're going to let them turn us over to the French authorities?"

"No. But I'm not going to let you off before we get to Curaçao either."

"I can't face starting out all over again," one of them said.

"Listen, take a look at the boat first. Maybe you just had a bad boat."

"O.K. We'll give it a try."

"All right. I'll ask the chief to let you look at the boat."

Together with Sergeant Willy, we went over to the port. The three *mecs* seemed to have more confidence once they saw the boat.

NEW DEPARTURE

We set sail two days later, we three and the three strangers. I don't know how they had got wind of it, but a dozen girls from the bars came to see us off, along with the Bowen family and the Salvation Army captain. As one of the girls was giving me a farewell kiss, Margaret laughed and said, "Henri, you're a fast worker!"

"Good-by, everybody. If we don't see you again, remember you have a big place in our hearts. We'll never forget you."

At four in the afternoon we were towed away from the quay. We were out of the port in no time and watched to the last moment the group that had come to see us off. They were now waving white handkerchiefs. The wind filled our sails, the towrope was dropped, and we breasted the first of the million waves that lay between us and our destination.

There were two knives on board, mine and Maturette's. The hatchet was near Clousiot and so was the machete. We were certain that none of the others was armed, but all the same we arranged things so that at least two of us would always be awake. About sunset the school ship appeared and kept us company for nearly half an hour. Then it saluted and moved off.

"What's your name?"

"Leroux."

"Which convoy?"

" 'Twenty-seven."

"Your sentence?"

"Twenty years."

"What's yours?"

"Kargueret, 'twenty-nine convoy. I'm a Breton."

"You're a Breton and you don't know how to sail a boat!"

"My name is Dufils. I'm from Angers. I got life because I said something stupid in court. If it hadn't been for that, I'd have got ten years maximum. I was in the 'twenty-nine convoy."

"What was it you said?"

"Well, it was like this. I killed my wife with a flatiron. During my trial one of the jury asked me why I hit her with the iron. I don't know why, but I said I killed her with the iron because she was a bad ironer. My lawyer said it was that stupid remark that got me my heavy sentence."

"Where did you escape from?"

"Cascade—the forest camp about fifty miles from Saint-Laurent. It was easy to escape from because we had a lot of freedom. There were five of us and it was a cinch."

"What do you mean, five? Where are the other two?"

There was an embarrassed silence.

Clousiot said at last, "Look, *mecs*, we're all in this together. We've got a right to know."

"I'll tell you," the Breton began. "Like he said, there were five of us when we left. But the two missing men—they were from Cannes—told us they were fishermen. They paid nothing toward the *cavale*, but they said they would make up for it by helping us sail the boat. Well, when we were under way, we saw that neither of them knew a damn thing about sailing a boat. We almost drowned twenty times. We hugged the coast, first Dutch Guiana, then British Guiana, then finally Trinidad. Between Georgetown and Trinidad I killed the one who said he could run the boat. And the *mec* deserved what he got—he didn't pay his share and he lied about what a good sailor he was. The other one thought he was going to be killed, too, so in the middle of a storm he dropped the tiller and jumped overboard. We did the best we could; the boat almost sank several times, we cracked up on a rock, but somehow pulled through. I swear that's the truth and nothing but the truth."

"That's right," the other two said. "That's the way it happened. We all agreed the *mec* should be killed. What do you think, Papillon?"

"I'm in no position to judge."

The Breton insisted. "But what would you have done?"

"I'll have to think about it. To really know, you'd have to be there. Otherwise you can't tell what's right."

Clousiot said, "I'd have killed him. His lie could have cost everybody's life."

"O.K. Let's not talk about it any more. But I get the impression you're still scared. You're back at sea only because they made you go, right?"

"Right," they answered together.

"All right then. But nobody panics here no matter what. At least, don't let on you're scared. If you are, shut up about it. This is a good boat; it's proved itself. We have a heavier load, but the gunwales are six inches higher. That pretty well takes care of the extra load."

We smoked and drank some coffee. We had had a good meal before leaving and decided we wouldn't eat again until the next day.

Clousiot, our official recorder, informed us that it was now forty-two days since we launched our *cavale* from our room at the Saint-Laurent hospital. Since then I had gained three precious possessions: a waterproof steel watch purchased in Trinidad, a very precise compass in a double suspension box and a pair of dark glasses with plastic lenses. Clousiot and Maturette each had a sailor's cap.

The first three days were without incident except for two meetings with schools of dolphins. A group of eight of them took it into their heads to play games with the boat; we all broke into a cold sweat. First they passed under the boat lengthwise, coming up just in front of the bow, sometimes grazing it. In another game three dolphins deployed themselves in a triangle, one in front and two in parallel positions behind. They would come at us with furious speed and just when they were almost on top of us, they would dive under the boat and come up on the opposite side. We had a strong wind and were tearing ahead under full sail, but they went even faster. The game lasted for hours; we were mesmerized. The three newcomers said nothing, but you should have seen their faces!

In the middle of the fourth night we were hit by a tremendous storm. It was terrifying. The waves ran in all directions, colliding every which way, some deep, others short. We didn't speak. Only Clousiot occasionally let out a "Go to it, pal! Get that one like you got the others!", or "Look out behind!" Every so often the waves came roaring from three directions at once, their crests exploding with spray. I'd figure out their speed and carefully anticipate the angle of attack. Then, as if from nowhere, a wave would stand us straight up and smack us on the ass. Several times the waves broke over my shoulders and flooded the boat. All five men would grab cooking pots and empty cans and bail like mad. But in spite of the heavy seas, the boat never filled more than a quarter way up and at no time were we in actual danger of sinking. This three-ring circus lasted half the night—almost seven hours. Because of the rain we couldn't see a thing, and the sun didn't break through until eight in the morning.

We greeted the storm's end, the return of the sun and the start of a new day with joy. To celebrate we must have coffee! We made some Nestlé café-au-lait boiling hot and drank it with hardtack as tough as iron but delicious when dunked in coffee. The night's struggle against the storm had exhausted me, and even though the wind was still strong and the waves high and unruly, I asked Maturette to take the tiller. I had to sleep. I wasn't down ten minutes when Maturette took a wave broadside and the boat filled three-quarters full. Everything was afloat—tin cans, stove, blankets. . . . I woke up with water up to my stomach, and was just able to grab the tiller before another wave broke over us. With one tug I turned our stern toward the wave—the impact pushed us a good thirty feet.

Everybody set to bailing. Maturette manned the big pot, which held four gallons. Nobody tried to save anything. We had only one idea: to bail, to bail as fast as possible, because the great weight of the boat made it difficult to fight the waves. I had to admit that the newcomers conducted themselves very well: when the Breton saw his suitcase carried off, he decided to further lighten the boat by cutting free the water barrel which he'd hung over the side. Two hours later we were dry, but we'd lost our blankets, the primus stove, our charcoal, fuel, and—voluntarily—our fresh water.

It was noon when I decided to change my pants and realized that my suitcase was gone, too, along with two of our three oil-skins. All our tobacco was lost or wet, even the cigarette papers had disappeared in their watertight aluminum box, but in the very bottom of the boat we found two bottles of rum.

"*Mecs,*" I said, "first a good slug of rum, then let's open our box of reserves and see what's left. There's fruit juice. Good. We'll ration it. Boxes of *petit-beurre* cookies: we'll empty one and make a stove out of it. We can put the canned food in the bottom of the boat and use the crate for firewood. We've all had a good scare, but the danger's over now. We have to pull ourselves together and get ready for what lies ahead. From here on, nobody's to say: 'I'm thirsty.' Nobody's to say: 'I'm hungry.' And nobody's to say: 'I wish I had a smoke.' All right?"

"All right."

Everybody understood, and mercifully the wind died down enough so that we could make a corned beef soup. A bowlful of that with dunked hardtack made a good warm lining for our stomachs, enough to last until the next day. Then each of us had a tiny portion of green tea. A carton of cigarettes turned up in the one undamaged case: twenty-four small packs of eight cigarettes each. My five companions decided that I should be the only one to smoke—it would help me stay awake. So that the others wouldn't be jealous, Clousiot gave up lighting my cigarettes. He just lit the matches. Thanks to his tact, we didn't have a single disagreeable moment.

We'd been gone six days and I hadn't really slept yet. This evening the sea was a millpond, so I slept. I slept like the dead for nearly five hours. It was ten at night when I woke up. The sea was like glass. The others had already eaten; I found a can of polenta, which I ate with some smoked sausages. Delicious. The tea was almost cold, but so what. I smoked and waited for the wind. The night was thick with stars. The North Star shone with all its brilliance; only the Southern Cross outdid it. You could clearly make out the Great and Little Bear. There wasn't a cloud and the full moon was already high in the sky. The Breton was in a bad mood: he had lost his jacket and was in shirt sleeves. I loaned him the oilskin. We moved into the seventh day.

"Well, we can't be far from Curaçao now. Though we may have gone too far north. From here on I'm going due west so we don't miss the Dutch Antilles. Otherwise we're in trouble."

"Do what you think best," the Breton said.

We waited for the wind the whole of that night. Finally, at four in the morning a good breeze started up, growing stronger as the day progressed. For thirty-six hours it kept us going at a good clip, yet the waves were so small that we had smooth sailing all the way.

CURAÇAO

Gulls. First only their cries, for it was dark; then the birds themselves, wheeling over the boat. One gull perched on the mast, flew off and came back again. This went on for over three hours until day broke with a radiant sun. Nothing on the horizon to indicate land. Where on earth had the gulls come from? We spent the whole day looking. No sign of land. A full moon rose as the sun went down, so brilliant that it hurt my eyes. I had lost my dark glasses; they'd been swept overboard by that broadside wave, along with our protective caps. Then about eight in the evening the moonlight picked out a black line far away on the horizon.

"It's got to be land!" I said.

There was general agreement that there was indeed a black line and that it must be land. For the rest of the night I kept us headed toward it. Its outline grew gradually sharper—we were getting nearer. Now, with a strong wind behind us, we rode a long, smooth wave and closed in rapidly. The black mass lay low in the water with nothing to show whether there were cliffs, rocks, or a sandy shore. The moon was about to set on the far side of the land, and that made it difficult to see. Then, at the water's edge, I saw a row of lights which broke up as we approached. We came nearer, then nearer still, and about half a mile from shore I dropped anchor. The wind was so strong that the boat spun around in circles, heading into waves which stood it on its stern as they passed by. The constant tossing was unnerving. We had lowered the sails and folded them and might have waited in this safe though disagreeable position until daybreak, but unfortunately the anchor came loose. To steer the boat, it had to be under sail. We put up the jib and spinnaker and suddenly the anchor caught again. My companions pulled on the rope and it came away without the anchor. We had lost it. I did what I could, but the waves pushed us so near the rocks I decided to put up the mainsail and head straight for them. My maneuver succeeded so well that we found ourselves wedged between two rocks with the boat completely disabled. As the next wave rolled in, we threw ourselves into the water and rolled to shore, battered but alive. Only Clousiot with his cast got a really bad mauling. His arms, face and hands were bruised and covered with blood. As for the rest of us, a few scrapes on the knees, hands and ankles. I had a bloody ear from crashing into a rock.

The important thing was that we were alive, out of the reach of the waves and on dry land. When the sun rose, we recovered the one oilskin and I returned to the boat, which was beginning to break up. I managed to pry the compass loose from the rear bench. No sign of life anywhere. We searched the place where we had seen the lights and found a row of lanterns, placed there—as we later learned—to warn fishermen that this was a danger area. We set off inland. There was nothing but cactus, enormous cactuses and donkeys. We came to a well. We were tired for we'd taken turns, two by two, carrying Clousiot in a seat we made of our hands. The dried carcasses of donkeys and goats lay scattered around the well. It was dry, and the blades of the windmill that had worked it once now beat the air aimlessly. Not a soul about; only donkeys and goats.

We continued on until we reached a small house whose open door seemed to invite us in. We called "Hello!" No answer. A cloth bag hung from the chimneypiece by its cord. I took it down and opened it. The cord broke and I saw that it was full of Dutch florins. Bonaire, Curaçao, or Aruba? Without touching its contents, we returned the bag to its place. We found water and everybody took turns drinking from a ladle. No one in the house, no one outside. We set off again—slowly because of Clousiot. Suddenly our path was obstructed by an ancient Ford. A large fat man was at the wheel.

"Who are you? Are you French?"

"Yes, sir, we are."

"Climb in." We laid Clousiot across the laps of the three men in the back seat; I sat next to the driver with Maturette next to me.

"You were shipwrecked?"

"Yes."

"Anyone drowned?"

"No."

"Where did you come from?"

"Trinidad."

"And before that?"

"French Guiana."

"*Bagnards* or *relégués?*"

"*Bagnards.*"

"My name is Dr. Naal; I own this spit of land. It's a peninsula that juts out from Curaçao. It's called Donkey Island. The donkeys and goats feed on the cactuses. They have very long thorns. The people here call the thorns 'the girls of Curaçao.' "

"That's not very flattering to the real girls of Curaçao," I said.

The man laughed noisily. Then with an asthmatic wheeze the Ford stopped dead in its tracks. I pointed to a pack of donkeys and said, "If the car has given up, we can be towed."

"I have harness in the trunk, but the problem is to catch them and get them in it. It's not so easy." The fat doctor lifted the hood and discovered that a big jolt had disconnected a wire. Before getting back into the car he looked around nervously. We set off again and after driving along a series of rutted roads we came to a white barrier. Next to it stood a small white house. The doctor spoke in Dutch to a light-skinned Negro in very clean clothes who kept repeating, "Ya, master. Ya, master." The doctor turned to us and said, "I've given this man orders to keep you company until I get back, and give you something to drink. Please get out of the car." We sat on the grass in the shade. The Ford coughed on its way. It hadn't gone fifty yards when the Negro told us in Papiamento—a dialect of the Dutch Antilles composed of English, Dutch, French and Spanish—that his boss, Dr. Naal, had gone for the police because he was scared of us and had warned him to look sharp since we were escaped thieves. So the poor fellow couldn't do enough for us. He made us some weak coffee, but in the heat it tasted very good. We had been waiting for over an hour when a big paddy wagon drove up with six policemen dressed in German style, and behind it, an open car driven by a chauffeur in a police uniform with two men and Dr. Naal in back.

They got out of the car and the shortest of the three—he had the closely shaved head of a priest—said to us, "I am the official responsible for security on the island of Curaçao. It is therefore my responsibility to arrest you. Have you committed an offense since your arrival? If so, what was it? And which of you committed it?"

"Sir, we are escaped convicts. We've come from Trinidad, and it's only a few hours since our boat smashed up on your rocks. I'm in charge of our little band and I can assure you that not one of us has committed even the smallest offense."

The police officer turned toward the fat doctor and spoke to him in Dutch. As they were talking, a man drove up on a bicycle. He spoke loud and fast, first to Dr. Naal, then to the officer.

I asked, "Dr. Naal, why did you tell this man we were thieves?"

"Because my man told me so before I met up with you. He stood behind a cactus and watched you go into his house. He's an employee of mine and looks after the donkeys."

"We're thieves because we walked into his house? That's a silly thing to say, sir. We drank some water in his house. Is that robbery?"

"What about the bag of florins?"

"I did open the bag; I even broke the string when I opened it. But all I did was examine the money to see what country we were in. Then I replaced the money and hung the bag back where I found it, from the ledge of the chimney."

The officer looked me in the eye, turned abruptly to the man on the bicycle and spoke to him sharply. Dr. Naal started to speak. In his dry German way the officer indicated he should stay out of it. The officer made the man on the bicycle get into his car and sit next to the chauffeur; he got in himself with two of the policemen and drove off. Naal and the third man stayed with us.

"May I explain?" Naal said. "My man told me that his money

was gone. The officer interrogated him before having you searched, suspecting that he might have lied. If you are innocent, I am truly sorry, but it wasn't my fault."

In less than fifteen minutes the car was back and the officer said, "You were telling the truth. That man is a liar. He'll be punished for this." The poor bugger was loaded into the paddy wagon, the other five got in behind, and I was about to follow when the officer held me back, saying, "Get into my car and sit next to the driver." We left ahead of the police van, and it was soon out of sight. We drove along well-surfaced roads and finally reached the town. The houses were built in the Dutch style, everything was very clean, and almost everybody seemed to be on bicycles. There were hundreds of people riding around. We entered the police station and walked through a large room where several police in white were sitting at desks, then into an air-conditioned office. It was very cool. A big, strong, fair-haired man of about forty sat in an armchair. He got to his feet and spoke to the officer in Dutch.

When the conversation was over, the officer said to us in French, "May I introduce the chief of police of Curaçao?" Then, turning to the police chief, he said, "Sir, this man is French and he is the leader of the six men we just arrested."

"As men shipwrecked on our territory, you are welcome to Curaçao. What is your name?"

"Henri."

"Henri, the business of the money bag must have given you a disagreeable moment. But the incident served to put you in a good light. It proved your honesty beyond the shadow of a doubt. I'm going to give you a room with a couch so that you can rest. Your case will be brought before the governor; he will decide what's to be done. This officer and I will speak up for you."

He held out his hand and we left. In the courtyard Dr. Naal apologized and promised to intervene on our behalf. Two hours later we were locked in a large room with a dozen beds and, in the middle, a long wooden table flanked by two benches. Through the barred window we asked a policeman to buy us tobacco, cigarette papers and matches with our Trinidad dollars. He wouldn't take the money, saying something we couldn't understand.

There was a long wait. "That spit-and-polish black isn't going to do us any favors," Clousiot said. "Where's our tobacco?"

I started to knock on the door and it opened at the same moment. A little coolie was standing there in a gray prison uniform with a number across his chest so there'd be no mistaking his status. He said, "Money cigarettes."

"No, tobacco, cigarette papers and matches."

He was back in a few minutes with our order plus a big steaming pot of cocoa.

I was summoned back to the office of the chief of police during the afternoon.

"The governor has given orders that you're to be allowed out in the prison yard. Tell your companions they're not to try to escape or there'll be serious consequences for all of you. As leader of the group, you can go into town for two hours every morning, from ten to twelve, and every afternoon from three to five. Have you got any money?"

"Yes. English and French."

"A policeman in civilian clothes will accompany you wherever you want to go."

"What are you going to do with us?"

"I think we'll try to put you separately on oil tankers of different nationalities. Curaçao has one of the biggest refineries in the world which processes the oil from Venezuela. From twenty to twenty-five tankers arrive and leave every day of the year. That would be your best solution, for then you'd be able to enter almost any country with no problem."

"Where do you mean? Latin America? North America? Countries under British rule?"

"No, they're out of the question. Europe is equally impossible. But don't worry. Trust us. We want to help set you on the way to a new life."

"Thank you, sir."

I reported all this faithfully to my companions.

Clousiot, the most skeptical of our band, said, "What's your opinion, Papillon?"

"I don't know yet. I'm afraid it's some sort of trick to keep us quiet, to keep us from trying to escape."

"I'm afraid you're right."

The Breton, however, thought the plan was great, and the *mec* of the flatiron was jubilant. "No more boats, no more adventures. We each arrive on a tanker in some country or other and disappear into the sticks with official sanction." Leroux agreed.

"What do you think, Maturette?"

And this kid of nineteen, this child accidentally turned convict with features more delicate than a woman's, said in his soft voice, "You really think those pigs are going to cook us up fake identity cards? I don't. At most, they might look the other way while we sneak aboard a tanker, but that's about it. And the only reason they'd do that is to get rid of us. At least, that's what I think. I don't trust them."

I went out very little—sometimes in the morning to do a few errands. We'd now been here a week and nothing had happened. We were getting nervous. One afternoon we noticed three priests escorted by the police going from cell to cell. They spent a long time in the cell nearest ours, where there was a black who had been arrested for rape. Assuming they were coming to us next, we went into our room and sat on our beds. Sure enough, the three of them came in, along with Dr. Naal, the chief of police and a man with white-and-gold braid who looked like a naval officer.

"Monsignor, these are the French," the chief of police said in French. "Their conduct has been exemplary."

"I congratulate you, my children. Let's sit around this table. It's easier to talk that way." Everybody sat on the benches, including the men who had come with the bishop. Someone brought in a stool from the courtyard and placed it at the head of the table so that he could see everybody.

"Most Frenchmen are Catholics. Are any of you not Catholic?" Nobody raised his hand. Thinking back to the priest at the Conciergerie and how I'd been virtually baptized, I decided I could consider myself a Catholic too.

"My friends, I am of French descent. My name is Irénée de Bruyne. My ancestors were Huguenots who fled to Holland when Catherine de Medici was on the rampage. So I have French blood, I am the Bishop of Curaçao, a city with more Protestants than Catholics but where the Catholics are devout. Tell me your situation."

"We are waiting to be put on board oil tankers."

"How many men like you have left here in this manner?"

"None yet."

"Hm. What do you say to that, Officer? Please answer me in French; you speak it so well."

"Monsignor, the governor sincerely believed he was helping these men, but I must confess that up to now not a single ship's captain has been willing to take on a convict, mainly because they have no passports."

"Then that's where we should start. Can't the governor issue special passports?"

"I don't know. We haven't discussed that."

There was a pause, then the bishop said, "I will say a mass for you the day after tomorrow. Will you come for confession tomorrow afternoon? I will personally hear your confessions so that I can intercede with the good Lord and ask him to pardon your sins." He turned to the chief of police. "Will you see that they're brought to the cathedral at three o'clock?"

"Yes."

"I want them brought by taxi or in a private car."

"I'll bring them myself, Monsignor," said Dr. Naal.

"Thank you, my son. My children, I can promise you nothing. Only this: from this moment on, I will do my utmost to help you." Seeing Naal kiss his ring and the Breton, too, we each placed our lips on it, then escorted him to his car, which was parked in the court.

The next day everyone confessed to the bishop. I was last.

"My child, what was your worst sin?"

"Father, to begin with, I was not baptized, but where I was in prison in France, a priest told me that whether I was baptized or not, we were all children of the Lord."

"He was right. Good. Go on."

I described my life in detail. This prince of the Church listened patiently and at length. He took my hands in his and looked at me intensely. When I came to the parts that were hard to confess, he looked down to make it easier for me. The expression in the eyes of this sixty-year-old priest was so pure that he seemed more like a child. His infinite goodness shone through his features and his pale gray eyes soothed me like balm on a wound. He talked softly, very softly, always my hands in his. "Sometimes God wills for one of His children to experience human wickedness so that he will emerge stronger and nobler than ever. Don't you see, my son, that if you hadn't had this Calvary to climb, you would never have been able to raise yourself so near to God's truth? Let me put it another way: the men, the system, the cogs of the machine that ground you down, the evil men who framed you and tortured you, have rendered you the greatest service possible. They brought forth a new man, superior to the first, and if today you recognize honor, goodness and charity, and realize the energy you will need to surmount the obstacles and become someone superior, you owe it to them. Your idea of vengeance, of punishing everybody according to the injury inflicted on you, goes against the grain of your character. You must be a saver of men, and not live in order to do evil, even though you think the evil is justified. God was generous to you. He told you, 'Help yourself and I'll help you.' He helped you in so many ways. He even allowed you to save other men and lead them to freedom. But most important, don't make so much of your sins. There are many people in higher positions who are guilty of much worse. Only they haven't experienced the weight of man's idea of justice and therefore have missed the opportunity to rise above it as you did."

"Thank you, Father. You've done me enormous good. I will never forget it." And I kissed his hands.

"You are leaving soon, my son, and will meet new dangers. I would like to baptize you before you go. What do you say?"

"Father, leave me as I am for now. My father raised me without religion. He has a heart of gold. When my mother died, he found new words, new ways to fill her place in my life. If I let myself be baptized now, it would be a kind of betrayal. Give me time to become completely free, to begin a normal life, then I'll write and ask him if he minds if I give up his philosophy and have myself baptized."

"I understand, my son, and I'm sure that God does too. I bless you and ask God to protect you."

*   *   *

"So what do we do now?" I asked Dr. Naal.

"I'm going to ask the governor to tell Customs to give me first choice of the smugglers' boats at the next auction. You'll come with me to choose the one you like best. As for the rest of it, the food and clothing, that will be easy."

After the bishop's sermon we had many visitors. Everybody wanted to get to know us. They usually came about six o'clock and brought us things which they left on our beds without comment. About two in the afternoon we had visits from the Little Sisters of the Poor, accompanied by their Mother Superior, who spoke very good French. They always brought baskets full of things they had cooked themselves. The Mother Superior was young—I'd say less than forty. Her hair was hidden under her white coif, but her eyes were blue and her eyelashes blond. She came from an important Dutch family (according to Dr. Naal) and had written to Holland to see if there were some way of setting us free other than sending us back to sea. We had good times together, and she loved to hear me tell the story of our escapes. If I forgot something or missed a detail, she brought me gently to heel: "Don't go so fast, Henri. You skipped the story of the *hocco*. . . . Why did you forget the ants today? The ants are very important, because without them you wouldn't have been caught by the Masked Breton!" These were wonderful moments, so completely different from all that had gone before, that they cast a strange and unreal glow over our fast dissolving past.

I saw the boat. It was magnificent: twenty-five feet long, a good keel and a very high mast with immense sails. It was fully equipped, not to mention a cluster of customs seals. At the auction someone had started at six thousand florins (about a thousand dollars). Dr. Naal whispered a few words in the man's ear and we got it for six thousand and one florins.

Five days later we were ready. Freshly painted, its wealth of provisions carefully stored in the hold, our boat was fit for a king. Six suitcases, one for each of us containing new clothes, were wrapped in waterproof cloth and stowed in the cabin.

THE PRISON IN RIO HACHA

We left at daybreak. The doctor and the sisters saw us off. We picked up wind immediately and moved swiftly away from the quay. The sun made its radiant appearance and an uneventful day was under way. I noticed right away that we hadn't sufficient ballast for the amount of sail we were carrying, so I decided to be cautious. The boat was a real thoroughbred: very fast, but jealous and irritable. I headed due west. We hajd thought to sneak our three new companions onto the Colombian coast. They wanted no part of a long crossing; they said they had confidence in me but not in the weather. In point of fact, we had learned from the newspapers that bad weather was on the way, including hurricanes.

It was agreed that we should let them off on a desolate, uninhabited peninsula called La Guajira. Then we would continue on to British Honduras. The weather was glorious, and the starry night that followed our first sparkling day had in addition a brilliant half-moon to help us see. We made straight for the Colombian coast, dropped anchor and took soundings to determine if it was safe to let them off. Unfortunately the water was very deep and we had to approach dangerously near the rocky coast to find water not over five feet. We shook hands, they each dropped over the side, found their footing and, holding their suitcases on top of their heads, waded toward dry land. We watched their progress with interest and some sadness. Our companions had behaved well and had risen to every challenge. It was too bad they were leaving. Then, as they neared land, the wind died abruptly. God damn. Just so long as we weren't anywhere near Rio Hacha, the first port with a police force. I thought we might already have cleared it, judging by the small lighthouse we had just passed which showed on the map.

We waited and waited. . . . The other three had disappeared after waving good-by. Wind! For God's sake, wind! Wind to get away from this Colombian coast and all its unknown dangers. We had no idea what they did with escaped prisoners. Finally at three in the afternoon the wind rose. I put up all the sails and, heeling perhaps a little too much, we skimmed along nicely for over two hours. Then suddenly a launch full of men appeared, heading straight for us and shooting over our heads to make us stop. I ignored them and ran on, trying to reach the open sea beyond territorial waters. No luck. The powerful launch overtook us, and with ten men aiming their guns, we had to give up.

If these were soldiers or policemen, they wore very strange uniforms: dirty pants that had once been white and wool sweaters full of holes that had certainly never been washed. They were barefoot except for their "commander," who was a little cleaner and better dressed. But if their clothes were ratty, their weapons were not. They were armed to the teeth, each with a cartridge belt full of bullets, an army rifle in first-class condition and, just in case, a handy large dagger in a sheath. Their "commander" looked like a half-breed assassin; he had a revolver hanging from a belt full of ammunition. Since they spoke Spanish, we had no idea what they were saying, but their expressions, gestures and voices were hostile.

We walked from the port to the prison, passing through a village which was indeed Rio Hacha. We were flanked by six of the cutthroats with three more behind, their guns aimed right at us.

We arrived in a prison yard surrounded by a low wall. About twenty filthy, bearded prisoners stood or sat around with equally hostile expressions. "*Vamos, vamos.*" We gathered that our guards were saying, "Get going, get going," which was not easy because, although Clousiot was improving, he was still in his cast. The "commander," who had stayed behind, now came up to us, our compass and the oilskin under his arm. He was eating our biscuits and chocolate, and we sensed immediately that we were going to be entirely cleaned out. We weren't mistaken. They locked us up in a squalid room with one heavily barred window. On the floor were planks of wood with wooden pillows—our beds. "Frenchies, Frenchies," a prisoner said through our window as soon as the police were gone.

"What do you want?"

"Frenchies, no good, no good!"

"What's no good?"

"Police."

"Police?"

"Yes, police no good." Then he went away. Night fell. The room was barely lit by a weak bulb. Mosquitoes buzzed in our ears and up our noses.

"This is great! We're going to have to pay a pretty price for letting those guys ashore."

"How were we to know? It was only because there was no wind."

"You went too far in," Clousiot said.

"Enough of that. This is no time to blame ourselves or anybody else. We've got to help each other out, stick together like we never did before."

"Sorry, Papi, I guess you're right. It wasn't anybody's fault."

Oh, it would be too damned unfair to have fought so hard, then have our *cavale* end like this! They hadn't searched us, though. I had my *plan* in my pocket and lost no time putting it in its place. Clousiot did the same. We were lucky to still have them.

By my watch it was eight in the evening. They brought us lumps of brown sugar as big as your fist and three different kinds of rice paste cooked in salted water. *"Buenas noches!"* "That must mean 'Good night,' " Maturette said. In the courtyard the next morning we were served excellent coffee in wooden bowls. The chief of police came by about eight. I asked him if I could go to the boat to collect our belongings. Either he didn't understand me or pretended not to. The more I saw of his ugly mug, the less I liked him. On his left hip he carried a small bottle in a leather case; he took it out and uncorked it, drank a gulp, spat and handed me the flask. As this was his first friendly gesture, I accepted it and drank. It was a good thing I didn't drink much: it was firewater and tasted like wood alcohol. I swallowed it quickly, started to cough, and the half-breed Indian laughed fit to burst.

At ten o'clock a group of white-clad civilians appeared. There were six or seven of them and they made for what appeared to be the prison administration building. We were summoned. The men were sitting in a semicircle under the large portrait of a much decorated officer: President Alfonso López of Colombia. One of the gentlemen asked Clousiot to sit down; the rest of us remained standing. The man in the middle, a thin man with half glasses resting on his eagle's beak, began the interrogation.

Instead of translating, the interpreter said, "The man who just spoke and who will conduct the interrogation is the judge of the town of Rio Hacha. The others are distinguished citizens and friends of his. I am Haitian and in charge of the electrical works for this department. I will serve as translator. Some of these men understand a little French—and maybe even the judge—but they won't admit it."

This preamble annoyed the judge. He interrupted and began his interrogation, the Haitian translating.

"You are French?"

"Yes."

"Where did you come from?"

"Curaçao."

"And before that?"

"Trinidad."

"And before that?"

"Martinique."

"That's a lie. Our consul in Curaçao warned us over a week ago to watch the coast because six convicts who'd escaped from the French penitentiary were going to try to land on our territory."

"O.K. So we escaped from the penitentiary."

"You are 'Cayeneros'?"

"Yes."

"If a country as noble as France has seen fit to send you this far and mete out such severe punishment, it must be because you are very dangerous bandits."

"Perhaps."

"Are you thieves or murderers?"

"Murderers."

"Same thing. So you're big shots? Where are the other three?"

"They stayed in Curaçao."

"That's another lie. You dropped them off thirty-five miles from here in a place called Castillette. Luckily they were arrested and will be here in a few hours. You stole your boat?"

"No, it was a present—from the Bishop of Curaçao."

"Very well. You stay here as prisoners until the governor decides what to do with you. For the offense of landing your three accomplices on Colombian territory and then trying to escape to sea, I sentence the captain of the boat to three months in prison and the other two to a month. And you'd better be on your good behavior if you don't want our police to beat you up. They're tough men. Have you anything to say?"

"No. All I want is to get my possessions and the provisions we left on the boat."

"Everything has been confiscated by the Customs except for pants, shirts, jackets and shoes for each of you. And that's that. There's nothing you can do about it: it's the law."

We returned to the prison yard. The miserable prisoners hovered around the judge: "Doctor! Doctor!" Swelling with self-importance, the judge swept through the group without saying a word. The men in white left the prison and disappeared.

At one o'clock the other three arrived in a truck together with seven or eight armed men. Looking ashamed, they climbed down with their suitcases. We followed them into our room.

"That sure was a dumb-ass thing we made you do," said the Breton. "We're really sorry, Papillon. You can kill me if you want to. I won't try to defend myself. We didn't behave like men; we behaved like a bunch of fags. We did it because we were scared of the sea. Well, from what I've seen of Colombia and Colombians, the dangers of the sea are a joke. Did they get you because the wind died down?"

"Yes, Breton. But I'm not about to kill anybody. We were in this thing together. I could have refused to drop you off, then nothing would have happened."

"You're too damn good, Papi."

"No, I'm just trying to be fair." I told them about the interrogation. "Maybe the governor will set us free."

"Well . . . let's hope so. As the fellow said, where there's life, there's hope."

I had the impression that the officials in this hole were not in a position to decide our case. Some higher authority would determine whether we stayed in Colombia, were returned to France, or were given back our boat so that we could move on. It would be a damn shame if these people we had done nothing to took the decision on themselves. After all, we had committed no offense of any kind on their territory.

We had now been here a week. Nothing new, except for talk that we might be transferred to a bigger town a hundred and twenty miles away called Santa Marta. Our guards with their ugly pirate's faces were unchanged in their attitude toward us. Yesterday one of them hit me with his rifle because I tried to claim my own soap in the washroom! We were still in the same mosquito-ridden room, though it was a little cleaner since Maturette and the Breton had taken to washing it down every day. I was beginning to lose hope and confidence. The Colombians were nibbling away at my self-confidence. One of the Colombian prisoners lent me an old issue of a Santa Marta newspaper. On the front page were photographs of the six of us and, below, the chief of police with his enormous felt hat and cigar, then the photograph of a dozen armed policemen. It was clear that our capture had been romanticized and that their role in it had been much amplified. It appeared that our arrest had saved all Colombia from a terrible threat. But I must say, the pictures of the so-called outlaws made us look much more sympathetic than the police. The "outlaws" looked like honest men, whereas the police, if you'll forgive me, starting with their chief—well, perhaps we were prejudiced. . . .

What should we do? I was beginning to understand a few words of Spanish: to escape, *fugar*; prisoner, *preso*; to kill, *matar*; chain, *cadena*; handcuffs, *esposas*; man, *hombre*; woman, *mujer*.

THE *CAVALE* FROM RIO HACHA

There was a *mec* in the courtyard who always wore handcuffs. I made friends with him. We would smoke the same cigar; it was long, thin and very strong, but I smoked it. I gathered that he smuggled contraband between Venezuela and the island of Aruba.

He had been accused of killing some guards on the coast and was awaiting trial. Some days he was very calm, others he was nervous and excitable. I began to realize that he was calm when he'd had a visitor and was chewing the leaves he was brought. One day he gave me half a leaf and I understood. My tongue, palate and lips lost all feeling. The leaves were coca. He was thirty-five, with arms and chest covered with curly jet-black hair, and unusually strong. His feet were so callused that he could step on a piece of glass or a nail without feeling it.

"You and me we *fuga*," I said to him one evening. (On one of the Haitian's visits I had asked him for a French-Spanish dictionary.) The *mec* understood and indicated he would like to escape, but what about his handcuffs? They were American handcuffs with a slot for a flat key. The Breton made me a hook out of metal thread flattened at one end. After a little practice I was able to open my friend's handcuffs whenever I liked. At night he was put in a dungeon with very thick bars. Those in our room were thin, and I was sure we could bend them easily. So there would be only one bar that needed sawing—Antonio's (his name was "Antonio, the Colombian"). "How do we get a saw?" "Money." "How much?" "One hundred pesos." "In dollars?" "Ten." So, for ten dollars, which I gave him, he got two hacksaws. I explained by drawing on the dirt in the yard that each time he had sawed a little, he was to mix the metal sawdust with some paste from our rice balls and fill the cut. Just before we went back in, I opened his handcuffs. If they were checked, he had only to press against them and they'd close by themselves. It took him three nights to cut almost through the bar. He said one minute would see him the rest of the way through and he was sure he could bend the bar back with his hands. When he was out of the dungeon he'd come by for me.

It rained often; he said that he'd get out on the first rainy night. My comrades knew what I was planning, but none of them wanted to go with me. I was going too far away for them. I wanted to get to a point on the Colombian peninsula next to the Venezuela frontier. On our map this territory was called Guajira and it appeared to be contested by Colombia and Venezuela. My Colombian friend said it was the land of the Indians; there were no police, either Colombian or Venezuelan, and only a few smugglers knew it. It was dangerous because the Guajiros Indians tolerated no civilized man on their territory. And the farther inland you went, the more dangerous they became. On the coast there were Indian fishermen who trafficked with the village of Castillette and a hamlet called La Vela through the intercession of less primitive Indians. Antonio didn't want to go there. Either he or his companions must have killed some of these Indians when their boatload of contraband was forced onto the Indians' coast. Antonio agreed to take me near Guajira, but I would have to go on from there alone. You can't imagine how laborious these arrangements were; so many of the words he used weren't in the dictionary.

So, that night it rained in torrents. I stood close to the window. We had pried away a plank from the partition to help separate the bars. We had tried it two nights before and found the bars gave easily.

"*Listo* [I'm ready]."

Antonio's face appeared between the bars. With the help of Maturette and the Breton, one tug was enough not only to bend the bars but to pry one loose. They lifted me up and pushed me through, giving me a few whacks on the rear in farewell as I disappeared. We were now in the yard. The torrential rain made an infernal noise as it fell on the tin roofs. Antonio took my hand and led me to the wall. Jumping over it was child's play: it was only six feet high. I did cut my hand on the glass imbedded on the top, but it didn't matter. That amazing Colombian managed to find the path even though we couldn't see ten feet ahead of us. Because of the rain, we were able to march straight through the village until we found a road that ran between the bush and the coastline. Very late we saw a light, forcing us to make a wide detour into the brush, which fortunately was sparse at that point. Then we picked up our path again and walked in the rain until daylight. Antonio had given me a leaf of coca as we left, and I chewed it the way I'd seen him do in prison. When daylight came I still wasn't tired. Was it the leaf? I'm sure it must have been. Even though it was now daylight, we continued walking. From time to time Antonio lay down and put his ear to the water-soaked earth. Then he'd start off again.

He had a curious way of walking. It wasn't a walk and it wasn't a run. It was a succession of little leaps of exactly the same length, and he used his arms as if he were rowing the air. At one point he must have heard something for he pulled me into the brush. Then, sure enough, along came a tractor dragging a roller to flatten the ruts.

It was now ten-thirty in the morning. The rain stopped and the sun came out. After walking perhaps a third of a mile on the grass, we lay under a thick bush full of thorns. I thought we were out of danger, but Antonio wouldn't let me smoke or talk even in a whisper. He kept swallowing the juice of his leaf and I did the same, though with greater moderation. He showed me his pouch, which had more than twenty leaves in it, and laughed silently, his magnificent teeth gleaming in the dim light. To fight the mosquitoes, he chewed on a cigar and we coated our faces with his nicotined saliva. That took care of them.

It was now seven in the evening. Night had fallen, but the moonlight was too bright for us to proceed. He pointed to nine o'clock on my watch and said, "Rain." I understood: at nine o'clock it would rain. And sure enough, at nine-twenty it started to rain, and we took off. In order to keep up with him, I copied his leaps and rowed with my arms. It wasn't hard to do, and you moved faster than at a fast walk, yet you weren't running. During the course of the night we had to hide in the brush three times, once to let a car go by, once a truck, and once a wagon pulled by two donkeys. Thanks to the leaves, I wasn't tired when day came. The rain stopped at eight and then, as before, we walked cautiously on the grass for over half a mile before going into the bush to hide. The one thing I didn't like about the l leaves was that you couldn't sleep. We hadn't closed an eye since we started. Antonio's pupils were so dilated that the irises had disappeared completely. Mine must have done the same.

It was now nine at night and the rain had returned. It was as if the rain were waiting for nine o'clock. I learned later that in the tropics, at whatever hour the rain first started to fall, it would start and stop at just about the same time during that moon's quarter. As we started the night's march, we heard voices and then saw lights. "Castillette," Antonio said. The extraordinary man took me firmly by the hand, led me into the brush, and after more than two hours' painful marching allowed us to return to the road. We marched, or rather leaped, the rest of the night and a good part of the next morning.

The sun dried our clothes. We had been wet for three days, and for three days we had eaten only some brown sugar, and that on the first day. Now Antonio seemed quite confident that we were out of danger. He was walking unconcernedly, and several hours had gone by since he last put his ear to the ground. The road followed the shore, and after a while Antonio cut himself a stick and we walked over to where the sand was wet. He stopped to examine a trail of flattened sand about twenty inches wide, running from the sea to the dry sand. We followed it to where it widened and made a circle. Antonio plunged his stick into the circle. When he pulled it out, the end was covered with a yellow liquid that looked like egg yolk. Which it was. We dug a hole in the sand with our hands and soon uncovered a mass of eggs, perhaps three or four hundred of them. They were sea turtles' eggs, covered with skin instead of shells. We filled Antonio's shirt with as many as it would hold, a hundred or so, left the beach, crossed the road and went into the brush. Once safely hidden, we began our feast. Following Antonio's instructions, I ate only the yolk. He would penetrate the skin with one snap of his teeth, allow the white to run out and suck in the yolk. One for him, one for me, and so on. He went on and on, opening, swallowing, first him, then me. Filled to bursting, we stretched out on the ground with our jackets for pillows. Antonio said in Spanish, "Tomorrow, you continue alone for two more days. From tomorrow on there won't be any more police."

At six o'clock we came to the last border outpost. We recognized it from the barking of dogs and the bright lights in the little house. Thanks to Antonio's masterful tactics, we managed a successful detour and walked the rest of the night without taking precautions. The path was narrow, but the lack of grass underfoot showed that it was used. It was about twenty inches wide and skirted the brush next to the beach, which was about six feet below us. From time to time we saw the hoofprints of horses and mules. Antonio sat down on a large root and motioned me to do the same. The sun was beating down hard. My watch said eleven, but when I stuck a small stick in the ground it made no shadow. It must therefore be noon. I reset my watch. Antonio emptied his pouch; he had seven leaves left. He gave me four and kept three. I went off into the brush and came back with a hundred and fifty Trinidad dollars and sixty florins. He was startled. He reached out and touched the bills, unable to understand how they could look so new and why they hadn't gotten wet. Holding them in his hands, he thanked me, thought for a long time, took six bills of five florins each and gave me back the rest. I insisted, but he wouldn't take more. At that point he seemed to change his mind: he had decided previously that we should go our separate ways; now he seemed to want to continue with me another day. After that he'd make a half-turn and go on alone. O.K. We swallowed a few egg yolks and lit a cigar after a half hour's struggle to get a fire going by rubbing two stones together and igniting a handful of dried moss. Then we set off.

We'd been walking three hours when we saw a man on a horse coming straight at us. He was wearing an enormous straw hat, boots, something that resembled a long leather slip instead of pants, a green shirt and a faded green jacket. He was armed with a beautiful carbine and a huge revolver hung from his belt.

"*Caramba!* Antonio, my son!" Antonio had recognized the rider from far away. The big bronzed cavalier dismounted and the two men slapped each other lustily on the shoulder. (This was the typical greeting of the region, I learned later.)

"Who is that?"

"A companion in escape, a Frenchman."

"Where are you going?"

"As near to the Indian fishermen as we can. He wants to go through the Indians' territory and into Venezuela to get back to Aruba or Curaçao."

"The Guajira Indians are bad people," the man said. "You're unarmed. Take this." He handed me a dagger with a polished horn handle in a leather sheath. We sat by the side of the path. I took off my shoes; they were bloody. Antonio and the rider talked very fast, and I could tell that they did not approve of my plan for crossing Guajira. Antonio motioned that I should get up on the horse and that I should hang my shoes over my shoulder to let my bleeding feet dry out. The rider got back on his horse and I climbed on behind. I had no idea what was going on. We galloped all that day and the following night. From time to time we stopped; he'd pass me a bottle of anisette and I'd take a swallow. When the sun rose, he stopped. He gave me a piece of cheese as hard as a rock, two biscuits, and six coca leaves. To carry them, he made me a present of a waterproof bag which I attached to my belt. He threw his arms around me and slapped me on the shoulders the way he had Antonio. Then he got back on his horse and galloped off.

THE INDIANS

I walked on until one in the afternoon. The bush ended, there wasn't a tree to be seen. The sea shimmered silver under the burning sun. I walked barefoot, my shoes hanging over my left shoulder. As I was deciding whether to lie down, I saw far away five or six trees—or perhaps they were rocks—set back from the beach. I tried to figure the distance: six miles or so. I took out a large piece of leaf and, chewing away, set off again. An hour later I was able to identify the five or six shapes: they were huts with thatched roofs of straw or some kind of light-brown leaf. Smoke was coming out of one of them. Then I saw people. They saw me. I could hear their voices and saw them gesturing in the direction of the sea. Then I saw four boats coming in to shore and about ten people getting out. Everybody gathered in front of the houses and looked in my direction. The men and women were naked except for small loincloths. I approached slowly. Three of the men were leaning on bows, the arrows in their hands. They made no motion of either hostility or welcome. A dog let out a bark and rushed at me in a fury. He bit my calf and tore off a piece of my pants. When he lunged again, a small arrow from somewhere nipped his rear (I learned later it was shot from a blowpipe); he ran off howling and disappeared into a house. I limped on—for he had given me quite a bite. I was now perhaps thirty feet from the group. Not one of them moved or spoke, and the children hid behind their mothers. Their bodies were splendid: bronzed and well muscled. The women had firm, hard breasts with large nipples. There was only one with sagging breasts.

One man had an especially noble bearing; he had fine features and was obviously superior to the rest. I went straight to him. He was not holding a bow. He was as tall as I and his hair was well cut. It hung down to his eyebrows and to his earlobes on the sides, so black it looked purple. His eyes were steel gray. There was no hair on his body. His bronzed thighs were well muscled and his legs beautifully proportioned. He was barefoot. I came to a stop about ten feet in front of him. He took two steps forward, his eyes looking directly into mine. The examination lasted two minutes. His motionless face with the hooded eyes was like a bronze bust. Then he smiled and touched my shoulder. That was the signal. Everybody came and touched me, and a young Indian girl took me by the hand and led me into the shade of one of the huts. All the others followed and sat in a circle. One of the men handed me a lighted cigar; I took it and smoked it. They all laughed at the way I smoked, for they—women as well as men—held the burning end in their mouths. The girl pushed up my pants leg. The bite had stopped bleeding, but a piece of me the size of a quarter was missing. She pulled out all the hairs, and once the skin was smooth, she washed the wound with sea water which another young Indian had brought. Then she squeezed the wound to make it bleed. Still not satisfied, she scratched each pore with a piece of sharpened steel. I made an effort not to flinch, for everyone was watching. Another young Indian girl wanted to help, but she was pushed away. For some reason everybody laughed. I gathered that the one dressing my wound wished to make it clear to the other girl that I was her property; this is what had made them laugh. Then she cut my pants well above the knee, prepared a poultice of seaweed on a stone and laid it on the wound, holding it in place with strips of cloth she ripped from my pants. Finally satisfied with her labors, she motioned me to get up.

I stood up and took off my jacket. It was then that she noticed the butterfly tattooed at the base of my neck. She examined it closely; then seeing there were more tattoos, she took off my shirt to see the rest. Everybody crowded around. On the right side of my chest I had a guard from Calvi; on the left, the head of a woman; just above the waist a tiger's head; on my spine, a crucified sailor, and across the kidneys, a tiger hunt with hunters, palm trees, elephants and tigers. To get a better look, the men pushed the women aside, touched me and examined each tattoo minutely. The chief expressed his opinion, then everyone else gave his. From that moment on it was clear that I'd been adopted by the men. The women had adopted me the minute the chief smiled at me and touched my shoulder.

We went into the largest of the huts and I was completely taken aback. The hut was made of brick-red earth. It was round, with eight doors, and in a corner hung a cluster of hammocks made of brightly colored wool. In the middle of the hut was a highly polished flat, round rock and around it smaller round rocks to sit on. Several double-barreled shotguns, a sword and a great variety of bows hung from the walls. There was also a turtle shell big enough for a man to lie in and a chimney constructed of identical stones without cement. On a table a split gourd held two or three handfuls of pearls. I was handed a wooden goblet filled with a fermented fruit juice; it was bittersweet and very good. Then I was brought on a banana leaf a five-pound fish cooked over the coals. I ate slowly. When I had finished the delicious fish, the Indian girl took me by the hand and led me to the beach so that I could wash my hands and mouth in sea water. When we returned, we all sat down in a circle, the young Indian girl at my side with her hand on my thigh, and tried through words and gestures to get to know each other.

Suddenly the chief rose, went to the back of the hut, returned with a white stone and started to draw on the table. First he drew naked Indians, then the village, then the sea. To the right of the Indian village he drew houses with windows, and men and women wearing clothes. The men carried guns or sticks. To the left, another village, men with guns and hats and ugly faces, their women also wearing clothes. I looked closely at the drawings. The chief noticed that he'd forgotten something and traced a path from the Indian village to the hamlet on the right and another path to the village on the left. To indicate their location in relation to his own village, he drew on the right side—the Venezuelan side—a round sun with rays shooting out in all directions; on the Colombian side, a sun on the horizon cut by a wavy line. His intention was clear: the sun rose on one side and set on the other. The chief examined his work with pride and everybody took turns looking at it. When he saw that I understood, he took his stone and covered the two villages with lines, leaving his own intact. I gathered that he was telling me that the men in the two villages were bad and that only his village was good. As if he needed to tell me!

He took a damp cloth and wiped the table. When it was dry, he put the stone in my hand to indicate that it was my turn. My drawing was more complicated than his. I drew a man with bound hands flanked by two armed men who were looking at him, then the same man running and the two men running after him, their guns pointed at him. I drew this scene three times, each time putting more space between me and my pursuers. In the last one the police had stopped and I was running to their village, which I identified by drawing the Indians and the dog and, standing in front of everybody, the chief with his arms held out to welcome me.

My drawings must have been pretty good because after a long discussion with the men, the chief opened his arms as in my picture. They had understood.

That same night the Indian girl took me into a hut where six women and four men were living. She hung a magnificent hammock of colored wool, so big that, crosswise, two could sleep in it comfortably. I lay in the hammock lengthwise while she installed herself in another one crosswise. Then I changed my position to crosswise and she came and lay down next to me. She touched my body, my ears, my eyes, my mouth. Her fingers were long and fine, but they were very rough and covered with small scars from the cuts made by the coral when she dived for oysters. When I stroked her face in turn, she looked at my hand with astonishment that it was so smooth. We spent an hour in the hammock, then we got out and went to the chief's hut. They had me examine the shotguns, twelve- and sixteen-bore from Saint Etienne. There were also six boxes of ammunition.

The Indian girl was of medium height, with gray eyes like the chief's, a fine profile and braided hair that fell to her hips. Her breasts were beautiful, high and pear shaped. The nipples were darker than her bronzed skin and very long. Her kiss was a bite; she didn't know how to kiss our way. I soon taught her. She wouldn't walk at my side but behind me, and there was nothing I could do about it. One of the huts was uninhabited and in poor condition. With the help of the other women, she repaired the roof of coconut-palm leaves and patched the walls with the red earth. They had a wide variety of cutting tools: knives, daggers, machetes, hatchets, hoes and forks with iron teeth. They also had cooking pots of brass and aluminum, watering cans, casseroles, a grindstone, an oven, metal and wooden barrels. Their hammocks

were of pure wool with braided fringes and vivid designs in blood
red, Prussian blue, canary yellow and a waxy black.

The house was soon ready and she started to fill it with contri-
butions from the other women: an iron ring on three legs for cooking over the fire, a hammock large enough for four adults, glasses,
tin pots, casseroles, not to mention a donkey harness.

We had been caressing each other for two weeks, but she refused
absolutely to go any further. I was mystified because, after all, she
was the one who had started it. But when the moment came, she
wouldn't. She never wore anything but her small loincloth which
hung from her slender hips by a narrow cord. Her buttocks were
entirely bare. Without ceremony, we installed ourselves in the little
round house. It had three doors: one in the center—the main one—
and two others facing each other. The three doors formed an isosceles triangle and had strict uses: I was always to come and go by the
north door, she by the south. I was never supposed to use hers or she
mine. The big door in the center was for our friends, and neither she
nor I was to use it unless we were with visitors.

It was only when we had moved into the house that she let me
take her. I won't go into details, but she was an ardent mistress
with intuitive skill; she enfolded me like a vine. When we were
alone, I would comb and braid her hair. She loved me to do this
and her face glowed with happiness. But there was fear in it, too,
fear that someone might discover us, for she gave me to understand that a man was never to comb his wife's hair, or rub her
hands with a pumice stone, and he must not kiss her mouth or
breasts in certain ways.

So Lali—for that was her name—and I installed ourselves in
our house. She never used iron or aluminum pots and never drank
from a glass, and she cooked everything in the earthenware pots
the Indians made themselves. We washed under the spray of the
watering can and went to the bathroom in the sea.

I helped open the oysters. This work was generally done by the oldest of the women. Each young pearl diver had her own sack. The pearls they found were shared: one portion went to the chief who represented the community, one to the fisherman, a half share to the woman who opened the oysters and a share and a half to the diver. When the diver lived with her family, she gave her pearls to her uncle, her father's brother. I never did understand the role of the uncle. He was also the first person to go into the house of the betrothed; he would take the arm of the woman and draw it around the man's waist and place the man's right arm around the woman, placing his index finger in her navel. Once this was done, he went his way.

So I helped with the opening of the oysters. I didn't fish, for I had not yet been invited into the canoe. The fishing was done quite far out, about a quarter of a mile from shore. Some days Lali came back with her thighs and ribs covered with scratches from the coral. Sometimes, if her cuts were bloody, she would crush some seaweed and rub it into the wounds. I did nothing unless invited. I never entered the chief's house unless someone led me in by the hand. Lali suspected that there were three young Indian girls sleeping in the grass near our door to see or hear what we did when we were alone.

Yesterday I met the Indian who acted as intermediary between our village and the first Colombian hamlet a mile beyond the border station. The hamlet was called La Vela. The Indian had two donkeys and a Winchester repeating rifle. He carried the pearls separated according to size in a cigar box. Like everyone else, he wore only a loincloth. He was small and dried up. He had an ugly scar that ran from under his chest on the left side across his body to his right shoulder. It formed a welt as thick as your finger.

The chief had asked me to tattoo him, so, with the help of the dictionary, I made out a list: needles, blue and red India ink and thread. But since the intermediary didn't speak a word of Spanish, I wondered how on earth he was able to do his business.

When the Indian was about to leave, the chief gave me permission to go along with him for a bit. To make sure I came back, the chief lent me a shotgun with six rounds of ammunition. He was convinced that I would feel obligated to return since naturally I would never take anything that didn't belong to me. The Indian got on one donkey and I on the other. We rode the whole day over the same path I'd used coming to the village; then when we were about two miles from the border station, we turned away from the sea and headed inland.

About five o'clock we came to the edge of a stream where there were five Indian houses. Everybody came and looked at me. The Indians talked on and on among themselves until a weird character appeared: his eyes, hair, nose and everything else were those of an Indian, except his color. He was the palest white and had the red eyes of an albino. He wore khaki pants. It was then that I understood that our intermediary never went farther than this.

The white Indian said in Spanish, "Hello. You are the killer who escaped with Antonio? Antonio is a relative of mine; we are bound by the pact of blood." (In order to become "bound," two men gash each other's arm with their knives, rub the two wounds together, then coat their hands with the blood and lick them.) "What you need?"

"Needles, red and black India ink, thread. That's all."

"I'll have it here at the beginning of the next quarter-moon."

His Spanish was better than mine and I had the feeling he knew how to strike a bargain that would benefit his people. As we were leaving, he gave me a necklace made of Colombian coins set in very white silver. He said it was for Lali.

"Come see me again." And to make sure I returned, he gave me a bow.

I started the trip back alone, but I hadn't gone more than halfway when Lali appeared with one of her sisters—a girl of about twelve or thirteen. Lali herself must have been somewhere between sixteen and eighteen. She pounced on me like a mad woman, clawed my chest—I was protecting my face—and bit my neck. Using all my strength, I was barely able to control her. Then she suddenly calmed down. I put the younger girl on the donkey, and Lali and I walked slowly back, our arms around each other. On the way I killed an owl. I shot it without knowing what it was; all I saw were two eyes gleaming in the shade. Lali was determined to have it and hung it from the saddle. We arrived at dusk. I was tired and wanted to wash. Lali washed me; then, right in front of me, she removed her sister's loincloth, washed her, and finally washed herself.

When they returned to the house, I was sitting waiting for water to boil to make some lemonade. Then a thing happened that I only understood much later: Lali pushed her sister between my legs, took my arms and placed them around the girl's waist—I noticed she wasn't wearing her loincloth and had the necklace I'd given Lali around her neck. I didn't really know what to make of this. I removed her gently from between my legs, took her in my arms and laid her down in the hammock. I took off the necklace and put it back on Lali. Then Lali lay down next to her sister, and I lay next to Lali. Long afterward, I learned that Lali had thought I was making inquiries about leaving because I wasn't happy with her and that she was hoping her sister might be able to hold me better. I woke up with Lali's hands shading my eyes. It was very late—eleven in the morning. The younger one had left. Lali looked at me, her large gray eyes full of desire, and bit me gently on the corner of my mouth. She wanted me to know how happy she was that I loved her and that I hadn't gone away because she had failed me.

The Indian who usually paddled Lali's canoe was sitting in front of the house, waiting for her. He smiled at me charmingly and closed his eyes to indicate that he knew Lali was still asleep. I sat down next to him and he started a conversation which, of course, I couldn't understand. He was young and had the powerful muscles of an athlete. He looked longingly at my tattoos and I gathered he wanted to be tattooed too. I nodded in agreement, but he seemed to get the idea that I didn't know how. Lali appeared. She had covered her body with oil. She knew I didn't like it, but she explained that with the cloudy weather the water would be very cold. Her mimicking—half laughing, half serious—was so engaging that I made her repeat it several times, each time pretending I didn't understand. When I asked her to do it yet again, she pouted as if to say, "Either you're stupid, or I'm no good at explaining."

The chief passed by with two Indian women. They were carrying a green lizard weighing at least twelve pounds. He had just caught it with his bow and arrow and invited me to come and help eat it later on. Lali spoke to him, then he touched my shoulder and pointed to the sea. I gathered that it meant I could now go with Lali if I wanted to. The three of us left together, Lali, her usual fishing companion and I. The boat was made of cork and was therefore very light. Carrying it on their shoulders, they walked into the water. The Indian got in the back, holding a huge paddle. Up to her chest in water, Lali held the canoe to keep it steady and prevent it from floating back to shore. I got in and sat in the middle; then with one bound Lali landed in the canoe, and the Indian gave a powerful shove with his paddle. The waves were rolling in and getting bigger and bigger the farther out we went. About fifteen hundred feet from shore there was a kind of channel where two boats were already fishing. Lali had tied her hair on top of her head with red leather laces. The Indian dropped the big iron bar that served as anchor and Lali followed the rope down into the water, a heavy knife in her hand. The boat was very unsteady and bobbed up and down with each roller.

For over three hours Lali dived and surfaced, dived and surfaced. You couldn't see the bottom—it must have been all of fifty feet down. She came up with oysters every time and the Indian emptied her sack into the canoe. During the whole three hours Lali never once got into the canoe. Her only rest was hanging onto the side for five or ten minutes. We changed our location twice. In the second spot the oysters were bigger and more plentiful. Then we went back to shore. Lali had got into the canoe and a wave rolled us in. An old Indian woman was waiting. She and Lali's fishing partner carried the oysters across the sand. When all the oysters had been gathered there, Lali pushed the old woman aside and started to open them herself. Using the point of her knife, she opened a good thirty before she found a pearl. (I had eaten at least two dozen by that time.) She gently pried it loose; it was in the largest category—as big as a chickpea. And how it gleamed! Nature had given it a great variety of subtle colors. Lali picked up the pearl, put it in her mouth, left it there a moment, then took it out and put it in mine. Then she went through some motions with her jaw, indicating she wanted me to crush it between my teeth and swallow it. I refused, but her pleading was so persuasive that I finally did what she asked. She opened four or five more oysters and gave them to me to swallow so that the crushed pearl would be washed down well inside me. Then, like a child, she opened my mouth to see if there were any fragments left between my teeth. After that we went off, leaving the other two to go on with the work.

I had now been here a month. The reason I knew was that I had marked each day and its date on a piece of paper. The needles and inks had arrived long ago. I discovered that Zato, the chief, had three razors. He didn't use them for shaving, the Indians being beardless, but for cutting his hair. Lali had removed all the hair on my body. The minute she saw one, she pulled it out and rubbed me with a paste made of seaweed mixed with ashes. This seemed to discourage growth. I tattooed the chief on the arm with an Indian crowned by a headdress of many colored feathers. He was ecstatic and gave me to understand that I was to tattoo nobody else until I'd done a larger tattoo on his chest. He wanted the same tiger I had, with its huge teeth. I laughed, for I didn't have the talent to do justice to the splendid head.

The Indians of Guajira lived on the coast and the inland plain up to the foothills of the mountains. There were other communities in the mountains called Motilones. Years later I was to have dealings with them. As I explained earlier, the Guajiros dealt with civilized people only through the medium of barter. The coastal Indians delivered their pearls and live turtles to the albino Indian. Some of the turtles weighed as much as four hundred pounds. They never reached the size or weight of those in the Orinoco or the Maroni—these sometimes weighed a thousand pounds and had shells six or seven feet long and over three feet wide. Once on their backs, turtles can't turn over. I've seen them stay on their backs three weeks without food or drink and still be alive. As for the big green lizards, they were very good to eat. Their flesh is deliciously tender, and when their eggs have been cooked in the sand by the sun's heat, they, too, have a fine flavor. Only their appearance makes them unappetizing.

Every time Lali went fishing, she brought her portion of pearls home to me. I put them in a wooden bowl, all sizes mixed together. The only ones I kept aside—in an empty matchbox—were two pink pearls, three black ones and seven of an extraordinarily beautiful metallic gray. There was also an unusual pearl the shape and size of our kidney beans. It had three colors superimposed one on the other and, depending on the weather, the dominant color was either black, a polished stainless steel, or silver with a pink cast. Thanks to the pearls and the occasional turtles, the tribe lacked for nothing. It's true they had some useless things and lacked some they could have used. For instance, there wasn't a single mirror in the village. I had to salvage one from a shipwreck—a nickel-plated board about fifteen inches square—so that I could see to shave or look at myself.

My manner with my friends was very simple: I never did anything that might diminish the authority of the chief or, even less, that of the old Indian who lived alone three miles inland surrounded by snakes, two goats, a dozen sheep and twenty chickens. He was the sorcerer for all the villages in Guajira. This way I kept their good opinion of me. By the end of the second month I had been completely accepted by everyone.

The two hamlets I was acquainted with had no goats, chickens, or sheep; having domestic animals seemed to be the privilege of the sorcerer. Each morning a different Indian woman set off to his house with freshly caught fish and shellfish in a basket on her head, together with corn cakes freshly grilled on hot stones. Sometimes, but not always, she returned with eggs and curdled milk. When the sorcerer wanted me to come and see him, he sent me three eggs and a highly polished wooden knife. Lali would accompany me halfway, then wait in the shade of a huge cactus. The first time I was summoned, she put the wooden knife in my hand and indicated with her arm the direction I should take.

The old Indian lived in revolting filth in a tent made of cowhide, hairy side in. Three stones in the middle stood around a fire that was always burning. He didn't sleep in a hammock but on a bed made of branches that stood at least three feet above the ground. The tent was quite large and without walls except for a few branches on the windward side. I saw the snakes: one was nearly ten feet long and as thick as your arm, the other about three feet with a yellow V on its head. "How those beasts must pack away the chickens and eggs!" I said to myself. It was beyond me how goats, chickens, sheep and a donkey could all live together in one tent. The old Indian looked me over, then made me take off my pants, which Lali had converted into shorts. When I was entirely naked, he had me sit on one of the stones. He threw some green leaves on the fire which made a thick smoke that smelled of mint. For the next ten minutes I thought I'd suffocate. Then he burned my pants and gave me two Indian loincloths, one of sheepskin and the other of snakeskin as supple as a glove. Around my arm he placed a bracelet made of goat-, sheep- and snakeskin laces braided together. It was four inches wide and held in place by a snakeskin lace which could be loosened or tightened at will.

I noticed that on his left calf the sorcerer had a sore the size of a silver dollar which was covered with gnats. From time to time he shooed them away, and if they got too much for him, he dusted the wound with ashes. My formal adoption over, I was on the point of going when he presented me with another wooden knife. This one was smaller than the one he had sent when he wanted to see me. Lali explained to me later that if I wanted to see him, I was to send him the smaller knife. If he was willing to see me, he would send me the larger one. As I was leaving the old Indian, I noticed how wrinkled his face and neck were. He had only five teeth left in his sunken mouth, three in the lower jaw and two in the upper, in front. His eyes, almond shaped like all Indians', had such heavy lids that when they were closed, they looked like two round balls. He had no eyelashes or eyebrows, but his hair hung straight, black and neatly cut to his shoulders. In front, like all the other Indians, he wore bangs to his eyebrows.

I started for home, somewhat ill at ease for my windswept buttocks. I felt like a fool. But it was a *cavale*, wasn't it? And I mustn't make fun of the Indians. Being free was worth a few inconveniences. Lali looked at my loincloth and laughed, showing her teeth, which were as white as the pearls she fished. She examined my bracelet and the snakeskin loincloth and sniffed to make sure I had passed through the trial by smoke. (I should mention that the Indians have a very highly developed sense of smell.)

I was getting used to this life and beginning to realize that if I stayed too much longer I might lose all desire to leave. Lali watched me constantly, hoping I might take a more active part in communal life. For example, she had seen me go fishing; she noticed that I paddled well and managed the little canoe with skill. From this she leapt to the idea that I should handle her pearl-fishing boat. But I didn't want to. Lali was the best diver among the village girls because she dived deepest and brought back more oysters and bigger ones than the others. But the young man in charge of her boat was the chief's brother. If I took Lali out, I would be doing him a disfavor, and that I must not do.

Whenever Lali saw me in a thoughtful mood, she'd go off in search of her sister. The young girl would come in joyfully through my door. This carried great significance. They'd arrive together at the big door facing the sea; then they'd separate, Lali turning and coming in her door and Zoraima through mine. Zoraima's breasts were hardly bigger than tangerines and her hair was still short. It was cut to the length of her chin and her bangs fell almost to her eyelids. Each time she was summoned by her sister, they would both bathe, after removing their loincloths as they entered and hanging them on the hammock. The younger one always went away disappointed because I hadn't taken her. One day the three of us lay together with Lali in the middle; then Lali got up and lay on the other side, leaving me glued to Zoraima's naked body.

The other day Lali's fishing companion cut his knee very badly. He was carried to the sorcerer and returned with a dressing of white clay. As a result, I went fishing with Lali. I launched the boat properly, but I took her a little farther out than usual. She was thrilled to have me in the boat with her. Before diving, she covered herself with oil; the bottom, which looked very black, was undoubtedly cold. I saw three shark fins pass near us and pointed them out to her, but she paid no attention. With her sack wrapped around her left arm, her knife in its sheath attached to her belt, she pushed off from the boat and, with amazing speed, disappeared into the blackness of the water. Her first dive was for exploration only, so she came up with very few oysters. Then I had an idea. There was a big ball of leather laces in the boat. I knotted one end to her sack and let it out as she went down. She got the idea, for she stayed down a long time, and when she came up again, she was without the sack. Tired from her long dive, she clung to the side of the boat and asked me to raise the sack. I pulled and pulled, but it suddenly stopped, caught probably on some coral. She dived down and freed it: the sack was half full and I emptied it into the canoe. By the end of the morning, aver eight dives, each fifty feet down, we had nearly filled the canoe. When she finally pulled herself in, the top of the canoe was almost flush with the water. We nearly went under when I started to pull up the anchor. We had to untie the anchor rope from the boat and attach it to a paddle to keep it floating until we returned.

The old lady and Lali's fishing partner were waiting on the sand to open the oysters. He was impressed with our haul. Lali explained how we'd done it, how the sack attached to the laces made her lighter and speeded her climb to the surface. And naturally she could gather more oysters. He carefully examined the way I had tied the sack and particularly the slipknot. He undid the knot and, on the first try, was able to make one himself. He was very proud of himself.

The old woman found thirteen pearls in the oysters. Lali seldom stayed for this part of the operation, usually letting them bring her her share at home. But this time she waited until the last oyster was opened. I must have swallowed three dozen, Lali five or six. The crone divided up the shares. The pearls were all about the same size—that of a good-sized pea. She put aside three for the chief, three for me, two for herself and five for Lali. Lali picked up my three and handed them to me. I gave them to her wounded partner. He didn't want to accept them at first, but I forced his hand open and closed his fingers over them. Then he accepted. His wife and daughter had been watching the scene from a distance. Silent before, they now burst out laughing and came over to us. I helped carry him to his hut.

We repeated this ritual for almost two weeks. Each time I gave my pearls to the injured Indian. Once I kept one. When I got back to the house, I had Lali eat it. She was ecstatic and spent the whole afternoon singing.

From time to time I would visit the albino Indian. He asked me to call him Zorrillo, which means "little fox" in Spanish. He told me that the chief had asked him to find out why I wouldn't tattoo the tiger's head on his chest. I explained that I wasn't a good enough artist. With the help of the dictionary, I asked him to get me a mirror the size of my chest, some tracing paper, a fine paintbrush, a bottle of ink, carbon paper and, if he couldn't get that, a soft pencil. I also asked him to get me some clothes, including three khaki shirts, which I would keep at his place. He told me that the police had questioned him about Antonio and me. He told them that I had gone over the mountain into Venezuela and that Antonio had been bitten by a snake and died. He had also found out that the other Frenchmen were in prison in Santa Marta.

Zorrillo's house had the same native crafts as the chief's: many earthenware pots decorated with typical Indian designs, handsome ceramics beautiful in form as well as design and color; tanned skins of snakes, lizards and buffalo, and braided baskets made of white or colored liana. He said they were all made by the Indians of my tribe, although these lived in the middle of the bush, a twenty-five days' march from here. That was where the coca leaves he gave me came from. I was to chew one if I got depressed. As I left Zorrillo, I asked him if he could bring me—in addition to my other requests—a few Spanish newspapers and magazines, for, with the help of my dictionary, I had learned a lot in two months. He had no news of Antonio; he knew only that there had been a new clash between coastal guards and smugglers. Five guards and one smuggler had been killed, but the boat had got away.

I had never seen a drop of alcohol in the village, except for their strange drink of fermented fruit. When I saw that Zorrillo had a bottle of anise, I asked if I could have it. He said no. I could drink it there if I liked, but I couldn't take it away. That old albino wasn't so dumb.

I left Zorrillo on a borrowed donkey, which he assured me would come back to him the next day all by itself. I took with me only a large box of colored candies, each wrapped in tissue paper, and sixty packs of cigarettes. Lali was waiting for me with her sister two miles from the village; there was no scene this time, and we walked back with our arms around each other. Every so often she stopped and gave me a "civilized" kiss on the mouth. When we reached the village, I went to the chief's and offered him the candy and cigarettes. We sat down in front of his door, facing the sea. We had some of the fermented drink, cold from its earthenware jug. Lali sat at my right, her arms around my thigh, and her sister did the same on my left. The box of candy was open in front of us, and the women and children came and shyly helped themselves. The chief pushed Zoraima's head toward mine, giving me to understand that she wanted to be my wife like Lali. Lali took her breasts in her hands, indicating that Zoraima's were small and that was perhaps why I hadn't desired her. I shrugged and everybody laughed. It was clear that Zoraima was sad. So I put my arms around her neck and caressed her breasts; this made her very happy. I smoked a few cigarettes; the Indians tried a few but soon rejected them in favor of their cigars. I took Lali by the arm and we left. Lali walked behind me and Zoraima behind her. We cooked some large fish over the fire, to which I added a five-pound lobster. It was a feast.

The mirror came and the tracing paper, the paper for my decalcomania, a tube of glue I hadn't asked for but which proved useful, several soft pencils, the inks and paintbrush. I hung the mirror by a string so that it was at the level of my chest when I was in a sitting position. There in the mirror was my tiger's head in all its glory. Lali and Zoraima watched me, full of interest and curiosity. I followed the lines on the mirror with the brush, but as the ink tended to run, I thought of the glue. So I made a mixture of ink and glue, and everything was fine. After three one-hour sessions I had painted an exact replica of the tiger's head on the mirror.

Lali went off to find the chief. Zoraima took my hands and placed them on her breasts. She looked so unhappy and her eyes were so full of desire that, without thinking what I was doing, I took her right there on the floor in the middle of the hut. She moaned and her body arched with pleasure. Then she wound herself around me and wouldn't let me go. I freed myself gently and went to bathe in the sea for I was covered with earth from the hut floor. She followed me and we bathed together. I rubbed her back, she rubbed my arms and legs, then we went back to the house. Lali was sitting on the spot where we had lain together; she understood. She got up, put her arms around my neck and kissed me tenderly. Then she took her sister by the arm and led her out through my door, turned and went out through hers. Soon there were sounds of banging on the outside of the house; I went out to see what was going on and found Lali, Zoraima and two other women trying to make a hole in the wall with a piece of iron. I figured they were making a fourth door. To keep the wall from cracking, they dampened it with the watering can. The door was quickly finished and Zoraima pushed the debris outside. From then on only she would use that door; she never used mine again.

The chief came, accompanied by his injured brother and three others. The brother's knee was almost healed. He looked at the picture on the mirror, then looked at himself. He marveled at how well I'd drawn the tiger and marveled, too, to see the reflection of his own face. But he had no idea what I had in mind. Since the picture was now dry, I placed it on the table, put the tracing paper over it and started to draw the outline. It was quickly done. The soft pencil faithfully followed every line. In less than a half hour, under everyone's fascinated gaze, I had a drawing as good as the original. Each in turn took the picture and examined it, comparing the tiger on my chest with the drawing. I had Lali lie down on the table. I rubbed her lightly with a damp cloth, placed a sheet of tracing paper on her belly and, on top of that, the drawing I had just made. I drew a few lines and everyone was filled with wonder to see a bit of the drawing come off on Lali's belly. Only then did the chief understand that all this effort was for him.

Those who haven't been exposed to the hypocrisies of a "civilized" education react to things naturally, as they happen. It is in the here and now that they are either happy or unhappy, joyful or sad, interested or indifferent. The superiority of pure Indians like these Guajiros was striking. They could outdo us in everything: when they adopted someone, everything they had belonged to him; and when anyone showed them the least attention, they were profoundly moved.

I decided that at the first session I would cut the broad lines with a razor so that the general outline of the tattoo would show right away. I'd do the pricking afterward, with three needles attached to a short stick. I started the next day.

Zato lay on the table. I transferred the drawing on the tracing paper to a heavier white sheet and made a decalcomania on his skin with a hard pencil. I had already covered it with a paste of white clay which I'd let dry. The decal left its imprint and I let it dry thoroughly. The chief was stretched out on the table like a ramrod, not daring to move—let alone flinch—for fear he might harm the drawing. I etched each line with the razor; his blood ran a little and I wiped it off each time. When I had done the whole drawing and fine red lines had replaced the black pencil, I coated his entire chest with blue India ink. The ink took everywhere but in the few places where I had cut too deep and it was washed away by the blood. The drawing came through beautifully. Eight days later Zato had his tiger's head with its big maw showing a pink tongue, white teeth, a black nose, mustache and eyes. I was very pleased with the result. It looked better than mine and the colors were brighter. As the scabs fell, I had to prick a few places again. Zato was so pleased that he asked Zorrillo to furnish us six mirrors, one for each of the other huts and two for his.

Days passed, then weeks, then months. It was now April and I had been here four months. I was strong and in excellent health. I was so used to going barefoot that I could walk miles looking for the big lizards without getting tired. I was never without a wife. When Lali was diving, Zoraima was at my side. If Zoraima was diving, Lali kept me company.

I forgot to say earlier that after my first visit to the sorcerer, I asked Zorrillo to get me some tincture of iodine, hydrogen peroxide, absorbent cotton, bandages, quinine tablets and some Stovarsol. I had seen a *bagnard* at the hospital with a sore the same size as the sorcerer's. Chatal, the orderly, had crushed a pill of Stovarsol and applied it to the sore. The medications arrived, plus an ointment that Zorrillo provided on his own. I then sent the sorcerer my little knife and he answered by sending me his big one. I had a hard time convincing him that he should be treated, but after a few days the sore was half its former size, and he volunteered to continue the treatment by himself. One fine day he sent me his big wooden knife so that I could see that he was completely healed. No one ever knew who had done it.

A son was born to Zato. As his wife went into labor, she walked to the beach and found herself a secluded place behind a big rock. Another of Zato's wives brought her a large basket of cakes, fresh water and a quantity of unrefined brown sugar in five-pound cones. She must have given birth about four in the afternoon, for she was on her way back to the village by sunset, shouting with joy and holding her baby high in the air. Thus Zato knew it was a boy before she arrived. Had it been a daughter, she would have returned to the village silently, holding the baby in the crook of her arm. Lali acted this out for me; that's how I knew. The wife approached Zato, raising the child high; Zato held out his arms and shouted, but otherwise remained motionless. She came forward a few more steps, lifted the baby, cried out again, and stopped once more. Zato shouted again, and again held out his arms. They did this five or six times over the hundred feet that separated them. Zato never moved from the threshold of his hut. He stood in front of his main door, flanked by all the Indians in the village. The mother stopped again—she was not more than five or six steps away now—raised the baby and cried out one last time. Then Zato moved forward, took the baby under its arms and lifted it up. He turned to the east and cried out three times, each time raising the child. Then he sat down with the child lying on his right arm across his chest, its head under his armpit and hidden by his left arm. Without turning, he backed through the big door into his hut. Everyone followed, the mother last. Then we drank all the fermented juice in the house.

For the next week, morning and evening, the Indians watered the ground in front of Zato's hut and tamped it with the heels of their feet. When they were finished, there was a large circle of red clay. The next day they set up a big cowhide tent, and I guessed there was to be a celebration. Stones were put in place and, near them, a pile of both dry and green wood that grew with each passing day. Much of the wood was old driftwood, dry, white and highly polished. There were three huge tree trunks salvaged from the sea, God knows how long ago. Two wooden forks of the same height were put in place to serve as supports for an enormous spit. Four overturned turtles, two sheep and over thirty large, live lizards, their claws tied to prevent their escaping, waited to be slaughtered. There were at least two thousand turtle eggs as well, and twenty huge earthenware jars of the Indians' favorite drink.

One morning fifteen Indians arrived on horseback, each wearing a collar around his neck, a large straw hat, the loincloth that left the thighs, legs, feet and buttocks bare, and a sleeveless sheepskin jacket. Each had a huge dagger stuck in his belt, and two of them carried double-barreled hunting rifles. Their chief wore a magnificent jacket with black leather sleeves and carried a repeating rifle and a well-stocked ammunition belt. Their horses were superb: small, high-strung, dappled-gray, and on the rump of each a bundle of hay. When they were still at some distance, they announced their coming with a barrage of rifle shots. Then, riding at a fast gallop, they were soon upon us. Their chief had a curious resemblance to Zato and his brother, with a few years added on. He got off his thoroughbred, went up to Zato, and each touched the other on the shoulder. Then the visitor went into the house alone, Zato following behind, and emerged with the infant in his arms. He held it out for everyone to see and went through the same motions Zato had made: he lifted it to the east where the sun rises, then hid it under his armpit with his left arm and went back into the house. All the riders got off their horses, tied them up and filled their feed bags with hay. Their wives arrived at noon in a big wagon pulled by four horses and driven by Zorrillo. There were at least twenty young Indian women and seven or eight children, all of them boys.

Before Zorrillo's arrival, I was introduced to all the visitors, starting with their chief. Zato showed me how the little toe of his left foot was twisted over the next toe and that the same was true of his brother and the chief who had just arrived. Then he showed me how each of them had the same mole under one arm. I gathered that the new arrival must be his brother also. Zato's tattoos were much admired, especially the tiger head. The Indian women had brightly colored designs on their faces and bodies. On some Lali placed coral necklaces, on others, necklaces of shells. I noticed one particularly handsome woman who was taller than the rest and had the profile of an Italian, like a cameo. Her hair was purple-black, her large eyes a true jade green fringed with very long lashes. Her hair was cut Indian-style with bangs and a part in the middle. Her breasts were the texture of marble, starting close together and spreading apart in a classically graceful way.

Lali introduced me to her and led her to our house, together with Zoraima and a young Indian girl who carried goblets and what looked like paintbrushes. The visitors had come to paint the Indians of my village. I watched as the beautiful Indian worked on Lali and Zoraima. The brushes were bits of wood tipped with a small piece of wool which she dipped in the different colors. I took out my paintbrush and, starting at Lali's navel, I painted a plant whose two branches ended below her breasts. I added pink petals and painted her nipples yellow like a half-opened flower showing its pistils. The other three wanted me to do the same design on them, but first I had to ask Zorrillo's permission. He said I could do what I liked as long as they all consented. What I got myself into! For over two hours I painted all the breasts of all our young Indian visitors and our own besides. Zoraima demanded that I do hers exactly like Lali's. Meanwhile the men roasted the sheep on the spit and cooked two of the turtles over the coals, having first cut them up into small pieces. The turtle meat was beautiful and red like beef.

I sat next to Zato and the visiting chief under the tent. The men ate on one side and the women on the other, except for those who waited on us. The celebration ended late in the night with dancing to the music of a shrill wooden flute and two sheepskin drums. Many were drunk—women as well as men—but not disagreeably so. The sorcerer arrived on his donkey and everyone took turns looking at the pink scar where his ulcer had been. They were amazed that the familiar sore had healed. And only Zorrillo and I knew how it had happened.

Zorrillo explained that the chief of the visiting tribe was actually Zato's father. His name was Justo, meaning "The Just." He was the one who administered justice to all the tribes in Guajira. When there was trouble with the Iapus (another Indian race altogether), they met to discuss whether they would go to war or settle the matter amicably. If an Indian was killed by someone of another tribe, it was agreed that in order to avoid war, the killer should pay for the death. It sometimes cost him as much as two hundred head of cattle, for the tribes had vast herds in the villages up in the mountains. Unfortunately they weren't vaccinated against foot-and-mouth disease, and epidemics carried off large numbers of them. But, according to Zorrillo, even this had its good side, for without these outbreaks they would be overrun. They were not allowed to sell their cattle in either Colombia or Venezuela for fear of spreading the disease, but Zorrillo said there was extensive smuggling through the mountains all the same.

Through Zorrillo, Justo asked me to visit him in his village. It had over a hundred huts, and Lali, Zoraima and I would be given one of our own. They would provide everything we might need, so I was to bring only my tattooing materials in order to make a tiger for Justo too. He took off his black leather wristband and gave it to me. According to Zorrillo, this gesture carried great significance: it meant that he was powerless to refuse my slightest wish. Justo asked me if I wanted a horse, and I said that I did but that I was in no position to accept one, for we had hardly any grass. He said that whenever we needed grass, Lali and Zoraima had only to go a half day's journey on horseback to find it. He explained where it was and that it was both tall and good. So I accepted the horse and he said he'd send it soon.

I took advantage of this long visit with Zorrillo to tell him that I trusted him not to tell anyone about my plan for going to Venezuela or Colombia. He described the dangers of the frontier, saying that from what the smugglers reported, the Venezuelan side was even more dangerous than the Colombian. He offered to accompany me himself into Colombia, almost to Santa Marta, pointing out that I had already made the trip once and that the way was better marked. He agreed that I should buy another dictionary or, better yet, a phrase book with standard Spanish expressions. He also suggested that it would be a good idea if I learned to stammer, because people would get bored listening to me and would finish the sentence for me; this way my accent wouldn't be noticed. So it was decided that he would provide me with the books and the most detailed map he could find, and that he would handle the selling of my pearls when I needed Colombian money. Zorrillo said that all the Indians from the chief down would approve my decision since it was what I wanted. They would be sorry to see me go but would understand my desire to return to my own people. The main problem would be Zoraima and Lali. Either one of them, but particularly Lali, was quite capable of finishing me off with one shot of the rifle. Then Zorrillo told me something else: Zoraima was pregnant. I hadn't noticed a thing and I was stunned.

The celebration was finally over; everyone left, the tent came down and things returned to normal, or so it seemed. My horse arrived, a magnificent dappled-gray with a tail so long it almost touched the ground and a wonderful platinum-gray mane. Lali and Zoraima weren't very happy about it. The sorcerer summoned me to tell me that Lali and Zoraima had asked him if it was all right for them to feed the horse broken glass in order to kill him. He had told them not to, that I was protected by an Indian saint, and that if they did, the broken glass would end up in their own bellies. He thought the horse was now out of danger but that I should be on the alert. If they saw me getting ready to leave, they had only to kill me with a shotgun—Lali in particular. Could I get them to let me go by promising to return? Impossible. Never let on that I intended to leave.

The sorcerer and I covered a lot of ground because he had asked Zorrillo to come and act as interpreter. Zorrillo's conclusion was that the situation was so serious that I must take every precaution. I went home. Zorrillo had come and gone by a different path. Nobody in the village knew that the sorcerer had summoned us together.

I had now been here six months and I was anxious to be on my way. One day I came home to find Lali and Zoraima bent over the map. They were trying to figure out the strange markings, especially the four arrows indicating north, south, east and west. They had guessed that this piece of paper had something very important to do with our lives.

Zoraima's belly was beginning to bulge. This made Lali jealous and she demanded that I make love to her at all hours of the day and night, regardless of where we happened to be. Zoraima also made demands, but fortunately only at night.

I went to visit Zato's father, Justo. Lali and Zoraima came too. Luckily I had kept the drawing of the tiger and was able to use it for his tattoo. In six days it was done, for the first scabs fell early, thanks to a solution of water and quicklime he had made. Justo was so pleased that he looked at himself in the mirror several times a day. Zorrillo came by during my stay. I gave him permission to tell Justo about my plan because I wanted a different horse. The Guajiros' horses were all dappled-grays, a type that did not exist in Colombia and would therefore be conspicuous. Justo had three Colombian chestnuts. As soon as he learned of my project, he sent for the horses. I picked the one that seemed the best tempered, and he had it saddled, spurred and bridled with an iron bit. (Generally the Indians rode bareback with a bit made of bone.) Equipped in true Colombian style, I mounted the horse. Justo handed me the leather bridle; then in my presence he counted out thirty-nine gold pieces worth one hundred pesos each, which he gave to Zorrillo. Zorrillo was to keep them until I was ready to leave. He also wanted to give me his Manchester repeating rifle, but I refused it and Zorrillo said I wouldn't be allowed to enter Colombia armed anyway. So Justo gave me two little arrows the length of a finger, wrapped in wool, and a small leather case to keep them in. Zorrillo told me they were poisoned arrows and that the poison was very quick-acting and very rare. He himself had never seen or owned a poisoned arrow. He was to keep these too until I left.

How could I express my gratitude for Justo's magnificent generosity? He told me that through Zorrillo he had learned something of my life, and that what he didn't know must be rich stuff indeed, for I seemed to be a completed man. I was the first white man he had ever known; he had assumed they were all his enemies, but from now on he would love them and try to find another one like me. "You should think twice before going to a country where you have many enemies when here you have only friends."

He said that he and Zato would watch over Lali and Zoraima and that Zoraima's child would always hold a place of honor in the tribe—if it was a son, of course. "I don't want you to go. If you stay, I'll give you the beautiful Indian girl you met at the celebration. She is a wonderful girl and she loves you. You can stay here with me. I'll give you a big hut and all the cows and cattle you want."

I left this extraordinary man and returned to the village. Lali was silent during the entire trip. She sat behind me on the chestnut, her thighs chafed by the saddle. Zoraima rode behind with an Indian. Zorrillo had left for his village by another road. It got cold as night fell so I handed Lali the sheepskin jacket Justo had given me; she let me put it around her without a word. She accepted the jacket but no more. The horse broke into a fast trot, but she wouldn't hold onto me. Once back in the village, I went to pay my respects to Zato. Lali took the horse home, tied him to the hut and placed a bundle of hay in front of him without removing his saddle or bit.

When they are sad, the Indians—and particularly their women—have closed faces. Not a muscle moves; their eyes may be swimming with tragedy, but they never cry. They may sometimes let out a moan, but that is all.

That night, in my sleep, I must have moved and jabbed Zoraima in the belly, for she cried out with pain. I didn't want this to happen again so I got up and lay down in another hammock. It hung very low, and as I got into it, I had the impression someone had been tampering with it. I pretended to be asleep. Lali sat down on a tree stump and watched me without moving. A moment later

I smelled Zoraima's presence (she was accustomed to scenting herself by crushing orange blossoms and rubbing them on her skin;
she bought these in little bags from an Indian woman who passed
through the village from time to time). When I woke up, both girls
were still there, motionless. The sun was up; it was nearly eight
o'clock. I led them to the beach and stretched out on the sand. Lali
remained seated; so did Zoraima. I stroked Lali's breasts and her
belly; she was as still as marble. I pulled her down next to me and
tried to kiss her; her lips were closed tight. Later the fisherman
came for Lali. One look at her face was enough: he turned around
and left. I was deeply troubled and didn't know what to do except
caress them and kiss them to show that I loved them. They
remained silent. It upset me that they should feel such grief at the
thought of living without me. Then Lali almost raped me, giving
herself with a kind of despair. Why? What was behind it? It could
only be one thing; she wanted me to make her pregnant too.

That morning, for the first time, I caught a hint of jealousy
between Lali and Zoraima. We were lying on the beach in a protected hollow. I was caressing Zoraima's breasts and belly and she
was biting my ears. Lali arrived, took her sister by the arm, passed
her hand over her sister's swollen belly, then over her own slender
flat one. Zoraima got up as if to say, "You're right," and gave her
place to her sister.

Each day my women prepared my food but ate nothing themselves. They had not eaten for three days. I took the horse and
almost committed a serious error—my first in more than five
months. I left for the sorcerer's without first asking his permission.
I realized it halfway there so, instead of going straight to him, I
passed back and forth in front of his tent at a distance of some two
hundred yards. He finally saw me and made a sign for me to come
in. I explained as best I could that Lali and Zoraima had stopped
eating. He gave me a kind of nut which I was to put in our drink-

ing water. I went home and placed it in the big earthen jar. They drank from it several times but still didn't eat. Lali also stopped fishing. Then, after four days of fasting, she stupidly swam two hundred yards out from shore and returned with thirty oysters for me to eat. Their silent grief was so disturbing that I had almost stopped eating too. This went on for six days. Then Lali took to her bed with a fever. During the six days she had sucked a few lemons and that was all. Zoraima ate once a day at noon. I didn't know what to do. I sat down next to Lali. She was stretched out on a hammock I had folded in two to make a kind of mattress and was looking fixedly at the roof. I looked at her, I looked at Zoraima with her bulging belly, and without quite knowing why, I started to weep. For me? For them? Who knows? I wept, and great tears ran down my cheeks. Zoraima saw them and began to moan, then Lali turned and saw them too. With one motion she got up and sat between my legs, all the while moaning gently. She kissed me and caressed me. Zoraima put an arm around my shoulder, and Lali started to talk; she moaned and she talked and Zoraima answered back. She seemed to be reproaching Lali for something. Lali took a piece of brown sugar as big as her fist, dissolved it in water and swallowed it in two gulps. Then she went out with Zoraima and I could hear them pulling on the horse. I went out and found him saddled, the bit between his teeth, the bridle over the pummel of the saddle. Zoraima gave me the sheepskin jacket, and Lali placed a folded hammock on the saddle. Zoraima was the first up and sat far in front, almost on the horse's neck; I sat in the middle and Lali in back. I was so confused that I set off without telling anyone good-by, without even speaking to the chief.

Lali pulled back on the reins, perhaps thinking we were going to the sorcerer's. But no, she pulled the reins again and said "Zor-rillo." So we were going to Zorrillo's. Hugging my waist as we rode along, she kissed me several times on the back of the neck. I held the reins in my left hand and caressed Zoraima with my right. We arrived at Zorrillo's village just as he was returning from Colombia with three donkeys and a heavily laden horse. We went into his house. Lali spoke first, then Zoraima.

According to Zorrillo, this was their story. Up to the moment I had cried, Lali believed that I was just a white man who didn't really care about her. She knew that someday I would leave, but it was deceitful of me not to tell her. She said she was deeply disappointed because she had thought she was capable of making a man happy, that a happy man didn't leave home, and that there would be no reason to go on living after such a calamity. Zoraima said more or less the same thing, but in addition, she was afraid her son would turn out like his father: a silent man and a false one, who made such difficult demands on his women that for all that they were ready to give their lives for him, they were unable to understand him. Why was I running away from her as if she were the dog who had bitten me the day I arrived?

I replied, "Lali, what would you do if your father were sick?"

"I would walk on thorns to take care of him."

"What would you do if you had been hunted like a dog and then the day came when you had a chance to get even?"

"I'd look for my enemy everywhere, and when I found him I'd bury him so deep he wouldn't even be able to turn around in his hole."

"Once you had accomplished this, what would you do if you had two wonderful women waiting for you?"

"I'd return on a horse."

"That's what I will do."

"What if I'm old and ugly when you return?"

"I'll return long before you're old and ugly."

"Yes, water ran from your eyes, and you can't do that on purpose. You may go when you wish, but you must leave in full daylight, in front of everybody and not like a thief. You must go as you came, at the same time in the afternoon, covered with clothes. You must say who is to watch over us night and day. Zato is our chief, but we must have another man to watch over us. You must tell them that the house will stay your house and that no man except your son—if it is a boy in Zoraima's belly—is ever to enter it. Zorrillo must come the day you leave so that he can tell us all the things you'll be saying."

We spent the night with Zorrillo. It was a deliciously warm and tender time. The sounds and murmurs that came from these daughters of nature were so full of love that I was very moved. We went home on the horse, but slowly, for the sake of Zoraima's belly. I was to leave eight days after the new moon so that Lali would know if she were pregnant. During the last moon she had not seen blood. She wanted to be sure; if there were still no blood during this moon, then she would know she had conceived. Zorrillo was to take my clothes. I would dress in his house after making my farewell speech "Guajira-style," meaning naked. On the eve of my departure the three of us would go to the sorcerer's to learn whether I was to leave my door open or closed. Our slow return—slow for Zoraima's belly—was not at all sad. It was better for them to know I was leaving than to look abandoned, objects of ridicule in the eyes of the village. After Zoraima had given birth, she would go out with a fisherman and find lots of pearls for me. Lali would fish longer hours to keep herself busy. I was sorry that I'd learned no more than a dozen words in Guajiro. I could have told them so much, things that can't be told through an interpreter.

We reached home. The first thing I had to do was see Zato and try to explain how sorry I was that I had gone without speaking to him first. Zato was as noble as his father. Before I opened my mouth to speak, he placed his hand on my neck and said "*Uilu*

[Quiet]." The new moon was due in twelve days. With the eight days I had to wait after that, it would be twenty days before I could set off.

As I was looking at the map once again and studying ways to bypass the various villages, my mind went back to what Justo had said. Where indeed would I be happier than here? Here I was loved by everybody. Wasn't I asking for trouble by returning to civilization? The future would tell.

The next three weeks were beautiful. We became certain that Lali was pregnant and that there would be two and maybe even three children awaiting my return. Why three? She told me that her mother had twice had twins. We went to the sorcerer's. No, we were not to close the door; we were only to place a branch across the opening. The hammock the three of us had slept in was to be stretched across the ceiling of the hut. Lali and Zoraima were to sleep together since they were now as one. Then he had us sit near the fire; he threw in some green leaves and left us in its smoke for ten minutes. We returned to our house to wait for Zorrillo. He arrived that same evening. We spent the whole night talking to the Indians around the fire in front of my hut. With Zorrillo as interpreter, I said something friendly to each of them, and each replied. As the sun rose, I retired with Lali and Zoraima. We spent the day making love. Zoraima straddled me the better to feel me in her; Lali coiled herself around me and, deep inside her, I could feel her beating like a heart.

It was the afternoon of my departure. I spoke, and Zorrillo translated:

"Zato, great chief of this tribe that welcomed me so warmly and gave me so much, I ask your permission to let me leave you for many days and nights."

"Why do you wish to leave your friends?"

"Because I must punish the people who hunted me down like an animal. I have found refuge in your village, I have eaten well, I have had noble friends, and wives who filled me with happiness. But I must not allow this to change me into an animal who, once he's found a warm refuge, stays in it the rest of his life for fear of being hurt. I am going to face my enemies and return to my father who needs me. I leave my soul here, in my wives Lali and Zoraima and in the fruits of our union. My hut belongs to them and the children soon to be born. I hope that if anyone forgets this, you—Zato—will remind him. And in addition to your personal vigilance, I ask that the man called Usli watch over my family day and night. I have loved you all and always will. I'll do everything I can to return soon. Should I die, my thoughts will fly to you, Lali and Zoraima and my children, and to you, the Indians of Guajira, who were my family."

I went back into my hut, followed by Lali and Zoraima, and put on my khaki shirt and pants, my socks and boots.

For a long time I sat gazing at the idyllic village where I had spent over six months. This Guajira tribe, feared as much by the other tribes as by the whites, had been a haven where I could catch my breath, an incomparable refuge from the wickedness of men. There I had found love, peace, tranquillity and nobility of spirit. Farewell, Guajiros! Be grateful that your vast lands are free of civilization. Your way of life has taught me something of great importance to my future: it is better to be a savage Indian than a judge with all his honors.

Good-by, Lali and Zoraima, incomparable wives, so close to nature, so spontaneous. I will surely come back. When? How? I don't know, but I promise myself I will return.

As the afternoon came to an end, Zorrillo got on his horse and we started for Colombia. I had on a straw hat and walked, holding my horse by the reins. Each of the Indians hid his face with his left arm and held out his right. This was to show me that they didn't want me to go, that it made them sad. The right arm was extended to try to keep me with them. Lali and Zoraima walked with me for about a hundred yards. I thought they were going to kiss me when suddenly they turned, sobbing, and ran toward the hut without looking back.

FIFTH NOTEBOOK

RETURN TO CIVILIZATION

THE PRISON IN SANTA MARTA

GETTING OUT OF GUAJIRA WAS easy, and we crossed the border at La Vela without incident. On horseback, we were able to do in two days what had taken me so long with Antonio. But it wasn't only the border patrols that were dangerous; there was also an area of about sixty miles between the border and Rio Hacha, the village I had escaped from.

With Zorrillo standing by, I had my first conversation with a Colombian in an inn. I didn't do too badly, and as Zorrillo had said, stammering helped a lot to hide my accent.

We set off again toward Santa Marta. Zorrillo was to leave me halfway and return home in the morning.

Now Zorrillo was gone. We decided that he should take my horse. Having a horse meant that you owned a house and belonged to a specific village, and as a result you might have to answer what for me would be embarrassing questions, such as:

"Do you know so and so?" "What is the mayor's name?" "What is Mrs. X up to?" "Who is running the *fonda* now?"

No, better for me to continue on foot, travel by truck or bus, and after Santa Marta, by train. I would be a stranger everywhere, no one knowing where I was from or what I did for a living.

Zorrillo gave me change for three of the gold pieces; I had a thousand pesos. A good workman earned from eight to ten pesos a day, so I had enough to keep me for a long time. I was picked up by a truck going close to Santa Marta, a good-sized port about eighty miles beyond where Zorrillo had left me. The truck was to pick up some goats.

Every five miles or so we came to a tavern, and every time we came to a tavern the driver got out and invited me to come with him. He did the inviting, I did the paying. And each time he drank five or six glasses of the local firewater while I pretended to drink one. By the time we had gone about thirty-five miles, he was drunk. He was so drunk that he took a wrong turn onto a muddy road and the truck bogged down. This didn't faze the Colombian: he lay down in the back and told me to sleep in the cab. I didn't know what else to do. We were still a good thirty miles from Santa Marta. If we met anyone, I was safer with him, and for all our many stops, it was faster than going on foot.

It was already morning, but I decided to get some sleep. The sun had risen, it was nearly seven o'clock. And there, suddenly, was a wagon drawn by two horses. It couldn't get past the truck. They thought I was the truck driver since I was in the cab, so I pretended to have just waked up, acting confused and stammering.

Then the real driver woke up and discussed the situation with the teamster. After several tries they still couldn't free the truck. The mud was up to the axle. In the wagon were two nuns dressed in black with coifs, and three little girls. After much talk, the two men agreed that we should clear a section of brush so that the wagon could get by, one wheel on the road, the other in the cleared brush.

They took out their machetes and cut the brush, and I laid it on the road to minimize the drop between it and the shoulder and to keep the wagon from sinking into the mud. After two hours' work the passage was cleared. The sisters thanked me and asked me where I was going.

"Santa Marta," I said.

"But you're on the wrong road. You must turn back and come with us. We will take you within five miles of Santa Marta."

I couldn't refuse; it would have seemed odd. On the other hand, I wanted to say that I would stay and help the truck driver, but the difficulty of saying all that compelled me to say instead, *"Gracias, gracias."*

So there I was, in the back of the wagon with the three little girls. The two kind sisters sat up front with the driver.

We made quick work of the three or four miles we had mistakenly taken with the truck; and once we reached the right road, we made really good time. As it approached noon we stopped at an inn to eat. The three little girls sat with the driver at one table and I sat with the sisters at another. The sisters were young, between twenty-five and thirty. One was Spanish, the other Irish, and their skin was very pale.

The Irish sister asked me gently, "I gather you're not from around here?"

"Oh, yes, I'm from Barranquilla."

"No, you can't be a Colombian. Your hair is too light and your skin is only dark from the sun. Where have you come from?"

"Rio Hacha."

"What did you do there?"

"Electrician."

"Ah! I have a friend at the electric company. His name is Perez; he's a Spaniard."

When the meal was finished, they got up to wash their hands. The Irish sister came back alone. She looked at me, then said in French, "I won't give you away, but my friend says that she saw your picture in the newspaper. You're the Frenchman who escaped from the prison in Rio Hacha, aren't you?"

To deny it would have made matters worse.

"Yes, Sister. But please don't turn me in. I'm not the bad guy they made me out to be. I respect God and love Him."

The Spanish sister arrived and the other one said, "Yes," and added something very fast that I didn't catch. For a while they seemed to be thinking things over, and then they got up and went back to the bathroom. During their five minutes' absence I thought fast. Should I go before they returned, or should I stay? If they had decided to give me away, it wouldn't much matter whether I left or not—they'd soon find me. This region had no real jungle or bush, and the approaches to the towns were all too visible. No, I would put myself in destiny's hands instead. Up to now it hadn't been unkind.

They returned, smiling. The Irish nun asked me my name.

"Enrique."

"All right, Enrique. You come with us to the convent. While we're in the wagon, you've nothing to worry about at all. Just don't talk; everyone will think you're a workman at the convent."

The sisters paid for our food. I bought a carton of cigarettes and a tinderbox. Then we left. The sisters didn't speak to me during the entire trip, for which I was very grateful. This way the driver wouldn't know how badly I spoke the language. Toward the end of the afternoon we stopped at a large inn. In front of it was a bus on which I read: "Rio Hacha—Santa Marta." Wanting to board it, I approached the Irish sister and told her my intention.

"That's a dangerous thing to do," she said. "Before it reaches Santa Marta, it stops at at least two police stations where they ask all the passengers for their identity cards. They won't do that to the wagon."

I thanked her warmly, and the anxiety I had felt since they discovered who I was disappeared completely. On the contrary, it was unbelievable luck to have run into the sisters. We arrived at our first police station as night fell. A bus going from Santa Marta to Rio Hacha was being inspected by the police. I lay in the wagon on my back, straw hat over my face, as if I were asleep. One of the little girls (she was about eight) had put her head on my shoulder and really was asleep. As the wagon passed through, the driver stopped just between the bus and the station.

"How are things with you?" asked the Spanish sister.

"Very well, Sister."

"I'm glad. Let's go, children."

At ten we came to a very brightly lit station. Two lines of vehicles of every description were drawn up here, one on the right, ours on the left. The police were opening all the car trunks. One woman had gotten out of her car and was rummaging through her bag. Then she was taken into the station. She probably had no identity card. I was sure I was lost. In front of us was a very small bus stuffed with passengers. On its roof were suitcases and large parcels, and at the rear a kind of net holding more parcels. Four policemen were forcing the passengers out. It had only one door, in front, from which the people stepped down, the women with babies in their arms. Then, one by one, they climbed back in.

Each had an identity card with his photograph on it.

Zorrillo had never told me about this. If I'd known, I might have been able to get myself a fake one. If ever I got through this checkpoint, I'd pay anything to get hold of one before going on to Barranquilla.

My God, but they were taking their time with that bus! The Irish nun turned to me and said, "Don't worry, Enrique." I was furious with her for speaking to me; the driver must surely have heard.

It was our turn to come under the blinding light. I decided to sit up. If I lay down, I would seem to be hiding. I leaned against the tailgate of the wagon, facing the sisters' backs. They would see only my profile and my hat was down over my face, but not too much so.

"How are things with you?" the Spanish sister said again.

"Very well, Sister. Why are you traveling so late?"

"It's an emergency, so please don't keep us waiting. We are in a great hurry."

"Go with God, Sisters."

"Thank you, my children. May God protect you."

"Amen," said the policemen.

And so we went peacefully through, without anyone asking us anything. But the strain of those minutes must have been too much for the sisters' stomachs, for a hundred yards beyond the control point they had the wagon stop and disappeared into the brush. This touched me so much that when the Irish sister climbed back into the wagon, I said, "I thank you, Sister."

She answered, "You're quite welcome. But we were so frightened that I'm afraid it affected our stomachs."

We arrived at the convent about midnight. A high wall, a large door. The driver unhitched the horses, and the wagon with the three girls was pulled inside. On the steps leading to the courtyard, a heated discussion broke out between my sisters and the nun who was keeping the gate. The Irish nun told me that she didn't want to wake the Mother Superior to ask her for permission to let me spend the night. And that's where I made my fatal mistake. I should have taken advantage of the situation and left for Santa

Marta, which I knew was only five miles away. That mistake cost me seven years in the *bagne*.

Finally they did wake the Mother Superior, and I was given a room on the third floor. I could see the lights of the town from the window. I could see the lighthouse and a large boat sailing out of the harbor.

I went to sleep and woke to a knocking on my door. I had had a terrible dream. Lali had ripped her belly open in front of me and our child had come out in pieces.

I quickly shaved and washed. I went downstairs, and there at the foot of the stairs was the Irish sister, a small smile on her lips.

"Good morning, Henri. Did you sleep well?"

"Yes, Sister."

"Please come to our Mother's office. She wants to see you."

We went in. The woman sitting behind the desk was about fifty; she had a very severe expression and unfriendly black eyes.

"Do you speak Spanish?"

"Very little."

"All right, the sister will serve as interpreter. You are French, I've been told."

"Yes, Mother."

"You escaped from the prison in Rio Hacha?"

"Yes, Mother."

"When?"

"About seven months ago."

"What have you been doing since then?"

"I've been living with the Indians."

"What? You, with the Guajiros? That's impossible. Those savages have never allowed anyone in their territory. Not even a missionary. I refuse to believe you. Where were you really? Tell me the truth."

"Mother, I was with the Indians and I can prove it to you."

"How?"

"With their pearls." I undid the bag which I'd pinned to the back of my jacket and handed it to her.

She opened it and took out a handful of pearls. "How many are there?"

"Oh, I don't know. Maybe five or six hundred."

"This is no proof. You could have stolen them somewhere else."

"Mother, to set your conscience at rest, I will stay here as long as it takes you to find out if any pearls have been stolen anywhere. I have money. I can pay for my room and board. I promise not to stir from my room without your permission."

She looked at me intently. I knew she must be thinking, what if he escapes? He escaped from prison; it would be much easier from here.

"I'll leave my bag of pearls with you. They are my entire fortune, but I know they're in good hands."

"All right, it's agreed. But you don't need to stay shut up in your room. You can go into the garden in the morning and afternoon while my girls are in chapel. You'll eat in the kitchen with the help."

The interview left me only partly reassured. I was about to go back up to my room when the Irish sister led me into the kitchen. Waiting for me was a large bowl of coffee, fresh black bread and butter. The sister watched me eat without speaking or sitting down. She simply stood there, looking troubled. I said, "Thank you for everything you've done, Sister."

"I wish I could have helped more, but I've done all I can, Henri." And with that she left the kitchen.

Sitting by the window, I looked at the city, the harbor, the sea. The countryside was well cultivated. But I couldn't rid myself of the feeling that I was in danger, so much so that I decided to run away the following night. To hell with the pearls. She could use them for the convent, or for herself—the old hag. I didn't trust her at all. Besides, how come she didn't speak French, she a Catalan and the Mother Superior of a convent and therefore supposedly well educated? That was most unusual. I would leave that very night. During the afternoon I'd go into the courtyard and study the best place to climb over the wall.

About one there was a knock on my door.

"Won't you come down and have something to eat, Henri?"

"Yes, thank you. I'm coming."

I sat down at the kitchen table and was just about to serve myself some meat and boiled potatoes when the door opened and there in front of me stood four policemen in white uniforms, armed with rifles, and an officer with a revolver in his hand.

"Don't move, or I'll shoot," the chief said. They put me in handcuffs. The Irish sister let out a scream and fainted. Two kitchen helpers picked her up.

"Let's go," said the chief. They took me up to my room. There they searched my belongings and right away found the thirty-six gold pieces I still had left, but they passed over the case containing the two arrows. They must have thought they were pencils. The officer put the gold pieces in his pocket with ill-concealed satisfaction, and we left. A vehicle—if it could be called that—was waiting in the courtyard.

The five policemen and I squeezed into the piece of junk and we set off at full speed. Our driver was in a police uniform, but he was as black as coal. I was crushed; I didn't try to resist, only to keep my dignity. There was no question of asking for pity or forgiveness. Just be a man and don't lose hope, I said to myself. I succeeded so well that, as I stepped out of the car, the first words of the police officer who met us were: "This Frenchman looks pleased with himself. He doesn't seem to care whether he was caught or not." I went into his office, took off my hat and sat down without being asked, my pack between my feet.

"Can you speak Spanish?"

"No."

"Call the cobbler."

A few moments later in came a small man in a blue smock, a shoemaker's hammer in his hand.

"You're the Frenchman who escaped from Rio Hacha a year ago?"

"No."

"You're lying."

"I'm not lying. I'm not the Frenchman who escaped from Rio Hacha a year ago."

"Take off his handcuffs. Remove your jacket and shirt." He took up a paper and examined it. All my tattoos were noted on it.

"You're missing the thumb of your left hand. Yes? Then it's you."

"No, it isn't me, because I didn't escape a year ago. I escaped seven months ago."

"Same thing."

"For you, yes. Not for me."

"I see. You're a real killer, aren't you? Frenchmen or Colombians, all you killers are alike—wild men. I'm only the assistant warden of this prison. I have no idea what they're going to do with you. But for the moment, I'll put you in with your old pals."

"What pals?"

"The Frenchmen you brought to Colombia."

I was taken to a cell which looked out over the courtyard. There I found my five friends. We hugged each other. "We thought you were safe forever, you old bastard," Clousiot said, and Maturette wept like the child he was. The other three were also excited. To see them again revived my morale.

"Tell us what happened," they said.

"Later. What about you?"

"We've been here three months."

"How are you treated?"

"So-so. We're waiting to be transferred to Barranquilla, where they say we'll be turned over to the French authorities."

"What a bunch of bastards. What about making a break?"

"You've just gotten here and you're already thinking about a break!"

"Why not? You think I give up all that easily? How closely watched are you?"

"During the day, not much, but at night there's a special detail."

"How many in the detail?"

"Three."

"How's your leg?"

"O.K. I don't even limp any more."

"Are you always locked up in the cell?"

"No, we get to walk in the yard two hours in the morning, three hours in the afternoon."

"What are the others like, the Colombian prisoners?"

"There are some really tough ones here. They say the thieves are just as bad as the murderers."

In the afternoon I was in the yard having a private talk with Clousiot when I was called away. I followed the policeman into the same office I'd been in that morning. The head warden was there with the man who had questioned me earlier. The seat of honor was occupied by a very dark-skinned man. His color was more like a Negro's than an Indian's. He had the short frizzy hair of a Negro too. He was almost fifty, with mean black eyes, thick lips and a small mustache. His shirt was open at the neck, and on the left side he wore a green and white decoration of some sort. The cobbler was there too.

"Frenchie, you escaped seven months ago. What have you been doing since then?"

"I've been living with the Guajiros."

"Don't give me that crap or you'll get the shit kicked out of you."

"It's the truth."

"Nobody's ever lived with the Indians. Only this year they killed more than twenty-five of our guards."

"No, the guards were killed by smugglers."

"How do you know?"

"I lived with them for almost seven months. They never left their territory."

"O.K. Maybe you're right. Where did you steal those thirty-six gold pieces?"

"They're mine. Justo gave them to me—he's chief of a mountain tribe."

"How could an Indian have such a fortune and then give it to you?"

"O.K., chief. Have any gold pieces been stolen in the last seven months?'

"No, you're right. We've had nothing about it in our reports. But that won't keep us from looking into it."

"Please do. You'll be doing me a favor."

"Frenchie, you committed a serious offense when you escaped from the prison in Rio Hacha, and a still more serious one when you helped Antonio escape. He was to be shot for the murder of several coastal guards. And we know that you're wanted by the French authorities and that you have a life sentence. You're a killer—and I'm not about to risk your escaping from here by putting you in with the other Frenchmen. You're going to be put in a dungeon until you leave for Barranquilla. You'll get your gold pieces back if we find you didn't steal them."

I was led to some stairs that went underground. We went down about twenty-five steps and arrived in a dimly lit passage with cages opening off to the right and the left. They opened one of them and I was pushed inside. When they had closed the door, I got the full benefit of the stink that rose from the slimy floor. I heard calls from all sides. Inside each barred hole were one, two, or three prisoners.

"Frenchie? Frenchie? What did you do? Why are you here? Do you know these dungeons are deathtraps?" they called in Spanish.

"Shut up! Let him talk!" a voice shouted.

"I'm here because I escaped from the prison at Rio Hacha." They seemed to understand my Spanish gibberish well enough.

"Listen, Frenchie, want a few facts? At the back of your cell there's a plank. That's to sleep on. To the right there's a can with water in it. Don't drink it too fast: you get a little each morning and you can't ask for more. To the left there's a pail to do your business in. Cover it with your jacket. You don't need your jacket here; it's too hot already. Cover the pail so it doesn't smell so bad. We all do it."

I drew closer to the bars to see their faces. I could make out only the two men opposite—they were glued to the bars, their legs planted outside. One was a Spanish-Indian type like the first policeman who arrested me in Rio Hacha; the other was a young and handsome light-skinned black. The black warned me that each time the tide came up, the water rose in the cells. I mustn't be scared because it never rose higher than your stomach. And I shouldn't try to catch the rats that crawled over me but just give them a whack on the head. If you tried to catch them, they bit you.

"How long have you been in this hole?" I asked him.

"Two months."

"What about the others?"

"Nobody more than three months. If you haven't been taken out before three months, it means you're here to die."

"Who's been here the longest?"

"One man eight months, but he's about had it. He hasn't been able to stand up for a month. The next time we get a real high tide, he'll drown."

"Are you a bunch of savages in this country?"

"I never said we were civilized. Yours isn't all that civilized either: they gave you a life sentence. Here in Colombia it's twenty years or death. Never life."

"Look, it's the same all over."

"Did you knock off a lot of people?"

"No, only one."

"I don't get it. They can't give you a long sentence like that for just one man."

"They did, though."

"So your country's as primitive as mine."

"O.K. So let's not argue about our countries. You're right. The police are shits all over. What did you do?"

"I killed a man, his son and his wife."

"Why?"

"He fed my kid brother to a sow."

"What! I don't believe it."

"My little brother used to throw stones at their kid and he hurt him in the head a couple of times."

"That's still no reason."

"That's what I said when I found out."

"How did you find out?"

"My little brother had been gone for three days. I kept looking for him, and then I found his sandal in the manure pile. It was the manure from the barn where the sow was. I dug around and found a white sock covered with blood. Then I understood. The wife confessed before I killed her. I made them say their prayers and then I shot them. The first shot shattered the father's legs."

"You were right to kill them. What will they give you for it?"

"Twenty years at the most."

"Why are you here in the dungeon?"

"I hit a policeman who was a member of their family. He was here in the prison. But he isn't here any more. They sent him away, so I'm O.K."

The door to the passage opened. A guard came in with two prisoners carrying a barrel hanging from two wooden bars. Behind them you could just make out two more guards carrying guns. Cell after cell, they brought out the pails that served as our toilets and emptied them into the barrel. Crap and urine reeked to the point of suffocation. Nobody spoke. When they got to me, the prisoner took my pail and dropped a small parcel on the floor. After they had moved on, I opened the package and found two packs of cigarettes, a tinderbox and a note written in French. First, I lit two cigarettes and threw them over to the two men across from me. Then I called to my neighbor and asked him to pass the cigarettes along to the other prisoners. After the distribution I lit my own and tried to read the paper by the light in the passage. It couldn't be done, so I made a tight roll of the paper the package was wrapped in and, after several tries, managed to set it on fire. I read fast:

"Chin up, Papillon. You can count on us. Tomorrow we're sending you paper and pencil so that you can write to us. We're with you to the death."

It warmed my heart. I wasn't alone after all; I could count on my friends.

Nobody talked. Everybody was smoking. The distribution of

the cigarettes showed there were nineteen of us in this deathtrap. So here I was, back on the road of the condemned for sure! Those little sisters of the Lord were really sisters of the devil. I was sure it wasn't the Irish or the Spanish sister who had turned me in. But what a damn fool I'd been to trust them all the same! No, it wasn't them. The man driving the wagon? We'd talked French two or three times. Had he heard us? Oh God, what's the difference! You're in it, you're really in it this time, Papillon. Sisters, the wagon driver, or the Mother Superior, it doesn't matter a damn.

So here I was, in a filthy hole that flooded twice a day. The heat was so stifling I took off my shirt, then my pants, then my shoes, and hung them all from the bars.

To think I'd gone fifteen hundred miles to fetch up here! Some great success that was. God had been good to me, but it looked as if He was abandoning me now. Maybe He was angry because He'd already done the best He could for me: He'd given me freedom, real freedom, and a community that adopted me completely. He'd given me not one but two wonderful wives. The sun, and the sea. A hut in which I was lord and master. And a life with nature, an existence that may have been primitive, but so calm, so peaceful. He'd given me the unique gift of freedom without police, judges, or mean and envious men. And I hadn't appreciated it. The blue of the sea—when it wasn't green or almost black—those dawns and sunsets that brought such sweet serenity, living without money yet lacking nothing essential—all that I had spurned. And for what? A society that had no intention of helping me. Men who couldn't be bothered to find out if I was worth salvaging. A world that had rejected me and cast me beyond the reach of hope, into holes like this, where they had only one thing on their minds: to kill me off, no matter what.

When the news of my capture got out, they'd have a good

laugh over it—those twelve cheeseheads on the jury, that rat Polein, the cops and the prosecutor. For there was bound to be some journalist who'd send the news to France.

And what about my own people? When the police announced my escape, they must have been so happy to learn that their boy had given his executioners the slip! And when they learned I'd been caught once more, they'd suffer all over again.

I'd been wrong to renounce my tribe. Yes, I have every right to say "my tribe," for they had truly adopted me. I'd been wrong and I deserved my fate. And yet . . . I hadn't done a *cavale* in order to increase the Indian population of South America! Dear God, you've got to realize that I must live among civilized people and show them I'm capable of taking part in their lives without being a threat to them. That's my real goal—with or without Your help.

I must prove that I can be, that I am and will be, a normal person. Perhaps no better, but certainly no worse than the rest.

I smoked. The water began to rise. It was about up to my ankles. I called out, "Heh, black man! How long does the water stay in the cell?"

"It depends on the tide. One hour. Two at the most."

I heard several prisoners cry out, "It's coming!"

Slowly the water rose. The half-breed and the black had climbed up the bars, their legs sticking out into the passage. I heard something in the water: a sewer rat as big as a cat was splashing around. It was trying to climb up the grill. I grabbed one of my shoes and clouted it over the head as it came near me. It squealed and moved on down the passage.

The black said, "Frenchie, if you think you can kill them all, you're out of your mind. Climb up the grill, grab the bars and wait it out."

I followed his advice, but the bars cut into my thighs, making it impossible for me to stay in that position for long. I took my jacket from the toilet pail, tied it to the bars and perched there. It made a kind of seat, and I could now stay in one position.

The invasion of the water, filled with rats, centipedes and tiny crabs, was the most disgusting thing I've ever experienced. When the water finally retreated after about an hour, the floor was covered with slime half an inch thick. I put on my shoes to protect my feet from the filth. The black threw me a piece of wood six inches long and told me to push the mud out into the passage, starting with the plank I slept on. This took me a half hour and kept me from thinking about anything else. It helped. Until the next tide I'd be free of water. That meant eleven hours. Six hours for the tide to go out and five to come back. A funny thought crossed my mind:

Papillon, you're destined to live with tides. Whether you like it or not, the moon has been a big thing in your life. It was thanks to the tides that you were able to sail out of the Maroni when you escaped from the *bagne*. You had to play the tides when you left Trinidad and Curaçao. You were arrested in Rio Hacha because the tide wasn't strong enough to take you out, and here you are permanently at its mercy.

Some will say, "He deserved it. If he had stayed in the *bagne*, this never would have happened to him." But let me tell you something: I hadn't lost hope, not at all. And I'll tell you something else. I was better off in the dungeon of this old Colombian fortress built by the Spanish Inquisition than on the Iles du Salut, where I should have been right then. In the dungeon there was still a lot I could do toward a *cavale*; even in this stinking hole I was fifteen hundred miles from the *bagne*. They would have to think up something really good to get me back there! I thought of my Indians and how it would never have occurred to them to invent this sort of

punishment, much less to punish a man who had never committed the slightest offense against them.

I smoked a couple of cigarettes lying on the plank at the rear of
my cell so that the others couldn't see me. I threw the piece of
wood back to the black and with it a lighted cigarette. Like me, he
hid while he smoked. Such details may not seem important, but to
me they meant a lot. It proved that although we might be outcasts,
we still had some manners and decency.

Who had told the police I was at the convent? If I ever found
out, that person would pay for it! Then I said to myself, "Don't be
a damn fool, Papillon! You have work to do in France—your
revenge. You didn't come to this filthy country to get into more
trouble. Life itself will punish whoever it was, and if you ever
come back, it won't be for revenge but to bring happiness to Lali
and Zoraima and perhaps the children they will have borne you. If
you ever come back to this hole, it will be for them and the Guajiros who did you the honor of adopting you. You may still be on
the road of the condemned, but even in this dungeon under water
you are—whether they like it or not—*en cavale*—on the road to
freedom. And that's God's truth."

I got my paper and pencil and two packs of cigarettes. I had
been here three days or, I should say, three nights, for it was always
night here. As I was lighting a Piel Roja, I couldn't help admiring
the extraordinary devotion of the prisoners to each other. The
Colombian who had delivered the parcels to me was running a big
risk: if he were caught, it would undoubtedly mean a stay in these
same dungeons. Since he was probably well aware of that, the way
he helped me through my ordeal was an act of unusual courage
and nobility. By the light of the burning paper I read: "Papillon,
we've heard you're holding up well. Bravo! Give us some news.
Nothing new here. A sister who spoke French came by to see you.

They wouldn't let her talk with us, but a Colombian reported that he just had time to tell her that the Frenchman was in the death cell. She said, 'I'll be back.' That's all. We send love. Your friends."

Answering wasn't easy, but I did manage to write, "Thanks for everything. I'm holding up. Write the French consul. You never know. Have the same man do all the errands so that if he's caught, only one man is punished. Don't anyone touch the points of the arrows. *Vive la cavale!*"

THE *CAVALE* AT SANTA MARTA

Thanks to the Belgian consul, a man named Klausen, I was out of that foul hole twenty-eight days later. The black, whose name was Palacios, had been let out three weeks after my arrival and had the brilliant idea of asking his mother to tell Klausen that there was a Belgian in the dungeon. He had thought of this one Sunday when the consul was visiting a Belgian prisoner.

So one day I was taken to the chief warden's office. He said to me, "You're a Frenchman. Why are you appealing to the Belgian consul?"

In the office with him was a man of about fifty dressed in white with a round rosy face and blond, almost white hair. He was sitting in an armchair, a leather briefcase on his lap. I immediately grasped the situation.

"It's you who said I was French. Admittedly I escaped from French justice, but I am in fact Belgian."

"Why didn't you say so in the first place?"

"I didn't think it would make any difference as far as you were concerned. I had committed no offense in your country except to escape, which any prisoner will try to do."

"Very well. I'll put you in with your friends. But I warn you,

Señor Consul, any attempt at escape and I put him right back where he came from. Take him to the barber, then put him in with his gang."

"Thank you, Consul. Thank you for going to all this trouble for me."

"God, how you must have suffered in that ghastly place! Now quick, on your way. Don't give that monster time to change his mind. I'll come see you again. Good-by."

The barber wasn't there, so they took me straight to my friends. I must have looked pretty strange because they kept saying, "It can't be you! It's impossible! What did those bastards do to you to make you look like that? Talk. Say something. Are you blind? What's the matter with your eyes? Why do you blink all the time?"

"I can't get used to the light. It's so bright here. My eyes are used to the dark. They hurt." I sat down with my back to the light. "That's better."

"You stink something awful."

I stripped and put my clothes near the door. My arms, back, thighs and legs were covered with red bites like a bedbug's, plus those from the tiny crabs that came in with the tide. I didn't need a mirror to tell me how horrible I looked. These five cons had seen plenty, yet they were so upset at my condition they couldn't speak. Clousiot called to a guard and said that even if there was no barber there was at least some water in the yard. The guard said to wait until it was time to go outside.

I went out naked. Clousiot carried the new clothes I was to put on. With the help of Maturette, I washed and washed with the local black soap. The more I washed, the more the scabs came off. Finally, after many soapings and rinsings, I felt clean. Five minutes in the sun and I was dry. I put on my clothes and the barber appeared. He wanted to shear me like a sheep, but I said, "No. Cut it in the normal way and give me a shave. I'll pay you."

"How much?"

"One peso."

"Do it well," Clousiot said, "and I'll give you two."

"How high did the water come? What about the rats? The centipedes? And the mud? What about the crabs and the crap? And what about the guys who died? Did they die naturally or did they hang themselves? Or did the guards help them 'commit suicide'?"

The questions kept coming, and talking so much made me thirsty.

There was a man selling coffee in the yard. During our three hours there I must have drunk at least ten cups of strong coffee sweetened with brown sugar. It tasted like the greatest drink in the world. My black friend from the dungeon came to say hello. Under his breath he explained the business of the Belgian consul and his mother. I shook his hand. He was very proud and happy to have helped me get out of the dungeon, and as he left, he said, "We'll talk more tomorrow. Enough for today."

My friends' cell seemed like a palace to me. Clousiot had a hammock he had bought with his own money and insisted I lie in it. I stretched out in it crosswise. He was astonished when I explained that this was the correct way to use a hammock.

We ate, we drank, we slept, we played checkers, we played cards; we talked Spanish among ourselves and with the Colombian police and the prisoners in order to learn the language. Our days on into the night were very active. It was hard to go to bed at nine. Then all the details of the *cavale* from the hospital at Saint-Laurent to Santa Marta would roll before my eyes, demanding a sequel. The movie could not stop there; it must go on. It will go on, *mecs*! Just give me time to get back my strength and you'll have some

new episodes, never fear! I found my small arrows and two leaves
of coca, one completely dried, the other still a little green. I chewed
the green one. Everyone watched me with curiosity. I explained
that these were the leaves from which cocaine was made.

"You're kidding!"

"Have a taste."

"I can't feel my tongue or my lips."

"Do they sell it here?"

"I don't know. Hey, Clousiot, how come you have so much
dough?"

"I'm a changed man since Rio Hacha. Everybody thinks I'm
rich now."

I said, "I've got thirty-six gold pieces in the head warden's
keeping, and each piece is worth three hundred pesos. One of these
days I'm going to get it back."

"I'd make a bargain with him. These people are starving."

"That's an idea."

I spoke to the Belgian consul and the Belgian prisoner on
Sunday.

The prisoner had broken a contract with an American banana
company. The consul promised to help us both. He filled out a
form which stated that I had Belgian parents living in Brussels. I
told him about the sisters and the pearls. Being a Protestant, he
didn't know the nuns, but he did know the bishop a little. As for
the money, he advised me not to claim it now. It was too risky. He
would be informed of our departure for Barranquilla twenty-four
hours before. "Claim the money in my presence—as I understand
it, there were witnesses."

"That's right."

"But for now, do nothing. They're quite capable of putting you
back in those terrible dungeons, or even killing you. Those gold

pieces are a small fortune. We mustn't tempt the devil. The pearls are something else again. Let me think about them."

I asked the black if he wanted to escape with me, and did he have any ideas on how to go about it. His skin went gray at the very thought.

"Man, don't you even think of it. If it goes wrong, it means slow death. You've had a taste of it. Wait until you're somewhere else, like Barranquilla. To try it here is suicide. You want to die? O.K., then, take it easy. In all of Colombia there's no dungeon like the one we were in. So why risk it here?"

"Yes, but the wall here is low. It should be pretty easy to climb over."

"Man, easy or not, don't count on me. I'm not going. And I'm not going to help you. I don't even want to talk about it." Then he added, his eyes full of terror, "Frenchie, you're not normal. You're crazy to think of such a thing at Santa Marta." With that he walked away.

Every morning and afternoon I watched the Colombians in the prison for serious offenses. They all had the faces of murderers, yet they seemed obsessed by something. They were paralyzed with terror at the thought of those dungeons. Four or five days ago a huge monster of a man had been let out of one of them. He was a good head taller than I and was called El Caiman. He had the reputation of being a very dangerous man. I talked to him, and after three or four walks together I asked him in Spanish, "Do you want to escape with me?"

He looked at me as if I were the devil himself and said, "To end up back where I just came from? No thanks. I'd rather kill my mother than go back down there."

That was my last try. I would never discuss escape with anyone again.

That afternoon the chief warden came walking by. He stopped, looked at me and asked, "How are you?"

"O.K., but I'd be better off if I had my gold pieces."

"Why?"

"Because then I could pay for a lawyer."

"Come with me."

He took me into his office. We were alone. He held out a cigar—not a bad one at all—and lit it for me. Things were getting better and better.

"Do you know enough Spanish to talk to me? We'll talk very slowly."

"All right."

"Good. You say you want to sell your twenty-six pieces?"

"No, my thirty-six pieces."

"Ah, yes; yes! And with this money you will pay for a lawyer? But only the two of us know you have these pieces."

"No, there's the sergeant and the five men who arrested me and the assistant warden who took them from me before giving them to you. Then there is my consul."

"Well, good. It's better if lots of people know. Then everything is out in the open. You know, I did you a great favor. I kept my mouth shut. I didn't even try to find out if there had been a theft of gold pieces in the places you passed through."

"But you should have."

"No, for your sake, it was better not to."

"Thank you, sir."

"You want me to sell them for you?"

"For how much?"

"Oh, three hundred pesos each—that's the price you said they paid you for three of them. You give me a hundred pesos apiece for the favor I did you. What do you say?"

"No. You give me back the pieces ten at a time, and I'll give you two hundred instead of a hundred apiece. That should pay you back for what you've done for me."

"Frenchie, you're much too clever. I'm only a poor Colombian officer. I'm stupid and too trusting. You're smart and, as I said already, too clever."

"O.K., then, make me a reasonable offer."

"Tomorrow I'll have the buyer come here to my office. He looks the pieces over, he makes an offer, and we go fifty-fifty. It's that or nothing. I send you off to Barranquilla with the gold pieces, or I keep them here for the investigation."

"No, this is my last offer: the man comes here, looks the pieces over, and everything over three hundred and fifty pesos each goes to you."

"Good enough. I give you my word. But where are you going to keep all this money?"

"The minute you get the money, you get the Belgian consul to come here. I'll give it to him to pay my lawyer."

"No, I don't want any witnesses."

"There's no risk in it for you. I'll sign on the dotted line that you gave me back my thirty-six pieces. You better accept the proposition, and if you're straight with me, I'll make you still another."

"What is it?"

"Trust me. It's as good as the other one, and this time we go fifty-fifty."

"What is it? Tell me."

"No, not now. Just do your best tomorrow, and at five o'clock, when my money is safe in the hands of the consul, I'll tell you about it."

Our interview had been a long one. When, very pleased with myself, I returned to the yard, my friends had already gone back to the cell.

"Well, what goes on?"

I repeated the whole conversation. We laughed like crazy in spite of our bleak situation.

"What a fox that *mec* is! But you beat him. You think he'll go for it?"

"I'll bet you one hundred pesos against two hundred that he does. Any takers?"

"No, I think he will too."

I thought long and hard the whole night. The first proposal was okay. The second was okay too—he would be only too happy to recover the pearls. The third: what about the third? All right, I'd offer him everything I'd got back if he'd let me steal a boat in the harbor. I could buy the boat with the money in my *plan*. We'd see how well he could resist that temptation. Was I running too great a risk? Hell, after the first two propositions, he couldn't even punish me. But we'd have to see. Don't count your chickens, etc. I could wait until Barranquilla. But why? Bigger city, therefore bigger prison, therefore more guards and higher walls. I should go back and live with Lali and Zoraima: I must escape quickly, spend a few years with the Indians, then go up into the mountains with the tribe that keeps its cattle there and make contact with the Venezuelans. This *cavale* must succeed at all costs. I spent the whole night figuring out the third proposal.

The next day things moved fast. At nine o'clock they came for me to see a man in the chief warden's office. The police stayed outside. I found myself in front of a man of almost sixty wearing a gray suit and a gray tie. On the table was a large gray felt cowboy hat. A large silvery gray-blue pearl was imbedded in his tie as if in a jewel case. Thin and dry, the man was not without a certain elegance.

"Good morning."

"Do you speak French?"

"Yes, I'm originally from Lebanon. I hear you have some gold pieces in one-hundred-peso denominations. I'm interested. Would you take five hundred for each?"

"No, six hundred and fifty."

"You've been misinformed, sir! The maximum price per piece is five hundred and fifty."

"Listen, if you'll take them all, I'll give them to you for six hundred."

"No, five hundred and fifty."

To cut it short, we agreed on five hundred and eighty. Sold.

The warden spoke up, in Spanish. "What did you say? How did it go?"

"Chief, we struck a bargain at five hundred eighty. The sale will take place at noon."

The man left.

The warden stood up and said, "All right. How much for me?"

"Two hundred fifty apiece. See, I'm giving you two and a half times what you asked for."

He smiled and said, "What about the other matter?"

"The consul has to come for the money first. This afternoon, when he's gone, I'll tell you about the second proposition."

"You mean it when you say there's a second proposition?"

"You have my word."

"It better be."

The consul and the Lebanese were there at two o'clock. The latter gave me 20,880 pesos. I gave the consul 12,600 and the chief warden 8,280. I signed a receipt for the warden showing he had given me back my thirty-six gold pieces. When they'd gone, I told the warden about my meeting with the Mother Superior.

"How many pearls did you have?"

"Between five and six hundred."

"That woman's a thief. She should have given them back to

you, or sent them here, or turned them over to the police. I'm going to expose her."

"No. Go see her and give her a letter from me written in French. But before you mention the letter, ask her to send for the Irish nun."

"I get it. The Irish nun will read the letter in French and translate it for the Mother Superior. Very good. I'm off."

"Hey! Wait for the letter!"

"Right! José, get the car ready. And I want two policemen," he called through the half-open door.

I sat down at the warden's desk and wrote the following letter on prison stationery:

"When God led me to your house where I thought I would receive the help which is owed the persecuted according to Christian law, I entrusted you with a sack of pearls that belonged to me as a pledge that I wouldn't run away. Some vile creature thought it his or her duty to expose me to the police who promptly arrested me on your premises. I hope that the miserable soul who committed this deed is not one of the daughters of God in your house. To tell you that I forgive this vicious soul would be a lie. On the contrary, I pray to God that He will punish whoever was capable of such a monstrous crime. I ask you to give Warden Cesario the bag of pearls I entrusted to you. I know he will return it to me faithfully. This letter will serve as a receipt. Sincerely yours, etc."

The convent was five miles from Santa Marta; the car was back in an hour and a half. The warden sent for me. "Here they are. Count them—see if any are missing."

"I think they're all here."

"You're sure none are missing?"

"I'm sure. Tell me what happened."

"When I arrived at the convent, the Mother Superior was in the courtyard. With the two policemen at my side, I said to her, 'Perhaps you can guess the serious matter that has brought me here. I wish to talk to the Irish sister in your presence.' "

"Then what?"

"The sister trembled as she read your letter to the Mother Superior. The Mother Superior said nothing. She looked down, opened the drawer of her desk and said, 'Here is the bag of pearls, untouched. May God forgive the person who committed this terrible crime. Tell Henri that we pray for him.' That was all there was to it!" The warden beamed with satisfaction.

"When do we sell the pearls?"

"Tomorrow. I won't ask you where they came from. I know you're a murderer, but I also know that you're a man of your word. Here, please take this ham, the bottle of wine and the French bread. I want you to celebrate this red-letter day with your friends."

I arrived in our cell with a two-quart bottle of Chianti, a smoked ham weighing a good eight pounds and four long loaves of French bread. We had a feast.

"Do you think a lawyer will be able to help us?"

I burst out laughing. The poor idiots. Even they had fallen for the business about the lawyer.

"I don't know. We have to study the situation, get some advice, before we give anybody any money."

"The best thing would be to pay only if the lawyer gets us off," Clousiot said.

"Good idea. We'll have to find a lawyer who'll go along with that." I said no more. I felt a little ashamed.

The Lebanese came back the next day. "It's very complicated," he said. "First, we have to classify the pearls according to size, color and shape—whether round or baroque." And, in addition, the Lebanese said he'd have to bring along another, more competent buyer. It took us four days. He paid thirty thousand pesos. At the last moment I took back a pink pearl and two black ones to give to the wife of the Belgian consul. They told me that those three pearls alone were worth at least five thousand, but I took them all the same.

The Belgian consul made a great to-do about accepting the pearls, but he agreed to keep the fifteen thousand pesos for me. So I was now in possession of over twenty-seven thousand pesos. All I had left to do was set up the third deal.

"Warden, how much would you have to pay to buy a business that would earn you more than you get now?"

"A good business would cost me between forty-five and sixty thousand pesos."

"Then why don't you go into business?"

"I haven't got half enough capital."

"Listen, Warden. This is my third proposition."

"You're not playing games with me?"

"I'm not, believe me. You want my twenty-seven thousand pesos? They're yours for the asking."

"How so?"

"Make it possible for me to escape."

"Look, Frenchie. I know you don't trust me. Maybe you were right before. But you've helped me out of the poverty I lived in, I'm able to buy a house, send my children to private school . . . Now I'm your friend. I don't want to rob you or see you killed, so I'll give it to you straight: here there's nothing more I can do for you, not for all the money in the world. I can't help you escape with any hope of success."

"And what if I prove you're wrong?"

"Then we'll see. But think about it first."

"Warden, do you know any fishermen?"

"Yes."

"Could you get one of them to sell me his boat and take me out to sea?"

"I don't know."

"What would a boat be worth?"

"Two thousand pesos."

"How would it be if I gave the fisherman seven thousand and you twenty thousand?"

"Frenchie, ten thousand is enough for me. Keep something for yourself."

"Will you make the arrangements?"

"Are you going alone?"

"No."

"How many then?"

"Let me talk to my friends."

I was astonished at the change in his attitude. Despite his sinister face, there were good things hidden in the bottom of his heart.

I talked to Clousiot and Maturette in the yard. They said they'd go with me, whatever I decided. The way they put their lives in my hands gave me deep satisfaction. I would never take advantage of their faith; I would always be prudent—it was a great responsibility. But I had to tell our other companions. We were just finishing a domino tournament. It was almost nine. I called out "Coffee!" and we were served six hot ones.

"I've got to talk to you. This is the way things are. I think I'm going to be able to get away on a *cavale*. But unfortunately only three of us can go. The natural thing is for me to go with Clousiot and Maturette because we escaped from the *bagne* together. If any of you don't like this, speak up. I'm listening."

"No," said the Breton, "it seems fair to me. You escaped from the *bagne* together. Besides you wouldn't be here if we hadn't asked to be let off in Colombia. But thanks all the same for asking our opinion. I hope to God you succeed—if you're caught, it's certain death."

"We know," Clousiot and Maturette agreed.

The warden spoke to me the next afternoon. He'd found someone. He wanted to know what supplies we wanted in the boat.

"A barrel with twelve gallons of fresh water, fifty pounds of cornmeal and six quarts of oil. That's all."

"Good God!" the warden exploded. "You can't go to sea with only that!"

"I sure as hell can."

"You're a brave man, Frenchie."

So it was settled. Then he added coldly, "Believe it or not, I'm doing this both for my children and for you. You deserve it because you have courage."

I thanked him.

"How can we arrange this so no one will know I'm involved?"

"You won't be involved. I'll leave at night when your assistant's on duty."

"What's your plan?"

"Tomorrow I want you to take one of the policemen off night duty. Then, in three days, take another one off. When only one's left, install a sentry box facing the cell door. On the first rainy night the guard will take shelter in the sentry box and we'll go out the rear window. The only other thing you have to do is short-circuit the lights on the wall. The way to do that is to take a yard of brass wire weighted with stones at either end and throw it over the two wires connecting the lights on the wall with the utility pole. As for the fisherman, see that he attaches the boat by a chain and that he forces the padlock himself so I don't have to waste time doing it. Also the sails should be ready to hoist and there should be three paddles to get us out into the open."

"But the boat has a small motor."

"Ah, so much the better. Have him leave the motor running as if he were warming it up, and then go to a nearby café for a drink. When he sees us coming, he should stand by the stern of the boat in a black oilskin."

"What about the money?"

"I'll cut your bills in half. I'll pay the fisherman his seven thousand in advance. I'll give you the halves of your bills ahead of time, and the other halves will be given you by one of the Frenchmen staying behind. I'll tell you which one."

"I see you don't trust me. That's not good."

"No, it's not that I don't trust you, but you might not do the short-circuit right. Then I don't pay you, because without the short-circuit, we can't get out."

"O.K."

Everything was ready. Through the warden I paid the fisherman his seven thousand pesos. For five days there had been just one guard, and the sentry box was installed. We waited only for the rain, but it wouldn't come. The bars had been cut with a saw donated by the warden. The cut was well disguised and, in addition, it was hidden by a cage which housed a parrot who had learned to say "Merde." We were in torment. Each night we waited, but no rain. At this time of year it was unbelievable. The smallest cloud beyond our window filled us with hope, then nothing. It was enough to drive you nuts. We had now been ready for sixteen days; sixteen nights of watching with our hearts in our mouths. One Sunday morning the warden came for me in the yard and took me back to his office. He gave me a packet of the half bills and three thousand whole pesos.

"What goes on?"

"Frenchie, my friend, tonight's your last chance. You leave for Barranquilla tomorrow morning at six. You get only three thousand pesos back from the fisherman because he spent the rest. If

God means it to rain tonight, the fisherman will be waiting for you, and when you take the boat, you can give him the rest of his money. I trust you."

It didn't rain.

THE *CAVALES* AT BARRANQUILLA

At six in the morning eight soldiers and two corporals accompanied by a lieutenant handcuffed us, and we set off for Barranquilla in an army truck. We did the hundred and ten miles in three and a half hours. At ten o'clock we were in the prison called the "80," Calle Medellin, in Barranquilla. So much effort to avoid going to Barranquilla, and there we were all the same! It was an important city, the biggest port in Colombia, situated inland on an estuary of the river Magdalena. Its prison was big too: four hundred prisoners and nearly a hundred guards. It was organized like a European prison, with double walls more than twenty-five feet high.

We were received by the prison's general staff and the director, Don Gregorio. The prison had four yards, two on one side, two on the other, separated by a long chapel which was used for mass as well as the visitors' room. We were put in the yard for the most dangerous prisoners. When they searched us, they found my twenty-three thousand pesos and the arrows. I thought it was my duty to warn the director that they were poisoned—it didn't exactly help our reputations.

"These Frenchies even have poisoned arrows!"

Barranquilla was the most dangerous stage of our adventure. From here we'd be turned over to the French authorities. Yes, Barranquilla was crucial. We had to escape from here no matter what the cost. It was all or nothing.

Our cell was in the middle of the yard. And it wasn't a cell; it was a cage. It had a cement roof resting on thick iron bars with the toilets and washstands in one corner. The other prisoners—about a hundred of them—were in cells recessed into the four walls, their grills opening onto the yard, which was about sixty by a hundred and twenty feet. At the top of each grill was a sort of metal overhang to keep the rain from coming into the cells. We six Frenchmen were the only occupants of the central cage and we were exposed night and day to the view of both prisoners and guards. We spent the day in the yard, from six in the morning until six at night. We could enter or leave the cage whenever we wanted. We could talk, walk about, even eat in the yard.

Two days after our arrival the six of us were taken to the chapel, where we found ourselves in the presence of the director, some policemen and seven or eight newspaper reporters and photographers.

"You are escaped prisoners from the *bagne* in French Guiana?"

"We never said we weren't."

"What were your crimes?"

"That's of no importance. What is important is that we've committed no offense on Colombian territory and that your country has not only refused to let us start a new life but has played bloodhound for the French government."

"Colombia doesn't want you in its territory."

"And we don't want to remain. We were arrested on the high seas; we weren't trying to come here. In fact, we were making every effort to get as far away from here as possible."

A journalist from a Catholic newspaper said, "The French, like the Colombians, are almost all Catholics."

"You may be baptized Catholics, but the way you act is hardly Christian," I said.

"What do you have against us?"

"You collaborated with the authorities who were out for our

necks. You did their work for them: you seized our boat with everything we owned—a gift, I might add, from the Catholics of Curaçao, represented by their noble bishop, Irénée de Bruyne. You weren't willing to let us try to rehabilitate ourselves, and, still worse, you prevented us from going anywhere else—to a country that might be willing to take that risk."

"You hold this against us Colombians?"

"Not the Colombian people, but their police and their judicial system."

"What do you mean by that?"

"That if there's a will, all errors can be corrected. Give us a chance to sail to another country."

"We'll try."

Once back in the yard, Maturette said, "Well, well! Did you get that? Let's have no illusions this time, *mecs*! We're in the soup all right, and it's not going to be easy to get out."

"Well, friends, I don't know whether we're stronger going it together or not. But remember you're all free to do what you think best. As for me, I've got to get out of here, and that's that."

I was called to the visitors' room on Thursday, where a well-dressed man of about forty-five was waiting for me. I looked at him hard. He had an uncanny resemblance to Louis Dega.

"Are you Papillon?"

"Yes."

"I'm Louis Dega's brother, Joseph. I read about what happened in the newspapers."

"Thank you."

"You saw my brother over there? You know him?"

I described Dega's odyssey in detail right up to the moment we separated at the hospital. Then he told me he had learned via Marseilles that his brother was on the Iles du Salut. He also told me there were about a dozen Frenchmen in Barranquilla who had come here with their women to seek their fortune. They were all pimps. In a special quarter of the town about twenty ladies carried on the distinguished French tradition of skilled prostitution. From Cairo to Lebanon, from England to Australia, from Buenos Aires to Caracas, from Saigon to Brazzaville, you found the same men and the same women practicing their specialty. So much for that.

He also told me that the Barranquilla pimps were worried: they were afraid our arrival might disturb their peace and endanger their flourishing trade. If one or all of us escaped, the police would immediately go after them, even if they were in no way involved. In the process the police might uncover a lot of things, such as false papers and invalid or expired visitors' permits. A few would be in serious difficulties if they were discovered.

He gave me all kinds of information, then added that he was at my disposal for anything I had in mind and would come to see me in the chapel every Thursday and Sunday. I thanked this stalwart friend, who was to give proof many times over that he was a man of his word. He also told me that, according to the newspapers, France had received permission to have us extradited.

When I got back to the cell, I gave them the news. "Gentlemen, let us cherish no illusions. Our extradition is on the books. A special boat is coming from French Guiana to take us back. In addition, our presence here appears to be a source of anxiety to some French pimps who have a nice business going on in this city. Not the man who just came to see me. He couldn't care less what happens to them, but his colleagues are afraid that if one of us escapes, they might all be in trouble."

Everyone laughed—they thought I was joking. Clousiot mimicked, "Dear Mr. Pimp, may I please have your permission to escape?"

"It's not funny. If any of the pimps come to see us, we must send them away. O.K.?"

"O.K."

As I've already mentioned, there were about a hundred Colombian prisoners in our yard. They were far from stupid. There were clever thieves, distinguished forgers, ingenious and spirited crooks, specialists in assault and battery, narcotics smugglers and a few specially trained assassins. In this part of the world the services of these assassins were in demand by the rich, the politicians and successful adventurers.

There was great variety in the color of their skin: from the black of the Senegalese to the tea color of the Martinique Creoles, from the brick red of the Indians with their straight, almost purple hair, to pure white. I made some contacts among them and tried to size up their desire or ability to make a break. Most of them were like me: they expected, or already had, long sentences and therefore were always ready for a *cavale*.

There was a walk along the top of the four walls that enclosed our yard; it was brightly lit at night, and at each of the four corners there was a small tower for the guard. So, night and day, there were four guards on duty, plus one more at the door to the chapel. This guard wasn't armed.

The food was adequate, and several prisoners sold food, coffee, or fruit juices—orange, pineapple, papaya, etc.—they got from the outside. From time to time they were the victims of assaults executed with amazing speed. Too fast for them to see it coming, a large napkin would be tied over their faces to keep them from crying out, and a knife held against their backs or necks, ready to plunge in at their slightest move. Before they knew what had hit them, they'd be cleaned out. Then they'd be given a sharp whack at the nape of the neck and the napkin removed. And that would be the end of it. No one ever mentioned it again. Sometimes, though, the "shopkeeper" would put away his goods—somewhat like closing shop—and go looking for his assailant. If he found him, there was always a battle with knives.

Two Colombian thieves came to me with a proposition, and I listened carefully. It appeared that some of the policemen doubled as thieves. When they were on duty in the town, they alerted their accomplices to come and go to work.

My visitors knew them all and explained that during the coming week it would be very likely that one of these policemen would be stationed at the door of the chapel. I should get hold of a revolver during visitors' hours. The policeman-thief could easily be persuaded to knock on the back door of the chapel, which opened on a small guardhouse. There were never more than six men in it. They'd be taken by surprise, and with the revolver in my hand, they wouldn't stop us from reaching the street. After that it would be a simple matter to get lost in the heavy traffic.

I didn't like the plan much. For me to hide a revolver, it would have to be a very small one, hardly big enough to intimidate the guards. Or one of them might have the wrong reaction and I'd be forced to kill him. So I said no.

I wasn't the only one tormented by a desire for action: my friends were too. Except that they had off days when they seemed all too ready to accept the arrival of the boat. From there to giving up altogether was a very short step. They even discussed what sentences we might get when we arrived at the *bagne* and what kind of treatment we could expect.

"I don't even want to listen to that crap. If you're going to talk like that, do it somewhere else. Do it in a corner where I can't hear you. What's happened to your balls? Have they been cut off? If so, please tell me. Because I want you *mecs* to know something: when I think *cavale*, I think *cavale* for all of us. And when my brain is bursting from planning how to escape, I'm thinking for all of us. . . . I'll tell you something else. When I see our time is almost up and we still haven't got going, I'll kill a Colombian policeman to gain some more. They won't turn me over to the French if I've killed one of their own. That'll get me extra time. And then I'll be escaping alone, so it'll be that much easier."

The Colombians had another plan in the works and this was a good one. On Sunday mornings the chapel was always full of visitors and prisoners. First there was mass, and when that was over, the prisoners with visitors stayed on in the chapel. The Colombians asked me to go to mass the following Sunday to see how things went so that I could coordinate our actions on the Sunday afterward. They suggested I be the leader of the revolt. I declined the honor—I didn't know the men involved.

I answered for us four Frenchmen. The Breton and the man of the flatiron wanted no part of it. No problem there: they wouldn't go to the chapel. We did. The chapel was rectangular. At the back, the chancel; in the middle on either side, two doors that opened on the yards. The main door opened on the guardhouse. It was covered by a grill behind which stood twenty guards. Behind them was the door to the street. Since the chapel was full to bursting, the guards left the grill open and stood in close ranks during mass. Among the visitors would be two men, and their women would be carrying the weapons between their legs. They'd give them—two guns, either .38 or .45 caliber—to the men as soon as the chapel was full. The leader of the plot was to get a heavy-caliber revolver from some other woman who would then leave. When the altar boy rang the bell the second time, we were all to attack at once. I was to put a large knife to the director's throat and say, "Give the order to let us pass or I kill you."

Another man was to do the same to the priest. The three others, from three different angles, were to aim their guns at the police standing at the grill of the main entrance. They were to kill the first guard who failed to drop his weapon. Those who weren't armed would go out first. The priest and the director would serve as shields for the last ones out. If everything went as expected, all the police would have laid down their arms. Then the men with revolvers would force them into the chapel. We'd leave, closing the grill first, then the wooden door. The guardhouse would be empty because the guards were obliged to attend mass. Outside, at a distance of fifty yards, there'd be a truck with a small ladder at the back to help us climb in faster. The truck would start up only after our leader was in. He would be the last one to leave the chapel.

I observed the mass and agreed to the plan.

Joseph Dega did not visit me on Sunday. He was preparing a fake taxi so that we wouldn't have to go in the truck but to a hideout instead. I was excited all week. I couldn't wait for the action to begin. Fernando, our leader, was able to get the revolver, a .45 belonging to the Colombian Civil Guard and a fearsome weapon. Thursday, one of Joseph's women came to see me. She was very nice. She told me the taxi would be yellow and that we couldn't miss it. She said "Good luck" and kissed me gently on both cheeks. She seemed quite moved.

"Enter, enter. Let this chapel be filled so that we may listen to the voice of God," said the priest.

Feeling very calm, I took my place. Clousiot stood close to me on one side, Maturette, his eyes glistening, on the other. Don Gregorio, the director, was right in front, sitting next to a fat woman. All of us were inconspicuously dressed in case we reached the street. The knife was open against my right forearm and held in place by a thick elastic band. It was covered by the sleeve of my khaki shirt, which was tightly buttoned at the wrist. Now it was time for the raising of the Host. Everybody bowed their heads as if they were looking for something on the floor; the altar boy gave the bell a quick shake, then let out three distinct peals. The second one was our signal. Each of us knew what to do.

First ring, second . . . I threw myself on Don Gregorio, the knife against his thick, wrinkled neck. The priest cried out, "God have mercy on me, don't kill me." I couldn't see the others, but I heard them order the guards to drop their guns. Everything was working fine. I took Don Gregorio by the collar of his suit and said, "Follow me. Don't be afraid, I won't hurt you."

The priest had a razor at his throat.

Fernando said to me, "Come on, Frenchie, let's make for the door."

Feeling triumphant, I was pushing my group toward the door to the street when I heard two shots at once. Fernando and one of the armed prisoners fell to the ground. I moved forward another three feet, but now the guards had picked themselves up and were barring the passage. Fortunately some women stood between us so they didn't dare shoot. More gunfire. Our third companion collapsed after shooting wild and wounding a young girl. Don Gregorio, pale as death, said to me, "Give me that knife."

I handed it to him. There was no point in continuing the battle. In less than thirty seconds the situation had been reversed.

More than a week later I learned that the revolt had failed because of a prisoner from another court who had been looking in at the mass from outside the chapel. During the first seconds of action he had alerted the guards on top of the wall. They jumped the twenty feet into the yard, took positions on either side of the chapel and shot between the bars of the side doors at the two men who were standing on a bench threatening the police. The third man was shot down a few seconds later when he happened to come within their range. What followed was a fine *corrida*. I stayed next to the director, who was shouting orders. Sixteen of us, we Frenchmen included, were put in a dungeon on bread and water.

Joseph Dega visited Don Gregorio. He called me in and said that to please Joseph he was putting me and my comrades back in the yard. So, thanks to Dega, ten days after the revolt we were once again in our cage in the yard. When we'd all got together, I asked for a few minutes' silence for Fernando and his two friends who had died in the revolt. During one of his visits Joseph told me that he had passed the hat among the pimps and had collected five thousand pesos to bring Don Gregorio around. The pimps went way up in our estimation.

But what to do now? What new plan could we dream up? I had no intention of admitting defeat, and I wasn't going to just sit there waiting for that boat!

I lay down in the washroom out of reach of the broiling sun where I could examine the guards on the wall without attracting attention. During the night, at intervals of ten minutes, they took turns shouting, "Guards, attention!" This was so the head guard would be certain that none of the four was asleep. If one of them failed to answer, the guard kept on shouting until there was a response.

I thought I'd found a vital flaw in the system. At each of the four corners of the wall a can hung by a cord from the sentry box. When the guard wanted some coffee, he called out "Coffee," and a prisoner poured some in the can. Then the guard pulled it up by the cord. Now the sentry box at the extreme right was a tower that hung out over the yard. If I could make a thick hook and attach it to a strong braided cord, it would catch on the overhang and in a few seconds I'd be over the wall and into the street. The only problem was how to neutralize the guard.

I saw him stand up and take a few steps along the wall. He seemed affected by the heat, fighting to stay awake. That was it! He must be put to sleep! First I'd make the cord, and when I found a strong enough hook, I'd put him to sleep and try my luck. In two days I had braided a cord almost seven yards long, using all the heavy cotton shirts I could lay my hands on, especially khaki ones. The hook was relatively easy to find. I took the bracket from one of the overhangs that protected the cells from rain. Joseph Dega brought me a bottle containing a powerful sleeping draught. The directions said that not more than ten drops should be taken at one time. The bottle held about six big spoonfuls. I got the guard to accept me as his coffee boy. He'd let down the can and I'd send him up three cups at a time. Since all Colombians loved alcohol and the sleeping potion tasted a little like anise, I got hold of a bottle of anisette.

"How would you like some coffee *à la française*?" I asked the guard.

"What's it like?"

"It has anisette in it."

"I'll try it."

Several of the guards had a taste of my coffee-anisette. Now when I offered them their coffee, they always said, "*À la française!*"

And so I'd pour in the anisette.

The time had come. It was a Saturday noon. The heat was unbearable. My friends realized there wouldn't be time for two people to escape, but a Colombian with the Arab name of Ali said he'd climb up after me. I said okay. This way, at least, none of the Frenchmen would appear to be accomplices. Also, Ali would carry the cord; it would be hard for me to hide the cord and hook while I was giving the guard his coffee. We figured the stuff would knock him out in five minutes.

It was now "minus five."

"How goes it?" I called up to the guard.

"O.K."

"Want some coffee?"

"Yes, *à la française*."

"Wait. I'll get it for you."

I went to the "coffee boy" and said, "Two coffees." I had already poured the whole bottle of sleeping potion into the can. If that didn't knock him out . . . ! At the foot of the tower I made a big show of pouring in the anisette.

"Want it strong?"

"Yes."

I poured in a little more and he pulled it up.

Five minutes went by, then ten, fifteen, twenty. He still wasn't asleep. Even worse, instead of sitting down, he was walking back and forth, gun in hand. Yet he had drunk the whole can. And his relief would come at one o'clock.

I watched his movements with a feeling of desperation. He gave no sign of being drugged. Ah! He staggered a little. Then he sat down in front of the sentry box, his gun between his legs, his head on one shoulder. All of us followed his reactions like hawks.

"Go to it," I said to the Colombian. "Now for the cord."

He was about to throw it when the guard stood up, let his gun fall to the ground, stretched and started working his legs as if he were running in place. The Colombian stopped just in time. Eighteen minutes until the change of the guard. Inwardly I called on God to help. "Just once more, Lord! I beseech you, don't let me down now!" But it was in vain that I called to this Christian God, whose ways were sometimes so mysterious, especially to me, an atheist.

"How do you like that!" Clousiot said, coming over to me. "Why doesn't the son of a bitch go to sleep?"

The guard started to pick up his gun and, just as he was bending down for it, he fell in a heap as if struck by lightning. The Colombian threw the cord, but the hook wouldn't hold and the cord fell down. He threw it a second time; it grabbed hold. He pulled on it to make sure it was firm. I checked it again and was just putting my foot against the wall to start climbing when Clousiot said:

"Beat it! The relief is here!"

I just had time to hide before he saw me. Moved by the instinct for self-preservation and the bond between prisoners, a dozen Colombians quickly surrounded me and drew me into their circle. We walked the length of the wall, leaving the cord hanging behind us. The relief took in the hook and the stricken guard at the same time. He ran a few yards and pushed the alarm button, convinced there had been an escape.

They came for the sleeping guard with a stretcher. More than twenty police stood on the wall. Don Gregorio was up there too and had the cord pulled up. He had the hook in his hand. A few moments later, their guns at the ready, the police fanned into the yard. They called the roll. After each name its owner was sent to his cell. Surprise! No one was missing.

Second check, cell by cell. No, nobody missing. At three o'clock we were allowed out in the yard. We learned that the guard was still out cold and that nothing would wake him. My Colombian accomplice was brokenhearted, as was I. He'd been so sure we'd succeed. He cursed all things American, for it turned out that the sleeping potion was American.

"What are we going to do?"

"Why, begin again, man!" It was all I could think of.

He thought I meant we should put another guard to sleep. "You think these guards are so stupid another one would take his coffee *à la française*?"

In spite of our sad situation, I had to laugh. "It wouldn't sur-prise me, *mec*!"

Our guard slept three days and four nights. When he finally woke up, he, of course, said I'd put him to sleep with my coffee *à la française*. Don Gregorio summoned me, and the guard and I confronted each other. The head guard raised his sword to strike me. I backed into a corner, egging him on. As the sword swung down, Don Gregorio came between us, took the blow on the shoulder and fell to the ground. The fall broke his collarbone. He let out such a yell that the head guard had to turn all his attention to him. He picked him up while Don Gregorio called for help. Civilian employees poured in from neighboring offices. Soon the head guard, two other policemen and the guard I had drugged found themselves in a pitched battle with a dozen civilians seeking to avenge their director. Several were slightly wounded. The only one who escaped unscathed was me. My case no longer mat-tered—only the one involving the director and the head guard.

The director's replacement—the director had been taken to the hospital—led me back to my yard. "We'll see about you later, Frenchie," he said.

The next day the director was back with his shoulder in a cast. He asked me for a written statement against the guard. I did every-thing he asked and with pleasure. The business of the sleeping draught was completely forgotten. Luckily for me, they couldn't have cared less.

A few days later Joseph Dega offered to try to organize some-thing from the outside. I had told him that a night break was impossible because of the lights on the walls, so he looked into the possibility of cutting the current. With the help of an electrician, he found it could be done by tripping the switch on a transformer outside the prison. I was to buy off the guard on the road side, the one in the yard and the one at the door to the chapel. It was more complicated than I expected. First I put pressure on Don Gregorio—via Joseph—to give me back ten thousand pesos under the pretext that it was for my family, not to mention "persuading" him to accept two thousand pesos to buy a present for his wife. Then I had to find out which guard was in charge of scheduling the tours of duty on the wall and buy him off. He was to get three thousand pesos, but he wanted no part of the negotiations with the other two guards. It was up to me to find them and deal with them myself. I would then give him their names and he would schedule their watch according to my directions.

The preparations for this *cavale* took over a month. At last every detail was worked out. Since we didn't need to worry about the guard in the yard, we cut the bars with a metal saw. It had three blades. The Colombian who had made the hook was alerted. He cut his bar in installments. On the designated night, a friend of his who had been pretending to be nuts for some time was to bang away on a piece of metal while singing at the top of his voice. The Colombian knew that the guard had complied only on condition that the break be limited to two Frenchmen. If there was a third man, he'd shoot him. But he wanted to try it all the same and thought that if the three of us stuck closely together, the guard wouldn't be able to make out in the dark whether we were two or three. Clousiot and Maturette drew lots to see who would go with me. Clousiot won.

The first moonless night came. The sergeant and two policemen had half their money. This time I didn't need to cut the bills in half; they were already cut. The police were to pick up the other halves at the Barrio Chino where Joseph Dega's wife worked.

The light went out. We went to work on the bar. It was sawed through in less than ten minutes. Wearing dark pants and shirts, we climbed out of the cell. The Colombian, naked except for a black undershirt, joined us in the passageway. I shimmied up the bars of our door, climbed around the overhang and threw the hook with its three yards of cord. I was on top of the wall in less than three minutes. I hadn't made a sound. Flat on my stomach, I waited for Clousiot. The night was blackest black. Suddenly I saw, or imagined I saw, a hand reaching up and pulled. There was a ghastly noise. Clousiot had climbed between the wall and the overhang and had caught the belt loop of his pants on the metal. I stopped pulling. The noise stopped. I pulled again, thinking that Clousiot was unhitched. But the metallic clatter continued. I pulled until he was free; then yanked him up and over.

Shots rang out from the other sentry posts. Unnerved by the noise, we jumped from the wrong part of the wall; here the street was twenty-five feet below, whereas farther along to the right there was a street only fifteen feet below. As a result, Clousiot broke his right leg again. I couldn't get up either. I had broken the arches of both feet. The Colombian dislocated his knee. The rifle shots brought out the guard on the street side. We were picked out by a big electric lantern and guns were aimed at us. I wept with anger. On top of that, the guards wouldn't believe I couldn't stand up. I crawled back to the prison on my knees, prodded on by rifle jabs. Clousiot and the Colombian hopped on one foot. My head was streaming blood from the whack of a rifle butt.

The shots had waked Don Gregorio, who luckily was on duty that night and therefore sleeping in his office. Without him the guards would have finished us off. The one who had roughed me up the worst was the sergeant I had paid to post our two accomplices. Don Gregorio put a stop to it. He threatened to haul them up before the tribunal if they did us real harm. This magic word brought everyone to heel.

The next day Clousiot's leg was put in a cast at the hospital. The Colombian's knee was set by a prisoner and strapped with an Ace bandage. During the night my feet swelled as big as my head and turned black and red from the clotted blood. The doctor made me soak my feet in warm salted water and applied leeches three times a day. When they were gorged with blood, the leeches let go by themselves and were put in vinegar to disgorge themselves. It took six stitches to close my head wound.

As a result of all this, a journalist wrote an article about me. He said that I'd been the leader of the chapel revolt, that I had poisoned a guard, and, to top it off, that I had mounted a mass break with the help of accomplices from the outside, since someone had cut off the electricity by tampering with the transformer. "Let us hope that France relieves us as soon as possible of its public enemy number one," he said in conclusion.

Joseph Dega visited me with his wife, Annie. The sergeant and the guards had each come to claim the other half of their money. Annie wanted to know what she should do. I said they should be paid since they had stuck by their word. It was not their fault that we had failed.

For a week now I'd been pushed around the yard in an iron wheelbarrow that also served as a couch. My feet were propped up on a length of material stretched taut between two sticks attached vertically to the handles of the wheelbarrow. It was the only position I could tolerate. Still swollen and congested with blood, my feet couldn't stand the slightest pressure even when I was lying down. Fifteen days later the swelling was down about half and I was taken for X-rays. It was then that I learned that I had broken both arches. I've been flat-footed ever since.

Today's newspaper announced that the *Mana* was coming for us at the end of the month with an escort of French police. It was now the twelfth of October. We had eighteen days left. We must play our last card, but what could we do with me and my broken arches?

Joseph was in despair. He told me that all the Frenchmen and the women of the Barrio Chino were dismayed at the thought of how hard I'd fought for my freedom and that in only a few days I'd be back in French hands. I drew comfort from the fact that so many people were on my side.

I abandoned the idea of killing a Colombian policeman. I couldn't bring myself to kill a man who had done nothing to me. Maybe he was helping out his mother and father, maybe he had a wife and children. I smiled at the prospect of having to search out an evil policeman with no family. How should I put it to him: "If I kill you, are you sure no one will miss you?" On the morning of the thirteenth I was really in the dumps. I examined the picric acid I was supposed to eat to get jaundice. If I was in the hospital, I might be able to escape with the help of some men Joseph would hire. The next day—the fourteenth—I was a beautiful lemon yellow. Don Gregorio came to see me in the yard. I was in the shade, lying in my wheelbarrow with my feet in the air.

Without beating around the bush, I attacked. "Ten thousand pesos for you if you can get me into the hospital."

"I'll try, Frenchie. Ten thousand pesos don't matter that much, but it hurts me to see you fight so hard and not get anywhere. The trouble is I don't think they'll let you stay at the hospital on account of that story in the paper. They'd be scared."

An hour later the doctor had me sent to the hospital. I was in and out in nothing flat. From the ambulance I was placed on a stretcher, and I was back in the prison two hours later after a detailed examination and urinalysis.

It was now the nineteenth, a Thursday. Joseph's wife, Annie, came to see me with the wife of a Corsican. They brought me cigarettes and candy. Their friendliness turned that dreary day into pure sunshine. I'll never be able to express how much the support of these people of the Barranquilla underworld meant to me, or how much I owe to Joseph Dega for risking his job and his own freedom to help me escape.

In the course of our conversation Annie said something that gave me an idea.

"Dear Papillon," she said, "you've done everything humanly possible to get back your freedom. Fate has been cruel to you. All that's left for you is to blow up the prison!"

"How about that! Why don't I blow up this old prison? I'd be doing the Colombians a great service. If I blew it up, maybe they'd build a new and cleaner one."

I kissed the charming ladies good-by for the last time and said to Annie, "Ask Joseph to come see me Sunday."

On Sunday, the twenty-second, Joseph was there.

"Listen, try to bring me a stick of dynamite, a detonator and a Bickford cord on Thursday. I'll see if I can get hold of a drill for brick."

"What are you going to do?"

"I'm going to blow the hell out of this prison wall. And in broad daylight. Promise five thousand pesos to that yellow taxi. He has to be in the street behind the Calle Medellin every day from eight in the morning until six in the evening. He'll get five hundred pesos a day if nothing happens and five thousand if it does. I'll be coming through on the back of a strong Colombian who'll carry me to the taxi. If the taxi driver is willing, send the dynamite. If he's not, then it's the end. I give up."

"Count on me," Joseph said.

At five o'clock I had myself carried into the chapel, explaining that I wanted to pray alone. I asked for Don Gregorio to come and see me. He came.

"It's only eight days until you go."

"That's why I wanted to see you. You have fifteen thousand

pesos belonging to me. I want to give them to my friend before I go so that he can send the money to my family, and I want you to take three thousand pesos in thanks for the way you've protected me from the guards. You'd be doing me a great service if you could get me the money today along with a roll of gummed tape so that I can get it ready for my friend by next Thursday."

"I'll do that."

He came back and handed me the twelve thousand pesos, still in halves, keeping three thousand for himself.

Back in my wheelbarrow, I called my Colombian friend over to a quiet corner. I described my plan and asked him if he thought he could carry me on his back for the twenty or thirty yards to the taxi. He gave me his word. So that part was all right. I made my plans on the assumption that Joseph would come through. I took up a position in the washhouse early Monday morning, and Maturette—who shared with Clousiot the "chauffeuring" of my wheelbarrow—went to find the sergeant to whom I had given the three thousand pesos and who had paid me back with such a savage beating.

"Sergeant Lopez, I'd like to talk to you."

"What do you want?"

"For two thousand pesos, I want a strong three-speed brace and six drills for brick. Two one-tenth of an inch thick, two four-tenths and two one-half inch."

"I have no money."

"Here are five hundred pesos."

"You'll have them tomorrow at one when the guard changes. Get the two thousand pesos ready."

The next day at one o'clock I received the tools in a wastepaper basket that was emptied when the guards changed. Pablo, my Colombian strong man, picked them up and hid them.

On Thursday there was no sign of Joseph. Then, toward the

end of visiting time, I was called in. Joseph had sent an old wrinkled Frenchman in his place.

"The things you're expecting are in this piece of bread."

"Here's two thousand pesos for the taxi. Five hundred for each day."

"The driver of the taxi is an excitable old Peruvian. Don't get into a fight with him."

They had put the bread in a big paper bag along with some cigarettes, matches, smoked sausages, a piece of butter and a flask of black olive oil. As the guard at the door was rummaging through the bag, I gave him a pack of cigarettes, some matches and two sausages. He said, "How about a piece of bread to go with it?"

That was all I needed!

"No, buy your own bread. Here's five pesos. Otherwise there won't be enough for the six of us."

Jesus, that was a close one! Whatever made me offer the *mec* sausages! We ducked him as fast as possible. I'd been so unprepared for the bread episode that I was covered with sweat.

"Tomorrow, the fireworks. Everything's ready, Pablo. You must make the hole exactly under the overhanging tower so the cop on top won't see you."

"But he'll hear me."

"I've thought of that. At ten in the morning that side of the yard is in the shade. We have to get one of the metal workers to hammer on something against the wall near you and in the sun. Two men would be even better. I'll give them five hundred pesos apiece. Try and find two men."

He found them.

"Two friends of mine have agreed to stand there hammering as long as necessary. The guard won't be able to hear the drill at all. You station yourself in your wheelbarrow a little away from the overhang and get into a discussion with the Frenchmen. That way you'll screen me from the guard on the other corner of the wall."

In an hour the hole was drilled. Thanks to the hammering and the oil on the drill, the guard suspected nothing. The dynamite was wedged into the hole and the detonator attached to an eight-inch wick. We moved away. If everything went well, the explosion would blow open a big hole, the guard would fall with his sentry box, and I'd be through the hole on Pablo's back and off to the taxi. The others would be on their own. Clousiot and Maturette would probably get to the taxi before me, even though I was going first.

Just before we lit the fuse, Pablo alerted a group of Colombians. "If you want to make a break, there'll be a nice hole in the wall in a few minutes."

That's good, I thought. The police will concentrate on the last ones through.

We lit the fuse. A terrific explosion shook the whole area. The tower fell. There were cracks over the whole wall, wide enough to see the street on the other side, but not one wide enough to let a man through.

I was finally forced to admit that all was lost. Obviously it was my fate to return to Cayenne.

The confusion that followed the explosion can't be described. More than fifty policemen filled the yard.

Don Gregorio had a pretty good idea who was responsible. "Well, Frenchie, I think this was your last try."

The head of the garrison was wild with exasperation: he could hardly order someone to hit a cripple lying in a wheelbarrow. I wanted to protect the others, so I declared in a loud voice that I had done it all by myself. Six guards were stationed in front of the wall, six in the prison yard, and six outside in the street. They stayed until the masons had repaired the damage. Fortunately the guard who fell with the tower was unhurt.

RETURN TO THE *BAGNE*

Three days later, at eleven in the morning on October 30, twelve white-uniformed guards from the *bagne* arrived to take possession of us. Before we left, there was a short official ceremony: each of us had to be identified. They had brought our descriptions, reports, photographs, fingerprints—the whole lot. Once they had verified our identities, the French consul stepped up to sign a document from the judge of the district—the official charged with giving us back to France. All of us were astonished at the friendly way we were treated by the guards. No animosity, no harsh words. The three in our group who had been there longest knew several of the *bagne* guards and joked with them like old buddies. The head of our escort, Commander Boursal, was worried about my condition. He looked at my feet and said he'd have them examined on the ship: there was a good orderly aboard.

We were put in the bottom of the old tub's hold, but the worst of it was the suffocating heat and the "bars of justice" to which our chains were attached. Only one interesting thing happened on the trip: the boat had to pick up coal in Trinidad. In port, a British naval officer demanded that our irons be removed. Apparently it was against British law to chain a man on board ship. I took advantage of the incident to slap a British officer in the face. I was trying to get myself arrested so they'd take me ashore. But the officer said, "I'm not going to have you punished for what you just did. Where you're going you'll get punishment enough."

Clearly, I was fated to go back to the *bagne*. It was very sad; eleven months of escapes, all that struggle, and all for nothing. But in spite of everything, my return to the *bagne*—no matter what happened there—could never wipe out the beautiful moments I had experienced.

We had just left Trinidad, which brought back memories of the incomparable Bowen family, and we passed near Curaçao, where that great man, Irénée de Bruyne, served as bishop. We must also have skirted the territory of the Guajiros Indians, where I'd known love in its purest and most spontaneous form. They saw things with the clarity of children, those Indians, and they were rich in human understanding and simple love.

And the lepers of the Ile aux Pigeons! Those wretched convicts with their terrible scourge, who still had the nobility to help us!

And, finally, the spontaneous goodness of the Belgian consul and Joseph Dega, who, without knowing me, constantly risked everything on my behalf! These people had made the *cavale* worth doing. Even though it was a failure, my escape was also a victory because of the way these extraordinary people had enriched my life. No, I didn't regret any part of it.

Now we were back on the Maroni and its muddy waters. It was nine in the morning and we were standing on the *Mana*'s bridge. The tropical sun was already burning the earth. We were sailing gently up the estuary I had left with such urgency. My comrades and I were silent. The guards were glad to be back. The sea had been rough during the trip, and they were happy to be in calm waters.

November 16, 1934

There was a wild crush at the landing. Perhaps everyone was just curious to see men who had been unafraid to make such a long trip. Also it was Sunday, and we were providing some distraction for people who didn't get much of it. I could hear people saying, "The one who can't walk is Papillon. That one's Clousiot. There, that's Maturette. . . ." And so on.

In the penitentiary camp six hundred men were lined up in front of their barracks. Guards stood beside each group. The first one I recognized was François Sierra. He was leaning from an infirmary window and looking straight at me. He was crying and making no attempt to hide the fact. It was plain that his grief was real. We were brought to a halt in the middle of the camp. The chief warden picked up a loudspeaker:

"Transportees, I hope this is proof that it is useless to try to escape. There is no country that will not arrest you and return you to France. Nobody wants any part of you. So it's better to stay here quietly and behave. What lies in store for these men? A heavy sentence in solitary on Saint-Joseph and then internment for life on the Iles du Salut. That's what their escape got them. I trust you get the idea. Guards, take these men to the disciplinary quarter."

A few minutes later we were in a special cell in the maximum-security section. As soon as we arrived, I asked them to look after my swollen feet, and Clousiot complained of the plaster cast on his leg. We could give it one more try. As if they'd ever send us to the hospital again! François Sierra arrived with his guard.

"Here's the orderly," the guard said.

"How goes it, Papi?"

"I'm sick. I want to go to the hospital."

"I'll try to get you in, but after what you did there it'll be just about impossible. Same goes for Clousiot."

He massaged my feet, rubbed them with ointment, checked Clousiot's cast and went on his way. We couldn't talk because of the guards, but his eyes were so full of sympathy that I was touched.

"No. Nothing doing," he told me the next day when he came

to give me another massage. "Want me to get you into a communal cell? Do they chain your feet at night?"

"Yes."

"Then it's better you go into a communal cell. You'll still be chained, but you won't be alone. It must be terrible for you to be in isolation at a time like this."

It was. Isolation was harder to bear than ever. I was in such a sorry state that I didn't even need to close my eyes to have my mind wander in either the past or the present. And not being able to walk made it that much worse.

So there I was right back on the road of the condemned. But hadn't I managed to get away once—and sail toward freedom, toward the joy of being a man again, and toward my revenge too? For I mustn't forget the debt I owed that trio—Polein, those pigs of policemen, and the prosecutor. As for the trunk, there was no need to hand it over to the police at the entrance to Headquarters. I would do it myself, dressed as an employee of Wagon-Lits-Cook, with the fancy company cap on my head. There would be a big tag on the trunk saying, "Commissioner Benoit, 36 Quai des Orfèvres, Paris (Seine)." I'd carry it up to the briefing room myself, having fixed it so the alarm wouldn't go off until I'd left. It couldn't possibly fail.

Finding this solution took a great load off my mind. As for the prosecutor's tongue, I had plenty of time to work that one out. In fact, it was as good as done. I'd tear it out in small pieces; that's what I'd do.

But, meantime, I had to heal my feet so I could walk as soon as possible. I wouldn't go before the tribunal for three months, and in three months a lot could happen. One month to get walking again, one month to make arrangements, then good night, gentlemen. Direction: British Honduras. But this time nobody would get his hands on me.

Yesterday, three days after our return, I was carried into the communal cell. There were forty men there, awaiting their fate. Among their crimes were theft, looting, arson, murder, attempted murder, attempted escape, escape and even cannibalism. There were twenty of us on each side, all chained to the same fifty-foot-long iron bar. At six in the evening each man's left foot was shackled to the bar. At six in the morning the shackles were removed, and we could spend the whole day sitting, walking about, playing checkers, and talking things over in what we called our "promenade"—a sort of alley six feet wide that went the length of the room. There wasn't time to be bored during the day. I had constant visits from people who wanted to hear about the *cavale*. They went out of their minds when I told them that of my own free will I had abandoned my tribe of Guajiros, and Lali and Zoraima.

"What the hell do you want, man?" a guy from Paris asked. "Métros? Elevators? Movies? Electricity? With high-tension wires for working the electric chair? Or did you want to take a bath in the fountain in the Place Pigalle? Are you crazy, man?" the guy continued. "You had two chicks, one more stacked than the other. The whole lot of you spent your time running naked through the woods; you ate, you drank, you hunted. You had the sea, the sun, warm sand, you even had the pearls and oysters free, and you couldn't think of anything better to do than give it all up? And for what? Tell me. So that you can dodge cars in the streets, so that you can pay rent, pay your tailor, your electricity and telephone bill, and if you want a secondhand wreck of a car, you steal or else work like a dog for somebody just to make enough to keep from starving? I don't get it, *mec*! You were in heaven and you willingly return to hell where, on top of the usual problems, you have to keep all those cops off your tail. It's true you're still full of that fresh French blood and you haven't had time to lose your faculties.

I've had ten years in the *bagne* and I don't understand you. Anyway, you're welcome here, and since I can see you want to start all over again, you can count on us to help you. That's right, isn't it, *mecs*?"

The *mecs* agreed, and I thanked them all.

I could see that these were men to be reckoned with. Because of the way we were jammed in together, it was hard to hide the fact that I had a *plan*. At night, since we were all chained to the same bar, it was easy to murder someone. All you had to do was slip a little something to the Arab turnkey during the day so he wouldn't quite close your shackle at night. Then when night came, the would-be killer did his bit, came back to his place, lay down quietly and closed his shackle. Since the Arab was indirectly an accomplice, he kept his mouth shut.

I'd now been back three weeks. The time had gone quite fast. I was beginning to walk a little, holding onto the bar in the passageway between the rows of bunks. Last week, at our interrogation, I caught sight of the three hospital guards we'd knocked out and disarmed. They were clearly delighted to see us back and expressed the fervent hope that we might all find ourselves together in some secluded spot where they could return the compliment. After our *cavale* they had been severely punished: their six months' holiday in France had been canceled, along with their supplementary colonial pay for a year. You might say that our reunion was not exactly cordial. We thought it wise to report this to our interrogators.

The Arab behaved better. He spoke only the truth without exaggerating and skipped over the role played by Maturette. The examining judge kept trying to find out who had provided us with the boat. We didn't help our cause when we told him the unlikely story that we had made a raft ourselves.

Because we had assaulted the guards, he said he would try his best to get Clousiot and me five years and three for Maturette.

"And since your name is Papillon, I think I'll clip your wings so you won't be flying off again very soon."

Only two months to go before I went before the tribunal. I was angry I hadn't put the small poisoned arrows in my *plan*. Maybe if I'd had them, I could have made it from the disciplinary quarter. However, I was making daily progress, walking better and better. François Sierra never missed his morning and evening visits to massage my feet with camphorated oil. He was a great help, both to my feet and to my morale. Thank God for true friends!

I've already mentioned that our long *cavale* had given us great prestige among our fellow convicts. I was certain that we were safe and ran little risk of being killed for our money. Most of the men wouldn't have tolerated it, and I had no doubt that if anybody tried, he'd be killed straight off. Without exception, everybody respected us; they even felt a certain admiration. And since we had dared to knock out the guards, they figured we'd do anything. It was an interesting sensation to feel safe.

Every day I walked a little longer, and Sierra left a little bottle with me so that my friends could massage my feet and the muscles of my legs, which were atrophied from long disuse.

THE *CAVALE* OF THE CANNIBALS

"They ate the wooden leg!" "A little wooden-leg stew, please!" Then a voice imitating a woman's: "Waiter, a piece of well-done *mec* without pepper, please!"

It was a rare night one of these strange phrases didn't shatter the silence. Clousiot and I wondered what it was all about.

I got the key to the mystery one afternoon when one of the men involved told me the story. His name was Marius de La Ciotat and he was a safecracker (like me). When he learned that I knew his father, Titin, he decided to talk to me.

I told him something of my *cavale*, and then I asked him casually, "What about you?"

"Me? Man, I'm really screwed up. I'm afraid I'm going to get five years for a simple escape. I was in the *cavale* they call the 'cannibals' *cavale*.' All that stuff you hear in the night is for the Graville brothers.

"There were six of us who escaped from Kilometer Forty-two. In our *cavale* were Dédé and Jean Graville, two brothers in their thirties from Lyon, an Italian from Marseilles, me from La Ciotat, a *mec* with a wooden leg from Angers and a kid of twenty-three who acted as his wife. We got out of the Maroni fine, but we could never get going once we reached the sea. In a few hours we were beaten back to the Dutch Guiana coast.

"We couldn't save anything from the wreck, no food or anything. We found ourselves in the bush. In that area there's no beach and the sea runs right up into the forest. It's a jungle, and impassable because of the fallen trees uprooted by the sea and all tangled together.

"We walked for a whole day before we reached dry land. Then we split up into three groups: the Graville brothers, me and Guesepi, and the wooden leg with his little friend each went in different directions. To make a long story short, after twelve days we met up with the Graville brothers in almost the exact same spot where we'd separated. The whole place was surrounded by a kind of quicksand and we couldn't find a way out. We had spent thirteen days with nothing to eat but roots and young shoots. We were dying of hunger and fatigue; we were at the end of our rope. It was decided that with what strength we had left Guesepi and I would go back to the coast and hang a shirt as high as possible on a tree and give ourselves up to the first Dutch coast guard that came

along. The two brothers were to rest a few hours, then try to pick
up traces of the other two.

"To make things easier, we agreed when we separated that each
group would indicate where it had gone by cutting branches along
the way.

"A few hours after we left, they saw the man with the wooden
leg coming toward them alone.

" 'Where's the boy?'

" 'I left him way back there; he couldn't walk any more.'

" 'You're a son of a bitch to leave him there alone.'

" 'It was his idea.'

"At that moment Dédé noticed that the guy was wearing the
queer's boot on his good foot.

" 'Along with everything else, you left him barefoot so that you
could wear his shoe? Congratulations! And you look in good
shape, not like the rest of us at all. You must have been eating
well.'

" 'Yes. I found a big wounded monkey.'

" 'Lucky you.' At that, Dédé got up with his knife in his hand.
Wooden-leg's knapsack looked well stuffed, too, and Dédé was
beginning to get the pitch.

" 'Open your knapsack. What you got in it?'

"He opened the sack and in it Dédé saw a piece of flesh.

" 'What's that?'

" 'A piece of the monkey.'

" 'You bastard, you killed your boyfriend and ate him!'

" 'No, Dédé, I swear I didn't. He died of exhaustion and I only
ate a little bit. Don't hold it against me . . . '

"He didn't have time to finish; Dédé's knife was already in his
gut. Then he searched the body and found a leather pouch with
matches and a striking pad.

"Dédé was wild with rage at the thought that the man hadn't

even shared his matches before they separated originally; then, with his hunger being what it was . . . To cut it short, they lit a fire, cooked the *mec* and started to eat him.

"Guesepi arrived in the middle of the feast. They invited him to join in, but he refused. He'd eaten some crabs and raw fish by the edge of the sea. So he watched without taking part as the brothers put more pieces of flesh on the fire, adding the wooden leg to keep the fire going. That day and the next the brothers ate the *mec* and Guesepi looked on, even noting which parts they ate: the shinbone, the thigh and the buttocks.

"I was still waiting by the sea when Guesepi came for me. We filled a hat with small fish and crabs and cooked them on the Gravilles' fire. I didn't see the corpse. They must have dragged it off somewhere. But I did see several pieces of meat scattered about in the ashes.

"Three days later a coast-guard boat picked us up and returned us to the penitentiary at Saint-Laurent.

"Guesepi couldn't keep his mouth shut. Everybody in this room knows the story, even the guards. That's why I've told you and that's why you hear those voices in the night.

"Officially, our offense is attempted escape, aggravated by cannibalism. The bad thing is that, to defend myself, I'd have to expose the others, and I can't do that. Everybody, including Guesepi, would deny it at the interrogation. They'd say that the others disappeared into the bush. And that's my situation, Papillon."

"I'm sorry for you, *mec*. Obviously your only defense is to accuse the others."

A month later, in the middle of the night, someone plunged a knife into Guesepi's heart. We didn't need to guess who'd done it.

* * *

Tonight I took another place along the bar. I replaced a man who had left, and by asking everybody to move over one, I got next to Clousiot.

Where I was now, by sitting up I could see what was going on in the yard, even with my left foot shackled to the bar.

Surveillance was so tight that the rounds had no rhythm. They never stopped, and guards were relieved at any and all times.

My feet bore my weight well now; they hurt only when it rained. I was even considering getting something new under way. But how? There were no windows in the room, only a grill that spanned the entire width and reached up to the roof. It was facing so that it was open to the wind from the northeast. After a week's careful observation I still couldn't find the smallest gap in the surveillance. For the first time I came close to admitting that they'd be locking me up in solitary on Saint-Joseph after all.

Everybody said it was a terrible place. They called it *la mangeuse d'hommes* [the devourer of men]. And another thing: in the eighty years of its existence, no one had ever escaped from it.

This partial acceptance that I'd lost the ball game made me look toward the future. I was twenty-eight, and the judge was going to give me five years in solitary. It would be hard to get away with less. So, by the time I got out, I'd be thirty-three. I still had a lot of money in my *plan*. Therefore, if I didn't escape—and it didn't appear I was going to—the least I could do was keep myself in good health. Five years of complete isolation would be hard to bear without going mad. From the first day of my sentence I would discipline my brain according to a carefully thought-out and varied program: I would avoid as much as possible all dreams of castles in Spain and, particularly, all dreams of revenge. From that moment on I would prepare to surmount the terrible punishment that lay ahead. Yes. I'd make it a big waste of their time. I'd leave solitary strong and in full possession of my mental and moral faculties.

I felt better for having set up my code of behavior and accepted with a certain serenity what lay ahead.

I was the first to feel the breeze that penetrated the room. It felt good. Clousiot knew when I didn't want to talk; he just went on smoking. A few stars were out. I asked him, "Can you see the stars from where you are?"

"Yes," he said, leaning forward a little. "I don't like to look at them. They remind me too much of our *cavale*."

"Don't take it so hard. You'll be seeing thousands of them on our next one."

"When? In five years?"

"Clousiot, don't you think the year we've just spent, the adventures and the people we got to know are worth five years in solitary? Would you rather have been on the islands all this time? Knowing what lies ahead—and I grant you it's going to be tough—how do you really feel about our *cavale*? Tell me the truth. Do you regret it or not?"

"Papi, you forget you had something I didn't: your seven months with the Indians. If I'd been with you, I might agree. But I was in prison."

"I'm sorry. I wasn't thinking."

"That's O.K. Sure, I'm glad we had our *cavale* because I had some good times too. It's only that I'm a little worried about what to expect at *la mangeuse d'hommes*. I don't know if it's possible to last five years there."

I explained my plan and he seemed to think it a good idea. I was glad to see his spirits pick up. We were to appear before the tribunal in fifteen days. According to rumor, the presiding officer was severe but fair. He wouldn't be a pushover for the Administration's lies, and that was good news.

Clousiot and I refused to use a guard as our lawyer. We decided that I should speak for the three of us and that I'd handle our defense myself.

THE JUDGMENT

I had a haircut and a shave and was dressed in new denims with red stripes; I was even wearing shoes. We were waiting in the courtyard to go before the tribunal. Clousiot had been without his cast for two weeks now and walked naturally, with no trace of a limp.

The tribunal had begun Monday. It was now Saturday morning. The first five days had been spent on a variety of cases. The Graville brothers got only four years, for lack of proof. Their case took over half a day. The other murder cases got four or five years. In general, among the fourteen cases tried, the sentences were on the severe side, but in proportion to the crime.

The tribunal started at seven-thirty. We were standing in the room when an officer came in dressed in the uniform of the Camel Corps and accompanied by an old infantry captain and a lieutenant who were to serve as assistant judges. On the President's right sat a captain representing the Administration.

"The case of Charrière, Clousiot and Maturette."

We were about twelve feet from the President. I could see the officer's face in detail: it was weathered by the desert, and his hair was silver about the temples. He appeared to be a little over forty years old, with bushy eyebrows and magnificent black eyes that looked right into your own. A real military man. But without meanness. He just looked at us, taking us in. My eyes met his, then I deliberately lowered mine.

The captain representing the Administration overstated his case, and that's what lost it for him. He labeled our knocking out the guards as attempted murder and claimed that it was a miracle the Arab hadn't died from our treatment. Another bad move was when he said that we had brought more dishonor on France than any convicts in the history of the *bagne*: "Mr. President! These men have covered fifteen hundred miles! Trinidad, Curaçao, Colombia—all these countries have had to listen to their smears and lies about the French penal administration! For Charrière and Clousiot, I ask for two sentences to be served consecutively for a total of eight years: five for attempted murder and three for escape. For Maturette, I ask only three years for escape, as the testimony indicates that he did not participate in the attempted murder."

The President spoke. "The tribunal would be interested in hearing a very brief recital of your odyssey."

So I described our trip to Trinidad, skipping over the Maroni part, and told them about the Bowen family and their kindness. I quoted the chief of police in Trinidad: "It's not for British authorities to judge French justice. But what we don't approve of is the way they send their convicts to French Guiana. It's inhuman and unworthy of a civilized nation like France." Then I told them about Irénée de Bruyne of Curaçao, the incident over the bag of florins, then Colombia and why and how we got there. Then I gave them a quick description of my life among the Indians. All the while the President listened without interruption, except when he asked for a few more details about the Indian episode, which seemed to interest him greatly. Then I told him about the Colombian prisons in general, and the underwater dungeon in Santa Marta in particular.

"Thank you. The court has found your recital both enlightening and interesting. We will now have a fifteen-minute recess. Where are your lawyers, the lawyers for the defense? I don't see them."

"We don't have any. I ask that you allow me to speak for our defense."

"You may. It's within the rules."

"Thank you."

The session resumed fifteen minutes later.

The President said, "Charrière, the tribunal authorizes you to present the defense for your friends and yourself. But we must warn you that the tribunal can revoke your right to speak if you show disrespect for the Administration. You are free to offer your defense, but you must do so in a suitable manner. You may begin."

"I ask the tribunal to lay aside only the charge of attempted murder. We don't deserve it, and I can prove it. Last year I was twenty-seven and Clousiot thirty. We were in very good condition, having just arrived from France. We're both big men. We hit the Arab and the guards with the iron legs from our beds. Not one of the four was seriously hurt. We tried as hard as we could not to do them serious harm, and we were successful. The prosecution forgot to say, or didn't know, that we wrapped the iron legs in cloth for that very reason. You men on the tribunal are career officers and you know what a strong man can do when he hits someone, even if it's only with a bayonet butt. So you can imagine what we could have done with these iron legs if we'd wanted to. I want to remind the tribunal that not one of the four men we attacked had to be hospitalized.

"On the second charge, since we all have life sentences, I believe that the offense of escaping is less serious than for a man with a short sentence. At our age it's very hard to accept the idea of never returning to a normal life. I beg the tribunal's indulgence."

The President whispered to the two assistants, then banged on his desk with the gavel.

"Will the accused please stand."

Stiff as ramrods, we stood, waiting.

The President said, "The tribunal has set aside the accusation of attempted murder. For the offense of escaping, we find you guilty in the second degree. The tribunal condemns you to two years in solitary."

We said, "Thank you, sir," and I added, "I thank the tribunal." The guards watching the trial couldn't believe their ears.

When we got back to our friends, everybody was pleased with our news. No one seemed jealous, and even those who hadn't been so lucky congratulated us. François Sierra came and hugged me. He was wild with joy.

SIXTH NOTEBOOK

THE ILES
DU SALUT

THE ARRIVAL

WE WERE TO SAIL TO the islands the next day. For all my long struggle, in a few hours I'd be interned for life, starting with two years in solitary on the Ile Saint-Joseph. I only hoped I could give the lie to its nickname, la *mangeuse d'hommes*.

I had lost the game, but I didn't feel like a loser. I could even be thankful that I'd have only two years in this prison within a prison. As I had promised myself, I would not give in to the mental aberrations that complete isolation induced. I had a good remedy: from the very start I would think of myself as free, healthy in mind and body—an ordinary convict on the islands. And I'd be only thirty when I got out.

I knew that escapes from the islands were few and far between. But even if you could count them only on one hand, some men had managed it. And so I'd escape, and that was that. I told Clousiot that in two years I'd make my escape.

"Papillon, there's just no way to keep you down, is there? I wish I had as much faith as you do. You've been trying *cavales* for a year now and you still haven't given up. No sooner does one go up in smoke than you start another. I'm surprised you haven't tried one from here."

"*Mec*, from here there's only one way: to start a revolt. And I don't have the time to organize all these bastards. I almost started one, and it damn near swallowed me up. The forty men here are old cons. They've been taken in by the system; they don't react the way we do. Take those cannibals, and the one who put poison in the soup and killed seven innocent men just to get one: they aren't like us."

"But everybody'll be like that on the islands."

"Sure, but to escape from the islands, I won't need anybody. I'll do it alone or, at most, with one other man. Why are you smiling?"

"Because of the way you won't give up. Because you're so fired up with the idea of getting back to Paris and getting even with your buddies that you won't believe it can't be done."

"Good night, Clousiot. See you tomorrow. I guess we're going to see the Iles du Salut after all. But what I want to know is why these goddamned islands are called 'the islands of salvation.' "

I turned away from Clousiot and leaned out to catch the night wind.

We set off for the islands early the next morning. There were twenty-six of us on a forty-ton tub called the *Tanon,* a coastal boat that shuttled between Cayenne, the islands and Saint-Laurent. Two by two, we were chained by the feet and handcuffed. Two groups of eight men in the bow with four guards, their guns at the ready. Then came a group of ten at the stern with six guards and the two escort leaders. Everybody was on deck, and the boat was clearly ready to go under at the first sign of bad weather.

I had decided not to think during the trip, so I looked around for some sort of distraction. Just to annoy him, I said to a gloomy-looking guard standing near, "With these chains, we don't have a prayer if the boat sinks. In view of its punk condition, that's very likely in a heavy sea."

Barely awake, the guard reacted as I had anticipated he would. "Go ahead and drown; we don't give a damn. We have orders to chain you and that's it. The responsibility is with the people who give the orders. We're in the clear."

"Quite right, sir. With or without chains, if this coffin splits open, we'll all go to the bottom together."

"Oh," the idiot replied, "this boat's been making this trip for a long time and nothing's happened yet."

"Exactly. It's been around so long that something's bound to happen sooner or later." I'd accomplished my goal; the nerve-racking silence was broken. Other guards and convicts immediately joined the conversation. One of the cons said, "This boat is dangerous, and on top of that, we're in chains. Without chains, we might at least have a chance."

The guards replied, "We're no better off. We have our uniforms, boots and guns. They're not all that light either."

"The guns don't count. If there's a shipwreck, you get rid of them right away."

Seeing that I'd hit the mark, I tried a second ploy. "Where are the lifeboats? I can only see one and it will take eight men at the most. The commander and the crew would fill it straight off. As for the others, who gives a damn?"

We were off and running.

"That's right. There isn't anything. It's the worst kind of irresponsibility to permit fathers of families to risk their lives for this batch of monsters."

I was in the group at the stern of the boat with the two leaders of the convoy.

One of them looked at me and said, "Are you Papillon, the one who came back from Colombia?"

"Yes."

"It doesn't surprise me you got so far. You seem to know a lot about the sea."

I stuck out my chest. "Yes, I do know a lot."

That cooled him. On top of that, the captain came down off the bridge to meet me. He had stayed at the helm while we were in the Maroni estuary: that was the most dangerous part of the trip. But now that we were out, he had turned it over to someone else. So this fat little black man asked to meet the jokers who had gone all the way to Colombia on a piece of kindling wood.

"It was this one, that one, and the one over there," said the convoy leader.

"Which one was the captain?" asked the little man.

"I was, sir."

"Well, kid, I want to congratulate you. You're no ordinary guy. Here!" And he put his hand in the pocket of his jacket. "Take this package of tobacco and the cigarette papers. Be my guest!"

"Thanks, sir. And I congratulate you for having the courage to sail this hearse."

He burst out laughing. This was more than the guards could stand.

He said, "You're right there! This tub should have been sent to the graveyard long ago, but the company's waiting for it to sink to collect the insurance."

I made a final thrust. "Aren't you lucky you and the crew have a lifeboat?"

"Yes, aren't we, though?" he said without thinking, and disappeared up the stairs.

The sea was fairly calm, but the wind was against us. We were going northeast, which meant heading into the wind and the waves, and this made the boat roll and pitch. Several guards and cons were sick. Luckily the man chained to me was a good sailor. There's nothing worse than having to watch someone throw up. My neighbor was a real street-type from Paris. He'd come to the *bagne* in '27, which meant he'd been on the islands seven years. He was relatively young—thirty-eight. "I'm called Titi la Belote, and if I do say so, belote is my strong suit. It's what I live on on the islands. Belote all night at two francs a point."

"You mean there's that much money on the islands?"

"You bet there is, *mec*! The islands are full of *plans* bursting with cash. Some have it all on them, others pay half and get the rest from guards who act as brokers. I can see you're new here, friend. You don't seem to know anything."

"No, I don't know much about the islands. All I know is it's hard to escape."

"Escape?" Titi said. "Forget it. I've been on the islands for seven years, and during that time there's been two *cavales*. Result: three dead and two caught. And nobody got away. That's why there's not too many candidates willing to take the chance."

"Why have you been on Grande Terre?"

"I went for X-rays to see if I had an ulcer."

"And you didn't try to escape from the hospital?"

"Look who's talking. You're the one who ruined everything. What's more, I ended up in the same room you escaped from. You should have seen the security! Every time I went near a window for a breath of air, somebody made me pull back. And when I asked why, they said, 'Just in case you start doing a Papillon.' "

"Tell me, Titi, who's the big guy sitting next to the leader of the convoy? Is he a stoolie?"

"Are you crazy? That *mec* is O.K. He may not be a 'pro,' but he knows how to handle himself. He doesn't hang around the guards and he asks no favors; he's very careful about his rank as a con. He gives good advice, he's a good pal, he keeps his distance from the pigs. Even the priest and the doctor can't get to him. He may look like a stoolie, but the fact is he's a descendant of Louis the Fifteenth. That's right, pal. He's a count, a real count, and his name is Count Jean de Bérac. After he arrived, it took him a long time to win the men over because what he did to get here was pretty awful."

"What did he do?"

"He threw his kid off a bridge into a stream. But the boy landed in a shallow place, so he went down, picked him up and dumped him where the water was deeper."

"Jesus! That's like killing the kid twice!"

"A friend of mine who's a trustworthy guy saw his file and says the *mec* was scared stiff because he was a blueblood. The little kid's mother was a servant in the castle, and his mother had kicked her out like a dog. Apparently the guy was dominated by his mother. The arrogant old bitch had humiliated him so much for having relations with a servant girl he didn't know what he was doing. So he threw the kid in the water, although he had told his mother he was taking him to the welfare people."

"What was his sentence?"

"Only ten years. I tell you, he's not like the rest of us, Papillon. The mother told the magistrates that killing a servant's kid wasn't really such a serious offense if it was done by a count trying to protect his family's honor."

"So?"

"Well, I'm just a street Arab from Paris, but here's what I think: basically this Count Jean de Bérac was a hick who had been brought up to think that the only thing that mattered was position. Maybe their servants weren't exactly serfs, but they were certainly beneath consideration. And his monster of a mother had ground him down and terrorized him to the point where he'd become almost like one of the servants. It's only in the *bagne* that this man with his *droits du seigneur* has become a true nobleman. It may sound crazy, but it's only now that he's really become Count Jean de Bérac."

In a few minutes the Iles du Salut would no longer be an unknown quantity. All I knew now was that they were hard to escape from, but not impossible. . . . As I took in great gulps of the sea breeze, I thought: When will this head wind turn into a tail wind and carry me back to freedom?

We had arrived. The islands made a triangle, with Royale and Saint-Joseph at the base and Diable at the top. The sun was already low, but it picked them out with that intensity of light you find only in the tropics. Royale had a flat coastline, then rose six hundred feet to a plateau. It looked like a Mexican hat with its crown cut off, floating on the sea. And everywhere, very green coconut palms. Small houses with red roofs gave the island an unusual charm, and if you didn't know what was there besides, you might want to live there the rest of your life. There was also a lighthouse on the coast to keep ships from breaking up on the rocks. Now that we were nearer, I could make out five large, long buildings. Titi told me that two of them were vast halls where four hundred cons lived. Then there was the maximum-security quarter with its cells and dungeons surrounded by a high white wall. The fourth building was the cons' hospital, and the fifth was where most of the guards lived, the others being scattered over the slopes in the small houses with the red tile roofs. Farther on, but very near the tip of Royale, was Saint-Joseph. Fewer palms there, less greenery and, on the top, one large building. I guessed it must be the Réclusion [Solitary], and Titi confirmed it. He pointed out, near the water's edge, the camp buildings where the cons with regular sentences lived. The watchtowers and battlements stood out clearly. It also had the tidy little white houses with red roofs.

The boat made for Ile Royale from the south and we lost sight of Diable. From what I'd been able to see, it was one enormous rock covered with coconut palms and no buildings of any size; only a few houses by the water's edge painted yellow with gray roofs. I learned later that this was where the political prisoners lived.

We were now coming into the port of Royale, which was protected by a big jetty made of huge blocks. To build it must have cost the life of many a con!

Three blasts of the siren and the *Tanon* dropped anchor about two hundred and fifty yards from the pier, which was a long, well-built quay ten feet high made of cement and large pebbles. Facing us was a row of white buildings, with signs painted in black: "Poste de Garde [Guard Station]," "Service de Canots [Navigation]," "Boulangerie [Bakery]," "Administration du Port [Port Administration]."

We could see convicts watching the boat come in. They weren't wearing stripes, but pants and a kind of white jacket. Titi la Belote told me that on the islands, if you had any money, you had yourself done up by the local tailors. They used flour sacks with the printing removed, which made comfortable outfits with even a certain chic. Hardly anybody wore the convict's uniform.

A launch approached the *Tanon*. There was one guard at the

tiller, two armed guards with carbines on his left and right, and behind him, six cons naked from the waist up and standing as they rowed. They made quick work of the crossing. A large empty lifeboat was roped to the stern. Once the launch was tied fast, the two convoy leaders got off and took up positions in the stern. They were followed by two armed guards who went to the bow. Still handcuffed, but with our feet unshackled, we got into the boat in pairs, first the ten in my group, then the eight who had been in the bow. The cons started to row away; they'd return for the rest of the group later. We were let off at the pier and waited in line in front of the building marked "Administration du Port." We had no packs. The cons standing about paid no attention to the guards and talked to us in loud voices, though at a safe distance of five or six yards. Several had been in my convoy and gave me a friendly greeting. César and Essari, two Corsican bandits I'd known at Saint-Martin, told me they were rowers for the Navigation Service. Then up came Chapar, who I'd known before my arrest in France. Without a thought for the guards, he said, "Don't you worry, Papillon! You can count on your friends. You won't lack for anything in solitary. What did they give you?"

"Two years."

"Not bad. It's over fast enough and you'll be back here before you know it. You'll see. Things aren't so bad here."

"Thanks, Chapar. Where's Dega?"

"He's a clerk up on the hill. I'm surprised he isn't here. He'll be sorry he missed you."

At that point Galgani came up to me. A guard tried to stop him, but he pushed him aside, saying, "You can't stop me from greeting my brother!" He embraced me and said, "Count on me."

"What are you doing here?"

"I'm in the Postal Service."

"How are things?"

"Not bad."

The last ones had arrived and joined us. Our handcuffs were removed. A guard said to Titi la Belote, Bérac and a few others, "Let's go. Off to camp." They had their packs from the *bagne*. They slung them over their shoulders and took the path that led to the top of the island. The warden arrived with six guards. They took the roll call. Everybody was present. Our escorts withdrew.

"Where's the clerk?" the warden asked.

"He's on his way, chief."

I saw Dega coming, handsomely dressed in white with a buttoned jacket. He and the guard accompanying him each carried a big book. One by one we stepped out of the line and were given our new classification: "Prisoner in solitary so-and-so, transportee identification number X, you are now solitary, identification number Z."

When it came my turn, Dega walked up and hugged me.

The warden asked, "Is that Papillon?"

"Yes, sir," Dega said.

"Good luck in solitary. Two years pass quickly."

SOLITARY

The boat was ready. Of the nineteen of us, ten were to go in the first lot. I was called. Dega said crisply, "No, he goes on the last trip."

I was astonished at the way the *bagnards* talked. There seemed to be no discipline; they didn't give a damn for the guards. Dega came over and we started talking. He knew all about my escape. He had heard it from some men I'd known in Saint-Laurent who had come to the islands. He didn't say he was sorry for me; that would have been beneath him. What he did say was, "You deserved to succeed, my boy. But you'll make it next time!" He didn't say "Chin up." He knew I didn't need it.

"I'm the chief clerk and I've got an in with the warden. Take care of yourself in solitary and I'll send you tobacco and food. You'll have everything you need."

"Papillon, let's go!" It was my turn.

"Good-by, everybody. Thanks for your kind words."

I stepped into the boat. Twenty minutes later we docked at Saint-Joseph. I took note of the fact that we had only three armed guards aboard for six rowers and ten solitaries. It would have been a cinch to take over the boat. . . . At Saint-Joseph we were met by a reception committee headed by the warden of the penitentiary on the island and the warden at the Réclusion. As we entered the large iron gate with "Réclusion Disciplinaire" written above, I realized that this prison was no joking matter. The gate and the high surrounding walls obscured at first a little building marked "Administration-Direction" and three other buildings marked A, B and C. We went into Direction. It was cold.

We were lined up in two rows and the warden said, "*Réclusionnaires*, as you know, this prison is for the punishment of offenses committed by men already condemned to the *bagne*. Here we don't try rehabilitation. We know it's useless. We try to break you. We have only one rule: keep your mouth shut. Absolute silence. If you get caught trying to 'telephone,' you risk an even heavier sentence. Unless you're seriously ill, don't ask to go to the infirmary. You'll be punished for an unwarranted medical call. That's all I have to say. Oh, one thing more—smoking is strictly forbidden. All right, guards, let's get going. Search them thoroughly, then put each one in a cell. Don't put Charrière, Clousiot and Maturette in the same building. Mr. Santori, will you see to this, please."

Ten minutes later I was locked up in my cell—number 234 in Building A. Clousiot was in B, Maturette in C. We said a mute good-by. Each of us understood that if we ever wanted to get out of here alive, we would have to obey their beastly rules. I watched them go, my companions of our long *cavale*, proud and brave comrades who never complained and never regretted what we'd brought off together. The fourteen months of our struggle for freedom had forged an unbreakable bond between us. I felt sick at heart.

I looked around my cell. It was hard to believe that a country like mine, France, the cradle of liberty for the entire world, the land which gave birth to the Rights of Man, could maintain, even in French Guiana, on a tiny island lost in the Atlantic, an installation as barbarously repressive as the Réclusion of Saint-Joseph. Imagine one hundred and fifty cells, back to back, their four thick walls pierced only by a small iron door with a wicket. Painted above each wicket was the warning: "Do not open this door without special permission." On the left was a wooden bunk with a wooden pillow, just like Beaulieu. The bunk folded back and hooked to the wall; there was a blanket, a cement block in the corner to sit on, a hand broom, a mug, a wooden spoon, and a metal sheet hiding a pail attached to it by a chain so that it could be pulled outside the cell to empty it, and pulled back in when you needed to use it. The cell was nine feet high. Its ceiling was made of iron bars as thick as streetcar tracks, so close together that nothing of any size could get through. Above that was the actual roof of the building, about twenty-two feet above the ground. Above the cells and looking down on them was a walk a yard wide with an iron railing, where two guards paced back and forth from opposite ends, stopping when they met and turning to retrace their steps. There was a little light at the top, but at the bottom of the cell you could barely see even in broad daylight. I started immediately to walk, waiting for the whistle to signal the lowering of the bunks. To avoid the slightest noise, both prisoners and guards wore slippers. I said to myself, "Charrière, you're here in number two thirty-four; try to live for two years without going crazy. That's seven hundred and thirty days. It's up to you to give the lie to that Réclusion nickname—*la mangeuse d'hommes*."

One, two, three, four, five and turn. One, two, three, four, five and turn. The guard just passed over my roof. I didn't hear him come. Suddenly he was there. The light came on, but very high up; it hung from the top roof twenty feet above. The walk was lighted, but the cells remained in the dark. I walked. The pendulum was back and swinging. Sleep in peace, you members of the jury who condemned me to this place; sleep in peace, for I do believe that if you had known what you were really doing, you would have pulled back. It was going to be difficult to keep my imagination from wandering. Almost impossible. Better to direct it toward less depressing subjects than to try to suppress it altogether.

The blast of a whistle announced that we could let down our bunks.

A deep voice said, "For the new men: Now you can let down your bunks and lie down if you want to." He said, ". . . if you want to." Therefore I kept on walking; it was too crucial a moment to sleep. I had to get used to this cage. One, two, three, four, five; right away I picked up the rhythm of the pendulum: head lowered, hands clasped behind my back, the length of the paces exactly right, a pendulum swinging back and forth, interminably. It was like sleepwalking. At the end of the five steps I didn't even see the wall but grazed it on the turn in this marathon without beginning or end.

It's a fact, Papi: *la mangeuse d'hommes* is no joke.

It was a weird effect when the guard's shadow hit the wall. If you lifted up your head to look at him, it was even worse: you felt like a leopard in a pit being watched by the hunter who'd just caught you. It took me months to get used to that awful sensation.

One year equals three hundred and sixty-five days, two years, seven hundred and thirty days, unless one's a leap year. I smiled at the thought. One day more wouldn't matter much. The hell it wouldn't! One day more is twenty-four hours more. And twenty-four hours is a long time. And seven hundred and thirty days each made up of twenty-four hours is one hell of a lot more. How many hours does that make? Can I figure it in my head? No, I can't; it's impossible. Why, of course, it's possible. Let's see. A hundred days, that's twenty four hundred hours. Multiplied by seven—it's easy—it makes sixteen thousand eight hundred hours, plus the thirty remaining days times twenty-four, which makes seven hundred and twenty hours. Total: sixteen thousand eight hundred, plus seven hundred and twenty, which makes, if I haven't made a mistake, seventeen thousand five hundred and twenty hours. My dear Mr. Papillon, you have seventeen thousand five hundred and twenty hours to kill in this cage with its smooth walls especially designed for wild animals. And how many minutes? Who gives a shit! Hours is one thing, but minutes? To hell with minutes. Why not seconds? What does it matter? What matters is that I have to furnish these days, hours and minutes with something, all by myself, alone! I wonder who's on my right, on my left, behind me. If those cells are occupied, the men in them must be wondering who just moved into 234.

I heard the quiet thud of something falling into the cell. What could it be? Could my neighbor be agile enough to throw something through the grill? I tried to figure out what it was. I could just make out something long and thin. Then as I was on the point of picking it up, the thing started to move toward the wall. I jumped back. As it reached the wall, it tried to climb up but fell to the ground. The wall was so smooth it couldn't get a grip. I watched it try three times; when it fell on the fourth attempt, I squashed it under my foot. It was soft. What could it be? I got down on my knees to see it as best I could and made out an enormous centipede over eight inches long and wider than two fat fingers. It was so disgusting I couldn't bring myself to pick it up and throw it into the pail. Instead I pushed it under the bunk with my foot. I'd do something about it tomorrow, in the daylight. I was to see plenty of centipedes; they fell from the upper roof. When I was lying down, I learned to let them walk over my naked body without disturbing them. I had learned what a tactical error could cost. One sting from the revolting beast and you had a terrible burn for almost six hours and a raging fever for twelve.

However, it was a distraction. If a centipede fell when I was awake, I'd torment it with the broom, or I'd amuse myself by letting it hide from me; then a few moments later I'd go find it. . . .

One, two, three, four, five. . . . Complete silence. Doesn't anybody snore here? Anybody cough? The heat is suffocating and it's night. It must be hell during the day! It seemed I was destined to live with centipedes. When the water rose in the dungeon at Santa Marta, they came in large numbers, but they were smaller. The same family, however. At Santa Marta we had the daily flooding, but at least we could talk, shout, sing, or listen to the screams of the ones who were going nuts. It wasn't the same. If I had to choose, I'd take Santa Marta. You're crazy, Papillon. Over there, there was a unanimous opinion that the most a man could stand was six months. Here there are lots who have to do four and five years and even more. It's one thing to give a man that sentence; it's quite another to serve it. How many kill themselves? I don't see any way to do it. Yes, I do. It wouldn't be easy, but you could hang yourself. You could make a cord out of your pants and tie one end to the broom. Then, by standing on the bunk, you'd be able to slip the cord around one of the bars. If you got flush with the wall, the guard might not see the cord. And immediately after he'd passed by, you'd let yourself go. By the time he came around again, you'd already be cooked. And besides, he'd be unlikely to hurry down to your cell to unhang you. How could he open the cell door? He couldn't. It says on the door: "Do not open this door without special permission." So, nothing to worry about. Anyone who wants to kill himself has all the time he needs before the "special permission" unhooks him.

All this may not be very interesting to people who like action and confrontations. You can skip these pages if you're bored. However, I feel obligated to describe as faithfully as possible my first impressions of my new cell and my reaction to those first hours of entombment.

I'd been walking a long time. My ears picked out a murmur in the night—the changing of the guard. The first guard was a tall, bony man; the new one was small and fat. He dragged his slippers. I could hear them scraping along two cells before mine and two after. He wasn't 100 percent silent like his comrade. I went on walking. It must be late. What time? I wondered. Tomorrow I'd get back some sense of time. I had to open the wicket in my door four times a day; that would give me an approximate idea. During the night, knowing when the first guard came on duty and the length of his watch, I'd be able to figure out the time by when the second came on, then the third, and so on.

One, two, three, four, five. . . . I automatically resumed my endless walk and, with the help of fatigue, took flight into the past. To fight the darkness of my cell, I sat down in the full sunlight of the beach with my tribe. The boat Lali was fishing from rocked on the opal sea about two hundred yards offshore. I dug my feet into the sand. Zoraima brought me a large fish cooked over the coals and wrapped in a banana leaf to hold in the heat. I ate with my fingers, and she watched me as she sat cross-legged in front of me.

She was happy to see that the big flakes separated neatly from the fish, and she read in my face how good it tasted.

I was far away from my cell. I hadn't heard of the Réclusion, or Saint-Joseph, or the islands. I rolled on the beach and cleaned my hands by rubbing them in the coral sand—so fine you would have said it was flour. Then I walked to the sea to rinse my mouth in that wonderfully clear and salty water. I cupped the water in my hands and splashed it on my face. As I rubbed my neck, I realized how long my hair had grown. When Lali came back, I'd have her cut it. I spent the whole night with my tribe. I undid Zoraima's loincloth, and there on the sand, in full daylight with the sea breeze caressing us, I took her. She moaned with love as she did when she felt special pleasure. Perhaps the wind carried this amorous music to Lali. Perhaps she saw us and knew we were making love. Yes, she must have seen us, for the boat was coming back to shore. She stepped out, smiling. On the way back she had untied her hair and shaken the wet strands with her long fingers to dry it in the glorious sun. I went up to her. She put her right arm around my waist and pulled me up the beach toward our hut. As we walked, it was clear what she was thinking: "What about me?" In the house she pushed me down on a folded hammock and, once inside her, I forgot that the world existed. Zoraima came in when she knew our lovemaking was over. Sated with love, we lay naked on the hammock. She sat down next to us and tapped her sister's cheek with her fingers, repeating a word that must have meant something like "glutton." Then she rearranged my loincloth and Lali's with a gesture of tender modesty.

I spent the entire night in Guajira, not sleeping a wink. I didn't even lie down. I just kept on walking in a kind of trance, transported to a delicious day I'd lived six months before.

The light went out and I could see daylight begin to invade the shadows of the cell, chasing away the floating mist that enveloped everything around me. Then came the sound of the whistle and the bunks slamming against the wall; I even heard my neighbor's hook as he fixed it to the ring. He coughed and I heard the sound of water. How did you wash in this place?

"Guard, please, how do you wash in this place?"

"*Réclusionnaire*, I'll excuse you since you're new. But remember, you get punished for talking to a guard. To wash yourself, you stand over the pail and pour from the pot of water with one hand as you clean yourself with the other. Didn't you unfold your blanket?"

"No."

"You'll find a towel inside it."

How about that! You can't even talk to a guard. Not for any reason. Not even if you're in pain, or about to croak, or if you have a heart attack, or appendicitis, or an attack of asthma. You can't call for help even if it's a matter of life or death? It's incredible. On the other hand, it's not really so incredible. It would be too easy to create a disturbance when you were at the end of your resistance, when your nerves had snapped. Just to hear voices, just to have somebody speak to you even if he only said, "Go ahead and croak, but shut up." But it's a sure thing that out of the two hundred and fifty poor bastards here, someone will provoke some kind of dialogue to let off—like a safety valve—the intolerable pressure in his head.

No psychiatrist could have thought up these cages; no doctor would have so disgraced himself. And certainly no doctor was responsible for the regulations. But the two who did plan this place—the architect and the bureaucrat—and worked out the details of the punishment must have been loathsome monsters, vicious and cunning psychopaths wallowing in sadistic hatred for the prisoners.

From the dungeons in Beaulieu and Caen, as deep as they were, there was a chance that echoes of the tortures and the horrible treatment inflicted on the prisoners might filter up and eventually reach the public's ear. The proof of this was that, when they'd taken off my handcuffs and thumbscrews, I saw real fear on the guards' faces—even if it was only the fear of troublesome complications.

But here, in the Réclusion, where only officials of the Administration knew what was going on, they were safe.

Clack, clack, clack, all the wickets opened. I moved over to mine, risked putting my eye to it, then stuck my head out a little, and finally put my whole head out in the corridor. There, on my left and my right, was a whole multitude of heads. Obviously, the minute the wickets opened, everybody did what I'd done. The one on my right looked at me without a trace of expression. Brutalized by masturbation, probably. His blank idiot's face was wan and sweaty. The one on my left asked quickly, "How long?"

"Two years."

"I have four. I've done one. What's your name?"

"Papillon."

"Mine's Georges, 'Jojo l'Auvergnat.' Where'd they get you?"

"Paris. What about you?"

He didn't have time to answer. The guards carrying the coffee and bread were two cells away from mine. He pulled in his head; I did the same. I held out my mug and they filled it with coffee and gave me my bread. But I wasn't quick enough: as they closed the wicket, the bread rolled onto the floor. In less than fifteen minutes silence had returned. At noon we got soup with a piece of boiled meat. At night, a bowl of lentils. For two years the menu changed only at night: lentils, kidney beans, split peas, chick-peas, white beans and rice with fat. The noon meal was always the same.

Every two weeks we put our heads out and a con with barber's shears cut our beards.

I'd been here three days. I began to worry. At Royale my friends had told me they'd be sending me food and tobacco. I hadn't received anything yet, and furthermore, I couldn't see how such a miracle could be brought off. I wasn't surprised I hadn't received anything. The cigarettes didn't matter; it would be dangerous to smoke, and besides, it was a luxury. But food was vital. The soup at noon was only hot water with two or three green leaves floating around and a little piece of meat weighing perhaps four ounces. At night we got a ladleful of water with a few dried peas or beans swimming about. To be honest, I didn't so much suspect the Administration of not giving us proper rations as I did the cons who prepared and distributed the food. This occurred to me because some nights there was a little guy from Marseilles who doled out the vegetables and his ladle went right down to the bottom of the pot, giving us more beans than water. The others did just the opposite. They stirred a little, then skimmed the water off the top. Lots of water, few beans. This undernourishment was very dangerous. To keep up your morale, a certain degree of physical strength was essential.

They were sweeping the corridor, and it seemed to me they swept a long time outside my cell. The broom kept pushing against my door. I looked closely and noticed a piece of white paper poking through. Somebody was trying to slip me something under the door and couldn't get it any farther. They were waiting for me to pick it up before moving on. I reached for it and unfolded a note written in phosphorescent ink. I waited until the guard had passed by and read:

"Papi, starting tomorrow you'll find five cigarettes and a coconut in your pail every day. Chew the coconut well if you want to get the most out of it, then swallow the pulp. Smoke in the morning when they're emptying the pails, or right after the noon and evening meals, but never after morning coffee. Enclosed is a pencil stub and a piece of paper. If you ever need anything, write it down, and when the man sweeps outside your cell, scratch the door with your fingers. If he scratches back, slip him the paper. Don't ever give him the paper before he's scratched back. Hide the paper behind your ear so you don't have to use your *plan*, and put the pencil somewhere at the base of the wall. Chin up. We send love. Ignace—Louis."

The message was from Galgani and Dega. A feeling of warmth crept up my throat. To have such faithful and devoted friends was a very warming thing. With even greater faith in the future and the certainty that I'd get out of this tomb alive, I started off with a gay and sprightly step: one, two, three, four, five and turn. . . . As I walked, I thought how remarkable those two men were. They must run a grave risk, perhaps even the risk of losing their jobs. What a wonderful gesture, not to mention how expensive it must have been. The number of people they must have had to buy off between Royale and my cell!

I should explain that dried coconut is so full of oil that if you grate six coconuts and soak the pulp in warm water, you can skim a quart of it off the top the next day. This oil made up for the lack of fat in our diet and was full of vitamins as well. A coconut a day almost guaranteed good health or, at the very least, prevented dehydration and death from starvation.

For over two months I received food and cigarettes without interruption. I took every kind of precaution when I smoked, inhaling the smoke deep down, then letting it out only a little at a time while fanning it away with my right hand.

A funny thing happened one day. I don't know whether I did the right thing or not. A guard up on the walk leaned over the railing and peered into my cell. He lit a cigarette and, after a couple of drags, let it fall into my cell. Then he walked on. I waited for him to come back and then made a big thing of crushing the cigarette with my foot. He stopped to watch me, then moved on. Had he felt pity for me? Was he ashamed of the Administration he belonged to? Or was it a trap? I didn't know, and it bothered me. When you're suffering, you're oversensitive to everything. If this guard was trying to be kind, I didn't want to hurt him with a gesture of contempt.

As I said, I'd been here over two months. It was clear to me that at the Réclusion escape was impossible. A deal, a "combination," was out of the question. So I worked on splitting myself in two and developed a foolproof method: in order to roam among the stars, to summon up various stages in my life or build my amazingly realistic castles in Spain, I first had to tire myself out. I would walk for hours without sitting down, never stopping, thinking about nothing in particular. Once I was truly exhausted, I stretched out on my bunk and wrapped the blanket around my head. This way, the little air there was in my cell was further cut off. My lungs became asphyxiated and my head started to burn. Suffocating with the heat and lack of air, I suddenly found myself in flight. Ah! What indescribable sensations! I spent nights of love that were more intense than real ones. I could sit down with my mother, dead these seventeen years. I could play with her dress while she stroked my curls, which she had left long to make me look like a girl. I caressed her slender fingers, her soft silky skin. She laughed over my foolish desire to dive into the river as I had seen the big boys do one day on a walk. I even saw the way she wore her hair, the love that flowed from her bright eyes, her gentle words: "My little Riri, you must be good, you must be very good so that your mummy can love you a lot. Later on, when you're a little bigger, you can dive into the river too. You're too small now, my treasure. The day will come soon, too soon, when you'll be a big boy."

Hand in hand, we followed the river home. I was actually there, in the house of my childhood. I held my hands over my mother's eyes so that she had to play the piano without looking at the music. I was there; it wasn't my imagination. I was with her, standing on a chair behind the piano stool, and I pressed my small hands against her large eyes so she couldn't see. Her nimble fingers continued to skim over the piano until she had played "The Merry Widow" to the end.

Neither you, inhuman prosecutor, nor you, dishonest policemen, nor you, miserable Polein, who bought your liberty for the price of a lie, nor the twelve jurymen who were such cheeseheads they believed the lot of you, nor the guards here in the Réclusion—worthy associates of *la mangeuse d'hommes*—no one, absolutely no one, not even these thick walls, nor the remoteness of this island lost in the Atlantic, nothing, nothing physical or mental, can stop my delicious wanderings, bathed in the rosy hue of bliss.

When I figured out earlier how much time I would be spending with myself, I was wrong to limit it to hours. There were times when it should have been measured in minutes. For example, the emptying of the pails took place about an hour after the distribution of the morning coffee and bread. It was with the return of the empty pail that I received the coconut, the five cigarettes and sometimes a note. Not every time, but often enough, I'd count the time in minutes. It wasn't hard, for I'd adjusted my steps to one to the second, and with my body acting as a pendulum, I arrived at the turn at the end of five steps and mentally registered "one." When I reached twelve, a minute had passed. But don't think it was the food I was worried about—the coconut my life depended on—or the cigarettes—the exquisite pleasure of being able to smoke ten times every twenty-four hours (for I cut each cigarette in half). No. About coffee time I was often seized with a fear that something might have happened to the people who were helping me at the risk of their own necks. It was only when I saw the coconut that I could relax. It was there; therefore all was well *with them*.

Slowly, very slowly, the hours, the days, the weeks, the months passed by. I'd been here almost a year. For exactly eleven months and twenty days I had not spoken with anyone for more than forty seconds, and then only in chopped sentences that were more murmured than said. I did have one exchange in a normal voice. I'd caught a cold and was coughing a lot. Thinking this justified a visit to the infirmary, I reported sick.

The doctor came. The wicket opened and a head appeared.

"What's the matter with you? Bronchitis? Turn around. Cough."

Was this a joke? No, it was true, absolutely true. Somewhere they'd turned up a doctor, and he'd come to examine me through my wicket at a distance of three feet and put his ear to the opening in order to listen to my chest. Then he said, "Stick your arm through." I was about to when I felt a sudden surge of self-respect and said, "Thanks, Doc, but don't bother. It isn't worth it." At least I let him know I didn't take his examination seriously.

"It's up to you," he replied in a cynical tone and left. Luckily, for I was about to explode with anger.

One, two, three, four, five and turn. One, two, three, four, five and turn. I marched, I marched without stopping, I marched with fury, my legs tense. After what had happened, I needed to trample on something. What? Under my feet was only cement. But there were still plenty of things to trample on. I trampled on that ass of a doctor who, to be in the good graces of the Administration, lent himself to such a farce. I trampled on the indifference of men to the suffering and pain of others. I trampled on the ignorance of the French people and their indifference to the human cargo that left Saint-Martin-de-Ré every two years—to where it went and how it was treated. I trampled on the reporters who spread a man's name all over the front page and forgot he existed a few months later. I trampled on the Catholic priests who heard the confessions and therefore knew what was going on in the *bagne* and said nothing. I trampled on the nature of our trials which were nothing but oratorical joustings between accuser and accused. I trampled on the League for the Rights of Man which wouldn't lift a voice to say, "Stop your dry guillotine, forbid the collective sadism of the Administration and its employees!" I trampled on the fact that no group or association ever asked those responsible for the system why 80 percent of its population disappeared down the road of the condemned every two years. I trampled on the death notices handed out by the official doctors: suicide, illness, death from continued undernourishment, scurvy, tuberculosis, raging madness, senility. I don't know on what else I trampled. But after what had just happened, I couldn't bring myself to walk normally. With every step I trampled on something.

One, two, three, four, five . . . and the slow passing of the hours gradually wore down my silent revolt.

Ten days later I was halfway through my sentence at the Réclusion. It was an anniversary worthy of a feast, for, my grippe aside, I was in good health. I wasn't crazy or anywhere near becoming so. I was even 100 percent certain that at the end of the next year I'd get out alive and sound of body and mind.

I was awakened by the sound of muffled voices:

"Monsieur Durand, he's dry as a bone. How could you have not noticed him?"

"I don't know, chief. The way he's hanging in the corner under the walk. I never saw him."

"It's not important, but you must admit it's pretty funny you didn't see him."

So my neighbor on the left had committed suicide. They carried him away. The door closed. It was all according to the rules, since the door was opened and shut in the presence of a "higher authority." (It was the head warden, for I recognized his voice.) The fifth loss from those around me in ten weeks.

On the day of my anniversary I found a can of Nestlé's condensed milk in my pail. It was a real extravagance on the part of my friends, expensive to buy and very risky to get to me. It was a day of triumph over adversity. In addition, I promised myself I wouldn't take my usual flight. I would stay in the Réclusion in mind as well as body. A year had passed since I'd arrived and I felt quite capable of leaving *en cavale* tomorrow if the opportunity arose. It was a positive assertion and I was proud of it.

The afternoon sweeper—that was most unusual—gave me a note from my friends: "Chin up. Only one more year. We know you're in good health. We're O.K. too. We send love. Louis—Ignace. If you can, send us a word through the man who gave you this."

On the small piece of paper attached to the note I wrote: "Thanks for everything. I feel strong, and thanks to you, I hope for the same a year from now. Have you any news of Clousiot and Maturette?" The sweeper came back and scratched on my door. I slipped him the piece of paper and it disappeared immediately. I spent the whole day and part of the night in the real world, something I promised myself I'd do more often. One year more and I'd be on one of the islands. Which one? Royale or Saint-Joseph? I'd get drunk with talking, smoking and planning my next escape.

I began the next day—the first of the three hundred and sixty-five that remained—with confidence, and for the following eight months all went well. But in the ninth there was trouble. One morning, when my pail was being emptied, the man was caught red-handed just as he was pushing the coconut and the five cigarettes into my cell.

The situation was so serious that for several minutes the rule of silence was forgotten. We could hear all too clearly the beating they gave the poor guy. Then the rattle of a dying man. My wicket opened and the flushed face of a guard bellowed at me: "You'll get yours, you son of a bitch!"

"Just try something, shithead!" I yelled back, furious at the treatment they'd given the poor devil.

All this happened at seven o'clock. It wasn't until eleven that I was visited by a delegation headed by the deputy warden. The door, which had been closed for twenty months, opened. I was in the rear of the cell with my mug in my hand, ready to fight. I wanted to give as good as I got and be knocked out as quickly as possible. No chance. "Get out!"

"If you want me, come and get me. I'm not going out there to be attacked from all sides. Here I can slug the first man who touches me."

"We're not going to hit you, Charrière."

"Whose word do I have?"

"Mine, the assistant warden's."

"What's your word worth?"

"Don't insult me. There's no point in it. I give you my word of honor you won't be touched. Come on now. Get out."

I held on to my mug.

"You can keep it. You won't be needing it."

"O.K." I came out and, surrounded by six guards and the assistant warden, I walked the length of the corridor. When I emerged into the courtyard, I felt dizzy and had to close my eyes against the brilliance of the light. Eventually I made out the little house where we had gone on arrival. A dozen guards stood by as I was led into the room marked "Administration." A man was moaning on the floor, covered with blood. The clock on the wall said eleven, and I thought, They've been torturing the poor bastard for four hours.

The head warden was sitting behind his desk with the deputy warden next to him.

"Charrière, how long have you been getting food and cigarettes?"

"Hasn't that guy already told you?"

"I'm asking you."

"I have amnesia. I have no idea."

"What the hell are you talking about?"

"Didn't you know? I'm surprised it isn't down in my file. I got amnesia from a blow on the head."

Totally unprepared for my reply, the warden turned to a guard and said, "Ask Royale if they have any record of this."

While they were telephoning, he continued, "You do remember that your name is Charrière?"

"That, yes." Then, very fast, to confuse him still further, I rattled out like an automaton, "My name is Charrière I was born in 1906 in the department of Ardèche I was given a life sentence in Paris Seine." His eyes grew as big as marbles and I knew I'd thrown him.

"You had your coffee and bread this morning?"

"Yes."

"What vegetable did you have last night?"

"I don't know."

"So, if we're to believe you, you have absolutely no memory?"

"For events, no. For faces, yes. For example, I know it was you who received me here once. But when, I don't remember."

"So you don't know how much more time you have to do?"

"Of my life sentence? Until I die, I suppose."

"No, no. Your sentence in solitary."

"I have a sentence in solitary? Why?"

"Now that's too much! Are you trying to tell me you don't remember you're doing two years for an escape? I don't believe it!"

At that point I really gave it to him. "Escape? Me? Warden, I'm no fool. I'm an intelligent person and perfectly capable of assuming my responsibilities. Come to my cell and see for yourself if I've escaped from it."

A guard broke in, "Royale on the line, Warden."

He picked up the phone. "Nothing there? That's funny. He claims to have been stricken with amnesia. . . . How? A blow on the head. . . . I see. He's faking. Well, we'll see about that. . . . O.K. Sorry, Warden. I'll check it. Good-by. Yes, I'll keep you informed.

"Hey, faker, let's have a look at your head. Yes, he does have a scar, and a long one. How is it you remember you lost your memory when you got hit? Answer me that!"

"I can't explain it. I only know that I remember being hit, that my name is Charrière, and a few other things."

"So what are you trying to tell me?"

"That's what we're talking about. You asked me how long I've been sent food and cigarettes. This is my answer: I don't know if it was the first time or the thousandth. Because of my amnesia, I can't tell you. That's all there is to it. You can make of it what you want."

"What I want is simple enough. You've had too much to eat for a long time. Now you're going to lose a little weight. No more supper until the end of your sentence."

That same day I received a note during the second sweeping. Unfortunately I couldn't read it because it wasn't phosphorescent. During the night I lit a leftover cigarette that had escaped the search. As I puffed it, it made enough light so I could read: "The guy didn't give us away. He said it was only the second time he'd given you food, and that he did it only because he'd known you in France. It hasn't bothered anybody at Royale. Chin up."

So I was now deprived of my coconut, cigarettes and news of

my friends at Royale. And on top of that, they'd taken away my evening meal. I'd got used to not being hungry, and, in addition, the ten smokes gave shape to the day. I was also worried about the poor devil they had beaten on my account. I hoped to God they didn't punish him further.

One, two, three, four, five and turn. . . . One, two, three, four, five and turn. . . . It wasn't going to be easy on these short rations. With so little to eat, I thought I ought to change my tactics. For example, if I stayed lying down, I could conserve my energy. The less I moved, the fewer calories I'd burn up. During the day I would just sit. I'd have to learn a whole new way of life. Four months: one hundred and twenty days. On this new diet, how long would it be before I became seriously anemic? Two months at least. So that would leave me with two crucial months. Once I became really weak, I'd be fertile ground for all kinds of sickness. I decided to stay down from six in the evening to six in the morning. I'd walk from after coffee till after they'd picked up the pails, or about two hours. At noon, after the soup, another two hours. Four hours' walking in all. The rest of the time I'd sit or lie down. It would be difficult to take my flights without the fatigue. But I had to try all the same.

I'd now been on my new regimen for ten days. I was permanently hungry. A constant weariness had taken hold of me like a chronic disease. I missed the coconut terribly, the cigarettes not so much. I went to bed very early and I soon escaped from my cell. Yesterday I was in Paris at the Rat Mort, drinking champagne with some friends, among them Antonio of London—originally from the Balearic Islands—who spoke French like a Parisian and English like a real "roast-beef." The day after—at the Marronnier on the Boulevard de Clichy—he killed one of his friends with five shots of his revolver. Things happened fast in the underworld, these changes from friendship to mortal hatred. Yes, yesterday I was in

Paris, dancing to the sound of an accordion at a ball in the Petit Jardin on the Avenue de Saint Ouen whose clientele consisted entirely of people from Marseilles and Corsica. On this particular trip my friends were so real that there was no question of their presence or mine in the many places where I'd had such good times.

So, without walking too much, I achieved the same results with my reduced diet that I had with fatigue before. And the pictures of the past caught me up with such force that I actually spent more hours free than in the cell.

One month to go. For three months I'd had only a piece of bread and hot broth with a bit of boiled meat at noon. In my state of perpetual hunger, I examined the meat the minute it was served to make sure it wasn't just skin, as so often happened.

I was very nervous this morning after drinking my coffee. I'd let myself eat half my bread, something I'd never done before. Usually I broke it in more or less equal pieces and ate one at six, one at noon, one at six in the evening and one during the night. I scolded myself: "Why did you do that? Why do you wait until it's almost over to have these lapses?" "I'm hungry; I feel weak." "What do you expect? How can you be strong on what you've been eating? What's important—and this puts you ahead of the game—is that you're weak but you're not sick. With a little luck, *la mangeuse d'hommes* isn't going to get you." I was sitting on the cement stool after a two-hour walk. Thirty more days, or seven hundred and twenty hours, and the door would open and someone would say: "Charrière, out. Your two years in solitary are over." And what would I say? "At last my two-years' Calvary is over." Oh, no! If it was the warden for whom I'd played the amnesia act, I'd have to keep it up. I'd say coldly, "What? I'm pardoned? Do I leave for France? Is my sentence over?" Just to see his face and impress him with the injustice of the fast he'd condemned me to. "My goodness me, what's happened to you?" What the hell! Injustice or not, the warden couldn't care less whether he'd made a mistake or not. What could it matter to that kind of man? Officers in the *bagne* weren't normal people. No man worthy of the name could belong to such a profession. Besides, you can get used to anything in this life, even to being a professional bastard. Maybe when he's got one foot in the grave, the fear of God—if he's religious—will make him repent. Not real remorse for his past actions, but fear that on the day of judgment it will be his turn to be condemned.

When I got out of this place, wherever they put me next, I'd have no truck with these types. A definite barrier divided people into two groups: on one side you had inertia, a soulless bureaucratic authority and instinctive sadism; on the other, me and men like me who might have committed crimes but who had learned certain qualities in suffering the consequences: pity, kindness, sacrifice, nobility and courage.

In all honesty, I preferred being a convict to being a *bagne* official.

Twenty more days. I was very weak. My bread ration seemed to be getting smaller. Who could lower himself to such a dastardly trick? For several days now my soup had been hot water and a bone with a tiny piece of meat or a bit of skin attached to it. I was afraid of getting sick. It was an obsession. I was so weak that I dreamed while I was wide awake. This deep weariness and the depression that went with it worried me terribly. I tried to fight it, but it was hard to get through the twenty-four hours of each day. I heard a scratching at my door. I quickly snatched the note. It was phosphorescent, from Dega and Galgani. It said, "Send us a word. We're worried about your health. Nineteen more days. Chin up. Louis—Ignace."

There was a small piece of paper and a pencil stub. I wrote, "Holding out but very weak. Thanks. Papi."

The broom brushed my door again and I pushed the note under it. Those words were better than the cigarettes, the coconut, better than all of it put together. This wonderful show of friendship and loyalty was the whiplash I needed. Out there someone knew about me, and if I fell sick, my friends would certainly see that a doctor took care of me. I was nearing the end of this exhausting race against death and madness. No, I wouldn't get sick. I would stay as still as possible in order to save calories. I'd cut out the two-hour walk in the morning and afternoon. It was the only way to hold on. I stayed down for twelve hours at night; the other twelve I sat on my stone bench without moving. From time to time I got up and flexed my arms, then sat down again. Ten days left.

I was taking a walk in Trinidad, the sound of Javanese violins soothing me, when a horrible scream brought me back to reality. It came from a cell behind mine, very near. I heard:

"You bastard, come down here in my cell. Aren't you tired of looking at me from up there? Don't you realize you're missing half the show because there's so little light in this hole?"

"Shut up or you'll get it good," the guard called down.

"Oh, don't make me laugh, you shithead! What's worse than this silence? Punish me as much as you like, cutthroat, beat me if it makes you happy, you'll never think of anything worse than this silence. I can't, I tell you! I can't go on without talking! For three years I should have been telling you sons of bitches to go fuck yourself. And I was so dumb I waited thirty-six months because I was afraid of being punished! Well, screw the whole lot of you, you rotten brown-nosers!"

A few moments later I heard the door open and a voice, "No, not that way. Put it on him inside out—it works better that way." And the poor bastard screamed:

"Put the hair shirt on any way you like, asshole! Inside out if you like, make it so tight it chokes me, pull the laces with your knees. It won't stop me from saying your mother's a whore and you're a pile of shit!"

They must have gagged him, for I heard nothing more. The door closed again. Apparently the scene had upset the young guard, because a few minutes later he stopped outside my cell and said, "He must have gone crazy."

"You think so? But everything he said made sense."

I suppose that stunned the guard, for as he left he said, "Are you next?"

The incident wrenched me from my island and its good people, from the violins, the breasts of the Hindu girls, the harbor at Port of Spain, and put me back in the sad reality of the Réclusion.

Ten more days: two hundred and forty hours.

Perhaps my tactic of not moving was doing the trick, or else the note from my friends had encouraged me. Whatever it was, I was feeling stronger, and this feeling was enhanced by the vivid contrast between me—two hundred and forty hours away from liberation, weak but whole in mind and body—and the poor bastard two yards away from me just entering the first phase of madness. He wouldn't live long because his rebellion gave them the green light to lavish on him their subtlest treatments, designed to kill in the most scientific way possible. I reproached myself for feeling stronger at his expense. I wondered if I, too, was one of those egotists who, warmly dressed, could watch a long line of poor suckers on their way to work, running like a flock of sheep to catch the first métro or bus, and because they were ill dressed, frozen with cold, their hands blue in the morning chill, could feel even warmer than before, my own sense of comfort intensified. But life is based on comparisons: I may have ten years, but Papillon is in for life; I'm in for life and he's got fifteen, but I'm twenty-eight and he's fifty. And so on.

I was almost at the end of solitary and I fully expected to be normal in every respect in six months—health, morale and energy—and ready for a spectacular *cavale*. They talked about the first one; the second would be inscribed on the walls of the *bagne*. I never doubted it. I was certain I'd be gone within six months.

It was my last night at the Réclusion: seventeen thousand five hundred and eight hours since I'd first entered cell number 234. My door had been opened once, to take me before the warden to be punished. Aside from my neighbor, with whom I'd exchanged a few short words for a few seconds each day, I'd been spoken to four times. Once to tell me I was to lower my bunk at the sound of the whistle—on the first day. Once the doctor: "Turn around. Cough." A longer and more animated conversation with the warden. And the other day, a few words with the guard who had been upset over the madman next door. That's not exactly overdoing the diversions! I fell into a quiet sleep with one thought: tomorrow that door will finally open. Tomorrow I'll see the sun, and if they send me to Royale, I'll breathe the air of the sea. Tomorrow I'll be free. I burst out laughing. What do you mean, free? Tomorrow you return to your regular sentence of hard labor for life. Is that what you call free? I know, I know. But it's one hell of a lot better than what I've just been through. I wondered how I would find Clousiot and Maturette.

My coffee and bread came at six o'clock. I wanted to say, "But I leave today, there must be some mistake." Then I quickly remembered that I was an amnesiac and if I let on I'd been fooling the warden, he was quite capable of giving me thirty days in the dungeon. And besides, it was the law: I had to be let out of the Réclusion of Saint-Joseph today.

It was eight o'clock. I ate all my bread. I'd find something to eat in the camp. The door opened. The assistant warden and two guards were there. "Charrière, your sentence is finished. Follow me."

I went out. In the courtyard the sun was already so strong it dazzled me. I felt weak. My legs were rubbery and black spots danced before my eyes. And I'd walked only a hundred and fifty feet.

As we neared the Administration Building, I saw Maturette and Clousiot. Maturette was a skeleton, his cheeks hollow, his eyes sunken. Clousiot was on a stretcher. He was ashen and had the smell of death. I thought, They don't look good, my old pals. Do I look like that? I was dying to see myself in a mirror.

"Well, how goes it?" I asked.

No answer.

I repeated, "How goes it?"

"O.K.," Maturette said softly.

I wanted to tell them our sentence in solitary was over and we could talk now. I kissed Clousiot on the cheek. He looked at me with bright eyes and smiled.

"Good-by, Papillon," he said.

"What do you mean, good-by!"

"I'm through. It's over."

He died a few days later in the hospital at Royale. He was thirty-two and had been given twenty years for the theft of a bicycle he hadn't stolen.

The warden arrived. "Have them come in. Maturette and Clousiot, you conducted yourselves well. I've put on your reports: 'Good conduct.' But you, Charrière, you committed a serious offense. I've put down what you deserve: 'Bad conduct.' "

"Excuse me, Warden, what was my offense?"

"Really, you don't remember the discovery of the cigarettes and the coconut?"

"No, I don't."

"Come on now. What have you lived on the last four months?"

"How do you mean? What have I eaten? Same as when I arrived."

"That's the end! What did you eat last night?"

"Per usual, what they gave me. I don't know. I don't remember. Maybe it was beans or rice, or some other vegetable."

"So you ate last night?"

"For God's sake, you think I throw my food away?"

"No, that's not what I mean. I give up. O.K. I'll scratch 'Bad conduct.' Make up another release paper . . . I'm putting down 'Good conduct.' Are you satisfied?"

"That's better. It's what I deserve." And with that we left the office.

The great door of the Réclusion opened to let us through. Escorted by one guard, we walked slowly down the path that led to the camp. The sea lay below us, sparkling. Royale was opposite, very green and dotted with red roofs. Diable was over there, grim and wild. I asked the guard if I could sit down for a few minutes. Maturette and I sat on either side of Clousiot and grasped each other's hands. The contact aroused a strange emotion and we embraced without speaking.

The guard said, "Come on, guys, we've got to get going."

Slowly, very slowly, we walked down to the camp. Maturette and I went in together, still holding each other by the hand, followed by the two stretcher-bearers carrying our dying friend.

LIFE AT ROYALE

As soon as we got to the camp, we were met by the welcoming

stares of the *bagnards*. Pierrot le Fou, Jean Sartrou, Colondini, Chissilia were all there. The guard told us we had to go to the infirmary, and twenty men escorted us across the yard. In a few minutes Maturette and I had been presented with a dozen packs of cigarettes, tobacco, hot café au lait and hot cocoa. Everybody wanted to give us something. The orderly gave Clousiot a shot of camphor oil, and adrenalin for his heart. An emaciated black said, "Orderly, give him my vitamins. He needs them more than me." Pierre le Bordelais said, "Do you need any money? Before you leave for Royale, I'll have time to scrape some up."

"No, thanks. I have some. But how do you know I'm going to Royale?"

"The clerk told us. All three of you. I think you're all going to the hospital there."

The orderly was a mountain bandit from Corsica. His name was Essari. I got to know him very well and later on I'll tell his story; it's an interesting one. The two hours in the infirmary went like a flash. We ate and drank our fill, then, full and happy, we set off for Royale. Clousiot's eyes stayed closed except when I came near him and put my hand on his forehead. Then he'd open them and say, "My friend Papi, we're real friends, aren't we?"

"We're more than that. We're brothers."

With our one guard, we started down the hill, Clousiot on the stretcher, Maturette and I on either side. At the entrance to the camp all the cons said good-by and wished us luck. Pierrot le Fou slipped a musette bag full of tobacco, cigarettes, chocolate and cans of milk around my neck. Someone gave Maturette one too. Only the orderly Fernandez and the guard went with us to the quay. Each of us got a slip for the hospital at Royale. I gathered that the two orderlies, Essari and Fernandez, had taken the responsibility for putting us in the hospital; no doctor had been consulted. The boat arrived. There were six rowers, two armed guards in the stern and another at the helm. One of the rowers was Chapar. We set off. The oars dipped into the water, and as he rowed, Chapar said, "How are things, Papi? You get the coconuts?"

"Not for the last four months."

"I know. There was an accident. The *mec* was good, though. He didn't squeal."

"What's happened to him?"

"He's dead."

"No. How?"

"The orderly said somebody kicked him and ruptured his liver."

We landed on the quay at Royale, the largest of the three islands. The clock over the baker's said three o'clock. The afternoon sun was hot, too hot. The guard asked for stretcher-bearers. Two hefty convicts spotless in white lifted Clousiot as if he were a feather, and Maturette and I followed behind. A guard carrying some papers walked with us.

The path was over twelve feet wide and covered with pebbles. It was hard for us to walk. Luckily the stretcher-bearers stopped from time to time and waited for us. I'd sit on the arm of the stretcher near Clousiot's head and pass my hand gently over his head and brow. Each time he smiled, opened his eyes and said, "Good old Papi."

Maturette took his hand.

He seemed happy to feel us near him. Near the entrance we were met by a gang on their way to work. Almost all the cons were from my convoy. As they passed, each said something friendly. We reached the level ground, and there in the shade in front of a square white building the islands' highest authorities sat waiting for us. We walked up to them.

Without getting up, Warden Barrot said, "So, it wasn't too

hard at the Réclusion? And the man over there on the stretcher, who is he?"

"It's Clousiot."

He looked at him and said, "Take them all to the hospital. When they're ready to leave, let me know. I want to see them before they go to the camp."

In the hospital we were given clean beds with sheets and pillows in a large, well-lighted room. The first man I saw was Chatal, who had been the orderly in the maximum-security ward at Saint-Laurent-du-Maroni. He began immediately to look after Clousiot and ordered a guard to call in a doctor. The doctor arrived about five o'clock. After a long and detailed examination he shook his head unhappily and wrote down some orders. Then he came over to examine me.

"We're not very good friends, Papillon and I," the doctor said to Chatal.

"I'm surprised. He's a good man, Doctor."

"That may be. But he made trouble for me."

"When?"

"When I examined him in the Réclusion."

"Doctor, you call that an examination?" I said. "Listening to my chest through a wicket?"

"It's an Administration rule that we can't open a prisoner's door."

"Perhaps so, Doctor, but for your sake I hope you're only on loan to the Administration, not a part of it."

"We'll discuss that another time. I'm going to try to get you well, you and your friend. As for the other one, I'm afraid it's too late."

Chatal told me that he was suspected of preparing an escape and had been interned on the islands. I also learned that Jésus, the one who had crossed me up on my *cavale*, had been killed by a leper. Chatal didn't know the leper's name and I wondered if it might have been one of those who had helped us.

The life of the convicts on the Iles du Salut was entirely different from what you might imagine. Most of the men were in the "dangerous" class. They ate well because there was a black market in everything: alcohol, cigarettes, coffee, chocolate, sugar, meat, fresh vegetables, fish, shellfish, coconuts, etc. As a result, everybody was healthy—as was the climate. Since only the cons with short sentences had any hope of being freed, the men with life sentences had nothing to lose. Everybody was involved in the daily black market, convicts and guards alike. It was all mixed up. The wives of the guards sought out young cons to work around the house—and often took them as lovers. They were called "houseboys," some working as gardeners, others as cooks. They became the middlemen between the camp and the guards' houses. There was no feeling against the houseboys because the trafficking depended on them. But we didn't consider them as "pure" underworld. No man from the real underworld would stoop to do that kind of work, or be a turnkey or work in the guards' mess. On the other hand, he would pay to get work where he didn't have to deal with the guards: for instance, as a cesspool cleaner, leaf raker, animal herder, orderly, gardener, butcher, baker, boatman, postman, lighthouse keeper, etc. These jobs were done by the real hardened cons. Also, a real con never worked with the gangs that maintained the prison walls, roads, stairs, or planted coconut trees. These gangs worked in the full sun and under the eyes of the guards. The workday was from seven to noon and from two to six. It was a strange mixture of people who lived together in this little village where everybody watched everybody else, judged everybody and observed the life around him.

Dega and Galgani came to spend Sunday with me in the hospital. We had an *ailloli* with fish, a fish soup, potatoes, cheese, coffee and white wine. We ate the meal in Chatal's room—Dega, Galgani, Maturette, Grandet and me. They asked me to describe my *cavale* down to the last detail. Dega had decided not to try to escape. He was hoping to get five years off. With the three years he had done in France and the three years here, he had only four years to go, and he was resigned to doing them. Galgani said some Corsican senator was doing something about him.

Then it was my turn. I asked them where the best places were around here for trying an escape. There was a great hue and cry. The question had never entered Dega's mind, and certainly not Galgani's. Chatal volunteered that a garden might be useful for making a raft. Grandet told me that he was a blacksmith in the workshop. He described it as a shop with a large variety of workers: painters, carpenters, blacksmiths, masons, plumbers—nearly a hundred and twenty men all told. They did the maintenance for the Administration buildings. Dega, who was head clerk, said he'd see to it that I had whatever job I wanted. Grandet offered to share his gambling operation with me so I could live off what I took from the players instead of spending my *plan*. As I learned later, it was interesting work but very dangerous.

Sunday went by like a flash. "Five o'clock already," Dega said, looking at his beautiful watch. "Time to get back to camp." As we were leaving, Dega gave me five hundred francs so I could play poker. Apparently there were some great games in our room. Grandet gave me a magnificent dagger he had tempered himself. It was an impressive weapon.

"You've got to be armed day and night."

"Don't they frisk you?"

"Most of the guards who frisk you are Arab turnkeys. If they know a man is considered dangerous, they see to it they never find anything on him, even if they've touched it."

"See you at camp," Grandet said.

Before leaving, Galgani said he had reserved a place for me so we'd be in the same *gourbi* (the members of a *gourbi* ate together and shared all their money). Dega didn't sleep in the camp but in a room in the Administration Building.

We'd been in the hospital three days, but since I had spent my nights with Clousiot, I didn't really know what went on in the ward. Clousiot was in bad shape—he was in an isolation room with another man. Chatal had pumped him full of morphine. He was afraid he wouldn't make it through the night.

In the ward there were thirty beds—most of them occupied—on either side of an aisle twelve feet wide. It was lit by two gas lamps. Maturette said, "They're playing poker over there." I went over. There were four players.

"Can I make a fifth?"

"Sure, have a seat. The ante's a hundred francs. You have to triple the ante to play, in other words, three hundred francs. Here's three hundred francs' worth of chips."

I gave two hundred to Maturette for safekeeping.

A man from Paris named Dupont said, "We play English rules. No joker. You know how?"

"Sure."

"O.K. Your deal."

The speed with which these men played was amazing. You had to bet like lightning or the dealer said, "Too late," and you had to sit it out.

These gamblers were a whole new class of *bagnards*. They lived for and off gambling. Nothing else interested them. They forgot everything: what they had been, their punishment, what they could do to change their lives. They didn't even care who they played with. The one thing that mattered was gambling.

We played all night, stopping in time for breakfast. I won three thousand three hundred francs. I was heading for bed when one of the guys—his name was Paulo—came up to me and asked if I could lend him two hundred francs so he could play two-handed belote. He needed three hundred and had only a hundred. "Here, take three hundred and we'll go halves."

"Thanks, Papillon. You really are the good guy they said you were. I can see we're going to be friends." He held out his hand, I shook it, and he went off happy.

Clousiot died this morning. During a moment of lucidity the night before he had told Chatal not to give him any more morphine. "I want to die conscious," he'd said, "sitting on my bed with my friends around me."

It was strictly forbidden to enter the isolation ward, but Chatal took the responsibility on himself so that Clousiot could die among his friends. I closed his eyes. Maturette was broken with grief.

"The companion of our adventures is gone. He was thrown to the sharks."

When I heard the words, "He was thrown to the sharks," my blood froze. It was true; there was no cemetery for *bagnards*. When a convict died, he was thrown into the sea at sunset between Saint-Joseph and Royale, in a place that was infested with sharks.

With the death of my friend the hospital became unbearable. I sent word to Dega that I wanted to leave in two days. He answered with a note saying, "Ask Chatal to get you two weeks' rest at camp. That way you'll have time to choose what work you want to do." Maturette would stay a while longer; Chatal was going to try to get him a job as infirmary aide.

I was taken from the hospital straight to the Administration

Building and into the presence of Chief Warden Barrot, known to the cons as "Coco Sec."

"Papillon, I want to have a few words with you before I let you go to camp. You have a very powerful ally here in Louis Dega, my chief clerk. He tells me you don't deserve the reports I've received from France and since, according to him, you're innocent, it's perfectly normal that you should be in a state of permanent revolt. I must say I don't entirely agree with him. But what I want to know is, what is your mental attitude right now?"

"In the first place, sir, to answer you I would have to know what the reports say."

"Have a look." And he handed me a yellow card on which I read the following:

"Henri Charrière, called Papillon, born November 16, 1906, in——, Ardèche, condemned for first-degree murder and sentenced to hard labor for life by the Assizes of the Seine. Extremely dangerous: to be closely watched. To be given no privileges.

"Centrale de Caen: Incorrigible. Likely to foment and lead a revolt. Keep under close observation.

"Saint-Martin-de-Ré: Had to be disciplined. Very influential among his friends. Will always try to escape.

"Saint-Laurent-du-Maroni: Committed savage act of aggression against three guards and a turnkey when escaping from the hospital. Was returned from Colombia. Good conduct during imprisonment there. Given light sentence of two years in solitary.

"Réclusion de Saint-Joseph: Good conduct."

"That, my dear Papillon," the warden said as I gave him back the report, "doesn't exactly recommend you as a boarder here. Will you make a deal with me?"

"Perhaps. It depends on the deal."

"I haven't the slightest doubt that you're going to do everything you can to escape from the islands. You may even succeed.

As for me, I have only five months more as warden here. Do you know what an escape costs the chief warden? A year's pay—the entire loss of colonial pay, plus having my leave put off six months and reduced to three. And if they investigate and find the warden guilty of negligence, it means a possible demotion. You see how serious it is. Now, if I do my job honestly, I have no right to put you in a cell just because I think you're likely to escape. Of course I could dream up some imaginary offense, but I don't want to do that. So I'd like you to give me your word you won't try to escape until I've left the islands. That's five more months."

"Warden, I give you my word of honor I won't leave while you're here unless it goes beyond six months."

"I leave in a little under five. It's definite."

"O.K. Dega will tell you that I keep my word."

"I believe you."

"But, in exchange, I have a request to make too."

"What's that?"

"That during the five months I have to stay I can have the kind of work that will be useful to me later, and that I can be allowed to change islands."

"All right. It's a deal. But strictly between us."

"Yes, sir."

He summoned Dega, who convinced him that I didn't belong with the "good" boys but with the men from the underworld in the building for dangerous prisoners, where all my friends were. I was given a pack with *bagnard* clothing, and the warden had them add some white jackets and pants.

So, carrying two pairs of brand-new very white pants, three jerseys and a hat of rice straw, I walked to the central camp accompanied by a guard. To get from the Administration Building to the camp, you had to cross the entire plateau. We skirted the sixteen-foot wall that surrounded the penitentiary, passed in front of the guards' hospital and, making an almost complete tour of the huge rectangle, arrived at the main entrance—"Pénitencier des Iles— Section Royale." The immense wooden door—it must have been at least eighteen feet high—was wide open. Two details of four guards each were on duty, and an officer sat on a chair nearby. No carbines; everybody carried revolvers. There were also four or five Arab turnkeys.

When I arrived at the door, all the guards came forward. Their leader—a Corsican—said, "He's new and he's some guy!" The turnkeys were about to frisk me, but he stopped them. "He doesn't have to empty his pack. Go on, Papillon. You have a lot of friends waiting for you in there. My name is Sofrani. Good luck on the islands!"

"Thanks, chief." I went into an enormous courtyard surrounded by three big buildings. The guard led me to one of the three. Above the door I read: "Bâtiment A—Groupe Spécial." The guard called through the wide-open door, "Guard!" and an old con appeared. "Here's a new man," the guard said, and went off.

I stepped into a huge rectangular room, home for a hundred and twenty men. Like in the barracks at Saint-Laurent, an iron bar ran the length of each of the longer sides, interrupted only by the door, a grill that was closed only at night. Stretched tightly between the wall and the bars were the "hammocks" that served as beds. They weren't like the hammocks I'd known, but they were clean and comfortable. Above each one were a couple of shelves, one for clothes, the other for food, dishes, etc. Between the two rows of hammocks was an alley three yards wide which we called "the promenade." The men lived in small communities called *gourbis*. Some had as few as two men in them, others as many as ten.

I was hardly in the room when the white-clad *bagnards* came at me from all sides. "Papi, come over here," or, "No, come to us." Grandet took my pack and said, "He's going to make *gourbi* with me." I followed him. My hammock was hung up and stretched good and tight. "*Mec,* here's a feather pillow for you," Grandet said. A lot of my old friends were there: men from Corsica and Marseilles, a few from Paris, all people I'd known in France, or at the Santé or Conciergerie, or in the convoy. "Why are you all here?" I asked. "Why aren't you out working?"

Everybody laughed. "Nobody here works more than an hour a day. Then we come back to our *gourbis.*"

I had a wonderful reception. But I soon realized something I hadn't anticipated: in spite of the four days I spent in the hospital, I would have to learn all over again how to live in a community.

Then, to my surprise, a man came in, dressed in white, carrying a platter covered with a white cloth and calling out, "Steaks, steaks, who wants some steaks?" He gradually made his way to us, stopped and lifted the white cloth, revealing neat piles of steaks just like in a butcher shop. It was clear that Grandet was a regular customer. He wasn't asked if he wanted any, but how many.

"Five."

"Sirloin or shoulder?"

"Sirloin. How much do I owe you? You better give me your bill because there's one more of us now."

The steak seller took out a notebook and started to add up. "A hundred and thirty-five francs all told."

"Here's your money. We'll start from scratch now."

When the man had gone, Grandet said, "If you don't have money here, you starve. But we have a system so you'll never be without it. We call it 'the deal.' "

In the hard-labor camps "the deal" was the way each person managed to get money. The camp cook sold the meat intended for the prisoners. When the meat arrived at his kitchen, he cut up about half. Depending on the cuts, he made steaks, or stew or soup meat. One part went to the guards—their wives did the buying—

and one part to the cons who could afford it. Naturally the cook gave a share of his earnings to the kitchen guard. The first building he went to with his merchandise was always ours—Special Building A.

So "the deal" was that the cook sold meat and fats; the baker sold the rolls and long loaves intended for the guards; the butcher sold meat too; the orderly sold injections; the clerk took money to get you a good job or to release you from a work gang; the gardener sold fresh vegetables and fruits; the cons who worked in the labs sold analyses and would even work up a fake tuberculosis, leprosy, dysentery, etc.; there were specialists in robbery who lifted chickens, eggs and French soap from around the guards' houses; the houseboys trafficked with their employers to provide you with whatever you asked for—butter, condensed milk, powdered milk, canned tuna fish, sardines, cheese, and of course wines and liquor (our *gourbi* was never without a bottle of Ricard, and English or American cigarettes); and the same for the men who fished for lobsters.

But the best and most dangerous "deal" was to be a croupier. There was a rule that no building could have more than five croupiers. If you decided you wanted to be one, you presented yourself at the start of the evening's game and said, "I want to be croupier."

The players would say, "No."

"Everybody says no?"

"Everybody."

"All right, then. I want So-and-so's place."

The man he singled out understood. He got up, they went to the center of the room, and there the two men fought it out with knives. Whoever won became croupier. Croupiers got 5 percent of each winning hand.

The gambling also gave rise to other smaller "deals." There

was the man who prepared the tightly stretched blanket we played on, someone else who rented out small benches for players who couldn't sit cross-legged on the floor, and the cigarette vendor who scattered cigar boxes containing French, English, American and even hand-rolled cigarettes on the blanket. Each cigarette had its price, and as the player took one, he dropped the exact amount in the box. And then there was the man who prepared the gas lamps and watched to see that they didn't smoke. (The lamps were made from milk containers with a wick that was stuck through a hole in the top. It needed a lot of trimming.) For non-smokers there were candy and cakes baked through a special "deal." Each building had at least one Arab-style coffee maker. Covered with a couple of jute bags, it kept hot the whole night. From time to time the coffee vendor passed through the door selling hot coffee or cocoa from a handmade pot.

Then there was *camelote*. It was a kind of artisans' "deal." Some worked the tortoiseshell from turtles caught by the fishermen. A shell with thirteen plates could weigh as much as four and a half pounds. They were made into bracelets, earrings, necklaces, cigarette holders, combs, the backs of brushes. I saw a small box of pale tortoiseshell that was really beautiful. Other craftsmen worked coconuts, cattle and buffalo horns, ebony and the wood on the islands. Still others did very fine cabinetwork using only joints—never nails. The cleverest of all worked in bronze. And there were also painters.

Sometimes several talents were combined to make one object. For example, a fisherman caught a shark and fixed his mouth in an open position, the teeth straight and well-polished. Then a cabinetmaker fashioned a small-scale anchor out of a smooth, fine-grained piece of wood, with enough space in the middle for a painting. The shark's jaw was attached to the anchor and the artist painted a scene showing the Iles du Salut surrounded by water.

One of the favorites was a view of the point of Ile Royale, the channel and Ile Saint-Joseph, with the setting sun casting bright rays over the blue sea and, in the water, a boat with six convicts naked from the waist up, their oars held upright, behind them three guards holding submachine guns. In the prow of the boat two men were raising a casket from which slid a flour sack containing the corpse of a dead con. Sharks were swimming about with their mouths open, waiting for the body. In the lower right-hand corner of the painting was the inscription: "Burial at Royale," and the date.

The *camelote* was sold in the guards' houses. The best pieces were often bought in advance or made to order. The rest was sold on the boats that shuttled between the islands. This "deal" was the boatmen's domain. There were also the forgers: someone would take a dented old mug and engrave on it: "This mug belonged to Dreyfus, Ile du Diable," and the date. They did the same with spoons and mess plates. Breton sailors fell for anything that had the name "Sezenec" on it.

This trade brought a lot of money into the islands and it was in the guards' interest not to interfere. Besides, the men were easier to handle and adapted better to *bagne* life if they were busy.

Homosexuality had official sanction. From the warden on down, everybody knew that So-and-so was So-and-so's wife, and if you sent one of them to another island, you made sure the other went with him.

Among all these men, not three in a hundred were interested in a *cavale*. Not even the ones with life sentences. The only possibility was to get disinterred and sent to Grande Terre, Saint-Laurent, Kourou, or Cayenne. And this worked only for those with short sentences. If you had life, you had to commit murder so you'd be sent to Saint-Laurent to appear before the tribunal. But since you had to plead guilty in order to go, you risked getting five years in solitary, and there was no knowing if you'd be able to use the short stay in Saint-Laurent—three months at the most—to bring off an escape.

You could also try to get disinterned for medical reasons. If you were found to be tubercular, you were sent to the camp for tuberculars called Nouveau Camp, about fifty miles from Saint-Laurent.

There was also leprosy or dysentery. It was fairly easy to fake these, but they carried with them the terrible danger of living isolated in a special ward for nearly two years with men who really had the disease. It was a short step from faking leprosy to having it, or from having healthy lungs to getting tuberculosis, but many took that step. Dysentery was the most contagious of all.

I was now installed in Building A with my hundred and twenty comrades. It was hard learning how to live in this community where you were so quickly pigeonholed. First you had to make it clear that you were dangerous. Once they were afraid of you, you had to win their respect by the way you handled yourself with the guards—you never accepted certain jobs, you refused to work with certain gangs, you never recognized the authority of the turnkeys, you never obeyed an order, even if it meant a run-in with a guard. If you gambled all night, you skipped roll call. The trusty for our *case* (the buildings were called *cases*) would call out "Sick in bed." In the other two *cases* the guards usually made the "sick" man take roll call. This never happened to us. Obviously, what everybody—from the highest to the lowest—wanted most was a peaceful *bagne*.

Grandet, my *gourbi* mate, was thirty-five and from Marseilles. He was very tall, as thin as a rail, but very strong. We had been friends in France and used to see each other around Toulon, Marseilles and Paris. He was a well-known safecracker and a good guy, although a little too dangerous perhaps.

Today I was almost alone in the huge room. The man in charge of our *case* was sweeping and mopping the cement floor. I noticed another man fixing a watch with a gadget in his left eye. Above his hammock he had a shelf with at least thirty watches hanging from it. His face looked thirty, but his hair was completely white. I went up to him and watched him work, then tried to start a conversation. He didn't open his mouth; he didn't even look up. This made me a little angry, so I left him and went into the yard to sit by the washhouse. Titi la Belote was there playing a card game. His nimble fingers shuffled the thirty-two cards with incredible speed. Without interrupting the rhythm of his magician's hands, he said, "How goes it, pal? You like Royale?"

"Sure, but today I'm bored. I think I'll go do a little work to get out of camp. I wanted to have a talk with that *mec* who fixes watches, but he wouldn't open his mouth."

"You can say that again, Papi. That *mec* doesn't give a damn for anybody. He lives for his watches and the hell with everything else. But after what happened to him, he has every right to feel bitter. You know they gave that kid—he's not thirty years old—the death penalty last year for supposedly raping the wife of a guard. It was a real phony. He'd been screwing her for a long time—she was the wife of a Breton guard. He worked for them as a houseboy, and each time the Breton was on duty, the watch repairer gave it to her. But they made a mistake: the broad wouldn't let him do the laundry or ironing any more. She did it herself, and since her husband knew she was bone lazy, he began to wonder what was going on. But since he couldn't prove anything, he thought up a scheme to surprise her in *flagrante delicto*, then kill them both. One day he left his post two hours after arriving and asked another guard to go home with him, saying he wanted to make him a present of a ham he'd just received from home. He crept up to his house and was just opening the door when his parrot shrieked: 'Here comes the boss!' which it did whenever the guard came home. Immediately the wife started to scream, 'Help, help! I'm being raped!' The two guards entered the room just as the woman was tearing herself from the con's arms; the con jumped through the window and the husband started to shoot, nicking him in the shoulder. Meanwhile the broad was clawing at her breasts and cheeks and ripping her dressing gown. The con fell, but just as the Breton was going to finish him off, the other guard disarmed him. When I tell you this guy was a Corsican, you'll understand right away that he knew the whole thing was a fake, that it was no more a rape than a twenty-five-franc lay. But he was in no position to tell this to the Breton, so he pretended he believed it was a rape. The watch fixer was condemned to death. Not that all this was particularly unusual. It was later that it became interesting.

"On Royale the cons with special punishments are kept in the same place they keep the guillotine. Every week the executioners and his aides go into the yard, mount the guillotine and slice a couple of banana trunks to make sure it's in good working order.

"The watch repairman was in a cell for cons with the death sentence along with three Arabs and a Sicilian. All five were waiting for verdicts on their appeals.

"One morning they set up the guillotine and threw open the watch fixer's door. The executioners jumped on him, bound his wrists and looped the rope around his feet. Then they cut away his collar and he shuffled out into the early-morning light. You probably know that when you arrive in front of the guillotine you face an upright board to which you're strapped. They were about to put his neck in the curved part when Coco Sec—the head warden has to be present at all executions—showed up. He was carrying a big hurricane lantern, and as he aimed it at the scene, he saw that the screwball guards had made a mistake: they were going to cut off the watch fixer's head when it wasn't his day at all.

" 'Stop! Stop!' Barrot hollered.

"He was so upset it was all he could get out. He dropped the lantern, elbowed past the guards and executioners and unstrapped the *mec* himself. Finally he managed to say, 'Orderly, take him back to his cell. Take care of him, stay with him, give him some rum. And you, you idiots, go get Rencasseu. He's the one you're supposed to execute today.'

"The next day the watch repairer's hair was white, as white as it is today. His lawyer, a guard from Calvi, wrote the Minister of Justice, telling him about the incident and asking for a new pardon. The *mec* was pardoned and given a life sentence instead. Since then he spends his time fixing the guards' watches. It's his passion. He tests them endlessly; that's why he's got them hanging from his shelf. Now you understand why he's a little peculiar?"

Every day I learned a little more about my new life. *Case* A was a concentration of really formidable men because of what they had done in the past and also because of the way they acted around the camp.

One morning they called out Jean Castelli's name on the list of people to work in the coconut plantation. He stepped out of ranks and asked, "What goes on here? You're putting me to work?"

"Yes," said the guard in charge of the work gang. "Here, take this pickaxe."

Castelli looked at him coldly. "You must be crazy. You have to come from the sticks to know how to use those things. I'm a Corsican from Marseilles. In Corsica we throw work tools into the sea. In Marseilles they don't even know they exist. Keep your pickaxe and leave me alone."

The young guard didn't know about our group yet and started

to raise the handle of the pickaxe over Castelli's head. With one voice a hundred and twenty men shouted, "Asshole, touch him and you're dead."

"Break ranks!" Grandet called out, and ignoring the guards who had taken up attack positions, we went back into our *case*.

Case B filed by on its way to work, followed by *Case* C. A dozen guards came to ours and closed the grill. An hour later we had forty guards flanking the door, submachine guns in hand. The assistant warden, the head guard, the guards, everybody was there except the head warden, who had left at six for an inspection tour of Diable.

The second-in-command said, "Dacelli, call up the men one by one."

"Grandet?"

"Present."

"Come out here."

He went out into the middle of the forty guards.

Dacelli said, "Go to your work."

"I can't."

"You refuse?"

"No, I'm not refusing. I'm sick."

"Since when? You didn't report sick at roll call."

"I wasn't sick this morning. But I am now."

The first sixty called up all said the same thing. Only one man refused without giving an excuse. He probably hoped to be taken to Saint-Laurent in order to go before the tribunal. When he was asked, "You refuse?" he answered, "Yes, I refuse."

"Why?"

"Because you make me puke. I refuse absolutely to work for shits like you."

The tension was mounting. The guards, especially the young

ones, couldn't take being humiliated by *bagnards*. They were waiting for the one threatening gesture that would justify their going into action with their guns.

"Everybody who was called up, strip! Then go to your cells." As our clothes hit the ground, you could hear the occasional clatter of a knife. Then the doctor arrived.

"O.K. Stop. Doctor, please examine these men. Those who are not really sick will go to the dungeons. The others will stay in their *case*."

"You have sixty sick?"

"Yes, Doctor, except for that one there who refuses to work."

To the first in line the doctor said, "Grandet, what's wrong with you?"

"I've got indigestion, Doctor. The guards make me sick to my stomach. All of us here have got long sentences, most of them life. We've got no hope of escaping, and there's no way we can stand it unless there's some give-and-take in the regulations. This morning a guard threatened a friend with a pickaxe handle. It wasn't a question of self-defense; the man hadn't lifted a finger. All he said was he didn't want to use the pickaxe. And that's the reason for this indigestion epidemic. You judge."

The doctor looked down, thought for a minute, then said, "Orderly, write down the following: 'Due to a widespread alimentary infection, I direct that the infirmary guard give twenty grams of sulfate of soda as a purgative to all those who reported sick this morning. As for convict X, place him under observation in the hospital so we may determine if his refusal to work was made when in full possession of his faculties."

Then he turned on his heel and was gone.

"Everybody inside!" the second-in-command called out. "Pick up your clothes. Don't forget your knives." For the rest of the day everybody stayed in the *case*. Nobody was allowed out, not even the man who sold us our bread. Toward noon the infirmary guard and two convict-orderlies came around with a wooden bucket full of the purgative instead of soup. Only three men swallowed the stuff. The fourth fell over the bucket in a perfect imitation of an epileptic fit, and the purgative, bucket and all, flew off in all directions. Our guard mopped up the mess and the incident was ended.

Jean Castelli came over to eat with us and I spent the afternoon talking with him. He was in a *gourbi* with a man from Toulon called Louis Gravon who had been convicted for stealing furs. When I brought up the subject of a *cavale*, his eyes glistened.

"I almost escaped last year," he said, "but it fizzled. I didn't think you were the type to stay here indefinitely. But talk *cavale* here and you might as well be talking Hebrew. I don't think you understand the *bagnards* on the islands yet; ninety percent are relatively happy here. But nobody will squeal on you, whatever you decide to do. Even if you kill somebody, there's never a witness. Whatever a man does, everybody comes to his rescue. The island *bagnards* are scared of only one thing: that a *cavale* might succeed. When that happens, there's just no peace: there are constant searches, no more cards, no more music—instruments are destroyed during the searches—no more checkers or chess, no books, no nothing. Not even making *camelote*. Everything stops. They search all the time. Sugar, oil, steak, butter, all that disappears. Every time a *cavale* has made it from the islands, the men have been picked up on Grande Terre. But in the eyes of the Administration, the *cavale* was successful: the *mecs* got away. And so the guards get hell and they in turn take it out on us."

I listened closely and didn't bring the subject up again. I had never thought of it that way.

"In short," Castelli said, "the day you decide to prepare a *cavale*, beware. Unless it's with a close friend, think twice before discussing it with anybody."

Jean Castelli was a professional burglar and a man of unusual guts and intelligence. He loathed violence. His nickname was "the Antique." He washed only with Marseilles soap. If I happened to wash with Palmolive, he'd say to me, "Say, you smell like a queer! You washed with whore's soap!" Unfortunately he was fifty-two, but his iron will was a joy to see. He told me one day, "Papillon, you're like my son. Life on the islands isn't for you. You eat well because you want to keep in shape, but you're never going to settle down and accept island life. I congratulate you. Among all these cons there aren't half a dozen like you. It's perfectly true that a lot of them would pay a fortune to get disinterned so they could go to Grande Terre and escape from there. But here nobody even gives it a thought."

Old Castelli gave me some good advice. He said I should learn English, and talk Spanish with a Spaniard as often as possible. He lent me a book that was supposed to teach me Spanish in twenty-four lessons, and a French-English dictionary. He had a very good friend, a man from Marseilles called Gardès who was nearly fifty and knew volumes about *cavales*. He'd done two, one from a Portuguese *bagne* and one from Grande Terre. He had one point of view on the subject, Jean Castelli another, Gravon yet another, all of them different. From that day on I decided to make up my own mind and stop talking about it.

The only thing they agreed on was that gambling was interesting only as a way to make money and that it was very dangerous: at any moment you could be forced into a battle of knives with the first troublemaker who came along.

Last night I gave my *case* a demonstration of the way I saw things. A little guy from Toulouse was challenged by a man from Nîmes. The little fellow's nickname was Sardine and the bully from Nîmes was called Mouton. Mouton, bare from the waist up, was standing in the middle of the alley with his knife in his hand: "You pay me twenty-five francs a hand or you don't play." Sardine answered, "Nobody's ever had to pay to play poker. Why take it out on me? Go fight the bankers."

"Never mind about that. Pay, don't play, or fight."

"I'm not fighting."

"You're chicken?"

"Yes. I don't want to risk being chopped up by someone like you who's never even been on a *cavale*. I'm a *cavale* man. I'm not here to kill or get killed."

We were all waiting to see what happened next. Grandet said, "The little guy's got guts. It's too bad we can't interfere." I opened my knife and placed it under my thigh. I was sitting on Grandet's hammock.

"O.K., chicken," the man from Nîmes continued. "What do you say?" He moved a step nearer Sardine.

I said, "Shut up, Mouton. Leave the guy alone!"

"You crazy, Papillon?" Grandet said.

Still sitting with the open knife under my left leg, my hand on the handle, I said, "No, I'm not crazy." Then in a louder voice, "Listen to me, Mouton. Before I fight you—which I'm prepared to do as soon as I've had my say—I want to get something off my chest. Since I've been in this case, I've come to realize that the most beautiful, the most important, the only true thing—yes, a *cavale*— is not respected here. I think every man who's given proof that he's a *cavale* man, who's got enough guts to risk his life in a *cavale*, deserves respect. Does anybody here disagree?" Silence. "You've got a lot of rules, but you lack the most important one: the obligation not only to respect but to aid and abet the *cavale* man. Nobody has to go, and I know most of you have decided to make your life here. But if you don't have the courage to start a new life, at least have some respect for the men who do. And I can guarantee serious consequences for anyone who forgets this rule. O.K., Mouton. Let's go!"

I jumped into the middle of the room, my knife in my hand.

But Mouton threw his knife down and said, "You're right, Papillon. But I don't want to fight with knives; I'll fist fight you to prove I'm not chicken."

I gave my knife to Grandet and we fought like wild dogs for almost twenty minutes. Thanks to a lucky jab to his head, I managed to beat him. We were standing next to each other over the washstands, washing the blood off our faces, when Mouton said, "It's a fact. We go to pieces here on the islands. I've been here fifteen years and I haven't even spent the thousand francs for a disinternment. That's not good."

When I returned to my *gourbi*, Grandet and Galgani jumped on me. "Are you crazy to insult everybody that way? It's a miracle somebody didn't jump into the alley and cut you up right there."

"It was no miracle. Our gang always goes along when they know you're right."

"That may be," Grandet said. "But I wouldn't fool around this volcano too much." All evening long, cons came by to talk to me. They dropped in as if by chance, talked of this and that, then, as they left, said, "You were right, Papi." After this incident the men had a higher opinion of me. From then on, although I was still considered one of the gang, my friends realized that I accepted nothing without first analyzing it and discussing the pros and cons. I also noticed that when I was croupier, there were fewer disputes, and when I gave an order, it was quickly obeyed.

One evening an Italian named Carlino was killed. He lived with a young kid as man and wife. They were both gardeners. Carlino must have known his life was in danger, for when he was asleep the kid watched over him, and vice versa. They had put some empty boxes under their hammock so nobody could sneak up without making a noise. But they got him anyway. We heard him scream and, right afterward, a wild racket of empty boxes.

Grandet was running a game with over thirty players sitting around him. I was talking to someone nearby. The scream and the noise of the boxes stopped the game. Everybody got up, asking what had happened. Carlino's friend had seen nothing. The leader of our *case* asked if he should call in the guards. No. Since Carlino was dead, there was nothing to be done. Guards could be summoned in the morning at roll call.

Then Grandet spoke up. "Nobody heard a thing, right? Not even you, kid. Tomorrow at reveille you notice he's dead."

Everybody went back to the game.

I was curious to see what would happen when the guards discovered there'd been a murder. The first bell rang at five-thirty. At six came the second bell and coffee. At six-thirty the third bell, and usually we went out for roll call. But today it was different. At the second bell our trusty said to the guard who accompanied the prisoner with our coffee, "Chief, a man's been murdered."

"Who?"

"Carlino."

"O.K."

Ten minutes later six guards appeared with a stretcher.

"Where's the dead man?"

"Over there."

The dagger had gone through the hammock and into Carlino's back. They pulled it out. "You two, take him away." Two guards lifted him and carried him off. Daylight came. The third bell rang.

With the bloody knife still in his hand, the head guard said,

"Everybody outside for roll call. There'll be nobody sick today."
Everybody went out. The wardens and head guards took the roll
call. When it got around to Carlino, our trusty said, "Died in the
night. Taken to the morgue."

"O.K.," said the guard calling the roll.

When everybody had been checked off, the head guard raised
the knife and asked, "Anybody recognize this knife?" No answer.
"Anybody see the killer?" Silence. "So nobody knows anything, as
usual. Hands out of your pockets and pass in front of me, then go
to your jobs. It's always the same, Warden—no way of finding out
who did it."

"All right. File it," the warden said. "But keep the knife and
put a label on it indicating it was the weapon that killed Carlino."

That was it. I went back to the *case* and lay down, for I hadn't
shut an eye the whole night. As I was falling asleep, I said to
myself, What's a *bagnard* to anybody? Even if he's killed, nobody
takes the trouble to find out who killed him. To the Administration
he's nothing. Just another *bagnard*. No better than a dog.

I decided to start my job as latrine cleaner Monday. At four-thirty
in the morning another man and I took the pails from our building. Regulations demanded that we empty them into the sea. But
we paid a man in charge of the buffaloes to wait for us by the edge
of the plateau, where a cement trough ran down to the water. In
less than twenty minutes the pails were emptied in the sluice. To
push the stuff along, we poured in gallons of sea water from a huge
barrel and helped it down with a stiff broom. The buffalo keeper
was a pleasant black from Martinique and we paid him twenty
francs a day for the water. On my first day of work, hauling those
buckets was very hard on the wrists. But I soon got used to it.

My new friend was very obliging, although Galgani warned me he was a dangerous man. It was said that he'd killed seven men on the islands. His "deal" was selling sewage. Each gardener was supposed to make his own manure pile. He dug a trench, put in dry leaves and grass, then the black sneaked in a couple of bucketfuls of sewage. Obviously it couldn't be done alone, so I helped him out. But I knew it was wrong because it could spread dysentery by contaminating the vegetables. I decided that once I knew him better, I'd try to stop him. I'd pay him to make up for what he lost from his business. He also carved cattle horns on the side. I asked him about the fishing, but he said he didn't know anything about it. I should get help from Chapar or someone down in the port.

So I was a cleaner of latrines. When I'd finished work, I took a good shower, put on shorts and, whenever I felt like it, went fishing. There was only one requirement: I had to be back in camp by noon. Chapar provided me with rods and hooks. As I started back with my catch of mullet strung on a wire, there was hardly a day when I wasn't hailed by the wife of some guard. They all knew me by name. "Papillon, sell me four pounds of mullet?"

"You sick?"

"No."

"Do you have a sick child?"

"No."

"Then I can't sell you any of my fish."

I usually caught enough to give some to my friends in camp. I traded them for rolls, vegetables and fruit. In my *gourbi* we ate fish at least once a day. Once, when I was returning with a dozen big langoustines and about fifty pounds of mullet, I happened to pass by Warden Barrot's house. A fat woman came out and said, "That's a fine catch, Papillon. The sea's been so rough no one's been catching anything. It's two weeks since I've had any fish. It's a shame you don't sell it. My husband tells me you won't sell your fish to any of the guards' wives."

"That's right, madame. But in your case I might make an exception."

"Why?"

"Because you're overweight and you shouldn't eat meat."

"I know. The doctor told me to eat only vegetables and poached fish. But I can't do it here."

"Here, madame. Please take these." I gave her about four pounds of *langoustines* and mullet.

From that day on, every time I made a good catch, I helped her with her diet. Although she knew that everything had to be paid for on the islands, she never offered me anything but thanks. She was right; she knew that I didn't want her money. Instead, she often invited me in for a pastis or a glass of white wine, and some figatelli from Corsica when she had some. Mme. Barrot never asked me about my past. She did let drop a comment once when we were discussing the *bagne*: "It's true you can't escape from the islands, but it's better here in a healthy climate than rotting like an animal on Grande Terre."

It was from her that I learned the origin of the islands' name. During an epidemic of yellow fever in Cayenne, a group of White Fathers and nuns from a convent there sought refuge on the islands and were saved. Hence the name, "Iles du Salut."

My fishing took me everywhere. I'd been on latrine duty for three months and I knew every corner of the island. I examined the gardens on the pretext that I wanted to exchange my fish for some vegetables and fruit. A member of my *gourbi*, Matthieu Carbonieri, worked in the garden next to the guards' cemetery. He worked alone, and it occurred to me that, when the time came, we might be able to assemble and bury a raft in his garden. Two more months and the warden would be gone. Then I'd be free to go into action.

I organized my activities: I made friendly overtures to a pair of brothers-in-law named Narric and Quenier. They were called "the wheelbarrow brothers." It seems they had been accused of encasing the body of a cashier they'd murdered in cement. Someone claimed to have seen them push a block of cement in a wheelbarrow and dump it in the Marne or the Seine, I don't remember which. The investigation proved that the cashier had gone to them to demand repayment of a loan and had never been seen again. The two men denied murdering him the rest of their lives. Even in the *bagne* they continued to protest their innocence. But, although the body was never found, the head had turned up in a large handkerchief. The "experts" asserted that the brothers had handkerchiefs of the same weave, thread, etc. However, they and their lawyers were able to prove that thousands of yards of the cloth had been made up into handkerchiefs. Everybody had them. In the end the brothers-in-law got life sentences.

I made friends with them. As masons, they were free to come and go from the workshops. Perhaps, piece by piece, they could furnish me with the makings of a raft. All that remained was to win them over.

Yesterday I met the doctor. I was carrying a huge fish weighing at least fifty pounds and very good to eat—it was of the same family as the black sea bass. We walked together toward the plateau. Halfway there we sat down on a low wall. He told me that my fish head made a wonderful broth, so I offered it to him along with a piece of the flesh.

My gesture surprised him and he said, "You don't hold a grudge, Papillon?"

"No, Doctor, I'm in your debt for what you did for my friend Clousiot."

We talked of other things, and then he said, "You'd like to escape, wouldn't you? You're not a real convict. I get the impression you're made of different stuff."

"You're quite right, Doctor. I don't belong here; I'm only visiting."

When he laughed, I plunged ahead. "Doctor, do you believe a man can make himself over?"

"Yes, I do."

"You accept the idea that I could become a member of society and not be a threat to it? That I could become an honest citizen?"

"I sincerely believe it."

"Then will you help to bring this about?"

"How?"

"By letting me be disinterned as tubercular."

"That I can't do, and I advise you not to try. It's far too dangerous. The Administration will disintern a man for reasons of illness only after he's spent a month in a ward for his particular disease."

"Why?"

"To prevent precisely what you want to do. If anyone tries to fake it, he runs the risk of being contaminated by the others in the ward. So I won't do it."

From that day on the doctor and I were friends. That is, until he almost killed my friend Carbonieri. After discussing it with me, my friend the gardener had taken the job of messcook for the head guards. He took it in order to steal three barrels—wine, oil, vinegar—it didn't matter as long as they could be fastened together and float us out to sea. Only after Barrot had left, of course. The difficulties were great because we would first have to steal the barrels, get them to the coast without being seen or heard, then lash them together with cables, all on the same night. It would work only during a storm when there was wind and rain to shield us. But by the same token, it would be that much more difficult to launch the raft because the sea would naturally be very rough.

So Carbonieri was now a cook. The chief cook gave him three rabbits to prepare for dinner the next day, a Sunday. Carbonieri sent one rabbit to his brother down in the port and two to us, already skinned. Then he killed three large cats and made a sensational stew.

Unfortunately for him, the doctor was invited to the dinner. He tasted the rabbit and said to the chief cook, "Monsieur Filidori, I congratulate you on your menu. This cat is delicious."

"You're joking, Doctor. These are three fine rabbits."

"I beg your pardon," the doctor went on, stubborn as a mule, "it's cat. See this breast? It's flat; a rabbit's is round. I'm sure I'm right. We're eating cat."

"Oh my God!" Filidori exploded. "I've got cat in my stomach!" He ran into the kitchen and thrust his revolver under Matthieu's nose, screaming: "Forget we're both Corsicans, I'm going to kill you. You fed me a cat."

He had a wild look in his eyes and, not realizing the cat was out of the bag—so to speak—Carbonieri said, "If you call what you gave me cat, it's not my fault."

"I gave you rabbits."

"And that's what I cooked. Look, I've still got the skins and heads."

Disconcerted, the cook looked at the rabbit heads and skins. "So the doctor doesn't know what he's talking about, eh?"

"The doctor told you that?" Carbonieri said, breathing again. "He's pulling your leg. But tell him it's no joking matter."

Appeased, Filidori went back to the dining room and addressed the doctor. "Say what you like, Doctor, I think the wine has gone to your head. I don't care whether those breasts are flat or round, I know it's rabbit I ate. I just saw their three fur coats."

It was a close call for Matthieu. He resigned as cook a few days later.

The day when I could begin my preparations was fast approaching. Only a few weeks and Barrot would be gone. I went to see his wife yesterday, and the good woman asked me to come in—she had a bottle of quinine she wanted to give me. Her living room was full of steamer trunks she was in the process of packing.

"Papillon," she said, "I don't know how to thank you for all you've done for me these last few months. I know that when the fishing was poor you gave me everything you caught. I can't thank you enough. Because of you, I've lost over thirty pounds and I feel much better. Is there anything I can do to show my gratitude?"

"There is something, but I'm afraid it may be a little difficult. Can you find me a good compass? It must be accurate but very small."

"That's little enough, Papillon, but it may not be easy to do in three weeks."

Upset because she hadn't been able to find me what I'd asked for, eight days before her departure she took the ferry to Cayenne. Four days later she was back with a magnificent antimagnetic compass.

The warden and Mme. Barrot left this morning. He handed over his post yesterday to a Tunisian officer named Prouillet.

There was good news: the new warden kept Dega on as head clerk, which was of great importance to everybody, especially me. Also, in his speech to the *bagnards* assembled in the big courtyard, the new warden gave the impression of energy and intelligence. Among other things, he said, "As of today, I am the new warden of the Iles du Salut. I'm satisfied that the methods of my predecessor were sound and I see no reason to change them. Unless your conduct forces me to do otherwise, I see no necessity to alter your way of life."

It was with understandable relief and pleasure that I saw the warden and his wife finally leave, even though the five months of forced waiting had passed with amazing speed. The false freedom we convicts enjoyed, our games, the fishing, conversation, new friends, arguments, fights, were all such powerful distractions that we had little time to be bored.

All the same, I wasn't really taken in by the life. Each time I made a new friend, I put him to the test: "Will he be a candidate for a *cavale?* Will he be useful in preparing one even if he doesn't want to come along?"

I lived only for that one thing: escape. It was my *idée fixe.* As Jean Castelli had advised me, I spoke of it to no one. But it obsessed me. I would never let my resolve weaken; never would I give up the idea of a *cavale.*

SEVENTH NOTEBOOK

THE ILES DU SALUT (CONTINUED)

A RAFT IN A TOMB

IN FIVE MONTHS I'D COME to know every inch of the island. It seemed to me that the garden near the cemetery, where my friend Carbonieri had worked before he became a cook, was the safest place to assemble a raft. I asked Carbonieri to go to work there again. He was willing. Thanks to Dega, he got the job back.

This morning, as I was passing by the new warden's house with a catch of mullet, I heard the young con who was working as their houseboy say to a young woman standing next to him, "That's him, madame. He's the one who brought Madame Barrot her fish every day." Then I heard the handsome woman—she was an Algerian type with bronze skin and dark hair—say to him, "So that's Papillon?" Then she spoke to me:

"Madame Barrot gave me some wonderful *langoustines* she said you'd caught. Won't you come in? Have a glass of wine? I'd like you to taste some of the goat cheese I just received from France."

"No, thank you, madame, I can't."

"Why not? You did when Madame Barrot was here."

"That was because her husband gave me permission to enter his house."

"Papillon, my husband is in charge of his camp, I'm in charge of my house. Don't be afraid to come in."

I had the feeling that this pretty woman would be useful, but dangerous too. I went in. She placed a plate of ham and cheese on the dining-room table and, without ceremony, sat down opposite me. She gave me wine, then some coffee with a delicious Jamaican rum.

While she was pouring, she said, "Papillon, when Madame Barrot was leaving, she took time out from the bustle of their departure and our arrival to tell me about you. I know she was the only woman on the island you gave fish to. I hope you will do me the same favor."

"I gave it to her because she wasn't well. From what I can see, you're in excellent health."

"I won't lie to you, Papillon. I am in good health, but I was brought up in a port and I adore fish. I come from Oran. But what troubles me is that I know you won't sell your fish. That's very annoying."

Well, the long and short of it was that I agreed to bring her fish.

I was smoking a cigarette, having just given her a good seven pounds of mullet and six *langoustines*, when the head warden came in.

He saw me and said, "I told you, Juliette, that, except for the houseboy, no *bagnard* is to come into the house."

I started to my feet, but she said, "Don't get up. This is the man

Madame Barrot recommended to me before she left. So it's no concern of yours. I'll allow nobody into this house but him. Besides, he's going to bring me fish when I need it."

"All right, then," the warden said. "What's your name?"

I was about to get up and answer, but Juliette put her hand on my shoulder and told me to stay seated. "This is my house," she said. "The warden is not the warden here. He is my husband, Monsieur Prouillet."

"Thank you, madame. My name is Papillon."

"Ah! I've heard of you and your escape from the hospital in Saint-Laurent three years ago. One of the guards you knocked out happened to be my nephew—mine and your protector's here."

With that Juliette let out a gay, young laugh and said, "So you're the one who knocked out Gaston! That won't change our relationship the least bit."

The warden, who was still standing, said, "The number of murders on the islands each year is unbelievable. Many more than on Grande Terre. How do you account for that, Papillon?"

"Sir, the men here have no hope of escape and that makes them testy. They live practically on top of each other for years on end and they naturally develop strong friendships and hatreds. Besides, less than five percent of the murderers are ever discovered, so no one's afraid of being caught."

"That sounds logical enough. How long have you been fishing? What work do you do that gives you the right to fish anyway?"

"I take care of the latrines. My work is over at six in the morning and then I fish."

"All the rest of the day?" Juliette asked.

"No, I have to be back in camp at noon, but I can go out again at three and stay until six. Of course, the tides vary and sometimes I miss the best fishing."

"You'll give him a special permit, won't you, darling?" Juliette said, turning to her husband. "From six in the morning until six at night, so that he can fish when he wants to."

"All right," the head warden said.

I left the house, congratulating myself on the way I'd managed things. Those three hours from noon to three were precious. It was siesta time and almost all the guards were asleep then.

Juliette all but took over both me and my fish. It got to the point where she'd send her young houseboy to find me and claim my catch. He'd say, "Madame wants everything you've caught because she's expecting company and wants to make a bouillabaisse." In fact, she not only took all my catch, but she also began sending me in search of special fish or after *langoustines*. It played havoc with the menu in our *gourbi*, though on the other hand, what protection! She was also full of little attentions: "Papillon, isn't it high tide at one o'clock?" "Yes, madame." "Then why don't you eat here so you don't have to go back to camp?" She was not as discreet as Mme. Barrot. Sometimes she'd try to question me about my past. I avoided the subject that interested her most—my life in Montmartre—and concentrated on my childhood and youth. Meanwhile the warden was asleep in his room.

Early one morning I had great luck and caught almost sixty *langoustines*. It was about ten when I stopped by her house. I found her in a white dressing gown with another young woman who was setting her hair. I said good morning and offered her a dozen *langoustines*.

"No," she said. "I want them all. How many are there?"

"About sixty."

"That's perfect. How many do you and your friends need?"

"Eight."

"Then you take eight and give the rest to the boy. He'll put them on ice."

I was on the point of going when she said, "Don't run away. Sit down and have a pastis. You must be hot."

It made me uncomfortable to sit down with this demanding woman. I drank my pastis slowly, smoked a cigarette and watched the young woman comb out Juliette's hair. From time to time the girl threw me a glance, and finally the warden's wife noticed it in the mirror. She said, "Isn't my beau handsome, Simone? You're all jealous of me, aren't you?" They both laughed and I didn't know where to look.

I said clumsily, "Luckily your beau—as you call him—isn't much of a threat. In his position he can hardly be anybody's beau."

"You're not trying to tell me you don't have a crush on me? I'm the first person who's been able to tame you, aren't I? And I can do anything with you I like. Isn't that right, Simone?"

"I don't know about that," Simone answered. "But I do know you're a terror to everybody but the warden's wife, Papillon. Last week the chief guard's wife told me you caught over forty pounds of fish and you wouldn't even sell her two miserable ones. There was no meat at the butcher's, and she wanted them like mad. And did you hear," she went on, "what he said to Madame Leblond the other day? She saw him going by with some *langoustines* and a big moray. 'Please sell me that moray, Papillon, or at least sell me half of it. It's a speciality with us Bretons.' 'Bretons aren't the only ones who appreciate it, madame. Lots of people, including those from Ardèche, have known it was a choice food since Roman times.' And he went on his way without selling her a thing."

They both laughed like mad.

I went back to camp in a rage and that evening told my *gourbi* the whole story.

"This is serious," Carbonieri said. "That broad is putting you on the spot. I'd advise you to go there as little as possible and then only when you're sure the warden is there." Everybody agreed, and I decided I would do just that.

I discovered a carpenter from Valence, which is almost my home country. He had killed a guard in the forest and water service. He was an inveterate gambler and always in debt. He spent his days feverishly making *camelote* and his nights losing what he'd earned. Often he'd make things to pay his creditors, but they took unholy advantage of him and paid him a hundred and fifty or two hundred francs for a rosewood box worth three hundred. I decided to go after him.

One day when we were in the washhouse together, I said, "I want to talk to you tonight. Let's meet in the toilets. I'll let you know when."

That night, as we were talking alone, I said, "Bourset, you know we're from the same neck of the woods?"

"How's that?"

"Aren't you from Valence?"

"Yes."

"Well, I'm from Ardèche. So we're neighbors."

"So what?"

"That means I don't like to see you taken advantage of when you're in debt, only getting half what your things are worth. Bring them to me—I'll give you full value. That's all."

"Thanks," Bourset said.

He was forever in hot water with the people he owed, so I was constantly helping him out. Things weren't too bad, though, until he got in debt to Vicioli, a Corsican mountain bandit and one of my good friends. Bourset told me that Vicioli was after him for the seven hundred francs he owed him. He had a small secretary that was almost finished, he said, but he wasn't sure when he'd be through with it because he had to work on it in secret. (They were not allowed to make large pieces because it took too much wood.)

I told him I'd see what I could do. With Vicioli's consent, I put on an act—Vicioli was to put the pressure on Bourset, even threaten him, and I'd jump in as Bourset's savior.

And that's exactly what happened. After that Bourset was my man and trusted me implicitly. For the first time in his life as a *bagnard* he could breathe freely. So I decided I'd take a chance.

One evening I said to him, "I'll give you two thousand francs if you'll do what I ask. I want a raft big enough for two men, in sections that will fit together."

"Listen, Papillon, I wouldn't do this for anybody else, but for you I'll even risk two years in solitary. The only thing is, I can't get the big pieces out of the workshop."

"I've got somebody to do that."

"Who?"

"The 'wheelbarrow brothers,' Narric and Quenier. Now, how do you plan to make the raft?"

"First I'll do a drawing to scale, then I'll make each piece tongue-and-groove so they'll all fit tight. All the wood on the islands is hardwood, though—I may have a little trouble finding wood that'll float."

"When will you know if you can do it?"

"In three days."

"Do you want to escape with me?"

"No."

"Why not?"

"I'm scared of the sharks and I don't want to drown."

"You promise you'll help me until it's finished?"

"I swear it on my children's heads. Only it's going to take a long time."

"That's all right. Now listen carefully. I'm going to copy the design for the raft on a piece of notebook paper, and underneath I'll write, 'Bourset, you make this raft just like this drawing or you die.' This'll be your alibi if something goes wrong. Later on I'll give you orders in writing on how to make every piece. Each time you've finished one, I want you to leave it where I tell you. It will then be taken away. Don't try to find out when." This seemed to make him feel better. "This way we avoid the risk of your being tortured if you're caught—the most you'll get is six months."

"What if you're the one who's caught?"

"Then it'll be the other way around. I'll admit to being the author of the notes. Naturally you'll keep the written orders. O.K.?"

"O.K."

"You're not afraid?"

"No, I'm glad to have the chance to help you."

I didn't say a word to anyone. I was waiting for Bourset's answer. An endless week passed before we talked again, alone in the library.

Right away Bourset put sunshine in my heart.

"The hardest part was to make sure I'd have wood that was light and dry. I solved it by designing a kind of wooden collar to fit around a bunch of dried coconuts—shells on, of course. The shells are the lightest thing there is and they're absolutely waterproof. When the raft is finished, it will be up to you to find the coconuts to put inside. I'll start on the first piece tomorrow. It should take me about three days. Have one of the brothers pick it up as soon as possible after Thursday. I won't start a new piece before the finished one has left the shop. Here's my design. You copy it and write the letter you promised. Have you talked to the brothers?"

"No, not yet. I was waiting for your answer."

"Well, you've got it. It's yes."

"Thanks, Bourset—I don't really know how to thank you. Here, take this five hundred francs."

He looked me straight in the eye and said, "No, you keep the money. If you make it to Grande Terre, you'll need it to set up your next *cavale*. Starting today, I'm not playing cards until you're gone. With the things I make here, I'll still have enough for cigarettes and steaks."

"Why won't you take it?"

"Because I wouldn't do this for ten thousand francs. For all the precautions we've taken, the risks are too great. I can do it only for free. You helped me, you were the only person who ever gave me a hand. It scares me, but I'm glad to do it."

As I copied the design, I began to feel very guilty. It had never even crossed Bourset's innocent mind that I'd helped him to gain my own ends. I had to keep telling myself—to make me look better in my own eyes—that escape justified everything, even the dishonorable way I'd behaved.

During the night I talked to Narric, who was to pass the word to his brother-in-law.

Right away he said, "You can count on me to carry the pieces out of the shop. Just don't be in too much of a hurry. We'll only be able to move them when there's big stuff going out for a masonry job. We won't miss a chance, though, I promise you that."

So far so good. Now I had only to talk to Matthieu Carbonieri, for he was the one I wanted to go with me on the *cavale*. He was for it 100 percent.

"Matthieu, I've found someone to make the raft and I've found someone to carry the pieces out of the shop. Now it's up to you to find a place in your garden where we can bury the raft."

"No, the garden's no good. The guards come at night to steal vegetables and they're likely to notice something. I'll fix up a hiding place in the retaining wall by taking out a big stone and digging out a space behind it. That way, when I get a piece, I'll only have to remove the rock and then put it back after I've stowed the piece inside."

"Should they carry the pieces straight to your garden?"

"No, that's too dangerous. The brothers don't have any good reason for going there. The best thing would be to have them leave the piece in a new place each time."

"Right."

Everything seemed to be working. The only thing lacking was the coconuts. I must try to figure out how to collect enough of them without attracting attention.

I felt myself coming back to life. The only thing left was to talk to Galgani and Grandet. I had no right to keep silent, for they might be accused of complicity at some point. To avoid this, I decided to leave our *gourbi* and live alone, but when I told them my plans they really bawled me out. "Get going on your *cavale* as soon as you can! We'll make out. But while you're waiting, stay with us. We've been through *cavales* before."

The *cavale* had now been in preparation for over a month. I had already received seven pieces, two of them quite big. I went to have a look at the retaining wall where Matthieu had dug his hiding place. He had taken the precaution of sticking moss around it so the rock didn't look as if it had ever been moved. The place was perfect, but the cavity looked too small to hold the whole raft. Still, there was room enough for the moment.

Having a *cavale* in the works was wonderful for my morale. I ate better than ever and the fishing kept me in good physical shape. In addition, I spent over two hours every morning doing exercises among the rocks. I concentrated on my legs, for the fishing took care of my arms. I discovered a good trick for the legs. If I fished further out where the waves broke against my thighs, the struggle to keep my balance was very good for the muscles.

Juliette, the warden's wife, was still very nice to me, but she noticed that I came in only when her husband was there. She said so right out, and to put me at ease, she explained that she had been joking the day she was having her hair done. And the young woman who had done her hair stopped me often on the way up from fishing to ask how I was, etc. So everything was all right in that department.

Bourset never wasted a moment. It was now two and a half months since we'd begun and, as I'd foreseen, the hiding place was full. We lacked only two pieces, but these were the longest—six and a half feet long and five feet. They would never fit into the hole in the retaining wall.

Looking around in the cemetery, I noticed a freshly dug grave with an ugly bouquet of faded flowers on it. It was probably the grave of the guard's wife who had died the week before. The cemetery guard, an ancient, half-blind con nicknamed Papa, usually spent the whole day sitting in the shade of a coconut palm on the far side; from there he couldn't see the grave or anyone coming near it. What if I used the grave for the raft after it was assembled, and to store as many coconuts as possible? But it would hold only about thirty-five—far fewer than I'd be needing. So I scattered over fifty in various other places—there were a dozen in Juliette's garden alone. The houseboy thought I'd left them there to make oil out of someday.

When I learned that the dead woman's husband had left for Grande Terre, I decided to dig the earth away from the grave.

Matthieu sat on the wall and acted as lookout. On his head he wore a white handkerchief, knotted at the four corners. Next to him he kept a red handkerchief, also knotted at the corners. He wore the white as long as there was no danger. If anyone came into view, he put on the red.

This risky work took me one whole afternoon and night. I didn't remove the earth as far down as the coffin because I had to enlarge the hole to make it big enough for the raft—another four feet plus a little room for maneuvering. The hours seemed endless, and the red handkerchief on Matthieu's head forced me to stop several times. Finally it was morning and I was finished. The hole was covered with woven palm leaves which made a fairly firm platform. On top of that I put a layer of earth with a small border. You could barely see it. By the time I was through, my nerves were on the point of snapping.

The preparations for the *cavale* had now been going on for three months. The labeled pieces had been taken out of their hiding place and laid above the poor woman's coffin, hidden by the earth that covered the matting. In the wall cavity we stored three bags of flour, a seven-foot rope for the sail, a bottleful of matches, a tinder box and a dozen cans of milk.

Bourset was getting more and more excited. You'd have thought it was his own *cavale*. Now Narric was sorry he hadn't said yes in the beginning. We could have made a raft for three people instead of two.

The rainy season began. It rained every day, which made it easier for me to visit the grave. Now only two side pieces for the frame were missing. Little by little I'd brought the coconuts nearer the garden, where they could be stored without danger in the buffaloes' open stable. My friends never questioned me. From time to time they simply asked, "How's it going?" "O.K." "It's taking a long time, isn't it?" "You can't do it faster without running a big risk." That was all.

Then one day Juliette saw me as I was moving the coconuts I'd stored in her yard. "Tell me, Papillon, when are you getting to work on your coconut oil? I don't see why you don't make it here in the yard. You've got a sledgehammer to open them with, and I can lend you a big pot for the pulp."

"I'd rather do it in the camp."

"That's funny. The camp isn't very convenient." She paused and then said, "Want me to tell you what I think? I don't think you're making coconut oil at all." I froze. She went on, "Why would you want it when I can give you all the olive oil you can use? The coconuts are for something else, aren't they?" Large drops of sweat rolled down my face. I was waiting to hear the word *escape*. I could hardly breathe.

"Madame, it was to be a secret, but your curiosity forces me to tell you. However, all I'm going to say is that I picked them out for their shells. I was going to make something as a present for you. That's all there is to it."

It worked. She said, "Papillon, you shouldn't go to all that trouble for me. I forbid you to spend your time and money making me something extravagant. I thank you sincerely, but you mustn't do it."

"That's for me to decide." Whew! I asked her for a pastis— something I'd never done before. Luckily she didn't notice my unease. God was on my side.

It rained hardest during the afternoon and evening. I was afraid the water would seep down through the thin layer of earth and lay bare the matting. Matthieu was forever having to replace the earth. I was certain it was flooded underneath, so we pulled back the matting and found that the water had almost reached the top of the coffin. It was a critical moment. Not far away was the grave of two children, dead for many years. We lifted off the tombstone; I crawled in and hacked away at the cement with a miner's pick on the side nearest my raft's grave. I had no sooner cracked the cement and prodded the earth with the pick than a great gush of water streamed in. It was the water from my flooded grave. I climbed out as it was reaching my knees. We replaced the stone and made it fast with some white mastic that Narric had found. With this operation we had got rid of half the water in our tomb.

That evening Carbonieri said, "We seem to have nothing but trouble with this *cavale*."

"Come on, we're almost there."

"Let's hope so." We were getting very nervous.

The next morning, as a cover-up, I went down to the quay and asked Chapar to buy me five pounds of fish. I told him I'd pick it up at noon. Then I walked over to Carbonieri's garden. As I came near, I saw three white caps. What were three guards doing in his garden? This was most unusual. Were they making a search? I'd never seen three guards around Carbonieri before. I waited almost an hour. Then I had to find out what was going on. Casually I walked down the path that led to the garden. The guards watched me come. When I was about forty yards away, Matthieu put the white handkerchief on his head. I breathed again and just had time to pull myself together before I reached them.

"Good morning, gentlemen. Good morning, Matthieu. I'm here for the papaya you promised me."

"I'm sorry, Papillon, but somebody stole it this morning while I was getting the poles for my beans. I'll have some more ripe ones in four or five days; they're already turning yellow. Gentlemen, don't you want some lettuce, or tomatoes, maybe some radishes for your wives?"

"Your garden is very well tended, Carbonieri. My congratulations," one of them said.

They accepted the lettuce, tomatoes and radishes and left. I made sure to leave before them, taking two heads of lettuce with me.

I passed by the cemetery. The rain had washed away the earth, leaving the tomb half uncovered. I could see the matting ten steps away. Only the good Lord had kept us from being caught this time. The wind blew like mad every night, roaring over the plateau and sometimes bringing gusts of rain. It was ideal weather for a *cavale*.

The six-foot piece of wood—the most important one and damnably cumbersome—joined its brothers. I slid it into place and it fitted like an angel. Bourset ran back to camp to find out if I'd received it. He was so relieved to know all had gone well, it seemed as if he'd been worried it might not arrive.

"Is something wrong?" I asked him. "Do you think somebody's onto us? Have you told anybody about this?"

"No, certainly not."

"But something's eating you. What is it?"

"A guy named Bébert Celier seems to be taking a little too much interest in us. I think he saw Narric put a piece of our wood under his workbench, then transfer it to a barrel of lime and carry it off. His eyes followed Narric to the door of the shop. That's why I'm worried."

So I said to Grandet, "Bébert Celier is in our *case*. He can't possibly be a stoolie, can he?"

"He's one of the boys in the Public Works Service. You know the kind: African battalion, *camisard*, one of those bullheaded soldiers who's been in every military prison in Morocco and Algeria. He's a fighter, dangerous with a knife, a passionate lover of young boys and a gambler. He's never been a civilian. Conclusion: he's a loser and a dangerous one. The *bagne* is his life. If you have any real doubts, take the bull by the horns and kill him tonight. Don't give him time to squeal."

"We've got no proof he's a stoolie."

"True," Grandet said. "But we've go no proof he isn't. His kind of *bagnard* don't like *cavales*. They don't like anything messing up their well-ordered lives. They might not be stool pigeons about anything else, but about *cavales*, who knows?"

I consulted Matthieu. His advice was to kill Celier that night. In fact, he volunteered to do it himself. I made the mistake of saying no. The idea of killing someone, or allowing someone to be killed, on the basis of appearances alone revolted me. What if

Bourset was imagining things? Fear might make him invent heaven knows what.

I asked Narric, "Have you noticed anything funny about Bébert Celier?"

"Me? No. I carried the barrel out on my shoulder so the turnkey at the door couldn't see inside. We figured that if I stood just in front of him until my brother-in-law arrived, the Arab would see I wasn't in a hurry and he'd trust me enough not to look inside the barrel. But later on my brother-in-law did tell me he thought Bébert Celier was watching us pretty closely."

"What do you think?"

"My brother-in-law was especially nervous because of the size of the piece and the fact that it looked too much as if it were for a raft. He thought he saw more than he actually saw."

"That's what I think. Let's forget it. When we get to the last piece, make sure Bébert Celier is not around when you leave. Take the same precautions with him you would with a guard."

I spent that night gambling for very high stakes and won seven thousand francs. The less attention I paid to the game, the more money I won. At four-thirty in the morning I left for work, though I actually turned the job over to the black from Martinique. The rain had stopped and I crept through the dark to the cemetery. I couldn't find the shovel, so I had to move the earth back with my feet. When I went down to fish, the sun was already shining bright. I went to the southernmost part of Royale, where I was planning to launch the raft. The tide was high and the sea rough; it was clear that it would be hard to get away from the island without being tossed back onto the rocks. I started to fish and right away caught a lot of rock mullet. In no time I had over twelve pounds. So I stopped and cleaned the fish in the sea. I was very uneasy, and tired from the long night of gambling. I sat down in the shade and tried to pull myself together. I told myself that the tension that had been building up for three months was soon coming to an end and, thinking about Celier, I decided I had no right to kill him.

Then I went to call on Matthieu. The grave could easily be seen from his garden. There was some earth on the path which he said he'd sweep off at noon. I passed by Juliette's and gave her half my fish.

She said, "Papillon, I had a bad dream about you last night. You were in chains and all covered with blood. Please don't do anything foolish. I'd suffer too much if something happened to you. See, the dream upset me so much I haven't washed yet or even combed my hair. I looked through my binoculars to see where you were fishing, but I couldn't find you. Where did you catch these?"

"On the other side of the island. That's why you didn't see me."

"Why do you go so far away where nobody can see you? What if you were carried away by a wave? There would be no one to save you from the sharks."

"Oh, you're exaggerating!"

"You think I'm exaggerating? Well, perhaps. But I forbid you to fish on that side of the island. If you don't obey me, I'll see that your fishing permit is taken away."

"Come, be reasonable. If it'll make you any happier, I'll let your houseboy know where I'm going fishing."

"All right. But why do you look so tired?"

"Because I am tired. And I'm going back to the camp to sleep."

"O.K., but I expect you for coffee at four o'clock. You'll come?"

"Yes, madame. I'll see you later."

Juliette's dream! That was all I needed! As if I didn't have enough real problems. . . .

Bourset told me he was sure he was being watched. We'd been waiting fifteen days for the last piece—the one five feet long. Narric and Quenier insisted there was nothing wrong, but Bourset was still afraid to make it. If it hadn't needed five joints that had to fit exactly, Matthieu could have made it in the garden. But it was into this plank that the five ribs of the raft had to be fitted. Narric and Quenier were repairing the chapel, so they were able to come and go from the shop with all kinds of material. Sometimes they even used a small wagon pulled by a buffalo. We had to take advantage of this opportunity.

Against his better judgment, Bourset started to make the piece. Then one day he said he was sure someone had moved it when he wasn't there. He still had to make one of the joints, and we decided he should do this and then put the piece under his workbench. He was to lay a hair on it to tell us if anyone touched it. He finished his work and left the shop at six o'clock, making sure that no one was left except the guard. The plank and hair were in place. At noon I was in the camp waiting for the eighty men to come out of the shop. Narric and Quenier were there, but no Bourset. A German came up to me and handed me a carefully sealed letter. I could see it hadn't been opened. I read: "The hair is gone; someone has touched the board. The guard is letting me stay to work during the siesta. I told him I had to finish a little rosewood box I've been working on. I'll take the board and put it with Narric's tools. You tell him about it. He must leave with the board at three sharp. Maybe we can steal a march on the guy who is taking such an interest."

Narric and Quenier agreed. Just before everybody was back in the shop, two men would start a fight outside the door. This task was allotted to two of Carbonicri's people—Corsicans from Marseilles named Massani and Santini. They didn't ask why, which was fine. Narric and Quenier would be first in line and they would take advantage of the incident to run in, then out, carrying a mixture of stuff as if they were in a hurry to get to work and the fight couldn't concern them less. We were all agreed that this was our last chance. If it succeeded, I wouldn't make a move for a month or two because it was clear that someone—or several people—knew that somebody was making a raft. It would be up to them to find out who and where.

It was now two-thirty and the men were getting ready. There were thirty minutes between roll call and the time the men actually filed off to work. Bébert Celier was in the middle of the twenty rows of four men each.

Narric and Quenier were in the first row, Massani and Santini in the twelfth, Bébert Celier in the tenth. It looked like a good setup, because when Narric was picking up his odd lengths of wood along with our board, others would still be going in. Bébert would be almost at the workshop door. When the scuffle broke out, everybody would turn around, Bébert included, and there'd be lots of shouting and shoving. And so it went. By four o'clock it was all over. The board was under a heap of stuff in the chapel. They hadn't yet been able to get it out of there, but it was well hidden.

I went to see Juliette; she wasn't home. On my way back I passed the Administration Building and saw Massani and Santini standing in the shade, waiting to be put in the dungeon. We had expected that.

I walked up to them and asked, "How much?"

"Eight days."

A Corsican guard said, "How about that! Two Corsicans fighting each other . . . !"

I went back to camp. Carbonieri and my friends were walking on air—they congratulated me on the way I had organized the operation. Narric and Quenier were pleased too. Everything was going great. I slept through the night even though I was asked to play poker. I pretended I had a headache. Actually I was just dead tired but overjoyed that success was around the corner. The most difficult part was behind me.

The next morning Matthieu put the board in the hole in the wall. The cemetery guard was raking the paths near our tomb. It would be risky to go too near it now. Every morning at daybreak I took a wooden bucket and replaced the earth on the grave. I tidied the path with a broom, then hurriedly hid the pail and broom in a corner and returned to work.

It was now exactly four months since we had started to prepare this *cavale* and nine days since we'd finally got the last piece for the raft. The rain had stopped except for a little at night. All my attention was turned to the next two stages: first getting the damned board out of Matthieu's garden, then fitting it into the raft. This could only be done during the day. Then, escape! But that had to wait until the raft was launched and packed with the coconuts and our supplies.

I brought Jean Castelli up to date. He was delighted to know that I was this near the end. He remarked, "The moon's in the first quarter."

"I know. At midnight there'll be no problem. The tide goes out at ten in the evening, so the best time to put the raft in the water will be between one and two in the morning."

Carbonieri and I decided to hurry things up a little. We'd make the final assembly the next morning. That night, escape.

The next morning I walked from the garden to the cemetery and jumped over the wall, carrying a bucket in my hand. While I was clearing the earth away from the top of the matting, Matthieu was moving the stone out from the wall to get at the board. Then together we lifted the matting and placed it to one side. The raft seemed to be in perfect condition. A little dirty, but that didn't matter. We took it out in order to have room to fit the last piece in, then we set in the five ribs, banging them into their grooves with a stone. Just as we were finished and about to put the raft back in its place, a guard appeared with a carbine in his hand.

"Don't move or I shoot!"

We dropped the raft and put up our hands. I recognized the guard. He was the one from the workshop.

"Don't try anything funny. I've got you. Admit it and at least you'll save your skin. It's hanging by just a thread right now—I'd really like to pump you full of lead. All right, get going. Keep your hands up."

As we passed the entrance to the cemetery, we met an Arab turnkey. The guard said to him, "Thanks for your help, Mohamed. Come by tomorrow morning and I'll give you what I promised you."

"Thanks," the old dog replied. "Don't worry, chief, I'll be there. But doesn't Bébert Celier owe me something too?"

"You work it out with him," the guard said.

So I said to him, "Was Bébert Celier the one who ratted on us, chief?"

"I didn't say so, did I?"

"It doesn't matter. It's just good to know."

Still aiming his carbine at us, the guard said, "Frisk 'em, Mohamed."

The Arab found my knife inside my belt, then took Matthieu's.

"Mohamed," I said to him, "you're pretty sharp. How'd you catch on to us?"

"I climbed a palm tree every day to see how you were doing with the raft."

"Who told you to do it?"

"First it was Bébert Celier, then Bruet, the guard."

"Let's go," the guard said. "That's enough talk. You can put your hands down now. Get moving."

The four hundred yards to the warden's were the longest road I'd ever walked. I wanted to die. All that struggle only to get caught like a pair of half-assed idiots. My God, but you're cruel to me! Our arrival at the warden's was a great occasion. As we were nearing the Administration Building, we kept meeting guards who fell into step with our guard. By the time we arrived, there must have been seven or eight of them.

The Arab had run ahead to give the warden the news. He was standing at the door with Dega and five guards. "What's going on, Monsieur Bruet?"

"I just caught these two red-handed. They were hiding a raft that looked to be about finished."

"What have you got to say for yourself, Papillon?"

"Nothing. I'll talk at the interrogation."

"Put them in the dungeon."

I was put in a cell with a blocked-up window near the entrance to the building. The cell was dark, but I could hear people talking outside.

Things moved fast. At three o'clock we were taken out and handcuffed. A kind of tribunal had been set up consisting of the head warden, his second-in-command and the head guard. Another guard served as clerk. Dega sat at a little table to one side, pencil in hand, ready to take down our statements.

"Charrière and Carbonieri, listen to Monsieur Bruet's allegations: 'I, Auguste Bruet, head guard and director of the workshops on the Iles du Salut, accuse the two *bagnards*, Charrière and Carbonieri, of the theft and misappropriation of material belonging to the State. I accuse the carpenter, Bourset, of complicity. I think I can also implicate Narric and Quenier. I wish to add that I caught Charrière and Carbonieri red-handed as they were violating the grave of Madame Privat, which they used as the hiding place for their raft.' "

"What have you got to say?" the warden asked.

"In the first place, Carbonieri had nothing to do with it. The raft was designed to carry only one man: me. I only asked him to help me lift the matting off the grave. Carbonieri is not guilty of theft or misappropriating material belonging to the State, or of complicity in an escape since there was no escape. Bourset was a poor bastard who was operating under pain of death. As for Narric and Quenier, I hardly know them. They had nothing to do with it."

"That's not what my informant told me," the guard said.

"Your informant was Bébert Celier. He might have been trying to get even with someone by implicating him falsely. Besides, how can you trust a stoolie?"

"All right," the warden said. "You are officially accused of theft and misappropriation of material belonging to the State, of defiling a grave, and attempting to escape. Sign here."

"I'll sign only when you've added my statement about Carbonieri, Bourset, Narric and Quenier."

"All right. Write it up."

I signed. I can't really tell you what happened after that. I was out of my mind. I barely ate, I couldn't move, I smoked constantly, one cigarette after another. Luckily Dega kept me well supplied with tobacco. Every day I had a morning walk in the sun in the yard of the maximum-security compound. The warden came to see me. The funny thing was that, although he would have been severely censured if the escape had succeeded, he wasn't angry with me at all.

Smiling all the while, he told me that his wife had said it was perfectly normal for a man to try to escape unless he had gone to pot. With great cleverness he tried to get me to admit Carbonieri's complicity. I think I convinced him. I explained how it was practically impossible for Carbonieri to refuse to help me when I needed to remove the matting.

Bourset disclosed my threatening letter and the design I'd made for the raft. In that matter the warden was completely convinced. I asked him what he thought the theft of State property would get me. "Not more than eighteen months."

So, gradually, I climbed out of the pit. A note came from Chatal, the orderly, informing me that Bébert Celier was in a special room in the hospital with a rare disease: an abscess of the liver. I was sure it was something cooked up between the doctor and the Administration to protect him from reprisals.

I was left alone in my cell and never searched, so I took advantage of this to get hold of a knife. I told Narric and Quenier to ask for a meeting of the shop guard, Bébert Celier, the carpenter and me. After the meeting the warden would decide whether they deserved imprisonment, punishment, or freedom.

During the morning walk Narric told me that the warden had agreed to the meeting. It was to take place the next day at ten. One of the head guards would act as examining judge. I spent the night trying to talk myself out of killing Bébert Celier, but I couldn't do it. It wasn't fair for him to be disinterned to Grande Terre for his service to the Administration and make a *cavale* from there as if in reward for having prevented mine. They'd probably condemn me to death. I didn't give a good goddam; I was that desperate. Four months of hope, of joy, the fear of being caught, ingenuity, then, on the brink of success, to have the whole thing collapse because of one stinking rat! Come what might, I'd kill Celier.

The only way to escape the death penalty would be to get him to pull his knife first. If I had mine out, he'd be sure to pull his. I would do it a little before or right after the meeting. During the meeting itself, it would be impossible because I'd risk being shot by a guard. I would have to count on the guards' chronic negligence.

I spent the whole night fighting this idea. I lost. After all, there were some things that could not be forgiven. I knew that nobody had the right to write his own laws, but that was for people of another social class. How could you not think of punishing a low-down bastard like him? I'd never harmed that bigmouth; he didn't even know me. He was condemning me to X number of years in solitary, and I'd never done a thing to him. He was burying me so he could live again. No, no, no! I couldn't let him profit from this. I felt lost. Tit for tat, let him feel lost, too, more than me even. But what if they condemned me to death? It would be damn stupid to die for a punk like him. I finally managed to promise myself one thing: if I couldn't get him to pull his knife, I wouldn't kill him.

I didn't sleep that entire night. I smoked a whole package of gray tobacco. When coffee arrived at six in the morning, I had two cigarettes left. I was so tense that, even though it was forbidden, I said to the coffee boy, "Could you give me some cigarettes or a little tobacco? I'm almost out, Monsieur Antartaglia."

The guard said, "Sure, give him some. I really feel sorry for you, Papillon. I'm a Corsican. I like people; I hate this kind of treachery."

By a quarter to ten I was in the yard waiting to enter the hall. Narric, Quenier, Bourset and Carbonieri were there. The guard in charge was Antartaglia, the coffee guy. He talked to Carbonieri in Corsican, and I gathered he was telling him that he stood a good chance of getting three years in solitary. At that point the door to the yard opened and in came the Arab of the palm tree, the Arab who guarded the door to the shop and Bébert Celier. When Celier saw me, he drew back, but the guard said, "Come on, stand over there on the right. Antartaglia, see they don't get too close." We were less than two yards apart.

Antartaglia said, "No talking between groups."

Carbonieri continued to talk to his fellow Corsican, who was watching both groups. The guard bent down to tie his shoelace; I made Matthieu a sign to step forward a little. He understood, looked at Celier and spat in his direction. The guard stood up and Carbonieri went on talking to him, commanding his attention so I could take a step forward without his noticing it. My knife slid down into my hand. Only Celier could see it. His knife was already open in his pocket and, faster than I'd anticipated, he swung at me and nicked me in the muscle of my right arm. But since I was left-handed, I was able to plunge my knife into his chest right up to the handle. There was an animal cry of "A-a-ah!" and he fell in a heap.

Antartaglia pulled out his revolver. "Get back, kid, get back. Don't hit him when he's down or I'll have to shoot you, and I don't want to do that."

Carbonieri went over to Celier and prodded his head with his foot. He said two words in Corsican. I understood them: "He's dead."

The guard said, "Give me your knife, kid."

I gave it to him. He put his revolver back in its holster, went over to the door and knocked. A guard opened it and he said, "Tell the stretcher-bearers to come pick up a dead man."

"Who's dead?" the guard asked.

"Bébert Celier."

"Ah! I thought it was Papillon."

We were put back in our cells. Meeting suspended. Before stepping into the hall, Carbonieri said to me, "Poor Papi, you're in for it this time."

"Yes, but I'm alive and he isn't."

The guard came back alone, opened the door and said in a husky voice, "Knock on the door. Tell 'em you're wounded. He attacked first. I saw him." He left.

These Corsican guards were amazing—either all good or all bad. I knocked on the door and shouted, "I'm wounded! I want to go to the hospital!"

The guard returned with the head of the disciplinary section. "What's the matter with you? Why all the racket?"

"Chief, I'm wounded."

"What? You're wounded? I didn't think he touched you."

"He got the muscle in my right arm."

"Open the door."

The door opened and I went out. The arm muscle was badly cut.

"Put him in handcuffs and take him to the hospital. But don't on any account leave him there. Bring him back here the minute he's patched up."

When he went out, there were more than ten guards standing around the warden. The shop guard said to me, "You murderer!"

Before I could say anything, the head guard answered for me. "Shut up, Brouet. He attacked Papillon first."

"I saw it too. I was a witness," Antartaglia said. "And you might as well learn now, Monsieur Bruet, Corsicans don't lie."

Once I was in the hospital, Chatal called for the doctor. With no anesthetic—either general or local—he sewed me up and attached eight clamps. When he was finished, he said, "I couldn't give you a local anesthetic. I'm all out." Then he added, "That was not a good thing you did."

"Well, you know, he couldn't have lived long with that abscess on his liver."

He started; he hadn't expected that one.

The interrogation was resumed. Bourset's participation in the plot was dismissed. It was agreed that he'd been terrorized. For lack of proof they dismissed the case of Narric and Quenier too. That left Carbonieri and me. In Carbonieri's case they dismissed the charge of theft and misappropriation, etc. There remained complicity in an attempt to escape. That wouldn't get him more than six months. In my case things got complicated. In spite of all the testimony on my behalf, the examiner would not accept legitimate self-defense. Dega had seen the full dossier and told me that, in spite of the examiner's vindictiveness, I couldn't be given the death penalty because I had been wounded. What the prosecution used to get me was the declaration of the two Arabs that I had been the first to pull my knife.

The interrogation ended. I waited to be sent to Saint-Laurent to appear before the council of war. I smoked. I hardly walked at all. At no time did the warden or the guards—except the shop guard and the examiner—show me the least hostility. Also I was allowed to have all the tobacco I wanted. I was to leave Friday.

On Wednesday morning at ten I had been in the yard almost two hours when the warden called me and said, "Come with me." We took the path to his house. As we walked, he said, "My wife wants to see you before you leave. I didn't want to upset her by having you brought by an armed guard. I hope you'll behave yourself."

We reached his house. "Juliette, I've brought your protégé, as I promised. Remember I have to take him back before noon. You have almost an hour." He discreetly went his way.

Juliette came up to me, put her hand on my shoulder and looked me in the eye. Tears made her black eyes sparkle all the more, but luckily she didn't cry.

"My friend, you really are crazy. If only you'd told me you wanted to leave, I could have helped you. I've asked my husband to do everything possible for you, but he said it wasn't up to him. I wanted you to come so I could see how you are. I congratulate you on your courage. You're in better shape than I could have hoped.

Besides, I wanted to tell you I intend to pay for all the fish you've given me. Here is a thousand francs. It's all I have. I'm sorry I can't do better."

"Madame, I don't need the money. I can't accept it. It would spoil our friendship." I pushed aside the two five-hundred-franc notes. "Please, don't insist."

"As you wish. Won't you sit down and have a small pastis?"

For more than an hour that admirable woman talked to me in her charming way. She was sure I'd be acquitted for murdering the punk, that the most I'd get would be eighteen months to two years for the rest.

As I was leaving, she squeezed my hand for a long time, then said, "Good-by. Good luck," and burst into tears.

The warden took me back to the cell block.

On the way I said, "Sir, your wife is the noblest woman I've ever met."

"I know it, Papillon. She wasn't made to live here; it's too hard on her. But what can I do? Well, we have only four more years to go."

"Now that we're alone, sir, I want to thank you for treating me so well in spite of all the trouble I would have caused you if I'd been successful."

"Yes, you could have been a real headache, Papillon. All the same, I'll tell you something. You deserved to succeed." At the door to the maximum-security section he added:

"Good-by, Papillon. God help you. You're going to need it."

"Good-by, sir."

I certainly was going to need God's help! The council of war was presided over by a police commissioner with four stripes, and it was tough. Three years for theft and misappropriation, defiling a grave and attempting to escape, plus five years—to be served consecutively—for Celier's murder. Total: eight years in solitary. If I hadn't been wounded, I would have got the death penalty for sure.

SECOND SOLITARY

I returned to the islands, handcuffed to a Polack named Dandosky. For two premeditated murders he'd got *five* years. I'd got eight.

There were sixteen of us, twelve condemned to solitary. The sea was very rough and the deck was often swept by huge waves. My despair was so deep I practically hoped the tub would sink. Absorbed in my fate, I talked to no one. The cold spray stung my face, the wind took my hat. So what! I wouldn't need it much for my eight years in solitary. At first I had hoped we'd all drown; now I took a different view: Bébert Celier was eaten by sharks; I am thirty and have only eight years to go. But can I survive eight years within the walls of *la mangeuse d'hommes*?

From my previous experience I had to say no. Four to five years had to be the absolute limit of human resistance. If I hadn't killed Celier, I'd have only three years to do, maybe only two, but that murder had messed up everything. I should never have killed the punk. My duty to myself was not to get even but, above anything else, to live—to live in order to escape. How could I have been such a dope? Even though he very nearly killed me, the filthy bastard. Live, live, live, that's what should have been, and must be from now on, my only religion.

Among the guards who accompanied the convoy there was one I remembered from the Réclusion. I couldn't recall his name, but I had a crazy desire to ask him a question.

"Chief, I'd like to ask you something."

Surprised, he came nearer. "What?"

"Have you ever known anybody who lived through eight years of solitary?"

He thought a moment and said, "No, but I've known several who did five years, and there was even one—I remember him very well—who got out in good health and sound mind after six years. I was at the Réclusion when he was freed."

"Thank you."

"You're welcome. You've got eight years, they tell me."

"Yes, chief."

"You'll make it only if you're never given extra punishment."

Those were very important words. I'd get out alive only if I was never punished. Punishment meant taking away part or all of your food for a certain length of time. After that, even when you were back on a normal diet, you could never make it up. A few mild punishments and you were dead. Conclusion: I would accept no coconuts, no cigarettes, not even write or receive notes.

For the rest of the trip I chewed this over. I would have nothing, absolutely nothing to do with the outside or inside world. Then an idea came to me: the only way to get better food without risk was to get someone on the outside to pay the soup distributor to give me the biggest and best piece of meat at noon. That was easy, because one man ladled out the broth and another man carried a platter of meat from which he chose the piece for your bowl. I had to get the first man to scrape the bottom of the pot and give me all the vegetables he could. This idea brought me comfort. If I could set this up, I'd be able to satisfy my hunger—or just about. Then, in order not to go mad, all I had to do was dream, flying as far away as possible and choosing only the most pleasant subjects.

We got back to the islands at three in the afternoon. I was no sooner off the boat than I noticed Juliette's pale-yellow dress next to her husband. The warden came up to me even before we had lined up and asked, "How many?"

"Eight."

He turned to his wife and spoke to her. She sat down on a rock, obviously stunned. Then her husband took her by the arm. She got to her feet and, looking at me somberly with her big eyes, walked away.

"Papillon," Dega asked, "how many?"

"Eight years in solitary." He was silent, and didn't even dare look at me. Galgani came up, and before he could speak I said, "Don't send me a thing. Don't write to me. With this long sentence I can't take any risks."

"I understand."

In a low voice I added quickly, "See if you can get me the best food possible at noon and at night. If you can manage it, maybe we'll see each other again someday. Good-by."

I headed for the boat that was to take us back to Saint-Joseph. Everybody looked at me as if I were a coffin being lowered into the grave. No one spoke.

During the short trip I repeated to Chapar what I'd said to Galgani. He replied, "That should be easy enough. Chin up, Papi." Then he asked, "What about Carbonieri?"

"I'm sorry I forgot to tell you. The President of the council asked for more information on his case before making a decision. Is that good or bad?"

"It's good, I think."

I was in the first row of the column of twelve men that climbed the hill to the Réclusion. I walked fast. It's strange, but I was actually in a hurry to get to my cell and be alone. In fact, I was rushing so fast that the guard said, "Slow down, Papillon. You look as if you were in a hurry to get home." Then we were there.

The guard said, "Strip, everybody. The chief warden at Réclusion will address you now."

He made his usual speech—"*Réclusionnaires*, here we . . ."—

then turned to me. "I'm sorry to see you back, Papillon. You're in Building A, cell one twenty-seven. It's the best one, Papillon. You're opposite the door to the hall so you have more light and you'll always have fresh air. I hope you intend to behave. Eight years is a long time, but who knows? If your conduct is good, you may get a year or two off. I hope so; you're a brave man."

So I was in number 127. It was exactly opposite a large barred door that opened into the passageway. Although it was already six o'clock, you could see quite clearly. Nor did this cell have the odor of rot that my first one had. That was encouraging. Old man, I told myself, these four walls will be watching you for the next eight years. Don't count every month and hour; that's a waste of time. Try six-month periods. Sixteen times six months and you're free again. You have one advantage anyway. If you croak in here, you have the satisfaction of dying in the light—if you die during the day, that is. It can't be much fun to die in the dark. If you're sick, here at least, the doctor can see your face. Don't blame yourself for trying to escape and live again, and for God's sake, don't feel guilty about killing Celier. Just think how you'd suffer if he left on a *cavale* while you were in here. Anyway, maybe there'll be an amnesty, a war, an earthquake; maybe a typhoon will destroy this place. Why not? Maybe some honest man, returning to France, will move the French to force the Penal Administration to put an end to this guillotining of men without benefit of guillotine. Maybe a doctor, sickened by what he has seen, will spill it to a journalist or to a priest. Who knows? In any event, Celier has been eaten by the sharks, but you're here, you have your pride, you'll get out of this tomb alive.

One, two, three, four, five and turn; one, two, three, four, five, another turn. I began to walk and suddenly it all came back to me: the position of the head, the arms, the exact length of each step to make the pendulum work properly. I decided to walk only two hours in the morning and two in the afternoon until I knew if I could count on the extra food. I mustn't waste energy.

Yes, it was heartbreaking to have failed at the end, even though it was only the first part of the *cavale*, with ninety miles on a frail raft ahead. And then, after arriving on Grande Terre, still another *cavale*. If I'd been able to launch the raft, the three flour sacks that had to serve as sails would have carried it at a speed of at least six miles an hour. In less than fifteen hours, maybe even twelve, we would have reached land. Assuming, of course, that it was raining that day, because only in the rain would we have dared to hoist sail. I seemed to remember that it rained the day after I was put in the dungeon. But I wasn't absolutely certain. I tried to think of what mistakes I'd made. Only two came to mind: first, the raft had been too well made; to house the coconuts, the carpenter had had to construct a framework which amounted to making two rafts, one inside the other. The whole thing had taken too many pieces and too much time.

The second mistake was more serious. The moment we began to have doubts about Celier—that very night—I should have killed him. If I had, just think what might have happened! Even if we'd been shipwrecked on Grande Terre or arrested as I put the raft in the water, I would have got only three years instead of eight, and I would have had the satisfaction of doing something toward a *cavale*. And where would I be if everything had gone well on the islands and Grande Terre? Who knows? Maybe having a chat with Bowen in Trinidad, or in Curaçao with Irénée de Bruyne. And we would have moved on only when we knew for sure which country was ready to accept us. If that hadn't worked out, I could easily have taken a small boat alone and rejoined my tribe in Guajira.

I went to sleep very late. It wasn't all that depressing. Live, live, live. Each time I was tempted to despair, I would repeat three times: "As long as there's life, there's hope."

A week went by. I began to notice a change in my food. A beautiful piece of boiled meat at noon and for supper a bowl of lentils with practically no water. Like a child, I recited: "Lentils are rich in iron. Lentils are very good for you."

If this lasted, I'd be able to walk ten to twelve hours a day, and by evening I'd be tired enough to fly where I wanted to. But actually I went nowhere. I stayed right on earth, thinking about all the *bagnards* I'd known on the islands. I thought of the legends that made the rounds, and there was one I promised myself I'd check on when I got out, the one about the bell.

As I've mentioned before, *bagnards* weren't buried but were thrown into the sea between Saint-Joseph and Royale in an area infested with sharks. The corpse was wrapped in flour sacks and a rock attached to his feet by a strong cord. A long, narrow crate— always the same one—rested in the bow of the boat. When the boat arrived at the right spot, the six rowers feathered their oars, one man tipped the crate, another opened the trap door, and the corpse slid into the water. It was a known fact that the first thing the sharks did was to saw through the cord. The corpse never had time to sink much below the surface. It soon bobbed up again and the sharks would begin to fight for the choicest pieces. They say that to watch a man being eaten by sharks leaves a lasting impression. When the sharks were especially numerous, they sometimes lifted the shroud and its occupant right out of the water, tore away the flour bags and carried off large hunks of the corpse.

I know that this part is accurate, but there was one thing I had not been able to verify. All the cons believed that what brought the sharks to this particular place was the sound of the bell which was rung in the chapel when a con died. They said that when you stood at the end of the jetty on Royale at six in the evening, there were sometimes no sharks at all. But when the bell rang in the chapel, the place was crowded with them in no time flat. There was no reason for them to rush to that particular spot at that hour. I hoped to God I would never be the sharks' "blue-plate special." If they ate me alive while I was making a *cavale*, okay, at least I was on the road to freedom. But to die in my cell of some disease—no, I couldn't allow that to happen.

Thanks to my friends, I ate well and stayed in perfect health. I walked from seven in the morning to six at night without stopping. And then came the evening soup bowl of lentils, split peas, rice, or whatever. I ate it all and happily. All that walking had a good effect: it brought on a healthy fatigue, and I even got to the point where I could spin off into the past while I was walking. For example, once I spent the whole day in the fields of a small village in Ardèche called Favras. After my mother died, I often used to go there to spend a few weeks with my aunt, my mother's sister, who was the village schoolteacher. Well, I was in the chestnut forest picking mushrooms. I heard my friend, the shepherd, call his sheep dog and order him to bring back a wandering sheep. I tasted the cool, slightly metallic water of the spring, felt the tiny droplets bounce up my nose. Such sharp recollections of moments and events fifteen years in the past, and the ability to relive them so intensely, can only be accomplished in a cell where you're cut off from all noise, in the most absolute silence.

I could even see the yellow of Aunt Outine's dress. I could hear the wind in the chestnut trees, the dry noise a chestnut makes when it falls on the ground, or its soft thump when it hits a pile of leaves. A huge wild boar appeared out of a field of broom and gave me such a fright that I ran off, dropping most of the mushrooms I'd picked. Yes, I spent the whole day in Favras with my aunt and my young friend, Julien. And there was no one to stop me from rolling around in these memories and drinking in the peace so necessary to my battered soul.

To the objective eye I was in one of the many cells of *la*

mangeuse d'hommes. But in point of fact I had stolen an entire day and spent it in Favras in the fields, among the chestnut trees.

Six months went by. I had promised myself to count only in intervals of six months. I kept my promise. This morning I reduced the figure from sixteen to fifteen. It was now only fifteen times six months.

To be specific: nothing had really happened in those six months. Always the same food, but in sufficient quantity to maintain my health. There were many suicides and lunatics around me, but luckily the latter didn't last very long. It was depressing to hear their screams, moans and complaints for hours and days on end. I found a good antidote, but it wasn't a very healthy one. I broke off two small pieces of soap and stuck them in my ears. The noise was gone, but my ears started to run after a couple of days.

For the first time since I'd arrived, I asked for something. One of the guards who ladled out the soup was from Montélimar, very near where I came from; I had known him at Royale. I asked him if he could bring me a ball of wax as big as a nut to drown out the madmen's racket. He did it the next day. It was a great relief not to hear those poor crazy bastards any more.

I established a good working relationship with the centipedes. In six months I'd been bitten only once. If I woke up and found one crawling over my body, I simply waited. You can get used to anything and it was only a matter of self-control, but the tickling of those legs and antennae was very disagreeable. It was better to let them go away by themselves, then look for them and crush them later; if you didn't catch them the right way, you got a terrible sting. There were always a few crumbs on my cement bench. They couldn't resist the smell of the bread, so that's where they went. I killed them there.

I had to get rid of one gnawing obsession: Why hadn't I killed Bébert Celier the day we began to suspect him? I'd argue endlessly with myself: When do you have the right to kill? Then I'd arrive at the conclusion that the end justified the means. My end had been to have a successful *cavale*; I'd been lucky enough to finish a good raft and hide it in a safe place. Our departure was only a few days away. I knew that Celier was dangerous. I should have finished him off. But what if I'd made a mistake? What if I'd been misled by appearances? I would have killed an innocent man. That would have been bad. But for a *bagnard* with a life sentence to get involved in questions of conscience . . . ! What's more, a con with eight years in solitary . . .

Who do you think you are, a piece of trash treated by society like so much garbage? I'd like to know if those twelve cheeseheads on the jury ever asked themselves if they'd done the right thing when they sentenced you to life. And whether the prosecutor—I still hadn't decided exactly how I'd tear out his tongue—had asked himself if he hadn't gone a little far with his indictment. Even my own lawyer probably didn't remember me. He might mention "that unfortunate business over Papillon at the Assizes in 'thirty-two" in general terms, saying, "You know, on that particular day I wasn't quite up to snuff, and besides, Prosecutor Pradel was having an especially good day. He argued his case in masterly fashion, truly a first-class adversary. . . ."

I heard all this as if I were standing right next to Raymond Hubert as he was conversing with some lawyers at a party, or more likely in the corridors of the Palais de Justice.

There was one man of honor, but only one—President Bevin. He might well have spoken to some of his colleagues about the danger involved in having a man judged by a jury. He might have said—choosing his words more carefully, of course—that the twelve yokels on the jury were not prepared to assume the responsibility of judgment, that they were too easily swayed by the lawyer's eloquence—that they acquitted too fast or convicted without really knowing why, according to the positive or negative atmosphere created by the more persuasive lawyer.

Perhaps my family felt aggrieved at the trouble I had caused them. Only my poor father probably didn't complain at the heavy cross his son had laid on his shoulders. Of that I was certain. He probably hadn't once criticized his child even though as a teacher he respected the law and taught his pupils to understand and accept it. I was positive that in the bottom of his heart he was saying, "You bastards, you've killed my child; worse than that, you've condemned him to a slow death at the age of twenty-five!" If he knew where his boy was and what they were doing to him now, he'd be quite capable of becoming an anarchist.

Tonight *la mangeuse d'hommes* really earned its name. Two men hanged themselves and one suffocated by stuffing rags in his mouth and up his nose. Cell 127 was near where the changing of the guard took place, and I could sometimes hear snatches of the guards' conversation. This morning I heard them discussing the events of the night. That's how I knew what had happened.

Another six months passed and I carved a handsome "14" into the wood. I had a nail which I used only for this purpose, hence every six months. I took stock and was glad to report that both my health and morale were good.

Thanks to my journeys among the stars, I rarely had long bouts of depression. Also, Celier's death was a great help in getting me through my moments of crisis. I would say to myself: I'm alive, I'm living, and I must continue to live, live now to live free again someday. The man who balked my escape is dead; he'll never be free. If I get out at thirty-eight, I won't be old. And the next *cavale* will work, that I know.

One, two, three, four, five and turn; one, two, three, four, five, another turn. For some days now my legs had been black and my gums were always bleeding. Should I report sick? I pressed my thumb against my calf and the thumbprint stayed. It was as if I were full of water. For the last week I hadn't been able to walk ten or twelve hours a day; six hours, even with a rest period, tired me out. I usually cleaned my teeth by rubbing them with the rough soapy towel, but now it hurt my gums, making them bleed. And yesterday a tooth fell out just like that, an incisor in the upper jaw.

This last six months wound up with a real revolution. Yesterday we were told to stick our heads out of our cells and a doctor came by and lifted everybody's upper lip. Then this morning, after only eighteen months in my cell, the door opened and I was told:

"Come out. Stand up against the wall and wait."

I was the man nearest the door. About seventy of us filed out. We were told to turn left, and I found myself at the tail of a line moving toward the opposite end of the building and out into the yard.

It was nine o'clock. A young doctor in a short-sleeved khaki shirt was sitting at a small wooden table in the middle of the yard. Near him stood two convict orderlies and an infirmary guard. I didn't recognize any of them. Ten armed guards kept us covered, and the chief warden and the head guards watched in silence.

"Everybody strip," the head guard called out. "Hold your clothes under your arms. First man. Your name?"

"X . . ."

"Open your mouth, spread your legs apart. Remove these three teeth. Apply some iodine, then methylene blue, and give him ascorbic acid twice a day before meals."

I was last.

"Name?"

"Charrière."

"That's interesting. You're the only one in good shape. Did you just arrive?"

"No."

"How long you been here?"

"Eighteen months today."

"Why aren't you as thin as the others?"

"I don't know."

"Well, I'll tell you. Either you eat better or you masturbate less. Open your mouth, spread your legs apart. Two lemons a day, one in the morning, one at night. Suck the lemons and rub the juice into your gums. You have scurvy."

They cleaned my gums with iodine, painted them with methylene blue and gave me a lemon. Left about-face and, last in line, I returned to my cell.

That was a real revolution, having sick cons go all the way into the yard, into the sun, to see a doctor face to face. Nothing like it had ever happened before at Réclusion. What was going on? Was it possible that a doctor had at last defied the inhuman regulations? That doctor, whose name was Germain Guibert, later became my friend. He died in Indochina. His wife sent me word in Maracaibo, Venezuela, many years afterward.

Every ten days we went into the sun. Always the same prescription: iodine, methylene blue and two lemons. I wasn't getting worse, but I wasn't getting better either. I twice asked the doctor for Cochlearia and twice he refused me. This made me mad; I still couldn't walk more than six hours a day and my legs were still black and swollen.

One day, as I was waiting my turn, I noticed that the spindly little tree I used for shade was a non-bearing lemon tree. I broke off a leaf and chewed it; then, without thinking, I broke off a twig with a few leaves on it.

When the doctor called me, I stuck the branch up my rear end and said, "Doctor, I don't know if it's because of all those lemons you've been giving me, but look what's growing out of my ass." I turned so he could see the little branch sticking out.

The guards broke out into guffaws, but the head guard said, "Papillon, you'll be punished for not showing the doctor the proper respect."

"Not at all," the doctor said. "You can't punish him if I don't lodge a complaint. So you don't want any more lemons? Is that what you're trying to tell me?"

"Yes, Doctor. I've had enough damn lemons. They aren't doing me any good. I want to try the Cochlearia."

"I haven't given it to you because I have very little and I've been saving it for the sickest men. However, I'll give you a spoonful a day, but you have to have the lemons as well."

"Doctor, I've seen the Indians eat seaweed. There was the same kind on Royale. There must be some here too."

"That's a good idea, Papillon. Yes, I've seen the kind you mean down by the edge of the water. I want you to distribute some daily to all the men. Did the Indians eat it cooked or raw?"

"Raw."

"Very good. Thank you. And, Warden, make sure this man isn't punished. I'm counting on you."

"Yes, Captain."

It was a miracle. To go into the sun for two hours every ten days and wait for the doctor, to watch the others file by, see faces, say a few words . . . Who would have dreamed that anything so glorious could ever happen? It wrought the most fantastic transformations: the dead rose and walked in the sun; men buried alive spoke a few words. It was like breathing a bottle of oxygen and feeling life flow back into us.

Click, click, many, many clicks, and one Thursday morning at nine all the cell doors opened. Everybody was to stand in his door. "Réclusionnaires," a voice called out, "the governor's inspection."

With five colonial officers in his train—probably all doctors—a large, elegant man with silver-gray hair moved slowly down the corridor, stopping at each cell. I could hear someone tell him each man's sentence and crime. Before he reached me, they had to lift up a man who hadn't been able to keep standing.

An officer said, "That man's a walking corpse!"

"They're all in terrible shape," the governor replied.

The group had now reached me. The warden said, "This man has the heaviest sentence at Réclusion."

"What's your name?"

"Charrière."

"Your sentence?"

"Eight years. Three for theft of material belonging to the State, et cetera, and five for murder, sentences to be served consecutively."

"How much have you done?"

"Eighteen months."

"How's his conduct been?"

"Good," the warden said.

"His health?"

"Fair," the doctor said.

"What have you to say for yourself?"

"That the life here is inhuman and unworthy of the French people."

"How so?"

"Absolute silence, no going outdoors and, until recently, no medical attention."

"Behave yourself and maybe you'll be pardoned if I'm still governor."

"Thank you."

From that day on, by order of the governor and the chief doctor, who had come from Martinique and Cayenne respectively, every morning we had an hour's walk and a swim in a kind of pool made with big blocks of stone to keep the sharks out.

Every morning at nine, in groups of a hundred, we walked down for our swim. The guards' wives and children were told to stay home so we could go down stripped.

This had been going on for a month, and a dramatic change had come over the men's faces. The hour in the sun, the swim in salt water, being able to talk for an hour each day, all had transformed this herd of morally and physically sick men.

One day I was among the last going back up after our swim when I heard the desperate shrieks of a woman followed by two revolver shots.

"Help, help, Lisette's drowning!"

The screams came from the quay, which was no more than a cement ramp leading down to the water where you got into the boats. More screams followed.

"Sharks!"

Then two more shots. Everybody had turned in the direction of the noise. Without thinking what I was doing, I pushed a guard aside and ran, naked, toward the quay. Standing there were two women screaming to wake the dead, three guards and a few Arabs.

"Jump in the water!" one of the women shouted at me. "She isn't far. I can't swim or I'd go. You pack of cowards!"

"Sharks!" a guard called out and shot again.

A little girl in a blue dress was being carried off by a gentle current. She was heading straight for the *bagnards'* cemetery. The guards kept on shooting. They must have hit a few sharks, for the water around her was boiling.

"Stop shooting!" I yelled and threw myself into the water. With the help of the current and vigorous kicking to keep the sharks away, I made quick time to the little girl, who was being kept afloat by her dress.

I wasn't more than thirty or forty yards away when a boat from Royale appeared. It reached the little girl before me and she was pulled out of the water, then me. I wept with anger. I had risked my life for nothing.

At least that's what I thought. But a month later, as a reward, Dr. Guibert was able to get my sentence in solitary suspended for medical reasons.

EIGHTH NOTEBOOK

THE RETURN TO ROYALE

THE BUFFALOES

IT WAS A KIND OF miracle to be back on Royale. I had left it with an eight-year sentence. Because of the attempted rescue I was back nineteen months later.

All my friends were there: Dega, who was still clerk; Galgani, still the postman; Carbonieri, who had been acquitted; Grandet; Bourset the carpenter; the "wheelbarrow boys," Narric and Quenier; Chatal in the infirmary—my accomplice in my first *cavale*—and Maturette, who was an infirmary aide.

All the bandits of the Corsican *maquis* were also there: Essari, Vicioli, Césari, Razori, Fosco, Maucuer and Chapar. All the headliners of the yellow press from 1927 to 1935 were there.

Marsino, the man who killed Dufrêne, had died the week before of an illness. That day the sharks had had a choice morsel. They had been served up one of the greatest experts on precious stones in all of Paris.

Also Barrat, nicknamed "La Comédienne," the millionaire tennis player from Limoges, who had killed his chauffeur and the chauffeur's intimate friend, his too intimate friend. Barrat was head of the laboratory and pharmacist at the Royale hospital. One facetious doctor claimed that the only way you got into the hospital was by *droit de seigneur*.

My arrival back on Royale was like a clap of thunder. It was a Saturday morning when I returned to the building of the "hardened criminals." Almost everybody was there and they all welcomed me with open arms. Even the *mec* of the watches, who hadn't spoken since that famous morning when he had almost been guillotined by mistake, came over to say hello.

"Well, boys, everybody okay?"

"Okay, Papi. Welcome back."

"Your place is still here," Grandet said. "It's been empty since the day you left."

"Thanks. Anything new?"

"One good thing."

"What?"

"Last night the punk who spied on you from the top of the palm was found murdered. A friend of yours must have done it, knowing you wouldn't want to see the devil alive, and wanting to spare you the chore."

"I'd like to know who it was so I can thank him."

"Maybe he'll tell you someday. They found the rat at roll call this morning with a knife in his heart. Nobody saw or heard a thing."

"It's better that way. How's the game going?"

"O.K. You still have your place."

"Great. So hard labor for life begins again. And who knows how or when the story will end."

"Papi, we were shocked as hell when we heard you got eight

years. Now that you're back, there isn't a man on the islands who won't help you, no matter how risky it is."

"The warden wants you," an old man said.

I went with him. At the guardhouse several of the men had kind words for me. I followed the old man and eventually found myself in front of Warden Prouillet.

"How are you, Papillon?"

"Fine, sir."

"I'm glad you got your pardon, and I must congratulate you for showing such courage in the matter of my colleague's little girl."

"Thank you."

"I'm going to put you in charge of the buffaloes until your old job is free again, along with your right to fish."

"I'd like that, if you can manage it."

"I'll make it my business. The workshop guard isn't here any more, and I leave for France in three weeks. O.K., you start tomorrow."

"How can I thank you?"

"By waiting a month before you try another *cavale*," Prouillet said, laughing.

In our room the same men were leading the same lives as before. The gamblers were a class apart, thinking and living only for cards. The men with young boys lived, ate and slept with them. These were real households, where passion and love between men dominated their thoughts day and night. There were scenes of uncontrolled jealousy where the "wife" and "husband" spied on each other. When one of them tired of the other and flew off to a new affair, inevitably someone was killed.

Last week, for love of beautiful Charlie Barrat, a black named Simplon killed a guy named Sidero. Sidero was the third man Simplon had killed for love of Charlie.

I hadn't been back for more than a few hours when a man called on me.

"Say, Papillon, I want to know if Maturette is your boyfriend."

"Why?"

"I have my own reasons."

"Listen. Maturette made a *cavale* with me, we covered fifteen hundred miles and he behaved like a man. That's all I have to say."

"I want to know if he belongs to you."

"No, I've never had sex with Maturette. He's my friend. The rest is none of my business, unless somebody does him harm."

"What if he becomes my wife?"

"If he consents, fine. But if you have to threaten him to get him, then you'll have to deal with me."

Passive or active, homosexuals are all the same; as soon as they settle into their passion, they think of nothing else.

I saw the Italian who had the gold *plan* on our convoy. He came to say hello.

"You're still here?" I asked.

"I've tried everything. My mother sent me twelve thousand francs, the guard took a commission of six thousand, I spent four thousand to get disinterned. I managed to get myself X-rayed in Cayenne, but nothing came of it. Then I got myself accused of wounding a friend. You know him—Razori, the Corsican."

"So what happened?"

"He agreed to do it. He wounded himself in the gut and we went to the council of war together, him the accuser and me the accused. We barely had time to look around. They were finished with us in fifteen days. I got six months and did them at Réclusion last year. You didn't even know I was there. Papi, I can't stand it any more. I want to kill myself."

"Better to die at sea in a *cavale*. Then at least you die free."

"You're right. I'm game for anything. If you get something going, just give me the word."

"O.K."

Life on Royale resumed. This time I was a buffalo herdsman. One of my charges was named Brutus. He weighed over four thousand pounds and was a killer—of other buffaloes. He had already killed two males. The guard in charge told me, "This is his last chance. If he kills one more, we finish him off."

I was introduced to Brutus. The black from Martinique who was taking care of him had to spend a week teaching me. I made friends with the bull right away by pissing on his nose: his long tongue went after anything salty. Then I gave him a few green mangoes I'd picked in the hospital garden. I led Brutus down, harnessed him like an ox to the thick shafts of a wagon so primitive it was worthy of the Merovingian kings. It carried a barrel holding almost a thousand gallons of water. My work, and that of my pal Brutus, was to go down to the sea, fill the barrel and climb back up the rugged slope to the plateau. Once there, I turned the barrel spigot and let the water run down the sluices, carrying with it whatever was left from the morning sewage. I started at six and was finished by about nine.

By the end of four days the man from Martinique had decided I was ready to go it on my own. There was only one problem with Brutus: at five in the morning I had to get him out of the pond where he hid because he didn't like to work. In his sensitive nostrils he wore an iron ring from which hung a chain about twenty inches long. When I was just about to reach him, he'd dive down and come up some distance away. Sometimes it took me over an hour to catch him in the revolting water of the stagnant pond full of insects and water lilies. I muttered in anger: "You bastard! You mulish Breton! Are you going to get out? If you're not, the hell with you." He was mine only when I could get hold of his chain. My insults left him unmoved. But when I had him out of the pond, he became my pal again.

I carried two grease buckets full of fresh water. First I'd give myself a bath to wash off the slimy pond water. When I had soaped and rinsed myself thoroughly, I usually had half a bucket left, so I'd scrub Brutus with a coconut branch. I'd rub all his sensitive parts and water him down. Then he'd rub his head against my hands and go get between the wagon shafts all by himself. I never goaded him the way the black had. Brutus must have been grateful, for he moved faster for me than he ever had for him.

There was a small female buffalo who was very much in love with Brutus. She was always tagging along, and I didn't chase her off the way the other herdsmen did. To the contrary, I let her snuggle up to Brutus and follow us everywhere. When they made love, I let them alone, and as a result Brutus was very beholden to me. He pulled his thousand gallons with extraordinary speed. It was as if he were trying to make up the time his licking sessions with Marguerite (that was her name) cost me.

I made three trips a day. The longest was when the barrel had to be refilled, but there were two men to help me, so it went fairly fast. By nine o'clock I was finished and free to go fishing.

I got Marguerite to help me lure Brutus out of the pond. When her ear was scratched, she let out a sound like a mare in heat. Then Brutus came out all by himself. I no longer needed to wash myself, but I washed Brutus better than ever. Clean and rid of the sickening smell of the water, Brutus was doubly attractive to Marguerite.

On our way back, about halfway up the cliff, we would stop at a little flat place where there was a big rock. I'd brake the wagon against it so Brutus could catch his breath. This particular morning another buffalo named Danton—as big as Brutus—was lying in wait behind some small coconut palms. As we approached, he bolted out and attacked Brutus. Brutus leapt to one side, dodging Danton's horns, one of which went right through the barrel. While Danton was desperately tugging to get free, I let Brutus out of his harness. Brutus backed up to higher ground—at least thirty yards away—and bore down on Danton at a furious gallop. Before my buffalo could reach him, Danton had yanked himself free of the barrel—leaving a piece of his horn behind. Brutus couldn't brake himself in time, collided with the wagon and turned it over.

Then the strangest thing happened. Brutus and Danton touched heads, not pushing, just rubbing their big horns together. It was as if they were talking, only they made no noise. Then Marguerite started slowly up the path, followed by the two males who would stop from time to time to rub and tangle horns some more. When this lasted too long, Marguerite gave an amorous moo and resumed her climb. The two mastodons followed. Three more stops, same ceremony, until we finally arrived at the plateau. We were in front of the lighthouse in a flat bare space about three hundred yards wide. At the far end was the *bagnards'* camp; to the right and left, the two hospitals—one for us, and one for the guards.

Danton and Brutus were still twenty paces behind. Marguerite went quietly toward the center and stopped. The two enemies came abreast. Marguerite let out a long, sexual lament. The males touched horns again, but this time it seemed they really were talking because their breathing was mixed with sounds that clearly meant something.

After their conversation one turned slowly to the right, the other to the left. They took up positions at the far ends of the clearing, three hundred yards apart. Marguerite, still in the center, waited. At last I understood: there was to be a duel, a formal contest, and the young female was the trophy. It was all right with Marguerite—she was proud to have two such suitors fighting over her.

A high, quavery moo from Marguerite started it; the two bulls threw themselves into the fray. I don't need to point out that, crossing the three hundred yards between them, their four thousand pounds multiplied as the speed increased. By the time their two heads crashed together, the shock was so great it knocked both of them out for five minutes. Brutus was the first one up and he galloped back to his place. This stage of the battle lasted two hours. Some of the guards wanted to kill Brutus then, but I said no. During the next set-to, Danton broke off the horn he had injured on the barrel. He started to run with Brutus after him. The next stage of the battle lasted until the following day. Wherever they went—garden, cemetery, or washhouse—they left a trail of destruction.

It wasn't until seven in the morning that Brutus finally pinned Danton against the wall of the butcher shop down on the quay and pierced his belly with his horn. Then to finish him off, Brutus rolled over twice, twisting his horn deeper into his victim's belly. Gushing blood and guts, Danton fell in a heap.

The battle between the monsters had so weakened Brutus that I had to disengage his horn for him to get up. He staggered down the path that wound along the shore, and Marguerite walked alongside, holding her hornless head high.

I did not share their honeymoon. The guard in charge of the buffaloes accused me of unharnessing Brutus and I lost my job as herdsman.

I asked to speak to the warden about Brutus.

"Papillon, what in God's name happened? Brutus has to be killed; he's too dangerous. We've lost three good buffaloes on account of him."

"That's why I came to see you. I want you to save Brutus. The field guard doesn't understand that Brutus was acting in legitimate self-defense. Will you let me explain?"

The warden smiled. "I'm listening."

I told him the story. ". . . so now you understand, sir, how my buffalo was the one who was attacked. Furthermore, if I hadn't unhitched Brutus, Danton would have killed him because Brutus was harnessed to his yoke and couldn't have defended himself."

"That's true," the warden said.

Then the field guard arrived. "Good morning, sir. Papillon, I was looking for you. You left this morning as if you were going to work. But you had no work to do."

"Mr. Angosti, I left because I wanted to try to stop the battle. Unfortunately it was past stopping."

"That may be, but I told you you're not to handle the buffaloes any longer. Besides, we're killing Brutus Sunday morning. He'll provide meat for the penitentiary."

"You can't do that."

"You can't stop me."

"No, I can't, but the warden can. And if that isn't enough, I'll ask Dr. Guibert to stop it."

"What does it matter to you?"

"None of your business. That buffalo is my responsibility, and he's my friend."

"Your friend? A buffalo? You trying to pull my leg?"

"Listen, Mr. Angosti, will you let me talk for a minute?"

"Let him defend the buffalo," the warden said.

"O.K. Go ahead."

"Do you believe that animals talk to each other?"

"Why not?—if they communicate at all."

"All right then. Brutus and Danton were fighting a duel."

I told the whole story again, from beginning to end.

"Christacho!" the Corsican said. "You're a strange guy, Papillon. Do what you like about Brutus, but one more death and nobody can save him, not even the warden. You can go back to being a herdsman. But see that Brutus does some work."

Two days later the wagon was repaired by the men in the shop, and Brutus, with his wife Marguerite at his side, resumed his daily carting of sea water. When we arrived at his resting place, and I anchored the wagon with the rock, I'd say, "Where's Danton, Brutus?" And that mastodon would free the wagon with one tug and, with the joyful step of the victor, finish the trip in a single bound.

REVOLT AT SAINT-JOSEPH

The islands were dangerous because of the false sense of security we enjoyed. I suffered at the sight of all those people settled into their comfortable lives. Some waited for the end of their sentences, others just indulged their vices.

One night I was stretched out on my hammock. At the back of the room a wild game was going on, so wild that Carbonieri and Grandet had to double up to run it. One man wasn't enough. I was out of it, trying to summon a few memories. But they wouldn't come; it was as if the Assizes had never existed. For all my efforts to focus the misty pictures of that fatal day, the only one I could see clearly was the prosecutor in all his cruel righteousness. Goddamn it, I really thought I'd beaten you when I arrived at Bowen's on Trinidad. You son of a bitch, what kind of evil eye did you put on me to make six *cavales* go sour . . . ?

As I was talking to my accuser, two men approached my hammock.

"You asleep?"

"No."

"We'd like to talk to you."

"O.K. Talk. If you're quiet, no one will hear you."

"Well, we're preparing a revolt."

"What's your plan?"

"We're going to kill all the Arabs, all the guards, all the guards' wives, and their kids. They're all rotten. Me, Arnaud, my friend Hautin and four other guys who are in on this are going to attack the warden's arms depot. I have a job there taking care of the weapons. There are twenty-three submachine guns and over eighty rifles and carbines. We'll begin the action—"

"Stop. You don't need to go on. I refuse. Thanks for your trust in me, but I won't go along."

"We thought you might take the lead. Let me fill in the details for you; we've studied everything carefully and we can't fail. We've been preparing this for five months. There are over fifty men with us."

"Don't tell me the names. I refuse to be the leader or even be involved."

"Why? You owe us an explanation after we've trusted you with our plan."

"I didn't ask you to tell me anything. Besides, I do only what I want to do, not what others want me to do. I'm not an assembly-line killer. I might kill somebody who had done something really bad to me, but not women and children who have done nothing. What's worse, and since you don't see it, I'll have to point it out to you: even if your revolt succeeds, you will fail in the end."

"Why?"

"Because you won't accomplish your main goal; you won't escape. Let's say a hundred take part in the revolt. How are they going to get off the island? There are only two boats here. Together they can carry at the most forty cons. What will you do with the other sixty?"

"We'll be among the forty who leave on the boats."

"That's what you think. But the others are no stupider than you. They'll be armed, too, and once you've eliminated all those you say you're going to eliminate, you'll be shooting each other to see who's going to get on the boats. And besides, no country is going to allow either boat to land. Telegrams will have gone out to every country you might try. Especially with all those dead left behind. No matter where you go you'll be arrested and returned to French authorities. I'm back from Colombia and I know what I'm talking about. I swear to you that after a business like that, nobody will keep you."

"O.K., then, you refuse?"

"Yes."

"This is your final word?"

"Yes."

"Well, we'd better go."

"One minute. Don't mention this to any of my friends."

"Why?"

"Because I can tell you beforehand they'll refuse. Save your breath."

"O.K."

"You can't put a stop to this project?"

"Frankly, Papillon, no."

"I don't understand what you're after. Seriously, as I said before, even if your revolt succeeds, you won't get your freedom."

"What we really want is revenge. And since you tell us that no country will accept us, well, we'll take to the bush, live as a group in the forest."

"I promise I won't speak of this even to my best friend."

"We know we can count on you."

"Good. And one last thing—give me eight days' warning so I

can go to Saint-Joseph. I don't want to be on Royale when this takes place."

"We'll give you time enough to change islands."

"You're sure I can't make you change your minds? Would you try another scheme with me? For instance, we could steal four rifles and attack the sentry who guards the boats at night. Without killing anybody, we could take a boat and leave."

"No. We've been through too much. The most important thing for us is revenge, even if we pay with our lives."

"All right. I don't want to talk about it any more."

"You don't want to wish us luck?"

"No. I repeat, give it up. There are better things to do than a half-assed scheme like this one."

"You don't agree we have the right to get even?"

"Sure, but not by killing innocent people."

"Good night."

"Good night. We'll pretend we haven't discussed it, all right, Papi?"

"All right, *mecs*."

Hautin and Arnaud went away. Jesus, how about that? What a pair of nuts! Already fifty or sixty men were involved, and at H hour there'd be a hundred. It was just plain crazy. None of my friends had spoken to me about it, so those two cons must have discussed it only with the squares. No man from the real underworld would get mixed up in a thing like that. And what made it worse, the squares were butchers. The ones like us were murderers, a different thing entirely.

I made some discreet inquiries about Arnaud and Hautin. Arnaud had been indicted, unjustly, it would seem, and condemned to life for something that wasn't worth ten years. The jury gave it to him because, the year before, his brother had been guillotined for murdering a cop. The prosecuting attorney had concentrated on the brother in order to create a hostile atmosphere. He was probably tortured at the time of his arrest, besides, all because of what his brother had done.

Hautin had never known freedom. He'd been in prison since the age of nine. At nineteen he had killed a guy just before he was due to get out of the reformatory, on the eve of joining up with the Navy. He was out of his mind: he was planning to get to Venezuela and work in a gold mine where he planned to blow off his leg in order to get a big compensation. The leg was already stiff from some injections he had cadged at Saint-Martin-de-Ré.

This morning there was a minor sensation. At roll call they called up Arnaud, Hautin and my friend Matthieu Carbonieri's brother. Jean was a baker down on the quay and had access to the boats.

They were sent to Saint-Joseph with no explanation. I tried to find out why, but in vain. Arnaud had been taking care of the weapons for four years, and Jean Carbonieri had been a baker for five. It couldn't be just a coincidence. There must have been a leak, but what kind of leak, and how far had it gone?

I decided to ask my three best friends—Matthieu, Grandet and Galgani. None of them knew anything. Just as I had thought, Hautin and Arnaud had involved only cons who weren't of the underworld.

"Why did they talk to me then?"

"Because everybody knows you'll escape at any price."

"But not at that price."

"They couldn't see the difference."

"What about your brother Jean?"

"God knows why he was such a fool to get mixed up in a business like that."

"Maybe the man who ratted said he was in it when he wasn't in it at all."

After that things moved fast. That night someone killed Girasolo as he was going to the toilets. They found blood on the Martinican's shirt. Fifteen days later, after a too-speedy interrogation and the testimony of another black in solitary, the herdsman was condemned to death by a special tribunal.

An old con named Garvel came to see me in the washhouse. "Papi, I killed Girasolo. I'd like to save the black, but I'm scared of the guillotine. That's too high a price to pay. If I could find some way of getting only three or five years, I'd confess."

"What's your sentence now?"

"Twenty years."

"How many have you done?"

"Twelve."

"Find some way to get life. That way you won't have to go to Réclusion."

"How do I do it?"

"Let me think about it. I'll tell you tonight."

That night I said to Garvel, "No, you can't get yourself accused and then confess."

"Why not?"

"You run the risk of the death penalty. The only way to avoid solitary is to get life. So you make your confession—say you couldn't in good conscience see an innocent man guillotined. Pick a Corsican guard to defend you. I'll tell you who later. But you've got to work fast. I just hope they don't cut the black's head off too soon. You'll have to wait at least two or three days."

I talked it over with a guard named Collona and he gave me a great idea: I was to take Garvel before the head warden and tell him that he had asked me to take on his defense, that I had promised to go with him while he made his confession and had guaranteed him that this noble act would make it impossible for him to get the death penalty, but that I had also warned him that his crime was very serious nonetheless, and he must expect life imprisonment at the very least.

The plan worked. Garvel saved the black, who was freed straight off. His false accuser found himself with a year in prison, and Robert Garvel got life.

Two months passed. Garvel told me all that had happened now that the affair was over. It seems that Girasolo had agreed to take part in the revolt and, after having been given all the details, had squealed on Arnaud, Hautin and Jean Carbonieri. Fortunately these were the only names he knew.

The accusation was so serious that, at first, the guards wouldn't believe it. But, to be on the safe side, they sent the three cons to Saint-Joseph—without a word, no questions, no nothing.

"What motive did you give for the murder, Garvel?"

"That he had stolen my *plan*. I said I slept opposite him—which was a fact—and that I took out my *plan* at night and hid it in the blanket I used as a pillow. One night I went to the toilet, and when I got back, my *plan* was gone. Now, in my area, only one man wasn't asleep and that was Girasolo. The guards believed me; they didn't even mention that he had squealed on the revolt."

"Papillon! Papillon!" somebody shouted from the yard. "Roll call!"

"Present."

"Get your gear together. You're going to Saint-Joseph."

"Oh, shit!"

War had broken out in France and had brought with it a new disciplinary measure: any officials in the penal service who allowed an escape were to be dismissed. Any cons arrested attempting an escape were to be condemned to death. It would be considered as motivated by a desire to join the Free French forces, who were traitors to the motherland. Anything was tolerated except escape.

Warden Prouillet had been gone two months. I didn't know the new man, so nothing doing there. I said good-by to my friends. At eight o'clock I was on the boat to Saint-Joseph.

Lisette's father was no longer at the camp on Saint-Joseph. He and his family had left for Cayenne the week before. The warden now was named Dutain and came from Le Havre. He met me at the dock.

"You're Papillon?"

"Yes, sir."

"You're a curious fellow," he said, leafing through my papers.

"Why do you say that?"

"Because on the one hand it says here you're extremely dangerous, with a note in red ink added: 'Always preparing to escape.' On the other hand, there's a footnote: 'Surrounded by sharks, attempted to rescue daughter of warden of Saint-Joseph.' I happen to have two small daughters, Papillon. Would you like to meet them?"

He called to two very blond children of about three and five who were entering his office in the company of a young Arab dressed in white and a very pretty, dark-haired woman.

"Darling, this is the man who tried to rescue your goddaughter, Lisette."

"Oh, let me shake your hand!" the young woman said.

To shake a *bagnard*'s hand is the greatest honor anyone can give him. You never put out your hand to a con. Her spontaneous gesture touched me.

"I'm Lisette's godmother. We're very good friends with the Grandoits. What are you going to do for him, dear?"

"He has to go to the camp first." He turned to me. "Then you must tell me what job you want."

"Thank you, sir. Thank you, madame. But could you tell me why I've been sent to Saint-Joseph? For me it's a kind of punishment, you know."

"There's no particular reason, so far as I know. The new warden on Royale is afraid you'll escape."

"He's right there."

"They've increased the penalties for those who allow escapes. Before the war you were liable to lose a stripe. Now you lose it automatically, and that's the least of it. He'd rather you escaped from Saint-Joseph, which is not his responsibility, than from Royale, which is."

"How much longer will you be here, Warden?"

"Eighteen months."

"I can't wait that long. But I'll find some way to get back to Royale so it won't be held against you."

"Thank you," his wife said. "That's very noble of you. If you need anything, count on us. Papa, give the guardroom orders that Papillon is to come and see me whenever he likes."

"All right, dear. Papillon, Mohamed will take you to the camp and you can pick out the *case* you want to be assigned to."

"No problem there. I want to be in with the dangerous cons."

"That isn't difficult," the warden said, laughing. He made out a slip and gave it to Mohamed.

I left the house on the quay which doubled as the warden's house and his office—Lisette's former home—and walked to the camp with the young Arab.

The man in charge of the guardroom was a violent old Corsican, a well-known killer. His name was Filisarri.

"So, Papillon, you're back. You know how I am, all good or all bad. Don't try any escape stuff with me, for if you fail, I'll kill you like a rabbit. I retire in two years and I don't want any trouble now."

"You know that all Corsicans are my friends. I'm not going to tell you that I won't try to escape, but if I do, I'll make sure it's when you're not on duty."

"It's all right, then, Papillon. We won't be enemies. You understand, the young guards are in a better position to take the flak that follows an escape. For me it's murder. At my age and just when I'm about to retire. . . . O.K. You understand. Now go to the building you've been assigned to."

There I was in a building exactly like the one on Royale with room for a hundred to a hundred and twenty cons. Pierrot le Fou was there, and also Hautin, Arnaud and Jean Carbonieri. Logically I should have made *gourbi* with Jean since he was Matthieu's brother. But Jean wasn't in the same class with Matthieu and, besides, I didn't like his friendship with Hautin and Arnaud. So I gave him a wide berth and settled next to Carrier, otherwise known as Pierrot le Fou.

The island of Saint-Joseph was wilder than Royale and, although really smaller, looked bigger because of its length. The camp was halfway to the top of the island, which had two plateaus, one above the other. On the lower level was the camp; on the higher level, the Réclusion.

Every day at noon the Arab who worked for the warden's family brought me three bowls on an iron platter and took away those he had left the day before. Every day Lisette's godmother sent me the exact same food she prepared for her own family.

I went to see her on Sunday to thank her. I spent the afternoon talking to her and playing with the little girls. As I stroked those blond heads, I was reminded of how hard it was to know where one's duty lay. A terrible danger threatened that family if those madmen held to their plan. The guards had put so little trust in Girasolo's accusation that they hadn't even bothered to separate Arnaud, Hautin and Carbonieri. If I were even to hint that they should, I'd be confirming the truth about the revolt. What would the guards' reaction be then? Better keep my mouth shut.

Arnaud and Hautin barely spoke to me. It was best that way: we were polite but not friendly. Jean Carbonieri didn't speak to me at all. He was angry that I hadn't made *gourbi* with him. There were four in our *gourbi*: Pierrot le Fou, Marquetti—who twice won the Prix de Rome for violin and often played for hours on end, which depressed me—and Marsori, a Corsican from Sète.

I didn't speak of it, but I had the impression that no one here knew about the abortive revolt on Royale. Had they changed their plans? Theirs was one of the worst jobs on the island: they had to pull, or rather haul, huge rocks that were being used to make a swimming pool in the sea. Chains were wound around the rocks to which another chain fifteen to twenty yards long was attached. Two cons wearing harnesses around their chests and shoulders stood on either side and inserted a long hook into one of the chain links. Then, like dumb beasts, they hauled the rock to its destination. In the hot sun this was hard work and terribly wearing.

One day we were sitting around when suddenly there was the crack of gunfire—rifles, carbines, revolvers—all going off together down by the quay. Christ! Those madmen were going through with it! What was happening? Who was winning? I sat in the room and didn't move. Everybody agreed, "It's a revolt!"

"A revolt? What do you mean?" I made it very clear that I knew nothing.

Jean Carbonieri had not gone to work that morning. He now came up to me, white as death for all that his face was deeply sunburned. In a low voice he said, "It's the revolt, Papi."

I said coldly, "What revolt? I guess I'm not up to date."

The carbine shots continued.

Pierrot le Fou came running into the room. "It's a revolt, but I think it fizzled. What a bunch of idiots! Papillon, get your knife ready. We might as well kill as many guards as we can before they finish us off!"

"Right! Let's kill as many as we can," Carbonieri agreed. Chissilia pulled out a razor. Everybody armed himself with something.

"Don't be a bunch of dopes," I said. "How many of us are there?"

"Nine."

"Seven of you put away your weapons. I'll kill the first man who threatens a guard. I'm not about to be shot down like a rabbit. You in on this?"

"No."

"You?"

"No, me neither."

"And you?"

"Didn't know a thing about it."

"O.K. All of us here are from the underworld. Nobody knew anything about this amateurs' revolt. Understand?"

"Yes."

"The minute anybody lets on he knows something, he's dead. So anyone who's fool enough to talk gains nothing. Throw your weapons in the pails. The guards'll be here soon."

"What if it's the cons who won?"

"If it's the cons, let's wait and see if they use their victory to make a *cavale*. The way I see it, the price is too high. How about you?"

They all agreed, including Jean Carbonieri.

I didn't let on about what I already knew—that, since the

shooting had stopped, the cons must have lost. If they'd won, the massacre would still be going on.

The guards swept past like a bunch of wild beasts, prodding the men who worked in the rock gang with rifle butts, sticks and feet. They herded them into the building next door, and soon guitars, mandolins, chess games, checkers, lamps, benches, bottles of oil, sugar, coffee, white uniforms, everything was trampled on, destroyed and thrown out the door. The guards took it out on everything that wasn't regulation.

Two revolver shots rang out.

There were eight buildings in the camp. In every one it was the same story. Guards crossed in front of us and entered the building to our right, the seventh *case*. We were the last one. The nine of us were each in our own place. None of the men who had been working outside had come back yet. We stood frozen to the spot. Nobody spoke. My throat was dry. All I could think was, Just so long as some bastard doesn't take advantage of this to shoot me. . . .

"Here they come," said Carbonieri, terrified.

They swept in, more than twenty of them, carbines and revolvers at the ready.

Filisarri shouted, "Why aren't you stripped yet? What are you waiting for, you shitheads? We're going to shoot the lot of you. Get moving! We don't want to have to undress you after you're corpses."

"Mr. Filisarri . . ."

"Shut your trap, Papillon! You'll get no pardon here. The little affair you cooked up this time is too serious. And, naturally, all of you here were in on it."

His bloodshot eyes bulged out of his head—there was no mistaking their murderous gleam.

Pierrot started to speak.

I decided to go for broke. "I can't believe that a Corsican like you would kill innocent men. You want to shoot? All right, then, but no more talking. We don't need it. Shoot, but shoot fast, for Christ's sake! I thought you were a man, Filisarri, a real Corsican, but I was wrong. Too bad. I don't even want to look at you when you shoot. I'm turning my back. Everybody turn your backs so they can't say we were attacking them."

To a man, they turned their backs. The guards were dumb-founded, all the more so because (as I learned later) Filisarri had killed two poor buggers in one of the other *cases*.

"Got anything else to say, Papillon?"

With my back still turned, I answered, "I don't believe your story about a revolt. Why should there be a revolt? To kill guards? Then leave on a *cavale*? Where could they go? I'm a *cavale* man; I've come back from as far away as Colombia. What country's going to offer asylum to a bunch of escaped murderers? Tell me its name. Don't be assholes. What man worthy of the name would get mixed up in a thing like this?"

"You, maybe not, but what about Carbonieri? I'll bet he was in on it. Arnaud and Hautin were surprised when he reported sick this morning instead of showing up for work."

"You're just guessing." Then I turned around. "But you'll find out. Carbonieri is my friend. He knows all about what happened to my *cavale*, and he knows perfectly well what would happen to a *cavale* that followed a revolt."

At that point the warden arrived. He remained outside. Filisarri went out and the warden called in:

"Carbonieri!"

"Present."

"Take him to the dungeon, but gently now, no rough stuff. Get everybody out. I want only the head guards to stay. Go bring back all the men still working around the island. Nobody's to be killed. I want everybody back in the camp without exception."

The warden, his second-in-command and Filisarri came into the room with four guards.

"Papillon, something very serious has happened," the warden said. "As chief warden of the penitentiary, I have to assume a very heavy responsibility. But before taking the next step, I need some information. I realize that in such a difficult situation you might think it unwise to discuss this with me in private, so I've come here. The guard, Duclos, has been murdered. They tried to take the arms from the depot—in my view that makes it a revolt. I have only a few minutes. I trust you. What's your opinion?"

"If it was a revolt, why weren't we in on it? Why weren't we told? How many were implicated? I think I can answer those three questions, but first I have to know how many men went into action after Duclos was killed and his weapon—I assume—taken."

"Three."

"Who were they?"

"Arnaud, Hautin and Marceau."

"All right, then. Whether you like it or not, there was no revolt."

"That's a lie, Papillon," Filisarri interrupted. "This revolt was supposed to take place on Royale. Girasolo squealed, but we didn't believe him. Now we know everything he said was true. You're playing us for suckers, Papillon!"

"Look, if there had been a revolt, we'd have been the ones in charge, not those jerks."

"You trying to tell me nobody else was involved? I don't believe it."

"All right, what did the other men do? Did anybody besides those three budge? Did anyone make a move to take over the guardhouse? How many boats are there on Saint-Joseph? One launch. One launch for six hundred men? That would be a little half-assed, wouldn't it? And killing people to make an escape? Even assuming twenty men got off, they'd be arrested and turned in. Warden, I don't know how many men your people have killed, but I'm almost certain they were all innocent. And now you want to destroy what little we have left. You may think your anger is justified, but don't forget that on the day you take away the little that makes our lives bearable, on that day—yes—there may be a real revolt. The revolt of the desperate, a collective suicide. Killing or killed, we'd all die together, guards as well as *bagnards*. Monsieur Dutain, I've spoken to you from the heart. I think you deserve it for having come here to find out what we think. Now leave us alone."

"What about those who were involved?" Filisarri said again.

"It's up to you to find them. We know nothing; we're of no use to you. I repeat, this was the folly of amateurs. It's not our kind of action."

"Mr. Filisarri, when the men return, keep them in until further notice. I want two guards at the door, no brutality and no touching what belongs to the men. Let's go." The warden left with the other guards.

Jesus, that was a close one. As he closed the door, Filisarri said to me, "You're damned lucky I'm a Corsican."

In less than an hour almost all the men who belonged in our building were back. Sixteen were missing—the guards were in such a hurry they had locked them up in the wrong buildings. Once everyone was back where he belonged, we learned what had happened, for these men had been in the same work gang. In a hushed voice a thief from Saint-Etienne told me the whole story:

"Here's the picture, Papi. We were hauling a rock weighing about a ton over a distance of four hundred yards. The path we used was fairly flat, and when we arrived at a well about fifty yards from the warden's house, we always stopped and rested. It was in the shade of some coconut palms and about halfway to where we were going. So we stopped per usual and pulled up a big bucket of fresh water. Some drank, others just wet the handkerchiefs they wore around their heads. The break usually lasted around ten minutes, so our guard sat down on the edge of the well. He took off his helmet and was wiping his brow and head with a big handkerchief when Arnaud came up behind him. Arnaud was carrying a hoe, but since he hadn't raised it, nobody thought to warn the guard. In a split second he lifted the hoe and brought the sharp edge down right in the middle of the guard's skull. The guard's head split in two, and he fell flat without making a sound. The minute he hit the ground, Hautin—who had taken up an advance position—grabbed his carbine and Marceau took his belt and revolver. With the gun in hand, Marceau turned toward the whole gang and said, "This is a revolt. Everyone who's with us, come on.' There wasn't a sound from the turnkeys, and not one man in the entire gang made a move to follow. Arnaud looked us over and said, 'You cowards, we'll show you what real men are!' He took the carbine from Hautin's hands and they both ran toward the warden's house. Marceau drew off to one side. He had the big revolver in his hand and ordered, 'Don't move, not a word, not a sound. You Arabs, down on the ground.' From where I was, I could see everything.

"Arnaud was about to climb the steps to the warden's house when the Arab who worked there happened to open the door, holding one of the warden's little girls by the hand and the other in his arms. Both men were caught by surprise. The Arab tried to kick Arnaud. Arnaud was about to kill him when the Arab held the child out in front of him as a shield. All this time there wasn't a sound. Five or six times Arnaud aimed the gun at different parts of the Arab. Each time the Arab held the child between him and the gun. Then Hautin grabbed the bottom of the Arab's pants. As he was about to fall, the Arab threw the child against the gun in Arnaud's hands. Arnaud was thrown off-balance, Hautin grabbed the Arab's leg. Arnaud, the Arab and the other child all fell in a heap. For the first time there were sounds: first screams from the kids, then from the Arab, then curses from Arnaud and Hautin.

"The gun had fallen to the ground. The Arab got to it first, but he had it only by the barrel and in his left hand. Hautin caught hold of his leg again. Arnaud grabbed his right arm and twisted it, but before they could get it away from him, the Arab threw the carbine a good ten yards.

"As the three of them were running after it, the first shot rang out, fired by a guard in charge of a leaf-raking gang. The warden appeared at his window and started to shoot, but for fear of hitting the Arab, he aimed where the carbine had fallen. Hautin and Arnaud fled toward the camp by way of the path that follows the shore. Hautin, with his stiff leg, couldn't run fast enough and was shot down before he reached the water. Arnaud rushed in between the guards' pool and the one under construction. The place is always swarming with sharks. As another guard came up, he hid himself behind a big rock.

" 'Give up,' the guard shouted, 'and your life will be saved.'

" 'Never,' Arnaud answered back. 'I'd rather be eaten by the sharks. Then at least I won't have to look at your ugly faces any more.'

"With that he waded into the sea—smack into the sharks. A bullet must have grazed him. Anyway he stopped for a second. But the guards went right on shooting and Arnaud kept moving farther out. The water wasn't up to his chest when the sharks hit. The guards saw him clearly, belting a shark that was coming at him half out of the water. He was literally drawn and quartered as the sharks yanked at him from all sides. In less than five minutes he'd disappeared.

"The guards must have shot at the pack a hundred times at least. One shark was killed; he floated up to the beach, belly side up. As guards began to move in from all sides, Marceau tried to save his skin by throwing the revolver into the well. But the Arabs got to their feet, beating him with sticks, fists and feet, and pushed him toward the guards, saying he was in the plot. Even though he was covered and had his hands up, the guards shot him dead. To finish him off, one of them crushed his head with the butt of his carbine, holding it like a bludgeon by the end of the barrel.

"As for Hautin, the guards completely unloaded their carbines into him, thirty men, six shots each, over one hundred and fifty bullets. The poor *mecs* killed by Filisarri were men the Arabs said had started to follow Arnaud, then thought better of it. That was an out-and-out lie, because, accomplices or not, no one moved."

We had now been locked up in our various buildings for two days. Nobody went to work. The guards at the door were changed every two hours. Between the buildings, more guards. We were forbidden to talk from one building to the next, forbidden to stand near a window. We could see the yard through the barred door only by standing to one side in the alley that separated the two rows of hammocks. Reinforcements were sent over from Royale. Not a single con was allowed outside. Nor a single Arab turnkey. We were all locked in. From time to time you saw a man stripped to the skin being led toward the maximum-security cells. Guards were constantly looking in on us through the side windows. The ones who stood at the door had short hours, but they never sat down or let go of their guns. They held their carbines under their arms, ready to shoot.

We decided to try playing in small groups of five. No big

games—it would make too much noise. Marquetti started to play a Beethoven sonata, but a guard made him stop.

"No music! We're in mourning."

An unnatural tension reigned not only in the *case* but throughout the camp. No coffee, no soup. A piece of bread in the morning, corned beef at noon, corned beef for supper, one can to four men. Nothing of ours had been destroyed, so we had coffee and a little food: butter, oil, flour, etc. The other *cases* had nothing left. We started a fire in the toilets to make coffee, but when he saw the smoke, a guard made us put it out.

An old con from Marseilles by the name of Niston made the coffee to sell. He had the gall to tell the guard, "If you want the fire put out, go in and do it yourself." The guard shot through the window. Coffee and fire disappeared quickly.

Niston was hit in the leg. We were so tensed up that we thought we were all going to be shot and threw ourselves flat on the floor.

Filisarri, who was still on duty as head of the guard detail, came running in like a madman, accompanied by his four guards. The one who had done the shooting was a Frenchman. Filisarri cursed him out in Corsican, but he didn't understand a word. All he could say was, "Don't understand."

We got back on our hammocks.

Niston's leg was bleeding. "Don't tell 'em I'm wounded. They might take advantage of the opportunity and finish me off out there."

Filisarri told Marquetti in Corsican, "Go make your coffee. Nothing more is going to happen." Then he left.

Niston was lucky: the bullet hadn't stayed in his leg. It had entered below the calf muscle and gone out farther up. A tourniquet was applied, the bleeding stopped, and he was given a vinegar dressing.

"Papillon, come." It was eight at night and dark outside. "The warden wants to see you."

"Tell him to come here. I'm not leaving."

"You refuse?"

"Yes, I refuse."

My friends came and stood around me in a circle. The guard spoke through the closed door. Marquetti went up to him and said, "We're not letting Papillon out unless the warden comes."

"But it's the warden who's sent for him."

"Tell him to come himself."

An hour later two young guards were at the door. With them they had the Arab who worked at the warden's, the one who had come to his rescue and broken up the revolt.

"Papillon, it's me, Mohamed. The warden wants to see you. He can't come himself so he sent me."

Marquetti said, "Papi, the *mec* has a gun."

I left the circle and went to the door. It was true that Mohamed was carrying a carbine under his arm. That was really something. A *bagnard* officially armed with a carbine!

"Come," the Algerian said to me. "I'm here to protect you."

I didn't believe him.

"Come along."

I went out. Mohamed stationed himself at my side and the two guards stood behind. As we passed the guards' house by the camp entrance, Filisarri said, "Papillon, I hope you're not holding anything against me."

"Not me. Or anybody else in our *case*. I wouldn't know about the others."

We went down to the warden's. The house and the quay were dimly lit by carbide lamps. On the way Mohamed gave me a pack of Gauloises. We entered a room brightly lit by two carbide lamps, and seated there were the warden of Royale, his deputy, the warden of Saint-Joseph, the warden of Réclusion and the deputy warden of Saint-Joseph.

Just outside I noticed four Arabs under guard. I recognized two of them as belonging to the work gang under discussion.

Mohamed said, "Here's Papillon."

"Good evening, Papillon," said the warden of Saint-Joseph.

"Good evening."

"Please sit down."

I sat down, facing the lot. The door of the room opened into the kitchen, where I saw Lisette's godmother making a gesture of greeting.

The warden of Royale began, "Papillon, Warden Dutain considers you a man he can trust. I know you only from official reports which describe you as a dangerous man. But I'd like to forget these and believe my colleague Dutain. Now, we know that a commission will be sent here to investigate the incident and that all the convicts will be asked to tell what they know. We also know that you and a few other men have great influence on the convicts and that they will follow your advice. What we want now is your view of the revolt and some information on what you think your *case* and the others are prepared to tell us."

"Sir, I can tell you nothing, nor can I influence the others. I might add that, if there is a serious investigation, with the situation the way it is now, you're all in trouble."

"What do you mean, Papillon? My colleagues and I stopped the revolt on Saint-Joseph."

"Maybe you're in the clear, but not the officials on Royale."

"Explain yourself!" The two wardens of Royale started to get up, then sat down again.

"If you continue to speak of it officially as a revolt, you're through. If you will accept my conditions, I can save you all—except Filisarri."

"What are your conditions?"

"First, that you let things get back to normal, starting tomorrow morning. It's only by talking among ourselves that we can influence the rest and decide what we'll tell the commission. Will you agree to this?"

"Yes," Dutain said. "But why do we need saving?"

"You on Royale are in charge, not only of Royale, but of all three islands."

"Right."

"Now, you were told by Girasolo that a revolt was being planned and that the leaders were Hautin and Arnaud."

"And Carbonieri."

"No, that's not true. Carbonieri has been an enemy of Girasolo's ever since their Marseilles days. He was implicated in this thing solely for revenge. Now, *you did not believe in this revolt.* Why? Because Girasolo told you that the object of the revolt was to kill women, children, Arabs and guards, and you thought this ridiculous. Also, a mass *cavale* was impossible. There were only two launches for eight hundred men at Royale and one for six hundred at Saint-Joseph. Nobody in his right mind would have gone along with such a stunt."

"How do you know this?"

"That's my business. But if you continue to talk about a revolt—even if you get rid of me, or especially if you do—it will all come out in the open. Therefore the responsibility lies with Royale, which sent these men to Saint-Joseph without separating them. The logical move would have been to send one to Diable and the other to Saint-Joseph. When the commission discovers this, you'll be in for it, even though I realize it was hard to believe such a wild scheme at the time. So I repeat, if you go on talking revolt, you're digging your own graves. Now these are my conditions: first, as I said before, that life return to normal starting tomorrow; second, that all the men now in dungeons be freed immediately and not interrogated as accomplices in a revolt *since there was no revolt*; third, that Filisarri be sent to Royale immediately, for his own safety and also because, if there was no revolt, how can you justify the murder of three men? And murder is what it was. That guard is a killer. When the incident took place, he was scared stiff and would have gladly shot us all. If you accept these conditions, I'll see to it that everybody states that Arnaud, Hautin and Marceau had decided to commit suicide by killing as many people as they could before they were killed themselves. They had no accomplices, no allies. Now, if you like, I'll go into the kitchen so you can talk it over by yourselves."

I went into the kitchen and closed the door. Mme. Dutain squeezed my hand and offered me some coffee and a brandy. Mohamed said, "Did you say anything about me?"

"The warden will take care of you. From the moment he allowed you to have a gun, it was clear he intended to see that you're pardoned."

Mme. Dutain said softly, "Well, well! So Royale won't get away with it, after all!"

"It was too damn easy for them to agree there had been a revolt on Saint-Joseph that everybody knew about except your husband."

"Papillon, I heard everything and understood right away that you were doing us a good turn."

The door opened. "Papillon, come in," a guard said.

"Please sit down," said the warden of Royale. "We've discussed the matter and it's our unanimous decision that you are correct. There was no revolt. The three convicts decided to commit suicide, first killing as many people as possible. So tomorrow life goes back to normal. Monsieur Filisarri goes to Royale this very night. His case is our affair and I will not ask you to collaborate. We depend on your keeping your word."

"You can count on me."

"Mohamed, you and the two guards take Papillon back to his *case*. Have Filisarri brought here. He will go to Royale with us."

As we were walking, I told Mohamed that I hoped he'd get his freedom. He thanked me.

Back in the *case*, there was absolute silence as I told what had happened, word for word, in a loud voice so that everybody could hear.

"If there's anybody here who doesn't agree, or wants to criticize the arrangements I made, let him speak up now." Nobody disagreed.

"You really think they believed no one else was involved?"

"No, but if they want to save their skins, they have to believe it. And if we don't want trouble, we'd better believe it too."

At seven the next morning they emptied every cell in the maximum-security section. There were over a hundred and twenty men. Nobody went to work, but all the buildings were open and the yard was full of *bagnards* talking, smoking, sitting in the sun or shade. Niston went to the hospital. Carbonieri told me that signs saying "Suspected of complicity in the revolt" had been hung on at least eighty of the doors.

Now that we were together once again, we learned what had actually happened. Filisarri had killed only one man, the other two had been shot by two young guards. The two cons had had their backs to the wall and, thinking they were about to be killed, they'd drawn their knives in the hope they could take at least one guard with them. The guards in turn felt threatened, so they shot them. That's how the revolt, luckily aborted at the start, was transformed into an unusual form of suicide. This theory was officially accepted by everybody, Administration as well as cons. It has since remained part legend, part true story.

Apparently the burial of the three men killed in camp, plus Hautin and Marceau, was effected in the following manner: Since there was only one sliding casket, the guards put them all in the bottom of the boat and the five were thrown to the sharks together. The guards had calculated that, while the first was being devoured, the others would have time to sink to the bottom, since their feet were weighted down with rocks. But I was told that none of the five sank and that, as daylight faded, they staged a ballet in their white shrouds—like five marionettes manipulated by the mouths and tails of the sharks. It was a spectacle worthy of Nebuchadnezzar. The horror of it sent the guards and boatmen beating it back to shore.

A commission came and stayed almost five days on Saint-Joseph and two days at Royale. I was not singled out for special examination but was treated like all the rest. I learned from Warden Dutain that everything went smoothly. Filisarri, given leave until the start of his retirement, would not be returning. Mohamed got a reprieve. Warden Dutain was promoted.

Some malcontent, a con from Bordeaux, asked me, "What did it get us to be so helpful to the guards?"

I looked the *mec* in the eye. "Not much. Only that fifty or sixty cons won't spend five years in solitary for complicity. That doesn't seem like anything to you?"

Fortunately the storm died down. A tacit understanding between guards and cons completely undermined the investigating commission, which perhaps wanted exactly that—for everything to work itself out.

Personally I won nothing and lost nothing, unless you count my comrades' gratitude. Some other good things happened: the hauling of rocks stopped—the work was now done by the buffaloes.

The cons only set them in place. And Carbonieri was allowed back in the bakery.

I tried to get sent back to Royale. There was no workshop on Saint-Joseph, therefore no way of making a raft.

Pétain's coming to power in France complicated relations between cons and guards. All the Administration people proclaimed themselves "Pétainists." One Norman guard even told me, "You want to know something, Papillon? I've never even been a Republican."

Nobody had a radio on the islands, so we were without news. On top of that, word went around that we were supplying German submarines at Guadeloupe and Martinique. There was no way of finding out the truth and arguments erupted all the time.

"Jesus, you want to know what I think, Papi? We should be staging a revolt now so we can give the islands back to de Gaulle and the Free French."

"You think *le grand Charlot* needs the *bagne*? What for?"

"He gets two or three thousand extra men!"

"Lepers, half-wits, tuberculars, men with dysentery? Don't make me laugh. He's not such a fool he wants an army of cons on his hands."

"What about the two thousand healthy ones?"

"That's something else again. They may be men, but that doesn't mean they'd be good for the firing line. You think war is like a knife fight. That takes ten minutes. A war lasts years. To be a good soldier you have to have a patriot's faith. Whether you like it or not, I don't think there's a single *mec* here who'd give his life for France."

"Why should we, after what she's done to us?"

"So you agree with me. It's a good thing old Charlot has other men besides you to fight the war. Though, goddammit, I don't like the idea of having all those German bastards in our country! And to think there are Frenchmen who've gone over to the side of the Boches! All the guards here say they're for Pétain."

The Count de Bérac said, "It might be one way of getting pardoned." No *mec* had ever spoken of trying to get a pardon. Now everybody—the underworld and the nonprofessionals both, even the hardened old criminals—was seeing flickers of hope on the horizon.

"How about staging a revolt so we can join up with de Gaulle, Papi?"

"I'm sorry, but I'm not looking for a pardon. Screw French justice and its ideas of 'rehabilitation.' I'll be the one to judge when I've been rehabilitated. My duty now is to make a *cavale* and, once I'm free, to be a normal man who is not a threat to society. I don't think there's any other way to prove yourself. I'm ready to leave at anytime, but only so long as it's on a *cavale*. I'm not interested in turning the islands over to *le grand Charlot* and I don't think he wants them anyway. Besides, if we did such a thing, you know what the boys at the top would say? That we did it for ourselves, not for France. Anyway, do we really know which one is right— Pétain or de Gaulle? I sure as hell don't. I suffer as much as the next guy, knowing that my country's been overrun. I think about my people, my father, my sisters, my nieces . . ."

"What right have these bastards to ask us to go to all that trouble for a society that doesn't give a damn about us?"

"It's perfectly natural. The pigs, the French judicial system, the guards—they aren't France. They're a class apart, made up of people with warped minds. Just guess how many of them are ready to grovel before the Germans! Want to bet the French police are arresting their own countrymen and turning them over to the German authorities? I tell you again, I'm not taking part in any revolt for any reason. Except for a *cavale*."

We had very serious discussions among our various factions.

Some were for de Gaulle, some for Pétain. But actually we knew nothing because, as I said before, neither guards nor cons had radios. News reached us only by the boats that brought in our food supplies. To us the war seemed very far away and difficult to understand.

There was a rumor that a recruiter for the Free French Forces had turned up at Saint-Laurent-du-Maroni. We on the islands knew nothing—only that the Germans were all over France.

There was one amusing incident. A priest came to Royale and preached a sermon after mass in which he said, "If the islands are attacked, you'll be given arms to help the guards defend French soil." He actually said it! That was some priest, all right, and he must have had a pretty funny opinion of us prisoners. To ask us to defend our cells! What next?

For us the war reduced itself to this: twice as many guards as usual, lots of inspectors, some with pronounced German or Alsatian accents; very little bread—we were down to less than a pound a day—and very little meat. The only increase was in the penalty for a failed escape: death, because added to the regular charge of attempted escape was "Attempt to go over to the enemies of France."

I succeeded in returning to Royale, where I made good friends with Dr. Germain Guibert. His wife, who was an extraordinary woman, asked me to plant a vegetable garden to supplement our restricted diet. I planted lettuces, radishes, green beans, tomatoes and eggplant. She was delighted and treated me like a close friend. The doctor had never shaken hands with a guard, whatever his rank, but he often shook mine and those of the few other *bagnards* he had come to know and respect.

Years later, when I was finally free, I made contact again with Dr. Guibert through Dr. Rosenberg. He sent me a photograph of himself and his wife taken on the Canebière in Marseilles. He was back from Morocco and congratulated me on my freedom. He was killed in Indochina trying to save a wounded soldier. He was an exceptional man and his wife was worthy of him. When I went to France in 1967, I thought about getting in touch with her, but decided not to. I had asked her for a letter of recommendation, which she had given me, but I hadn't heard from her since. I don't know why she stopped writing, but I still feel the deepest gratitude to both of them for the way they welcomed me into their home on Royale.

NINTH NOTEBOOK

SAINT-JOSEPH

CARBONIERI'S DEATH

YESTERDAY MY FRIEND MATTHIEU CARBONIERI was stabbed to death. His murder set off a whole series of other murders. He had been in the washhouse, naked, and his face was covered with soap when he was hit. When we showered, we were in the habit of opening our knives and hiding them under our clothes so we could reach for them quickly if a suspected enemy appeared. Carbonieri forgot to do this and it cost him his life. The man who killed him was an Armenian pimp.

With the permission of the warden and the help of another con, I carried my friend down to the quay. He was heavy and we had to stop three times to rest. I had a big rock attached to his feet and had used steel wire instead of the usual rope. That way the sharks wouldn't be able to cut it and he'd sink to the bottom without being eaten.

The bell tolled as we reached the quay. It was six o'clock. The sun was setting. We got into the boat. In the all too familiar crate, under the closed lid, Matthieu slept his final sleep. For him it was all over.

"Let's go. Start paddling," said the guard at the tiller. In less than ten minutes we were in the channel between Royale and Saint-Joseph. Suddenly my throat tightened. Dozens of sharks' fins were cutting through the water, whipping around in tightening circles. They were ready for their appointment.

Dear God, don't give them time to get at him! Our oars were raised as if in farewell. We lifted the crate. Wrapped in flour sacks, Matthieu's body slid into the water.

Jesus! He was no sooner in the water—for good, I thought—than he rose above the surface, lifted by, I don't know, seven, ten, maybe twenty sharks. The flour sacks were torn off, and for perhaps two or three seconds Matthieu appeared to be literally standing on the water. His right forearm was already gone. With half his body out of the water, he was bearing down on our boat when an eddy caught him and he disappeared. The sharks shot under the boat and, as they hit its bottom, one of our men lost his balance and almost fell in the water.

Everybody, guards included, was terror-stricken. For the first time in my life I wanted to die. It wouldn't have taken much to get me to throw myself to the sharks and leave this hell forever.

I walked slowly back to camp, alone. I was carrying the stretcher on my shoulder, and as I reached the place where Brutus had attacked Danton, I stopped and sat down. Night had fallen, although it was only seven, but in the west the sky was still glowing with a few licks of sunlight from below the horizon. Everything else was black but for the regular beam from the lighthouse. My heart was heavy.

Well, you wanted to see a burial and you saw one, the burial of your pal. O.K., you saw it, the bell and the whole bit. Now are you satisfied?

But I still had to get the *mec* who had killed my friend. When? Tonight? No, it was too early; he'd be on his guard. No point in moving too quickly. There were six men in his *gourbi*. How many men could I count on? Besides myself, four. O.K. We could do it. Yes, then if possible, I'd leave for Diable. On Diable, no rafts, no preparations, nothing—two sacks of coconuts and off into the sea. From there to the coast the distance was relatively short—twenty-five miles as the crow flies. With the waves, wind and tides, figure about seventy-five miles. It would be just a matter of endurance. I was strong, and I should certainly be able to last the two days astride my sacks.

I picked up the stretcher and continued on my way. When I arrived in front of the door, I was searched. Very unusual. That had never happened before. The guard removed my knife.

"You want me to be killed? Why are you taking away my knife? I guess you realize you're sending me to my grave?" Nobody answered, not the guards or the Arab turnkeys. They opened the door and I entered our *case*. "I can't see a thing. Why only one lamp?"

"Papi, come here." Grandet pulled me by the sleeve. The room was strangely quiet, as if something serious had just happened or was about to.

"I don't have my knife. They took it away from me at the door."

"You won't need it tonight."

"Why?"

"The Armenian and his friend are in the can."

"What are they doing there?"

"They're dead."

"Who did it?"

"Me."

"That was fast work. What about the others?"

"There are still four left in their *gourbi*. Paulo gave me his word he wouldn't do anything until he'd talked to you."

"Give me a knife."

"Take mine. I'll stay here."

I went over to their *gourbi*. My eyes were now used to the semi-darkness. I finally made out the group. They were standing glued to each other in front of their hammocks.

"Paulo, you wanted to speak to me?"

"Yes."

"What do you want?"

Prudently I left a good four feet between us. The knife was open inside my left sleeve and its handle was well cradled in the hollow of my hand.

Paulo said, "I wanted to say I think your friend has had his revenge. You lost your closest friend; we've lost two. In my opinion that's enough. What do you say?"

"Paulo, I'll consider your offer. What we could do, if you agree, is call off any action between our two *gourbis* for the next week. During that time we can consider what to do next. Is that all right with you?"

"Yes."

I left.

"What did he say?"

"They think Matthieu got his revenge with the death of the Armenian and Sans-Souci."

"No," Galgani said.

Grandet didn't speak. Jean Castelli and Louis Gravon agreed to the peace treaty. "What do you think, Papi?"

"In the first place, who killed Matthieu? The Armenian, right?

I suggested an agreement. I gave my word and they gave theirs that, for the next week, nobody moves."

"Don't you want to avenge Matthieu?" Galgani asked.

"Look, *mec*, Matthieu has been avenged enough. Two men died for him. Why kill still more?"

"Were they in on it or not? That's what we have to find out."

"Excuse me, but good night everybody. I've got to get some sleep."

Or, at least, I needed to be alone. As I stretched out on my hammock, I felt a hand slide over me and gently remove the knife. A voice whispered, "Try to sleep, Papi, and don't worry. We're taking turns keeping watch."

There was no real motive behind my friend's brutal murder. The Armenian had killed him because Matthieu had made him pay up a hundred and seventy francs for a poker hand. And the son of a bitch had felt humiliated because he had to do it in front of thirty or forty players. Given the squeeze by Matthieu and Grandet, he had to cough up. So, like a coward, he killed Matthieu, a born adventurer with his life before him. It was a heavy blow for me, and my only satisfaction was that his murderer had survived him by only a few hours. But it wasn't much.

With the speed of a champion fencer, Grandet had plunged his knife into their throats before they found time to protect themselves. The place where they fell must be damn bloody, I thought to myself. Then I wondered who had dragged them into the toilets. But I didn't want to ask. Behind closed lids I saw the sun go down again, tragically purple and red, casting its last rays on that Dantesque scene—the sharks fighting over my friend . . . the mutilated torso swaying toward the boat. . . . So it was true that the bell summoned the sharks and those bastards knew dinner was ready when the bell rang. . . . I saw again the dozens of fins, flashing a dull silver, scooting like submarines around and around. . . . There must have been over a hundred.

It was all over for my friend; he had come to the end of the road of the condemned.

To die for nothing at forty! My poor old buddy. I couldn't stand it here any more. I didn't care if the sharks ate me so long as I was trying for my freedom. There'd be no flour sacks, no rock, no rope. No spectators either, no convicts, no guards. And no bell. If I had to get eaten—well, let them eat me alive, fighting the elements on the way to Grande Terre.

I'm through, I told myself. No more overplanned *cavales*. Just Diable, two sacks of coconuts, and off into the arms of fate.

After all, it was only a matter of physical endurance. Forty-eight to sixty hours. Would that long immersion, plus the muscular effort to stay upright on the coconuts, end by paralyzing my legs? If I had a chance to go to Diable, I'd experiment with it. At all costs, I must get off Royale and go to Diable. After that we'd see.

"Are you asleep, Papi?"

"No."

"Want some coffee?"

"If you do." I sat up in my hammock and took the mug of hot coffee and the lighted Gauloise Grandet handed me.

"What time is it?"

"One o'clock. I started my watch at midnight, but since you were thrashing around, I figured you weren't asleep."

"You were right. Matthieu's death really hit me, but his burial and the sharks were even worse. That was horrible."

"I don't want to hear about it, Papi. I can imagine what it was like. You shouldn't have gone."

"I thought the story about the bell was so much crap. And I thought the wire around the rock would keep the sharks from reaching him on the way down. Poor Matthieu. I'll see that ghastly scene for the rest of my life. Tell me, Grandet, how did you manage to rub those two out so fast?"

"I was at the end of the island, fitting an iron door in the butcher shop, when I heard they'd killed Matthieu. It was noon. Instead of going up to camp, I went to the shop, pretending I needed to get something for the door. I was able to slip a double-edged dagger into a yard-long tube. The handle of the dagger and the tube were both hollow. I carried the tube back to camp at five. The guard asked me what it was for, and I told him that the wooden bar of my hammock was broken and I was going to replace it with the tube. It was still daylight when I entered our room, so I left it in the washhouse. I went and got it before roll call, when it was beginning to get dark. The Armenian and Sans-Souci were standing in front of their hammocks, with Paulo a little behind. You know, Jean Castelli and Louis Gravon are brave men, but they're getting old and can't move fast enough for that kind of close infighting.

"I wanted to have it done before you got back so you wouldn't be involved. With your record, if things didn't work out right, you'd get the maximum. Jean put out the light at one end of the room, Gravon at the other. It was almost dark, the only light coming from the gas lamp in the middle. I had a big flashlight that Dega had given me. Jean moved forward with me following. When he reached the two men, he aimed the light right in their eyes. The Armenian was blinded and raised his arm to protect his eyes—it gave me just enough time to plunge my knife into his throat. We did the same thing to Sans-Souci. He pulled out his knife but couldn't see to aim it. I gave it to him so hard the knife came out the other side. Paulo threw himself on the floor and rolled under the hammocks. Jean had turned off the flashlight, so I couldn't see Paulo. That's what saved him."

"Who pulled them into the can?"

"I don't know. I suspect it was the men in their *gourbi* who wanted to get their *plans* out of their gut."

"There must have been damn near a sea of blood."

"You're not kidding. They were stuck like pigs. They must have been drained to the last drop. The idea of using the flashlight came to me when I was preparing my knife. A guard in the shop was changing the batteries in his. I got in touch with Dega right away and asked him to get me one. Now they can do a routine search; it doesn't matter. An Arab turnkey returned both the flashlight and dagger to Dega. That part was easy. And I have nothing to be sorry about. They killed our friend when his eyes were blinded by soap; I killed them when their eyes were blinded by light. We're quits. What do you say, Papi?"

"You did right. I'm grateful to you for going at it so fast and especially that you kept me out of it."

"Never mind about that. I did my duty. You'd suffered enough, and you want your freedom so much I had to do it."

"Thanks, Grandet. It's true, and I want to get out now more than ever. But first we have to make sure this business ends right here. To be frank, it wouldn't surprise me if the Armenian didn't tell his *gourbi* before he killed Matthieu. Paulo would never have gone along with such a cowardly murder. He knows the consequences much too well."

"I agree. Galgani is the only one who thinks they're guilty."

"We'll see what happens at six o'clock. I won't do the latrines. I'll pretend I'm sick so I can watch developments."

Five A.M. Our *case* leader came up to us and said, "*Mecs*, think I should call the guardhouse? I just found two corpses in the toilets." That seventy-year-old *bagnard* wanted us—of all people—to think that, since six o'clock when the *mecs* were bumped off, he had known nothing. The room must be covered with blood; the men couldn't have helped tracking it around.

Grandet gave the old man some of his own back. "What? You mean to tell me there are two stiffs in the toilets? How long they been there?"

"How should I know?" the old man said. "I've been asleep since six o'clock. Just now I was going in to piss and slipped on a slimy puddle and landed on my face. I lit my lighter, saw it was blood, then I found the *mecs* in the toilets."

"Why don't you call for help and see what happens?"

"Guards! Guards!"

Guards came running. "What you yelling about, you old goat? Is your *case* on fire?"

"No, chief, but there're two corpses in the can."

"What you expect me to do? Bring 'em back to life? It's five-fifteen now. We'll do something about it at six. Don't let anybody near the toilets."

"That's impossible. How can I? The men have to piss."

"I suppose you're right. Wait. I'll report it to the duty guard."

Five guards appeared. We thought they were coming into the room, but they stopped by the grill.

"You say two dead men are in the toilets?"

"Yes, chief."

"Since when?"

"I don't know. I just found them now."

"Who are they?"

"I don't know. I just found them now as I was going to piss."

"Well, then, stupid, I'll tell you. One of them is the Armenian. Go have a look."

"Yes, you're right. It's the Armenian and Sans-Souci."

"O.K. We'll wait for roll call." And they left.

At six o'clock the first bell rang. The door opened and the two men who distributed coffee went from place to place with the bread man immediately behind.

Six-thirty, second bell. It was now daylight and the alley was full of bloody footprints.

The two wardens arrived. They were accompanied by eight guards and the doctor.

"Everybody strip and stand at attention in front of your hammocks! My God, this is a real slaughterhouse. There's blood everywhere!"

The deputy warden was the first to go into the toilets. When he came out, he was as white as a sheet. "They were completely drained. Of course, nobody saw or heard anything?"

Absolute silence.

"You, you old fool, you're supposed to be the guard here. These men are bone-dry. Doctor, how long would you say they've been dead?"

"Eight to ten hours."

"And you didn't find them until five? You saw nothing, heard nothing?"

"No. I'm hard of hearing; I can barely see. Besides, I'm seventy years old, and forty of them I spent in the *bagne*. So you see, I sleep a lot. I go to sleep at six, and it was only because I needed to piss that I woke up at five. It was pure luck, because usually I only wake up with the bell."

"You're right there. It was pure luck," the warden said with heavy irony. "Everybody slept peacefully the whole night through—guards and convicts alike. Please have the stretcher-bearers take the two corpses to the hospital amphitheater. I'd like you to do autopsies, Doctor. As for the rest of you, file out into the yard as you are."

We each filed past the wardens and the doctor. They examined every inch of our bodies. No one had a wound, although many were splattered with blood. They explained it was from slipping on the way to the toilets. Grandet, Galgani and I were examined even more minutely.

"Papillon, which is your place?" They searched through everything I owned. "Where's your knife?"

"My knife was taken from me by the guard at the door. Last night at seven."

"That's true," the guard said. "He made a big stink about it, too, said there were people who wanted to kill him."

"Grandet, is that knife yours?"

"Well, it's here in my place, so it must be."

The warden examined it carefully and saw that it was as clean as a new penny.

The doctor returned from the toilets. "It was a double-edged dagger that killed the men. They were knifed standing up. It's hard to understand. No *bagnard* would let himself be killed like a rabbit without trying to defend himself. Somebody here has to have been wounded."

"But you saw for yourself, Doctor. No one has so much as a nick."

"Were these two men dangerous?"

"Very. The Armenian was almost certainly Carbonieri's murderer. He was killed in the washhouse at nine yesterday morning."

"We'll shelve it," the warden said. "But keep Grandet's knife. Everybody to work now, except those of you who are sick. Papillon, did you report sick?"

"Yes, sir."

"You didn't waste much time avenging your friend. I'm not a fool, you know. Unfortunately I have no proof and I know we'll find none. For the last time, does anybody have anything to say? Anyone who can cast light on this double crime will be disinterned and sent to Grande Terre. You have my word."

Absolute silence.

The Armenian's entire *gourbi* reported sick. When they saw that, Grandet, Galgani, Jean Castelli and Louis Gravon became sick at the last minute. The room emptied. We were the five in my *gourbi*, the four in the Armenian's, plus the watch repairer, the old fellow who kept muttering about the cleanup he had in store, and two or three others, including the Alsatian—big Sylvain.

Sylvain lived alone and had only friends in the *bagne*. He was a highly respected man of action and the author of a singular deed that had got him twenty years at hard labor. All by himself, he had attacked the mail wagon on the Paris-Brussels Express, knocked out the two guards, and thrown the mail sacks onto the bank where his accomplices picked them up. They had netted a very pretty sum out of it.

Seeing the two *gourbis* whispering in their respective corners and unaware that we had agreed not to fight for a week, Sylvain spoke up. "I hope you don't have a pitched battle à la The Three Musketeers in mind?"

"Today, no," Galgani said. "That's for later on."

"Why later on?" Paulo said. "Never put off till tomorrow what you can do today. Though for myself, I don't see the point of us killing each other. What do you say, Papillon?"

"I have just one question. Did you know what the Armenian was going to do?"

"On my word of honor, Papi, we didn't know a thing. And you want to know something else? If the Armenian weren't dead already, I'm not sure I would have let him get away with it."

"Well, if that's the way it is, why don't we bury the hatchet right now?" Grandet said.

"It's O.K. with me. Let's shake on it and forget the whole sad mess."

"Agreed."

"I'm a witness," Sylvain said, "and I'm glad it's over."

At six o'clock the bell rang. When I heard it, I couldn't help seeing last evening's scene once again: my friend's body, upright, bearing down on our boat. The picture was so vivid, even twenty-four hours later, that I couldn't wish the same fate even on the Armenian and Sans-Souci.

Galgani wasn't speaking. He too knew what had happened to Carbonieri. He was sitting astride his hammock, staring straight ahead. Grandet hadn't come in yet. Still looking off, Galgani said in a low voice, "I only hope that Armenian son of a bitch isn't eaten by the same sharks that got Matthieu. It would be too much if the two of them ended up in the same shark's belly."

The loss of that wonderful friend left a big empty space. I had to get away from Royale as soon as possible.

THE MADMEN'S *CAVALE*

"Now there's a war on and the punishment is even tougher, this is no time to louse up a *cavale*, is it, Salvidia?"

I was talking with the Italian of the gold *plan* I'd known on the convoy. We were sitting in the washhouse, having just read the bulletins describing the new measures pertaining to escapes.

I told him, "But no death sentence is going to keep me from trying. What about you?"

"Papillon, I can't take any more of this. I've got to go, no matter what. I've asked for a job as orderly in the lunatic asylum. In the storeroom there they have two fifty-five-gallon barrels which would make a very nice raft. One is full of olive oil, the other of vinegar. If they were carefully tied together, I think you'd have a good chance of reaching Grande Terre. There's no surveillance on the outside wall surrounding the building. Inside there's only one infirmary guard with a few cons who concentrate on the patients. Why don't you go up there with me?"

"As an orderly?"

"Not a chance, Papillon. You know damn well they'll never give you a job at the asylum. It's too far from camp and there's very little surveillance—they'd never let you near the place. But you might get in as a lunatic."

"That would be a really tough one, Salvidia. When a doctor classifies you as loony, he's giving you the right to do anything you like. You're no longer responsible for your actions. Just think of the responsibility the doctor takes on when he admits that and signs the diagnosis. You can kill a con, a guard, a guard's wife, a kid, anyone. You can escape, commit any crime in the book, and justice has no recourse. The worst they can do is wrap you up in a straitjacket and put you in a padded cell. And they can't even do that for very long; after a certain time they have to relax the treatment. So, no matter how serious your crime, even if it's an escape, you get off scot-free."

"Papillon, I trust you, I'd really like to do a *cavale* with you. Do your damnedest to join me at the nuthouse. I realize it must be pretty grim to find yourself, a well man, in with all those nuts. But since I'd be an orderly, I'd be able to back you up and help you through the tough spots."

"You go to the asylum, Roméo. I'll look into it and study the early symptoms of madness so I can convince the doctor. It wouldn't be such a bad idea to have him class me as irresponsible."

I embarked on a serious study. There was no book on the subject in the *bagne* library, so at every opportunity I discussed it with men who had been sick. I gradually arrived at a pretty clear idea of what was involved:

1. All lunatics had terrible pains in the cerebellum.

2. Often they had buzzing sounds in the ears.

3. Since they were very nervous, they couldn't lie in the same position for any length of time. Their bodies were racked with nervous spasms, and the strain on them was intolerable.

The important thing was to have *them* discover these symptoms, not to display them openly. My madness must be just dangerous enough to make the doctor commit me to the asylum, but not so violent that it justified the extreme measures of hair shirts, beatings, withholding of food, hot or cold baths, etc. If I played my cards right, I might manage to fool the doctor.

I had one thing going for me: why would I want to fake madness? Since the doctor would not be able to think up a logical answer to this question, I might be able to get away with it. Anyway, it was my only chance. They had refused to send me to Diable, and I couldn't stand the camp after my friend's death. To hell with procrastination! I made my decision. I'd go to the doctor on Monday. No, I mustn't report myself. Better if someone else did it, someone who could be trusted. I would do a couple of slightly strange things in our *case*. Then our guard would report it and put me down for a doctor's visit.

For three days I didn't sleep, didn't wash and didn't shave. I masturbated several times each night and ate practically nothing. Yesterday I asked my neighbor why he'd removed a picture of mine that never existed. He swore he'd never touched any of my things. It made him so nervous he changed places. Our soup often sat for a while in the pot before being distributed. I walked up to the pot and pissed in it in front of everybody. The look on my face must have impressed everyone because there was absolute silence.

My friend Grandet said, "Papillon, why did you do that?"

"Because they forgot to salt it." And paying no further attention to the others, I got my bowl and held it out for the guard to serve me.

The silence continued while everybody watched me eat my soup.

Those two things did it. I was taken to the doctor without my saying a word.

I asked him, "Are you O.K., Doc?" Then I repeated the question. The doctor looked at me, stupefied. I looked at him perfectly naturally.

"Yes, I'm O.K.," the doctor said. "Are you sick?"

"No."

"Then why did you come to me?"

"For no reason. They told me you were sick. I'm glad to see it isn't true. Good-by."

"Wait a minute, Papillon. Sit down. Now, look at me." And the doctor examined my eyes with a lamp that gave off a small ray of light.

"You didn't see what you expected to, did you, Doc? Your lamp isn't powerful enough, but I think you understand all the same, right? Tell me, did you see them?"

"See what?" the doctor asked.

"Don't be an ass. Are you a doctor or a vet? You're not going to tell me you didn't see them before they hid? Maybe you don't want to tell me, and you're playing me for a fool."

My eyes glistened with fatigue. My appearance—unshaven, unwashed—helped. The guards listened, transfixed, but I refrained from any act that might have justified their intervention.

The doctor went along with the game so as not to excite me. He stood up and put his hand on my shoulder. "Yes, Papillon, I didn't want to tell you, but I did see them."

"Doc, you lie with your goddam colonial self-control. You didn't see a damn thing! You were looking for three black specks in my left eye. I see them only when I'm looking into space or reading. When I look in the mirror, I see my eye clearly, but not a sign of the three specks. They hide the second I pick up the mirror to look for them."

"Put him in the hospital," the doctor said. "Take him there immediately without going back to camp. Papillon, you said you weren't sick. Maybe so, but I think you're very tired and I want you in the hospital for a few days' rest. Is that all right with you?"

"What's the difference? Hospital or camp, it's still the islands."

I had taken the first step. A half-hour later I was in the hospital in a well-lighted cell with a clean bed and white sheets. The sign on the door said, "Under observation." Little by little, helped by the power of suggestion, I became a lunatic. It was a dangerous game: I had worked up a tic that twisted my mouth, and I bit the inside of my lower lip. I studied how in a mirror and got so good at it that I found myself doing it without thinking. Mustn't play this game too long, Papi. The effort to seem unbalanced could have serious consequences, even leave permanent damage. Still, I had to play the game with my whole soul if I was to achieve my goal. I had to get into that asylum, have myself classified as irresponsible and leave *en cavale* with my pal. *Cavale*! The magic word carried me away; I already saw myself astride my two barrels, being carried to Grande Terre with my buddy, the Italian orderly.

The doctor stopped by every day. He took a long time examining me; we always spoke to each other politely and nicely. He was troubled, but not yet convinced. So I told him I had the first symptoms—the shooting pains in the neck.

"How are you, Papillon? Slept well?"

"Yes, thank you, Doctor. Pretty good. Thanks for lending me your copy of *Match*. But sleep, that's something else again. The trouble is that in back of my cell there's a pump for watering something, and the shaft goes pang-pang all night, right through the back of my neck, and there's a kind of echo inside me going pang-

pang too. It keeps going all night long. I can't stand it. I'd be very grateful if you could get my cell changed."

The doctor turned to the orderly guard and muttered, "Is there a pump?"

The guard shook his head.

"Guard, put him in another cell. Where would you like to go?"

"As far as possible form the damned pump. At the far end of the hall. Thanks, Doc."

The door closed; I was alone in my cell. But I was aware of an almost imperceptible sound. I was being watched through the spy hole. It had to be the doctor, for I hadn't heard his steps moving off when he left. Quickly I stuck my fist out against the wall which my imaginary pump was behind and cried out—but not too loud: "Stop, stop, you filthy bastard! When will you finish that watering, asshole?" Then I threw myself on my bed and hid my head under the pillow.

I didn't hear the small brass plate close over the hole, but I made out the sound of retreating steps.

I changed cells that afternoon. I must have put on a good show because two guards and two orderlies were assigned to accompany me the few feet to my new one. They didn't say a word, so I didn't speak to them. I just followed them silently. Two days later I produced the second symptom: noises in the ear.

"How are you, Papillon? Did you finish the magazine I gave you?"

"No, I couldn't. I spent the whole day and most of the night trying to smother some mosquitoes or gnats or something. They've made their nest in my ear. I stuffed it with a piece of cotton, but it doesn't work. I can't seem to stop the zzin-zzin-zzin sound their wings make. But even worse is the buzzing. It never stops. It gets on your nerves, Doc. What do you think? Maybe asphyxiation, and if it doesn't work, we could try to drown them. What do you say?"

The tic in my mouth was working and the doctor made a note of it. Then he took my hand in his and looked into my eyes. I could feel that he was troubled.

"Yes, my friend, we'll drown them. Chatal, see that his ears are given a lavage."

I repeated these scenes every morning, with variations, but the doctor was still undecided about sending me to the asylum.

While Chatal was giving me an injection of bromide, he warned me, "It's going well for the moment. The doctor is definitely worried about you, but it could still be a long time before he sends you to the asylum. If you want to speed things up, show him you can be dangerous."

"How are you, Papillon?" The doctor was accompanied by Chatal and a couple of infirmary orderlies and greeted me in his friendly way as he opened the door to my cell.

"Don't give me that crap, Doctor!" I was very aggressive. "You know damn well how I am. I want to know which of you is in cahoots with my torturer?"

"Who's torturing you? When? How?"

"Doc, do you know the works of Dr. d'Asonval?"

"I should hope so."

"You know that he invented a multiple-wave oscillator for ionizing the air around a patient with duodenal ulcers. The oscillator gives off electric waves. Well, I think some enemy of mine filched one from the Cayenne hospital. Each time I go to sleep, he pushes the button and the charge hits me right in my gut. In one swoop I'm lifted five-inches off my bed. How do you expect me to sleep with that thing? It doesn't leave off the whole night long. The minute I close my eyes—pang—the current is on. My whole body lets go like a spring. I can't stand it any more, Doc! You tell everybody that the first man I suspect, I kill. It's true I don't have a weapon, but I've got enough strength to strangle him, whoever he is. They're warned! So to hell with you and your hypocritical 'How are you, Papillon?' I repeat, don't give me any of that crap!"

The incident bore fruit. Chatal told me that the doctor had warned the guards to watch me closely. They must never open my cell door unless there were two or three of them, and they were always to talk to me gently. I was suffering from a persecution complex, and I should go to the asylum immediately.

"With one guard I can take charge of moving him to the asylum," Chatal suggested, to keep me out of a straitjacket.

"Did you eat well, Papi?"

"Yes, Chatal, it was very tasty."

"You want to come with me and Monsieur Jeannus?"

"Where we going?"

"We're taking medicine up to the asylum. It will be a nice walk for you."

"Let's go then."

And the three of us set off toward the asylum. We were almost there when Chatal asked, "Aren't you tired of camp, Papillon?"

"I'm sick to death of it, especially since my buddy Carbonieri isn't there any more."

"Why don't you spend a few days at the asylum? Maybe that way the *mec* with the machine won't be able to find you."

"It's not a bad idea, but do you think they'll accept me when there's nothing wrong with me?"

"Leave it to me. I'll do the talking," said the guard, all too happy to see me fall into Chatal's supposed trap.

So I found myself in the asylum with one hundred lunatics. Living with nuts is no bed of roses. We got an airing in the yard in groups of thirty or forty while the orderlies cleaned the cells. Everybody was stark naked, day and night. Luckily it was hot. They let me wear socks.

An orderly had just handed me a lighted cigarette. I sat in the sun and reflected on the fact that I had been there five days and had not yet been able to make contact with Salvidia.

A lunatic came up to me. I knew his story. His name was Fouchet. His mother had sold her house in order to send him fifteen thousand francs through a guard so he could make his escape. The guard was to keep five and give him ten, but instead the guard took the lot and left for Cayenne. When Fouchet found out that his mother had sacrificed everything for nothing, he went off his rocker and attacked some guards. They subdued him before he could do any harm. That was three or four years ago. He had been in the madhouse ever since.

"Who are you?" he asked.

I looked at the poor bastard standing there in front of me. "Who am I? A man, like you, nothing more, nothing less."

"That's a stupid answer. I can see you're a man because you've got a prick and balls. If you were a woman you'd have a hole. I'm asking who you are. That means, what's your name?"

"Papillon."

"Papillon? You're a butterfly? Well, you're a lousy butterfly. A butterfly flies, it has wings. Where are yours?"

"I lost them."

"You've got to find them. That way you can escape. The guards don't have wings. That way you play them for suckers. Give me your cigarette." He grabbed it from me before I had time to hand it to him. Then he sat down and smoked it with a look of rapture.

"They gypped me. Every time I'm supposed to get something, they gyp me."

"Why?"

"Because. I've been killing a lot of guards. I hanged two last night. But don't tell anybody."

"Why did you hang them?"

"They stole my mother's house from me. D'you know, my mother sent me her house and they thought it was pretty so they kept it and moved in. I was right to hang them, eh?"

"Right. That way they won't be able to use your mother's house."

"You see that fat guard over there, behind the grill? He lives in the house. And you see that other guard over there? I'm going to bust him up, too, you can believe it." Then he got up and left.

Christ! It's no joke living with lunatics, and it's not very safe either. They shout and yell all night, and during the full moon it's even worse. Why the moon agitates a lunatic, I don't know. But I've noticed it often.

The guards made reports on the men under observation. With me they double-checked. For instance, they'd deliberately forget to let me out in the yard and wait to see if I complained. Or they'd forget a meal.

I had a stick with a string hanging from it and made motions as if I were fishing.

The head guard would say, "Are they biting, Papillon?"

"They can't. There's this little fish following me around, and when a big one comes to bite, the little one warns him, 'Watch out, don't bite. That's Papillon fishing.' So I never catch anything. But I go on fishing all the same. Maybe one day there'll be a fish that doesn't believe him."

I heard the guard say to an orderly, "That guy's really got it!"

When they made me sit at the communal table in the dining hall, I was never able to eat my lentils. A giant at least six feet eight, with arms, legs and torso covered with hair like a monkey, had picked me out for his victim. He always sat next to me. The lentils were served very hot so you had to wait until they'd cooled off. I'd take up a few in my wooden spoon and blow on them. That way I got down a few spoonfuls. Meanwhile Ivanhoe—he thought he was Ivanhoe—picked up his plate, made a funnel of his hands and swallowed the lot in five gulps. Then he grabbed mine and did the same, after which he banged the plate down in front of me and looked at me with his enormous bloodshot eyes as if to say, "See how I eat lentils?" I was beginning to get pissed off at Ivanhoe, and since I hadn't yet been classified mad, I decided to let him have it.

It was another lentil day. Ivanhoe was sitting there next to me, his batty face ecstatic at the prospect of downing my lentils after his. I pulled a big heavy jug of water toward me. The giant had just begun to lift my plate to his mouth when I stood up and with all my strength brought the jug down on his head. He screamed like a wounded animal and collapsed on the floor. Immediately all the lunatics jumped on each other, armed with their plates. There was a ghastly hassle to the accompaniment of screams and yells.

I was picked up bodily by four husky orderlies and returned to my cell with speed and few courtesies. I shouted that Ivanhoe had stolen my wallet with my card of identity. That did it. The doctor decided to classify me as not responsible for my actions. The guards agreed that I was a peaceful nut but with occasional dangerous moments. Ivanhoe had a splendid dressing on his head. Apparently I'd opened up more than five inches of his skull. It's a good thing we didn't take our walks at the same time.

I finally managed to talk to Salvidia. He'd already got hold of a duplicate key to the storeroom where the barrels were kept and was trying to find enough wire to tie them together. I told him I was afraid that, once we were afloat, the tugging of the barrels would break the wire; rope would be better since it had more give. I would try to get some and we could use both—wire and rope. He also needed three keys: one for my cell, one for the corridor that led to it, and one for the main door of the asylum. We weren't heavily guarded. One lone guard went on duty every four hours, from nine to one at night and from one to five. Two of the guards slept through their rounds. They counted on the convict-orderly who was on duty at the same time to cover for them. So everything was fine; we had only to be patient. A month at most and we'd be off.

The head guard gave me a terrible cigar as I was going into the yard. But terrible as it was, it seemed delicious. I looked at the herd of naked men, singing, weeping, making convulsive motions, talking to themselves. They were still wet from the showers they had to take before coming into the yard; their pathetic bodies were battered from the beatings they'd received or had inflicted on themselves, or from the marks left by straitjackets. This was the last circle of hell all right. I wondered how many of these crazy bastards had been unfairly held responsible for their actions in France.

Titin had been in my convoy in 1933. He had killed a guy in Marseilles, hailed a cab, put his victim inside and driven to the hospital where he announced, "Take care of him. I think he's sick." He had been arrested immediately, and the jury had had the gall to hold him responsible. But clearly he must have been mad already to do a thing like that. Only a madman wouldn't have known he'd get arrested. So here Titin was, sitting next to me. With his chronic dysentery he was a walking corpse. He looked at me with his blank, iron-gray eyes. "I got little monkeys in my belly, pal. The bad ones bite my gut and then I bleed. That's when they're angry. The other ones are covered with hair and have hands as soft as feathers. They caress me gently and keep the bad ones from biting me. When the gentle little monkeys defend me, there's no blood."

"Do you remember Marseilles, Titin?"

"What do you mean, do I remember Marseilles? I remember it very well. The Place de la Bourse, with the pimps and thieves . . ."

"Do you remember any of their names? L'Ange? Le Lucre? Le Gravat? Clement?"

"No, I don't remember any names. I only remember the fucking cabby that took me to the hospital with my sick friend and told me I was the reason he was sick. That's all."

"Your friends?"

"I don't remember."

Poor Titin. I gave him the butt of my cigar and got up, feeling an immense pity for this poor bastard who was dying like an animal. Yes, it was dangerous to live with lunatics, but what could I do? It was the only way I could see to make a *cavale* without risking another sentence.

Salvidia was almost ready. He had two of the keys and needed only the one for my cell. He had also found a stout rope and had made another with strips of hammock which he braided together, five strands thick. That part of our *cavale* was looking good.

I was in a hurry to start the action. It was too hard keeping up this game and, to stay in my section of the asylum, I had to put on an occasional performance.

I brought off one that was such a success the orderlies put me in a hot bath with two injections of bromide. The bath was covered with a very strong canvas to keep me from getting out. Only my head poked through a hole. I'd been in it for about two hours when Ivanhoe came in. The look he gave me was terrifying. I was sure he was going to strangle me, and I had no way of defending myself with my arms inside the canvas.

He came nearer, his big eyes scrutinizing me as if he were trying to place the head sticking out of the strange contraption. The stink of his breath engulfed me. I wanted to cry for help, but I was afraid that would only enrage him. I closed my eyes and waited, convinced he was about to strangle me with his giant hands. It will be a long time before I forget those few seconds of terror. Finally he moved away toward the faucets. He turned off the cold water and opened wide the hot. I screamed. I was being literally scalded to death. Then Ivanhoe left. The room was full of steam. I was choking and making superhuman efforts to tear my way out of the death-dealing canvas. Finally the guards came to my rescue. They had seen the steam rolling out of the window and came to pull me out of the cauldron. I was seriously burned and suffered like the damned, especially around the genitals, where the skin had been literally boiled away. They basted me with picric acid and put me to bed in the small infirmary in the asylum. The doctor gave me some injections of morphine which got me through the next twenty-four hours. When he asked me what had happened, I said a volcano had erupted in the bathtub. Nobody was able to figure out what had really happened. The infirmary guard accused the man who had prepared the bath of not properly regulating the flow of water.

Salvidia just left, having smeared me with picric ointment. He was ready, and he remarked that it was a lucky thing I was in the infirmary because, if the *cavale* was a bust, we could return to this part of the asylum without being seen. He had just made a print of the infirmary key on a piece of soap and he'd have it by tomorrow. It was up to me to let him know when I was sufficiently healed; then we'd take advantage of the first watch by one of the guards who slept through his tour.

It was to be tonight, during the one-to-five watch. Salvidia was off duty. To save time, he was going to empty the vinegar barrel about eleven. The oil barrel we'd leave full because the sea was very rough and the oil might help calm the water as we put out to sea.

I had some pants made of flour sacks, a wool sweater and a

good knife in my belt. I also carried a waterproof bag around my neck containing cigarettes and a tinderbox. Salvidia had filled a waterproof musette bag with tapioca flour saturated with oil and sugar. He had about six pounds of it.

It was late. I sat on the bed waiting for my buddy, my heart thumping in my chest. In a few moments the *cavale* would begin. If only luck and the good Lord would be with us so that I could leave this hell forever!

As the door opened, in spite of myself, I saw Matthieu looming out of the darkness, held high by the sharks.

"Papi, let's go!" I followed. He quickly closed the door and hid the key in the corner of the corridor. "Quick! Get moving!" We reached the storeroom; the door was open. The empty barrel was a cinch. He wrapped the rope around his shoulder and I did the same with the wire. I took the bag of flour and started to roll my barrel through the inky night toward the sea. Salvidia followed with the oil barrel. Luckily he was very strong so he was able to brake the heavy barrel as it rolled down the almost vertical drop.

"Watch it, watch it. Make sure it doesn't pick up speed." I waited in case he had to let go of his barrel so I could stop it with mine. I made the descent backward, me in front, the barrel behind. We got to the bottom without difficulty. There was a narrow access to the sea; the rest was rocks and impossible to get through.

"Empty the barrel. You'll never get it over the rocks full." The wind was howling and the waves were crashing against the rocks. It was done; the barrel was empty. "Push the stopper in hard. Wait, put this metal cap on too." The holes were made. "Hammer the nails in deep." The noise of the wind and waves muffled the sound of the hammer.

Tightly joined, the two barrels were hard to lift over the rocks. Each alone held over fifty gallons. The place my friend had picked for the launching didn't make things easier. "Push, for Christ's sake! Lift it up a little. Look out for that wave!" It picked us both up and, together with the barrels, we were pushed back violently against the rocks. "Look out! Look out!" Salvidia yelled.

"Calm down, pal. Either get out on the water side or come back behind. There, you're in a good spot now. When I yell, pull toward you. I'll push at the same time and we'll be free of the rocks. But we have to hold it for a minute even if a wave hits."

As I was shouting orders to Salvidia through the din of the wind and waves, a huge wave covered us completely—the barrels, him and me. Then, with furious energy, I pushed the raft forward, he pulled, and with one heave we were free. He was up on the barrel before me, and at the moment I was hoisting myself up, an enormous wave rolled under us and pitched us like a feather against the rocks. We hit so hard that the barrels cracked open and scattered in fragments. When the wave rolled back, it carried me over thirty yards back into the sea and then, as I started to swim, another wave rolled me back to shore. I landed in a sitting position between two rocks and just had time to grab hold before I was carried off again. Bruised all over, I managed to crawl out, but once on dry land, I realized I'd been carried over a hundred yards from where we'd launched the raft.

Without thinking I cried out, "Roméo! Salvidia! Where are you?" No answer. I collapsed on the path and took off my pants and sweater, leaving myself naked except for my socks. For Christ's sake, pal, where are you? And I started again at the top of my lungs: "Where are you?" Only the wind, waves and sea answered. I lay there, I don't know how long, numb and completely exhausted, physically and emotionally. I broke into tears of rage and tore off the little bag around my neck that held the tobacco and lighter—a brotherly gesture on the part of my friend who didn't smoke.

Standing with my face to the wind, facing the monstrous waves that had swept everything to perdition, I shook my fist and cursed God. "You son of a bitch, you swine, stinker, fag, aren't you ashamed of the way you treat me? You, a *good* Lord? You're a bastard, that's what you are! You're a damned sadist. Pervert, filthy bastard! I'll never speak your name again! You don't deserve it!"

The wind died down and the comparative calm helped me return to reality.

I'd go back up and try to get into the asylum. With a little luck I could manage it.

I climbed back up the bank with but one idea: to get back into my bed, unseen, unheard: I arrived in the infirmary corridor without trouble after jumping over the asylum wall, for I had no idea where Salvidia had put the key to the main door.

I didn't have to look long to find the key to the infirmary. I entered and double-locked the door, then went to the window and threw the key as far as I could. It fell on the far side of the wall. Then I got into bed. The only thing that could give me away was my wet socks. I got up and wrung them out in the toilet. Back in bed, I pulled the sheet over my face and gradually warmed up a little. The wind and the sea had congealed me. Had my friend really drowned? Maybe he'd been carried even farther than I and was able to grab hold at the far end of the island. Did I come back too soon? Should I have waited a little longer? I reproached myself for giving up too easily on my friend Roméo.

There were two sleeping tablets in the drawer of my night table. I swallowed them without water. I had just enough saliva to do the job.

I was sound asleep when I felt myself being shaken and saw an orderly standing in front of me. The room was filled with sunlight. Three inmates were looking in through the open window.

"What goes on, Papillon? You're sleeping like the dead. It's ten in the morning. You haven't drunk your coffee! It's stone cold. Come on, drink up."

Even half asleep, I realized that as far as they were concerned, this was nothing out of the ordinary.

"Why did you wake me up?"

"Because your burns are healed now and we need your bed. You're to go back to your cell."

"O.K., chief."

I followed him. He left me in the yard, and I took advantage of the opportunity to dry my socks in the sun.

It had been three days since the *cavale* went on the rocks. I hadn't heard so much as a word. I shuttled from my cell to the yard, from the yard to my cell. No sign of Salvidia. The poor bastard must be dead, crushed against the rocks. I'd had a narrow squeak; I must have been saved because I was behind instead of in front of the raft. But there was really no way of knowing. I had to get out of the asylum. It was going to be tough to make them think I was well or, at least, that I was better off in the camp. Now I'd have to convince the doctor.

"Monsieur Rouviot—" he was the head of the infirmary—"I'm cold at night. If I promise not to soil them, will you give me some pants and a shirt?"

Rouviot was dumbfounded. He looked at me carefully and said, "Papillon, sit down. Tell me, what's going on?"

"I don't understand why I'm here, chief. Isn't this the asylum? Why am I with the crazies? Did I go off my rocker? Why am I here? Please tell me, chief. I'd be much obliged."

"Old man, you were sick, but I can see you do look better. Do you want to work?"

"Yes."

"What kind of work?"

"I don't care."

They gave me clothes and put me to work cleaning the cells. My door was left wide open in the evening until nine o'clock when the guard on night duty came and locked it.

A man from the Auvergne, a *bagnard* orderly, addressed me for the first time last night. We were alone in the guardhouse. The guard hadn't turned up yet. I didn't know the guy, but he said he knew me well.

"There's no point in your carrying on any more, *mec*."

"What do you mean?"

"Come off it! You think I wasn't on to your act? I've been in the lunatics' infirmary here for seven years and I knew from the word go you were faking. I'm really sorry your *cavale* with Salvidia didn't come off. It cost him his life. It hurts me because he was a good friend, even though he didn't tell me about it. But I don't hold that against him. If you need any kind of help, tell me. I'll be glad to do what I can."

The look in his eyes was so honest that I felt he must be O.K. Poor Salvidia! The guy said there'd been quite a fuss when they found he was gone. They had found bits of the barrels thrown back by the sea and they were certain he had been eaten by sharks. The doctor threw a fit over the lost olive oil. He said that, what with the war, it would be a long time before we got any more.

"What's your advice?"

"I'm going to suggest they put you in the gang that goes to the hospital every day for our food. It'll be a nice walk for you. Be on your good behavior. And out of every ten conversations, see that eight make sense. You mustn't seem to be getting well too soon."

"Thanks. What's your name?"

"Dupont."

"Thanks, *mec*. I won't forget your advice."

The botched *cavale* was a month past. They had found

Roméo's body six days afterward. For some reason the sharks hadn't eaten him. But other fish had apparently devoured his middle and a part of one leg. Also his skull was bashed in. Because of the state of decomposition, no autopsy was performed.

I asked Dupont if he could get a letter mailed for me. He should get it to Galgani so that he could slip it into the bag just before it was sealed.

I wrote the following letter to Salvidia's mother in Italy:

> Madame, your son died without chains on his legs. He died at sea, bravely, far from prison. He died a free man fighting courageously for his liberty. We promised each other that we would write to the other's family if anything happened to one of us. I perform this painful duty and kiss your hands,
>
> Your son's friend, Papillon.

With this chore behind me, I decided to stop thinking about the nightmare. That was life. All that remained was to get out of the asylum, get to Diable no matter how, and try another *cavale*.

One of the guards put me in charge of his garden. For two months now I'd behaved normally, and the guard thought so highly of me he wouldn't let me go. Dupont told me that the doctor—when he saw me the last time—wanted to let me out of the asylum and put me back in the camp, on a "trial basis." But the guard opposed the move, saying his garden had never been better tended.

So one morning I pulled up all his strawberry plants and threw them into the garbage heap. In place of each plant I set a small cross. So many absent strawberries, so many crosses. The furor was indescribable. The fat guard was so upset he almost popped. He frothed and spluttered in his attempt to talk, but no words came. He sat down in a wheelbarrow and cried real tears. Perhaps I'd gone a bit far, but I had had to do something. . . .

The doctor took it calmly. He insisted that the patient be put on trial back at the camp so he could adapt himself to normal life. It was being all alone in the garden so much that had given him this strange idea.

"Tell me, Papillon, why did you pull up the strawberries and put the crosses in their place?"

"I can't explain it, Doc, and I asked the guard to forgive me. He loved his strawberries so much that I'm really sorry. I'll ask God to send him more strawberries."

So I found myself back in the camp among my friends. Carbonieri's place was still empty; I hung my hammock next to the empty space as if he were still there.

The doctor had "Special Treatment" stitched on my sweater. Only he was to give me orders. I was to rake leaves in front of the hospital from eight to ten every morning. Often I sat and drank coffee and smoked with the doctor and his wife in front of their house. Together they tried to find out about my past. By forcing me to talk about it, they believed they could cure me. I decided to ask the doctor to send me to Diable.

The thing was done. I was to leave the next day. The doctor and his wife knew why I wanted to go. They had been so good to me I couldn't deceive them. "Doc," I had said, "I've had it here at the *bagne*. Get me sent to Diable. Whether I go on *cavale* or die, I don't care as long as this comes to an end."

"I understand, Papillon. The system here revolts me too. The Administration is rotten to the core. Good-by and good luck!"

TENTH NOTEBOOK

DIABLE

DREYFUS' BENCH

DIABLE [DEVIL'S ISLAND] IS THE smallest of the three Iles du Salut. It is also the northernmost, and the most exposed to wind and waves. After a flat coastal area it rises rapidly to a high plateau where there was the guardhouse and one lone barracks for the *bagnards*, who numbered about ten. Officially Diable was not supposed to receive ordinary criminals, only those condemned and deported for political reasons.

Each political prisoner had a small house with a tin roof. On Monday he was given his food for the week and, every day, a loaf of bread. There were about thirty of these men. Their orderly was a Dr. Leger who had poisoned his family somewhere near Lyon. The political prisoners had nothing to do with the regular *bagnards* and sometimes wrote to Cayenne, complaining about this or that *bagnard* on the island. He was then returned to Royale.

There was a cable connecting Royale with Diable because often the sea was so rough that the launch from Royale couldn't dock at the cement pier.

I was greeted by the head guard at the camp (there were three), who was a big brute with an eight-day beard named Santini.

"Papillon, I hope you behave on Diable. Don't give me any trouble and I'll leave you in peace. Go on up to the camp. I'll see you later." There were six cons in my room: two Chinese, two blacks, a man from Bordeaux and another from Lille. One of the Chinese knew me well. He'd been at Saint-Laurent under suspicion of murder. Actually he was from Indochina and a survivor of the revolt in the *bagne* at Poulo Condor.

He had been a professional pirate. He used to attack sampans and sometimes murder everybody on board—men, women and children. Although he was very dangerous, he was a good man to live with; something about him inspired sympathy and confidence.

"How things go, Papillon?"

"How about you, Chang?"

"Not bad. It's okay here. You eat with me. You sleep there, next to me. I do cooking two times a day. You catch fish. Here many fishes."

Santini arrived. "So you're all moved in. Tomorrow morning you go with Chang to feed the pigs. He'll carry the coconuts. You split them open with the hatchet. Save the milk for the piglets. You do it again at four in the afternoon. Except for those two hours you're free to do anything you like. All the men who fish have to give my cook two pounds of fish or *langoustines*. That way everybody's happy. Is that okay with you?"

"Yes, Monsieur Santini."

"I know you're a *cavale* man, but I'm not going to worry about it—escape from here is impossible. You're locked up at night, but I know some get out all the same. Watch out for the political prisoners. They all have machetes. If you go near their houses, they think you've come to steal their eggs or chickens. You can get hurt or even killed. They can see you, remember, and you can't see them."

After feeding a good two hundred pigs, I spent the rest of the day wandering over the island with Chang, who knew every inch of it: An old man with a long white beard crossed our path as we were circling the island down by the shore. He was a journalist from New Caledonia who had written pro-German pieces during the First World War. We also met the bastard who had had Edith Cavell shot—the English or Belgian nurse, I forget which, who saved the lives of English fliers in 1917. He was a repulsively large, fat man and he was beating a huge eel about five feet long and as thick as my thigh with a stick.

The orderly also lived in one of the little houses, even though these were supposed to be only for political prisoners.

Dr. Leger was a big husky fellow. He was always dirty except for his face, and he had long graying hair that hung down over his neck and temples. His hands were covered with badly healed cuts and gashes he must have gotten from the rough rocks along the coast.

"If you need anything, come to me and I'll give it to you. But only come when you're sick. I don't like being visited, and I like being talked to even less. I sell eggs and sometimes a hen or chicken. If you ever happen to slaughter a baby pig on the sly, bring me a leg and I'll give you a chicken and six eggs. Since you're here, take this bottle of quinine tablets—there are a hundred and twenty capsules in it. You must have come here to escape, so if by some miracle you manage to succeed, you'll need these in the bush."

Morning and evening I caught a vast number of rock mullet. I sent seven or eight pounds a day to the guards' mess. Santini was in heaven. He had never had so much fish or so many *langoustines*.

A couple of times, at low tide, I caught as many as three hundred of them.

Dr. Germain Guibert came to Diable yesterday. The sea was calm, so he came with the warden of Royale and Mme. Guibert. This extraordinary person was the first woman ever to set foot on Diable. I talked to her for over an hour, and she walked with me to the bench where Dreyfus had gazed out over the sea toward the France that had cast him out.

Dreyfus' bench was high on the northernmost point of the island, a good hundred and twenty feet above the sea.

"If this polished stone could only tell us what Dreyfus' thoughts were . . ." she said, stroking the stone. "Papillon, this *is* probably the last time we'll see each other if you're going to try a *cavale* soon. I shall pray to God that He let you succeed. And before you go, I ask that you come back and spend a last minute on this bench as a farewell to me."

The warden gave me permission to send the doctor *langoustines* and fish by the cable any time I wanted to. Santini agreed.

"Good-by, Doctor. Good-by, madame." I tried to act natural as I said good-by before the launch pulled away from the pier. Mme. Guibert looked at me with wide-open eyes as if to say, Don't ever forget us. We'll always remember you.

I didn't go fishing today. I was holding over two hundred pounds of mullet in a natural pool and about five hundred *langoustines* in an iron barrel chained to a rock. No need to fish. I had enough to send the doctor and enough for Santini, the Chinese and me.

It was 1941. I'd been in prison eleven years. I was thirty-five. I'd spent the best years of my life in either a cell or a dungeon. The only freedom I'd had was the seven months with my Indian tribe. The children I had by my two Indian wives must be eight years old.

Jesus! How the time had flown! But as I looked back, those hours and minutes became cruelly long, each one separately imbedded in my stations of the cross.

Thirty-five years! Where were Montmartre, Pigalle, the Place Blanche, the ball at the Petit Jardin, the Boulevard de Clichy? Where was big Nénette with her madonna's face, like a cameo, and her huge black eyes filled with despair as she cried out at the trial, "Don't worry, baby, I'll get you out of there!" Where was Raymond Hubert with his "We'll be acquitted"? And the prosecutor? How were my father and my sisters' families doing under the German occupation?

So many *cavales*. How many had there been?

The first was when I knocked out the guards and escaped from the hospital.

The second was in Colombia, at Rio Hacha.

That was a beautiful *cavale*. A real success. Why did I leave my tribe? A quiver of physical longing flowed through my body. It was as if I were feeling again the sensations of making love to my wives.

Then there were the third, fourth, fifth and sixth at Barranquilla. What lousy luck I had had with those *cavales*! The stunt at mass that ended so badly. . . . The dynamite that fizzled, and the next time when Clousiot's damn pants caught . . . and the sleeping potion that wouldn't work. . . .

The seventh was on Royale when that filthy bastard, Bébert Celier, ratted on me. That one would have worked for sure if it hadn't been for him. If he had kept his trap shut, I'd be free with my poor buddy Carbonieri.

And the last one, the eighth, from the asylum. A mistake, a stupid-ass mistake on my part. I should never have let the Italian choose our launching place. Two hundred yards farther down, near the butcher's, would have been a much better place. . . .

Dreyfus' bench, where that innocent man condemned to death had found the courage to go on living, would inspire me. I would not admit defeat. I would try another *cavale*.

Right. This silky, polished stone hanging out over the rocky shore, where the waves pounded and broke without letup, would inspire me. Dreyfus never gave up; he fought for his vindication to the very end. True, he had Emile Zola and his famous *"J'accuse."* But all the same, if he hadn't had a will of iron, the injustices he suffered would surely have sent him hurtling into the abyss from this very bench. He had held on. I could not be a lesser man than he. But I would give up the idea of a "win or die" *cavale*. I'd forget about the "dying" and concentrate exclusively on winning and being free.

During the long hours I spent sitting on Dreyfus' bench, my brain shuttled between dreams of the past and of a rosy future. Often my eyes would become dazzled by the glare and the platinum reflections of the breaking waves. From looking at the sea so long—almost without seeing it really—I came to know every quirk of the wind and waves. Tirelessly the sea attacked the island's exposed rocks. It worked away at them, searched and stripped them as if to say, Diable, go, disappear, you're in my way, you bar my passage to Grande Terre! That is why, every day, relentlessly, I remove a little piece of you.

When there was a storm, the sea gave Diable the full force of its fury, raging in to snatch its piece of the island, then sweeping it away. It hurled its water into every nook and cranny so as to undermine little by little the giant rocks that seemed to say, You shall not pass.

And that's how I made a very important discovery. Immediately opposite Dreyfus' bench were some enormous craggy rocks that the waves broke against with particular violence. The tons of water had no place to go because the two rocks formed a horseshoe about five or six yards wide and a cliff rose directly above them, leaving the waves no exit except back out into the sea.

What made this important was that if, just as the wave was flinging itself into the chasm, I was to take a sack of coconuts and jump from the rock directly into its center, it would beyond the shadow of a doubt take me with it as it retreated.

I knew where I could find the jute bags for the coconuts; there were plenty of them in the pigsty.

The first thing was to test my theory. During the full moon the tides were higher, hence the waves were bigger. I would wait for the full moon. I hid my carefully sewn bag of dry coconuts in a cave I knew which could only be reached from the water. I had come upon it one day when I was looking for *langoustines*. The shellfish clung to its ceiling, which was completely under water except at low tide. To the bag of coconuts I strapped another bag containing a rock weighing between eighty and ninety pounds. Since I'd be leaving with two bags instead of one, and I weighed a hundred and fifty-five pounds, the proportions were about right.

I was very excited about the experiment. This side of the island was taboo. Nobody would ever suspect that the most windswept and dangerous spot on the island would be used for an escape.

Besides, it was the only place where, if I did manage to get clear of the coast, I would be carried out into the open sea without the hazard of cracking up on Royale.

This had to be the place.

The bag of coconuts and the rock were heavy and hard to carry. I wouldn't be able to do it alone so I spoke to Chang, who said he'd come and help me. He brought along some fishing tackle and heavy lines; if we were caught, we could say we were setting up traps for sharks.

"Keep pushing, Chang. A little farther and we're there."

The light of the full moon made it as bright as day. The noise of the waves was deafening. Chang said, "Ready, Papillon? Into this next one?" A fifteen-foot wave lunged at the rock as if possessed and broke just below us, but the shock was so violent that the crest passed over us and drenched us. Still we were able to throw the sacks in at the moment the wave went into reverse. Like a straw, the bag was swept back toward the open sea.

"That's it, Chang! It works."

"Wait and see if it comes back."

Sure enough. My heart sank when, five minutes later, I saw my bag riding back on the crest of a wave over twenty feet high. It smashed against the rocks, scattering the coconuts in every direction and tumbling the rock into the chasm below.

Wet to the bone, battered and almost swept off our feet, Chang and I left that bedeviled place without so much as a backward glance.

"No good, Papillon. No good, *cavale* from Diable. Royale better. Leave from south coast, much better."

"Yes, but an escape from Royale would be discovered in less than two hours. The bag of coconuts moves only with the waves—they'd catch me in no time. Here there's no boat, and I have the whole night before they find out I'm gone, and even then they'll probably think I drowned while fishing. Also there's no telephone on Diable. If I leave in a heavy sea, they'll have no way of communicating with Royale. So here is where I have to leave from. But how?"

The noon sun was leaden—a tropical sun to boil the brain in your skull; a sun that shriveled the plants not yet grown strong enough to resist it; a sun that, in a few hours, dried up all but the deepest salt-water pools, leaving only a white film of salt; a sun that set the air to dancing—it literally moved before my eyes—its reflection on the water burning my pupils. But that did not prevent me from returning to Dreyfus' bench and taking up again my study of the sea. It was then I discovered what an idiot I'd been.

Only one wave out of every seven was as large as the monster that had flung my sack back against the rocks. The others were little more than half its size. From noon to sundown I watched to see if this was always so, if there wasn't an occasional shift or whim that altered the regularity.

There wasn't. The ground swell never came sooner, never came later. There were six waves about twenty feet high, then, forming about three hundred yards from shore, the ground swell. It came in straight as a cannonball, growing in size and height as it approached. There was hardly any spray on its crest compared to the other six, very little, in fact. It had its own special noise, like far-off thunder. When it broke on the two rocks and hurled itself into the passage between them, crashing against the cliff, its great mass caused it to choke and turn on itself. Then, after ten or fifteen seconds, the eddies would work their way out with a wild churning, tearing off huge stones and rolling them back and forth, making a rumble like a hundred wagonloads of stones being dumped.

I put a dozen coconuts in a sack and added a fifty-pound rock. As the ground swell broke, I threw the sack in. I couldn't follow it with my eyes because of the spray, but I saw it for a second as the water was sucked back to the sea. It did not return. The next six waves lacked the strength to throw it back on shore, and by the time the seventh had formed three hundred yards out, the sack must have drifted beyond it, for I didn't see it again.

Bursting with excitement, I went back to camp. I had it! I had found the perfect launching. No question of luck here. Still I would do another trial run, this time under the conditions of the real *cavale*: two sacks of coconuts tied together and; on top, two or three rocks weighing a total of a hundred and fifty-five pounds. I told Chang about it and he listened closely.

"It's good, Papillon. I think you got it. I help you for real thing. Wait for high tide twenty-five feet. Soon equinox."

With Chang's help and that of the twenty-five-foot equinoctial tide, we threw the two sacks and three rocks into the famous wave.

"What was name of little girl you tried save on Saint Joseph?"

"Lisette."

"We call wave that take you away Lisette. O.K.?"

"O.K."

Lisette arrived with the roar of an express train pulling into a station. Standing straight as a rampart, she grew larger with every second. It was an impressive sight. She broke with such power that Chang and I were swept off the rock and the sacks fell into the chasm. In the flash of a second we realized we couldn't hold onto the rock, so we threw ourselves back—which didn't protect us from a mighty soaking but did prevent our falling into the chasm. This happened at ten in the morning. We weren't taking any risk because the three guards were busy doing inventory at the other end of the island. The sacks were carried off—we could see them clearly far out from shore. Were they beyond the ground swell? We waited. The six waves that followed Lisette were not able to catch them. Lisette came and went a second time, but still no sacks. They were beyond her reach.

We climbed quickly up to Dreyfus' bench to see if we could see them again and, to our joy, we caught sight of them four different times riding the crest of the waves. And these waves were not coming toward Diable but heading west. We had the proof. I would sail toward the great adventure on the back of Lisette.

"Look, there she comes." One, two, three, four, five, six . . . then Lisette.

The sea was always heavy below Dreyfus' bench, but it was especially bad today. Lisette was advancing with her usual noise.

She seemed even bigger, carrying more water than ever. Her monstrous mass struck the two rocks faster and straighter than ever before. And when she crashed against them, the noise was even more deafening, if that was possible. "That's where you want us to jump from? Well, pal, you sure found a great spot! But not for me. I want to go on a *cavale*, not commit suicide."

Sylvain was impressed with my description of Lisette. He had come to Diable three days before and, naturally, I suggested we leave together, each of us on our own raft. If he accepted, I'd have a companion on Grande Terre to help with the second stage of the *cavale*. Being alone in the bush was no picnic.

"There's no point in being scared ahead of time. I realize that on first thought any man might hesitate a little. But it's the only wave that'll take us far enough out."

"Calm down. Look, we tried it," Chang said. "It's sure thing. Once off, you never pushed back on Diable or Royale."

It took me a week to convince Sylvain, a man with the body of an athlete, all solid muscle and six feet tall.

"O.K. I can see we'll be carried far enough out. But after that, how long will it take us to get to Grande Terre?"

"To be honest, Sylvain, I don't know. The speed of the drift depends on the weather. The wind'll have little effect because we'll be so low in the water. But if we have heavy weather, the waves will be bigger and push us faster. Seven, eight, ten tides at the most and we should reach the mainland. It could take anywhere between forty-eight and sixty hours."

"How do you figure?"

"From the islands to the mainland isn't more than twenty-four miles. The drift is the hypotenuse of the triangle. Look at the direction of the waves. We have to do between seventy-five and ninety miles maximum. The nearer we get to shore, the more directly the waves aim us at the coast. Wouldn't you guess that a piece of drift-wood at this distance from the coast would travel at least three miles an hour?"

He listened very attentively to my explanations. The big guy was pretty intelligent.

"It sounds all right to me. If it wasn't for the low tides, which will pull us back, it wouldn't take more than thirty hours to reach the coast. Taking them into account, I think you're right—it'll take somewhere between forty-eight and sixty hours."

"Are you convinced?"

"Almost. But once we're on Grande Terre, in the bush, what then?"

"We have to find our way to the outskirts of Kourou. It's a fairly big fishing village, and there are also people there searching for gold and balata trees. You have to be careful, though, because it has a camp for *bagnards*. There'll be some kind of path going toward Cayenne, and also toward the Chinese camp called Inini. We'll have to force a con or a black civilian to take us to Inini. If he behaves himself, we'll give him five hundred francs—then make him beat it. If it's a con, we'll make him join our *cavale*."

"What do we do in Inini in a camp for Chinese?"

"Chang's brother is there."

"Yes, my brother there. He leave on *cavale* with you. He find boat and food. When you meet Cuic-Cuic, you got everything for *cavale*. Chinese never squeal. Any Annamite you find in bush, tell him to tell Cuic-Cuic."

"Why's your brother called Cuic-Cuic?" Sylvain asked.

"Don't know. French baptized him Cuic-Cuic." Then he added, "Be careful. When you almost Grande Terre, there's quick-sand. Never walk on quicksand; it bad, it suck you up. Wait next tide to push you in bush so you grab liana and branches. If not, you finished."

Sylvain said, "O.K., Papillon. I'm going with you."

"All right, then. Our rafts will be alike and weigh about the same—we shouldn't be separated by much. But you never know. If we do get separated, we've got to have a way of finding each other. You can't see Kourou from here. But when you were on Royale you must have noticed that to the right of Kourou, about twelve miles away, there are some white rocks—they stand out clearly when the sun hits them."

"Yes."

"They're the only rocks on the whole coast. To the right and left, for miles and miles, there's nothing but quicksand. The rocks are white because of bird shit. There are thousands of birds, and since no man ever goes near it, it's a good place to catch our breath before we start into the bush. We can eat eggs and our coconuts. We mustn't make a fire. The first one there waits for the other."

"How many days?"

"Five. It won't take more than five days, not possibly."

The rafts were ready. We lined the sacks to make them stronger and then decided to take the next ten days to practice riding them. We soon realized that it would take a special effort to keep the sacks from turning over. Whenever possible, we would have to lie flat but be careful not to fall asleep. If we fell off, we might not be able to get back on. Chang made me a small waterproof bag to hold cigarettes and a lighter to hang around my neck. We would grate ten coconuts for each of us. The pulp would take care of thirst as well as hunger. Santini had some kind of skin for carrying wine. Chang, who occasionally visited the guard, was going to pinch it.

It was all set for Sunday at ten in the evening. There would be a full moon, hence a twenty-five-foot tide, and Lisette would be at full strength. Chang was going to feed the pigs alone that Sunday morning. I would sleep all of Saturday and Sunday. Departure at ten—the tide would have started to ebb two hours before.

My two sacks couldn't possibly rip apart. They were bound together with braided hemp rope and brass wire and sewn with the heavy thread used for making sails. We had found some unusually large sacks and joined them at the neck so the coconuts couldn't possibly work their way out.

Sylvain was forever doing exercises, and I lay in the sea for long hours for the little waves to massage my thighs. The continuous pounding and the contractions necessary to resist the pull gave me legs and thighs of iron.

I found a chain about three yards long in a dried-up well and wove it in and out of the rope that held my sacks together. Then I attached a bolt to one of the links. If I reached the point where I'd had it, I would chain myself to my sacks. That way I could sleep without falling into the water and losing my raft. If the sacks turned over, the water would automatically wake me up and I'd be able to right the raft.

"Papillon, just three more days." We were sitting on Dreyfus' bench watching Lisette.

"Yes, just three more days. I really believe we're going to make it. Don't you?"

"I'm sure of it, Papillon. Tuesday night or Wednesday morning we'll be in the bush. Then we're all set!"

Chang was to grate our coconuts—ten each. Besides our knives, we had two machetes we'd lifted from the tool house.

The Inini camp was east of Kourou. We must walk into the morning sun to be sure of our direction.

Chang said, "Monday morning we fool Santini. I say nothing; only Papillon and Sylvain disappear before Monday three o'clock in afternoon when guard have siesta."

"But why can't you say a wave swept us away while we were fishing?"

"No. Want no complications. I say, 'Boss, Papillon and Sylvain not come work today. Me all alone feed pigs.' No more, no less."

THE *CAVALE* FROM DIABLE

It was Sunday, seven o'clock in the evening. I had just waked up. I'd been asleep since Saturday morning. The moon would be rising at nine. It was blackest night, with very few stars, and large clouds heavy with rain rushing overhead. We had just left the barracks. Since we often sneaked out to fish at night or take a walk around the island, the others thought this perfectly normal.

A queer was going into the barracks with his lover, a big, hairy Arab. They must have been making love in some dark corner. As I watched them raise the plank to go back into the room, it crossed my mind how, for the Arab, being able to screw his friend two or three times a day must be the last word in bliss. The fact that he could satisfy his erotic needs transformed prison into paradise. Same for the fairy. He must have been twenty-four or -five, but his body had lost its youthful beauty. For all that he probably spent the whole day in the shade to protect his milk-white skin, he was no longer any Adonis. But here in the *bagne* he had more lovers than he had ever dreamed of when he was free. In addition to the Arab, he took on others at twenty-five francs a lay, exactly like a whore on the Boulevard Rochechouart in Montmartre. So, besides the pleasure his clients gave him, he made enough dough to live a comfortable life with his "husband." From the day they first set foot in the *bagne*, he and his clients had given themselves entirely to this occupation. They had only one thing on their minds: sex.

The prosecutor who had got them convicted came out the loser if he thought he was punishing them by heading them down the road of the condemned. Here they'd found their real happiness.

Once the plank had closed behind the kid's pretty ass, we were alone—Chang, Sylvain and I.

"Let's go!" We quickly made for the northern tip of the island.

We took the two rafts out of the cave. In no time all three of us were drenched. The wind howled with hurricane force. Sylvain and Chang helped me push my raft to the top of the rock. At the last moment I had the idea of tying my left wrist to the rope around the sack. I was suddenly frightened at the thought of losing my sack and being carried off without it. Sylvain, with Chang's help, climbed up onto the rock opposite. The moon was already quite high. We could see clearly.

I tied a towel around my head. We had to wait out six waves. More than thirty minutes.

Chang came back to me. He hugged me around the neck and kissed my cheek. Then he stretched out flat on the rock and, wedged in a crack, prepared to hold my legs to help me resist the shock when Lisette broke.

"One more," Sylvain called out, "and then the good one!" He was standing in front of his raft to protect it with his body from the coming deluge. I was in the same position, with the added bracing of Chang's hands. His nails were puncturing my calves in the excitement.

She was on her way; Lisette was coming straight for us, standing up like the spire of a church. With her usual deafening roar she broke over our rocks and swept toward the cliff.

I threw myself in a fraction of a second before my buddy, but we were close together as Lisette sucked us out into the open sea with dizzying speed. In less than five minutes we were over three hundred yards from shore. Sylvain hadn't climbed onto his raft yet, but I had been up and astride within two minutes. Chang had scampered up to Dreyfus' bench and, holding a white rag in his hand, was waving a last good-by. Now we were a good five minutes beyond the dangerous area where the waves heading for Diable formed. The ones we were riding were much wider, almost without crests and so regular we could drift with them without bouncing and with no danger of the rafts turning over.

We rose and fell from immense heights to great depths, all the while moving smoothly out with the ebb tide into the open sea.

As I rose to the top of one of the waves, I looked back and saw the white cloth in Chang's hand for the last time. Sylvain was quite near me, perhaps forty yards farther out. I caught sight of him several times waving his arm in triumphal joy.

The night went smoothly. Then we felt a powerful change in the direction of the sea. The tide which had drawn us out had turned and was now pushing us toward Grande Terre.

The sun rose; it was about six o'clock. We were too low in the water to see the coast, but I knew we were far from the islands because, even with the sun on their summits, they were barely visible. Also they looked like one continuous island. Since I could make out no details, I figured they must be at least twenty miles away.

I smiled at the thought of our triumph.

If I sat up on my raft, would the wind on my back help me go faster?

I freed my chain and wound it once around my waist. The bolt was well greased, and it was easy to screw the nut on. I held my hands in the air to dry them off. I wanted a cigarette. Done. I inhaled in long, deep puffs and let the smoke out slowly. My fear was gone. There's no need to try to describe the agonies in my gut just before, during and after the leap. The real point is that I wasn't afraid any longer. In fact, after I'd finished the cigarette, I decided to eat a few mouthfuls of coconut pulp. I chewed a big handful, then smoked another cigarette. Sylvain was quite far away. We caught a glimpse of each other now and then when we crested a wave at the same time. The sun was striking the top of my head with hell's own heat; my skull was roasting. I wet the towel and wrapped it around my head. Then I took off my wool sweater. Even with the wind the heat was suffocating.

Christ! My raft just turned over and I almost drowned. I took in two huge gulps of sea water. Try as I could, I couldn't right the sacks and climb back on. The chain was constricting my movements. Finally, by letting it hang from one side, I was able to tread water and take a few deep breaths. I tried to get free of the chain, but my fingers couldn't work the nut and bolt. Furious, my nerves on edge, I didn't have the strength to unscrew them.

Finally I did it. That was a bad moment. I had nearly gone out of my mind thinking I couldn't get free of the damn chain.

I didn't bother to straighten the raft. I was too exhausted. I just hoisted myself up. What difference did it make whether it was the top or the bottom? I'd never attach myself to it again, not with the chain, not with anything. What a fool I'd been to tie myself to the raft by my wrist! That experience should have taught me.

The sun seared my arms and legs. My face was on fire. And it seemed to be worse when I wet it because the water evaporated immediately and made it burn even more.

The wind died down. This made the going more comfortable but much slower. Better lots of wind and a heavy sea than this calm.

I got such a violent cramp in my right leg that I yelled out. I made crosses on the cramp with my finger, remembering how my grandmother had said that would make the cramp go away. It didn't work. The sun was now low in the west. It must be about four in the afternoon, and there had been four tides since we started. This one seemed to be pushing me harder than the others.

Now Sylvain and I could see each other all the time. He had taken off his shirt and was making signs at me. He was over three hundred yards farther out to sea. He seemed to be rowing with his hands, because I could see little whitecaps around his raft. Was he trying to slow his raft so that I could get closer to him? I got down on my stomach, plunged my arms into the water and rowed. If he braked and I rowed, perhaps we could close the gap between us.

I'd chosen a good partner for this escape. Sylvain had certainly risen to the challenge—100 percent.

I stopped rowing; it was tiring work. I must conserve my strength. I would try to right the raft. The food bag was underneath with the leather bottle containing the fresh water. I was thirsty and hungry. The best way to turn over the raft was to hang on, facing the waves, then give it a mighty shove with my feet as it was about to take the swell.

After five tries I finally made it. The effort exhausted me and I barely made it back onto the raft.

The sun was on the horizon and would soon be gone. Six o'clock. I hoped the night wouldn't be too rough, for I realized that the continued drenchings were sapping my strength.

I took a long drink of water from Santini's leather bottle and downed two fistfuls of coconut pulp. Full up, my hands dry in the wind, I took out a cigarette and smoked with deep delight. Before night fell, Sylvain waved his towel and I mine to say good night. We were still about the same distance from each other. I was sitting with my legs straight out. I wrung out my sweater as hard as I could and put it on. Even wet, those sweaters held the heat, and with the sun gone, it got cold right away.

The wind picked up. Only the low clouds in the west still glowed; everywhere else it was dark and getting darker with every minute. There were no clouds in the east, where the wind was coming from, therefore no danger of rain for the moment. My one thought was to hold on tight and not to get any wetter than necessary. I wondered if it would be a good idea to tie myself to the sacks in case fatigue got the better of me. Or, in the light of my recent experience, was it too risky? Then I suddenly realized that the reason I'd had trouble maneuvering was that the chain was too short: one end was being wasted in a tangle of rope and wire. I quickly freed it, then straightened the chain and attached it to my belt. There was still plenty of grease on the bolt and it worked perfectly. I mustn't screw it so tight, that was all. Now I felt better, for I'd been scared stiff of falling asleep and losing the raft.

Yes, the wind was building up to something, and so were the waves. It was becoming a real toboggan ride.

Now it was completely dark. A million stars flickered in the sky, the Southern Cross the brightest of them all.

I couldn't see Sylvain. This night was very important, for if the wind kept up its strength, we would have made real progress by morning.

The wind grew stronger as the night advanced. A reddish-brown moon rose slowly out of the sea. When, round and enormous, it finally floated free, I could clearly see the lines of its face.

It was about ten o'clock. The night grew increasingly clear, and gradually, as the moon rose in the sky, the light of the lunar day became more intense. The waves were dipped in platinum and their strange reflections burned my eyes, already inflamed by the scorching sun and salt water. Even so, I couldn't keep from looking. I knew it was foolish, but I just couldn't resist the incredible effect.

I smoked three cigarettes, one right after the other.

The raft behaved perfectly, rising and falling gracefully on the swollen sea.

But what to do about my physical problems? For one thing, if I kept my legs stretched out too long, the terrible cramps returned. Also, most of the time I was wet to the crotch. But at least my chest was almost dry, since the wind dried my sweater and no waves came higher than my waist. My eyes were burning more and more. I kept them closed. From time to time I slept. "Don't sleep!" Easy to say, but I was beyond caring. Oh Christ, how I fought against it! And every time I returned to reality, I felt a terrible pain in my head. Then I'd take out my lighter and burn myself on my arm or my neck. I was racked with a fearful anxiety that I couldn't get rid of. What if I fell asleep? If I tumbled into the sea, would the cold of the water wake me up? It was a good thing I had tied myself with the chain again. I must not lose these two sacks; they were my life. Wouldn't it be great if I toppled into the sea and didn't wake up!

I'd been thoroughly drenched for several minutes. A freak wave, one that had run across the path of the others, had just broken against my right side. Not only had it soaked me, but it had thrown me crosswise so that the next two waves washed over me from head to foot.

It was late into the second night. What time was it, I wondered. From the position of the moon in the west, it had to be around two or three in the morning. We had been in the water through five tides, or thirty hours. The soaking turned out to be a good thing: the chill of the water woke me up. I was shivering, but I could keep my eyes open without effort. My legs were almost paralyzed, so I decided to draw them up under me. With both hands I pulled the first one, then the other. Finally I managed to get myself into a squatting position. My toes were frozen; maybe sitting on them would warm them up.

I sat for a long time in this Arab squat. The change helped. I looked for Sylvain across the brightly moonlit sea, but the moon was so low that it shone in my eyes and made it hard to see. I couldn't find him. He had nothing to attach himself to his sacks.

Could he have fallen off? It worried me and I kept looking for him, in vain. The wind was strong, but steady and without gusts. This was very important. I had caught the rhythm now and my body was as one with the sacks.

Staring into the night, I became obsessed with the idea of finding my partner. I dried my fingers in the wind and whistled through them with all my might. Then I listened. No answer. Did Sylvain know how to whistle through his fingers? I had no idea. I should have asked him before we left. It would have been so easy to make two whistles. Damn it, why hadn't I thought of that? I cupped my mouth with my hands and yelled, "Yoo-hoo!" The only answer was the noise of the wind and waves.

Finally I couldn't stand it any more so I stood up on my sacks, grasping the chain with my left hand and holding my balance through five waves. When I reached the crest of a wave, I stood straight up; when I went up or down, I squatted. Nothing to the right, nothing to the left. Could he be behind me? I didn't dare turn around while I was standing up. The one thing I was sure of was a dark line that the moon picked out on my left. It must be the bush.

By daytime I'd be seeing trees! I rubbed my toes and stretched my legs again. Then I decided to dry my hands so that I could have another cigarette. I smoked two. What time could it be? The moon was very low. I couldn't remember how much time there had been last night between the setting of the moon and sunrise. I closed my eyes and tried to bring back the impressions of our first night. No go. Wait a minute! Suddenly I had a picture of the sun rising in the east at the same time a sliver of moon still showed in the west. So it must be about five o'clock. But the moon was taking its time about setting. The Southern Cross had disappeared long ago, as well as the Big and Little Bear. Only Polaris was still there, outshining them all. Now that the Southern Cross was gone, Polaris was queen of the skies.

The wind seemed to be rising. Or, at least, it seemed heavier—if you can call a wind heavy. The waves were stronger and deeper and the whitecaps bigger than at the beginning of the night.

I'd been at sea thirty hours. I had to admit that, for the moment at least, things looked better rather than worse. But the day that was about to begin would be the real test.

Yesterday I'd been exposed to the sun from six in the morning until six at night. When the sun came up today and started cooking me again, it wasn't going to be any fun. It was still night, but my lips were already burning, as were my eyes, arms and hands. If I could manage it, I wouldn't expose my arms. That would depend on whether I could stand to wear my sweater. I was also raw between my buttocks from the salt water and the constant rubbing against the sacks.

In any event, old pal, burned or not, you're on *cavale* and it's worth a few discomforts. The prognosis on your arriving on Grande Terre alive is 90 percent favorable and that's something, isn't it? Even if you arrive literally scalped, with half your body raw flesh, it will be a small price to pay. And you haven't seen a single shark. Are they all on vacation? This time luck is really with you, and if you don't admit it, you're a damn peculiar fellow. This time it's going to work. All the other *cavales* were too carefully thought out, too well prepared; when all is said and done, the successful *cavale* will have been the stupidest: two sacks of coconuts and let the wind and sea take you! To Grande Terre. You don't have to be a graduate of Saint-Cyr to know that all wrecks end up on shore.

If the wind and waves could keep this up all day, I would almost certainly reach land by afternoon.

The monster of the tropics was looming up behind me. Today he seemed determined to burn everything to a crisp. He had the lunar day on the run in no time, not even waiting to get out of bed to proclaim himself master, the undisputed King of the Tropics. In no time at all the wind had gone from cool to warm. In another hour it would be hot. A marvelous sensation of well-being crept through my body. The first rays of the sun had no sooner touched my skin than I felt a gentle warmth suffuse me from my waist to my scalp. I removed the towel from around my head and exposed my cheeks to the sun as if to a log fire. Before the monster burned me to the quick, he was letting me know he was Life. Soon he would be Death.

The blood flowed through my veins and even my aching rear began to revive with the renewed circulation.

I could see the bush clearly, or at least I could see the tops of the trees. They seemed fairly near. I'd wait for the sun to rise a little higher before I stood up on my sacks to look for Sylvain.

In less than an hour the sun was high. Christ, it was going to be hot! My left eye was almost glued shut. I scooped up some water and wet it; it stung. I took off my sweater; I wanted my chest bare for a few moments before the sun got too hot.

An unusually strong wave lifted me high. In the split second before it broke and I started down, I caught sight of Sylvain. He was sitting bare-chested on his raft. He didn't see me. He was less than two hundred yards away, a little ahead on my left. The wind was still strong, so I decided to try to catch up with him by taking off my sweater, keeping only my arms in the sleeves and holding it up in the air like a sail with the bottom in my mouth.

I kept this up for almost half an hour until my teeth began to hurt and I became exhausted trying to resist the wind. But it did look as if I'd narrowed the distance between us.

Hallelujah! I just saw him again, less than a hundred yards away. But what was he doing? He didn't seem to care where I was. Another wave came, lifting me up, and I saw him once, twice, three times. I distinctly made out that he had his hand over his eyes as if he were looking around. Look back, you bastard! He looked toward me but didn't seem to see anything.

I stood up and whistled. When the raft climbed out of the trough, I saw Sylvain standing facing me. He raised his sweater in the air. We waved hello at least twenty times before we sat down again. Each time a wave peaked, we hailed each other, for luckily we were rising and falling to the same rhythm. On the last two waves he held his arm out toward the bush, which was now very distinct. It couldn't be more than six or seven miles away. I lost my balance and fell in a sitting position on the raft. I was so overcome with joy to see my buddy and the bush so near that I wept like a child. The tears in my pus-filled eyes became a thousand little crystals of every color. Like stained-glass windows, I thought. God is with you today, Papi! In the midst of nature's monstrous elements, in the wind, the immenseness of the sea, the depth of the waves, the imposing green roof of the bush, you feel your own infinitesimal smallness, and perhaps it's here, without looking for Him, that you find God, that you touch Him with your finger. I had sensed Him at night during the thousands of hours I had spent buried alive in dank dungeons without a ray of sun; I touched Him today in a sun that would devour everything too weak to resist it. I touched God, I felt Him around me, inside me. He even whispered in my ear: "You suffer; you will suffer more. But this time I am on your side. You will be free. You will, I promise you."

I never had any religious instruction, I didn't know the ABC's of the Christian religion, I was so stupid I didn't know who Jesus' father was or whether His mother was really the Virgin Mary, or whether His father was a carpenter or a camel driver; yet being ignorant of all that didn't keep me from finding God when I really needed Him, in the wind, the sea, the sun, the bush, the stars, in the very fish He had placed in the sea to nourish man.

The sun had risen fast. It must be ten o'clock. I was bone-dry

from my waist up, so I soaked my towel and wrapped it—
burnoose style—around my head. Then I put my sweater on to
cover my burning shoulders, back and arms. Even though my legs
were constantly doused with water, they, too, were as red as lobsters.

Because the shore was nearer now, the waves were moving
faster, racing toward it in long, straight lines. I could now see the
bush in detail, and it made me realize how quickly we had narrowed the distance. I had learned how to figure distances on my
first *cavale*: when details are sharp, you're less than three miles
away. I could see the difference between the thicknesses of the various trees, and from the crest of an especially high wave I made out
a giant one that had fallen, its branches awash in the sea.

Suddenly dolphins and birds! Just so long as the dolphins didn't
play any games with the raft. I had heard they were in the habit of
pushing driftwood and men toward shore, but the men often
drowned from their well-intentioned prodding. No, they spun
around me a few times, three or four of them come to have a look
and see what was up, but they left without even grazing the raft.

It was noon, the sun directly overhead. Plainly it intended to
poach me in sea water. My eyes oozed pus and the skin was gone
from my nose and lips. The waves were shorter now and rushed
toward shore with a deafening roar.

Since the waves were so much smaller, I could see Sylvain most
of the time. Once in a while he turned toward me and raised his
arm. He was still naked from the waist up, the towel around his
head.

Then the waves turned into rollers. There was a sand bar which
they hit with a terrible roar, and then, once past it, they advanced
on the bush in an explosion of spray. The sea was an ugly yellow
covered with muddy foam. We were so close I could see the dirty
line it left on the tree trunks at high tide.

Even the noise of the breakers couldn't deaden the shrieks of thousands of wading birds. Two or three yards more, then ploof! I had run aground; I was stuck in the quicksand. There wasn't enough water to carry me farther. From the position of the sun it looked to be about two o'clock, or forty hours since I'd set out. That was the day before yesterday, at ten in the evening, after two hours of ebb tide. The tide would turn in about three hours and, by night, I'd be in the bush. I must keep the chain attached to avoid being swept off the raft when the breakers started to roll over me. It would take two or three hours of rising tide before I'd have draft enough to float.

Sylvain was about a hundred yards ahead on my right, making motions in my direction. It looked as if he were trying to tell me something, but he couldn't have made any sound or I would have heard it. With the breakers behind us, the only noise was the cries of the birds. I was about five hundred yards from the bush and Sylvain was still a hundred yards or so ahead of me. But what was the stupid ox doing? He was standing up and leaving his raft. Had he lost his mind? If he started walking, with each step he'd sink a little deeper until he wouldn't be able to get back to his raft. I tried to whistle but couldn't. There was a little water left in the gourd; I drank it, then tried to call to him to stop. I couldn't get a sound out. Bubbles of gas were rising from the quicksand, which meant it was shallow and there was mud underneath. The poor bugger who got stuck in it was done for, for sure.

Sylvain turned toward me, making signs I didn't understand. I flung my arms about in an attempt to tell him, "No, no, don't leave your raft, you'll never reach the bush!" Since he was between me and his raft, I couldn't tell how far he was from it. At first I thought he must be fairly near, that if he started to sink he could still grab hold.

Suddenly I realized he was too far away, that he was being

sucked in and was unable to free himself. The sound of a wail reached me. I lay down flat on my sacks, dug my hands into the quicksand and pulled with all my might. The raft started to move and I crept forward perhaps twenty yards. I was now where, from a standing position, I could see that Sylvain, my pal, was at least ten yards from his raft and buried up to his waist. Terror gave me back my voice and I yelled, "Sylvain! Sylvain! Don't move! Lie flat on the quicksand! Try to free your legs!" He heard and his head bobbed up and down as if to agree. I lay down on my stomach again and clawed at the sand. Rage gave me superhuman strength, and I moved another thirty yards. All this must have taken an hour, but I was getting very close to him, perhaps fifty or sixty yards away. I had trouble seeing him, though, because my hands, arms and face were covered with mud. I tried to wipe away the salty muck that stung my left eye and prevented me from seeing; the right eye was weeping. Finally I managed to see him. He wasn't lying flat, he was standing up, and only his upper torso still showed above the quicksand.

The first breaker passed over me, leaving my raft exactly where it was, and subsided ahead, covering the quicksand with foam. It swept over Sylvain; now only his chest was above the level of the sand. I realized that the more the breakers rolled in, the softer the sand would become. I had to reach him.

With the desperate energy of a mother trying to save her baby from danger, I pulled and pulled and pulled against the sand to reach Sylvain. He looked at me without speaking, without moving, his eyes wide open and glued to mine. I wanted only not to lose those staring eyes. Not looking to see where my hands were going, I dragged forward a little, but two more breakers rolled over me, and when they had passed, the sand was so much softer it was hard to keep moving. A huge wave hit me, knocking the breath out of me and almost sweeping me off the raft. I sat up. Sylvain was up to his armpits. I was less than forty yards away now and Sylvain was still staring at me. I saw that he knew he was dying there in the muck, three hundred yards from the promised land.

I lay down again and went back to clawing at the sand, which was almost liquid now. Our eyes stayed riveted on each other. He made a sign as if to say, "No, give up, you can't make it." But I kept on until I was about thirty yards away, when another giant breaker covered me with an avalanche of water and I floated another five or six yards forward.

When the breaker had passed on, I looked up. Sylvain was gone. The quicksand was covered with a thin layer of foamy water. There was not even a hand raised in a final farewell. Suddenly I was seized with a shameful animal reaction: the instinct for survival swept all sentiment away. I said to myself, You may still be alive. But when you're in the bush alone, without a friend, your *cavale* will be in trouble.

A roller broke over my back—I was sitting now—and brought me back to reality. The wave was so powerful that it doubled me over and for several minutes I couldn't get my breath. The raft slid forward another few yards, and it was only then, when I saw the wave die beneath the trees, that I wept for my friend: We were so near. If only you hadn't gotten off! Less than three hundred yards! Why? Why did you do it? What on God's earth made you think you could walk to shore? Too much sun? The blinding reflections? Did you lose the strength to endure this hell? Why couldn't a man like you take the punishment for a few more hours?

The breakers kept on rolling in with a thunderous roar. They were bigger still and coming closer and closer together. Each time I was drenched completely, but each time I slid a few yards forward. Once the wave moved on, I was grounded, but I was determined not to budge from my raft until I had a branch or liana in my hand. Twenty yards to go. It must have been another hour before the last wave literally hurled me into the trees. I unscrewed the bolt and freed myself from the chain. But I held on to it. I might need it again.

IN THE BUSH

Quickly, before the sun went down, I crept into the bush, half swimming, half walking, for there was quicksand everywhere. The water penetrated so deeply into the bush that, as night fell, I was still far from dry land. The odor of rot assaulted my nose and the gas was so strong it stung my eyes. My legs were covered with grass and leaves. Each time I took a step, I first felt the ground under the water. I moved forward only when I met resistance.

My first night was spent on the trunk of a fallen tree. I hung my sack high on a branch and closed it tight. That sack was my life—without the coconuts it contained, I'd never survive. I strapped my machete to my right wrist. Then, exhausted, my body burned and itching, I stretched out in a crook of the tree and fell asleep without a thought in my head. Perhaps I murmured "Poor Sylvain!" a couple of times, but I can't be sure.

The sound of the birds woke me up. The sun was filtering into the bush at such an angle that it must have been seven or eight in the morning. There was water everywhere—the tide was rising. It was probably the end of the tenth tide, or roughly sixty hours since I'd left Diable. I couldn't tell how far I was from the sea. In any event, I had to wait for the water to subside before I ventured into the sun. I was out of drinking water. I ate my last three handfuls of coconut pulp and rubbed some of it over my burns and bruises. The oil in the pulp was soothing. Then I smoked two cigarettes and thought about Sylvain, this time without the earlier selfishness. After all, hadn't I planned originally to escape alone? So . . . nothing was really changed, except for the great sadness in my heart. I tried to close my eyes against the memory of his sinking—as if that could help. For him it was all over.

My sack had survived nicely in its nook and I took out a coconut. Sitting with my legs spread out, I brought it down against the tree with all my might until I finally managed to crack the shell. You can do it with a machete, but it's better just to bang it on the point. I ate a whole fresh coconut and drank the sweet liquid inside. The sea was retreating fast now; I could walk on the mud to reach the beach.

The sun was at its most radiant and I'd never seen the sea so beautiful. I looked long and hard at the spot where I figured Sylvain had disappeared. I washed in sea water and the sun soon dried both me and my clothes. After a cigarette and a last look at my friend's grave, I started into the bush. The walking was quite easy. My sack slung over my shoulder, I moved slowly through the thick vegetation until after two hours I finally reached permanently dry ground. No tidemarks at the base of the trees. I decided to camp here and rest for twenty-four hours. I would open the coconuts one by one, take out the nuts and put them in my sack, ready to eat whenever I was hungry. I could light a fire, but that probably wasn't too good an idea.

The rest of the day and the night was uneventful. When the birds woke me up with the sun, I finished extracting the coconut pulp and, with my much reduced sack on my shoulder, headed west.

Toward three in the afternoon I came upon a path. It must have been for either balata prospectors or prospectors after hardwoods, or maybe for bringing supplies to gold panners. The path was narrow but well cleared—apparently it was used often. Every so often I came across the hoofprints of a donkey or an unshod mule and sometimes the prints of human feet, the big toe clearly outlined in the dried mud. I walked until nightfall. Occasionally I'd chew some coconut, which was both nourishing and thirst-quenching, and then I'd use a mixture of oil and saliva to coat my nose, lips and cheeks. My eyes, full of pus, often stuck together. As soon as I got the chance, I'd rinse them out with fresh water. Along with the coconuts in my sack, I had a waterproof box containing a piece of Marseilles soap, a Gillette razor, twelve blades and a shaving brush.

I walked with my machete in hand although the path was so clear I didn't need it. On either side of me I noticed what seemed to be freshly cut branches. There must be a lot of activity on this path. I'd better be careful.

The bush here was different from the bush I'd known during my first *cavale* from Saint-Laurent-du-Maroni. This one had two levels and was not as thick. The first level rose to a height of fifteen to twenty feet; above that was the green vault at a height of over sixty feet. Daylight reached only the right-hand side of the path; the left was in almost total darkness.

I was walking fast now, sometimes coming to a clearing—whether made by man or by lightning, I couldn't tell. The slant of the sun's rays indicated that it was near dusk. I turned my back to the sun and headed east toward the blacks' village of Kourou, where the penitentiary of the same name was located.

Night was about to fall, so I went into the bush to find a place to lie down. I found one not thirty yards off the path, well protected by a thick cover of shiny leaves like those of a banana tree. I cut some down and made a kind of bed. This time I would be really dry—there was a good chance it wouldn't rain. I smoked two cigarettes.

I was less tired tonight and the coconut pulp had eased my hunger. If only my mouth weren't so dry! I had almost no saliva.

The second stage of my *cavale* was under way and I was starting my third night on Grande Terre without unpleasant incident. If only Sylvain were here! Well, *mec*, he isn't, and there's not much you can do about it. Since when have you ever needed advice or support, anyway? What are you, a general or a private? Don't be a fool, Papillon. It's fine to grieve for your friend, but you're no worse off in the bush for being alone. It's five days since you left the islands. They must have alerted Kourou by now—first the guards in the forest camp, then the blacks in the village. There may be a police station there as well. Is it wise to be heading for this village?

I knew nothing about the surrounding country, only that the camp was wedged in between the village and the river.

On Diable I had planned to hold up the first man I came across and force him to lead me to the edge of Camp Inini, the Chinese camp where I was going to look up Cuic-Cuic, Chang's brother. Why change the plan now? If Diable was convinced I had drowned, there'd be no trouble. But if they suspected a *cavale*, Kourou would be dangerous. Since it was a forest camp, there'd be a lot of Arabs and therefore plenty of people available for a man-hunt. Watch out for them, Papillon! No mistakes now. Don't be caught in a vise. Make sure you see them before they see you. So I came to the conclusion that I'd better not walk on the path but stay parallel to it in the bush. It was damn stupid to go galloping down that trail armed only with a machete; worse than stupid, insane. From now on I'd keep to the bush.

I woke up early to the cries of the beasts and birds greeting the morning, and shook myself to the sounds of the waking bush: another day was starting for me too. I carefully chewed a handful of coconut, spread some on my face and started out.

I kept very close to the path but well hidden in the bush. It was difficult walking because, even though the liana and branches were not very thick, they still had to be separated to make a passage. For all these difficulties, however, I had done well to leave the path, for I suddenly heard someone whistling. I peered out; fifty yards of path stretched before me. Nobody. Ah yes, there he was! A Negro black as coal carrying a pack on his shoulder and a gun in his right hand. He was wearing a khaki shirt and shorts and was barefoot. He didn't take his eyes off the path and his back was bent under the weight of his heavy burden.

I hid behind a thick tree by the edge of the path and waited for him, my knife open in my hand. As he passed by the tree, I leapt on him. My right hand grabbed his rifle in midair and I twisted his arm until he dropped it. "Don't kill me! For the love of God, have pity on me!" Holding the point of my knife against his neck, I bent down and picked up the gun—an ancient single-barreled shotgun undoubtedly loaded to the muzzle with powder and lead.

I raised the hammer of the gun, stepped back a couple of yards and ordered, "Drop your pack. You try to run away, I'll kill you like a dog."

Terrified, the poor black did as he was told. Then he looked at me. "You escaped from the *bagne*?"

"Yes."

"What you want? You can have everything I got. But, please, don't kill me. I got five kids. Let me live."

"Oh, stop that crap. What's your name?"

"Jean."

"Where you going?"

"I'm carrying food and medicine to my two brothers. They're cutting wood in the bush."

"Where did you come from?"

"Kourou."

"You live in the village?"

"I was born there."

"Do you know Inini?"

"Yes. I sometimes do business with the Chinese in the prison camp."

"See this?"

"What is it?"

"It's a five-hundred-franc note. You've got two choices. If you do what I tell you, the five hundred francs is yours and you get your gun back. If you don't, or if you rat on me, I'll kill you. Which do you choose?"

"What you want me to do? I'll do anything you ask, even for free."

"I want you to take me to the edge of Camp Inini. When I make contact with a certain Chinese, you can go on your way. O.K.?"

"O.K."

"But rat on me and you're a dead man."

"I won't. I swear I won't."

He had some condensed milk with him. He took out six cans and gave them to me, along with a two-pound loaf of bread and some smoked ham.

"Hide your pack in the bush—you can pick it up later. I'll make a mark on this tree with my machete so you'll know where it is."

I drank a can of milk. He also gave me a brand-new pair of blue work pants. I put them on, never letting go of the rifle.

"O.K., Jean, let's go. Be careful no one sees us. If we're caught it'll be your fault and your tough luck."

Jean walked better in the bush than I did; he was so nimble at ducking liana and branches that I had trouble following him. In fact, the bugger walked with the greatest ease.

He said, "Did you know Kourou has been warned that two *bagnards* escaped from the islands? I must be honest with you: it's very dangerous around Kourou and we have to go near there."

"You seem like an honest man, Jean. I hope you're being square with me. What's your advice as to how we get to Inini? Remember, your life depends on my safety. If I'm caught, I'll have to kill you."

"What do I call you?"

"Papillon."

"O.K., Monsieur Papillon. We must go deep into the bush and make a big detour around Kourou. I can guarantee I'll get you to Inini if we go through the bush."

"I'm in your hands. Pick the path you think safest."

It was slower going in the bush, but since we'd left the vicinity of the path, the black had seemed more relaxed. He wasn't sweating so much and his face was less tense. It was as if he'd taken a tranquilizer.

"Jean, you don't seem so scared any more."

"I'm not, Monsieur Papillon. Being so near the path was very dangerous for you—and for me too."

We made good headway. The black was smart; he never let us get more than twelve feet apart.

"Wait a minute. I want to roll a cigarette."

"Look, I've got a pack of Gauloises."

"Thanks, Jean. You're a good man."

"It's true. I am a good man. You see, I'm a Catholic. It hurts me to see how the white guards treat the *bagnards*."

"You've seen a lot of them? Where?"

"At the forest camp in Kourou. It breaks your heart to see them dying a slow death from cutting that wood, or from yellow fever or dysentery. You're much better off on the islands. You're the first really healthy convict I've ever seen."

"It's true. It is better on the islands."

We sat down for a bit on a big branch. I offered him one of his cans of milk, but he refused it, preferring to chew on a coconut.

"How old is your wife?"

"She's thirty-two. I'm forty. We've got five children—three girls and two boys."

"Do you make a good living?"

"We don't do so badly with the rosewood, and my wife does washing and ironing for the guards' wives. That helps a little. We're very poor, but we always have enough to eat and the children all go to school. And they all have shoes to wear."

The poor devil! He thought everything was O.K. because his children had shoes. He was almost as tall as I and his black face was not unsympathetic. To the contrary, his eyes said clearly that here was a man who was full of the right sentiments, a strong worker, good family man, good husband, good Christian.

"What about you, Papillon?"

"Jean, I'm going to start a new life. I've been buried alive for ten years and I keep on trying to escape so that someday I can be like you, a free man with a wife and kids, without harming anyone, even in my thoughts. You said it yourself: the *bagne* is rotten, and any man with a shred of self-respect has to try to escape."

"I'll do my best to help you. Let's get going."

With never a second's hesitation and with an extraordinary sense of direction, Jean guided me straight to the Chinese camp. We arrived about two hours after dusk. We could hear some banging in the distance but saw no lights. Jean explained that to get near the camp we would have to skirt a couple of sentry posts. We decided to stop and spend the night where we were.

I was dead tired but afraid to fall asleep. What if I were wrong about the black? What if he were putting on an act and took the gun while I was sleeping and killed me? It would be a double victory for him—he'd be shed of the danger I represented, and he'd win a bonus for killing an escaped con.

Yes, he was smart all right. Without a word he lay right down and went to sleep. I still had the chain with the bolt. I thought of binding him with it, but there was no point in that; he could undo it as easily as I could. So I would have to try to stay awake. I had Jean's pack of Gauloises. I'd do everything I could think of not to fall asleep. I couldn't trust Jean; after all, being an honest man, he must classify me as a criminal.

The night was very dark. Jean was lying only six feet away, but all I could see of him was the white of his bare soles. I listened to the night sounds of the bush and the constant chattering of the large-goitered monkeys with their powerful, raucous cry that you could hear miles away. This was very important, for as long as the cries were regular, the troop was eating and sleeping in peace. Therefore, we too were safe from man and beast.

Stretched out rigid, I held my own against the temptation to sleep without too much effort, aided by an occasional cigarette burn, but even more by a swarm of mosquitoes determined to drain me of my last ounce of blood. I could protect myself with a lotion of saliva mixed with nicotine, but without them buzzing around me I was sure to fall asleep. All I hoped was they weren't carrying malaria or yellow fever.

I passed the time in reflection. Here I was, provisionally at least, off the road of the condemned. When I started down that path, it was 1931 and I was twenty-five. It was now 1941. Ten years had passed. In 1932 that fiendish prosecutor, Pradel, had thrown me, a young man at the height of his powers, into the sink-hole that was the French penal system, there slowly to dissolve in the slime until I had disappeared altogether. I had brought off the first part of the *cavale*. I had climbed out of the hole and was clinging to the edge. Now I must commit all my energy and intelligence to success in the second part.

The night was long, but it was drawing to a close. I had stayed awake and was pleased with myself for successfully guarding my liberty against the threat of fatigue. It was a victory of spirit over matter and I was full of self-congratulations when I heard the first cries of the birds announce the coming of morning. Their awakening was soon followed by another: the black stretched, sat up and rubbed his feet.

"Good morning. You didn't sleep?"

"No."

"That was foolish. You got no reason to be afraid of me. I decided straight off I wanted to help you."

"Thanks, Jean. How long do we have to wait for daylight to reach us here?"

"Another hour at the very least. Only the animals know when daylight's coming. We'll be able to see about an hour from now. Lend me your knife, Papillon?"

I gave it to him without hesitation.

He cut a branch off a thick plant, handed me a piece and kept another for himself. "Drink the liquid inside, then spread some on your face."

I drank, then washed. Jean gave me back my knife. Day came. We each smoked a cigarette and set off. We arrived on the outskirts of Inini about midday, after an uneventful morning except for the huge mud puddles we had to wade through.

We ventured near the main access road to the camp. A narrow-gauge railway track ran along the side of a wide, cleared space. Jean told me it was used for wagons pulled by the Chinese and that they made such a racket you could hear them from far away. We watched one go by. Two guards sat on a bench, and behind them two Chinese braked the wagon with long poles. The wheels threw off sparks. Jean explained that the poles had steel points and that they were used for both pushing and braking.

It was a well-used path. Chinese passed by carrying rolls of liana on their shoulders; one carried a wild pig, others bundles of palm leaves. Everybody was heading toward the camp. Jean described the variety of things the men did in the bush: hunting wild game, cutting liana for cabinetwork, cutting palm leaves to weave into matting to protect the vegetable gardens from the heat of the sun. Some hunted butterflies, others flies or snakes, etc. They were allowed to go into the bush after they had finished the work assigned them by the Administration. Everybody had to be back at camp by five in the evening.

"Jean, here's the five hundred francs and your gun." I had unloaded it earlier. "I've got my knife and machete. You can go now. Thanks for everything. I hope God repays you better than I can for helping a man back to life, that when you tell your kids about this, you'll say, 'That *bagnard* was a good man. I'm not sorry I helped him.' "

"Monsieur Papillon, it's late. I can't get very far before night. You keep the shotgun, and I'll stay with you till morning. If you like, I'll stop one of the Chinese and tell him to pass the word to Cuic-Cuic. He'd be less afraid of me than a white man on *cavale*. Let me go out on the road. Even if a guard comes along, he won't think anything of me being there. I'll tell him I'm looking for rosewood for the Symphorien lumberyard in Cayenne. Trust me."

"O.K., but take your gun. They'd think it pretty funny for a man to go into the bush unarmed."

"You're right."

Jean planted himself in the middle of the road. I was to give a low whistle when I saw a Chinese I liked the looks of.

"Hello, Mouché," said a little old Chinese carrying a banana trunk on his shoulder—probably for its delicious palmetto. I whistled, for this polite old man looked okay to me.

"Hello, Chink. Stop a minute. I want to ask you something."

"What you want, Mouché?"

They talked for almost five minutes. I couldn't hear a thing. Two Chinese went by carrying a big doe on a pole. It hung by its feet and its head scraped along in the dirt. They didn't speak to the black, but said a few words to the Chinese, who answered briefly, all of it in Chinese.

Jean led the old man to where I was in the bush. As he came up to me, he held out his hand.

"You *froufrou* [escaped]?"

"Yes."

"From where?"

"Diable."

"Good." He laughed and looked at me hard through his slanted eyes. "That good. Your name?"

"Papillon."

"Never heard of you."

"I'm a friend of Chang, Chang Vauquien, Cuic-Cuic's brother."

"Ah! Good." He shook my hand again. "What you want?"

"I want you to tell Cuic-Cuic I want to see him here."

"Not possible."

"Why?"

"Cuic-Cuic stole sixty ducks from chief of camp. Chief wanted to kill Cuic-Cuic. Cuic-Cuic *froufrou*."

"Since when?"

"Two months."

"Did he go out to sea?"

"Don't know. I go to camp talk to Chinese very good friend of Cuic-Cuic. He tell me. You don't move. I come back tonight."

"What time?"

"Don't know. But I bring food, cigarettes. No make fire here. I whistle 'La Madelon.' When you hear, you come out on road. Understand?"

"Understand." And he went. "Jean, what do you think?"

"You haven't lost a thing. If you want, we can still go back to Kourou. I'll get you a dugout there, food and a sail."

"Jean, I'm going very far away. I can't do it alone. But thanks for your offer. If worse comes to worst, I may have to take you up on it."

We ate a big piece of the palmetto the Chinese had given us. It was wonderfully cool, with a definite nutty flavor. Jean said he'd take the watch. I trusted him. I spread tobacco juice over my face and hands, for the onslaught had already begun.

Jean woke me up. "Papillon, someone's whistling 'La Madelon.' "

"What time is it?"

"Not very late. Nine o'clock maybe."

We went out onto the road. The night was still very dark. Whoever was whistling was coming nearer. I answered back. He was still nearer now, though I couldn't see him yet. Taking turns whistling, we finally met. There were three of them. Each in turn touched my hand.

"Let's sit here by the side of the road," one of them said in perfect French. "Nobody can see us here in the shadows." Jean came and joined us.

"Eat first, then we'll talk." This was from the educated member of the group. Jean and I lapped up a piping-hot vegetable soup. It warmed us so well we decided to leave the rest of the food for later. We drank a delicious hot, sweet tea with a mint flavor.

"You're a friend of Chang?"

"Yes. He told me to come here and find Cuic-Cuic so we could escape together. I've already done one long *cavale*, all the way to Colombia. I'm a good sailor. That's why Chang wanted me to take his brother along. He trusts me."

"Maybe. Describe Chang's tattoos."

"He's got a dragon on his chest and three dots on his left hand. He told me the dots meant he had been one of the leaders of the revolt at Poulo Condor in Indochina. His best friend is another leader of the revolt, named Van Hue. He's got only one arm."

"That's me," the educated one said. "You've proved you're Chang's friend, therefore you're our friend. Now listen carefully. Cuic-Cuic hasn't gone out to sea yet because he doesn't know how to sail a boat. He's alone in the bush, about seven miles from here. He makes charcoal. Friends sell it for him and give him the money. When he's earned enough, he's going to buy a boat and find somebody to escape with him. Where he is now, he's safe. Nobody can get to his island because it's surrounded by moving quicksand. Anyone who tries to cross is sucked down into the muck. I'll come for you at sunrise and take you to him. You come with us now."

We followed the edge of the road, for the moon was up and it was bright enough to see fifty yards ahead. We came to a wooden bridge and Van Hue said, "Go down under the bridge. Sleep there, and I'll come for you in the morning."

We shook hands and parted. They walked out into the road. If they were caught, they were going to say they had gone to check some traps they'd set in the bush.

Jean said, "Papillon, don't you sleep there. You sleep in the bush, I sleep there. When they come, I'll call you."

"Fine." I went into the bush, smoked a few cigarettes, and fell asleep happy and my stomach warm from the good soup.

Van Hue turned up before daybreak. To gain time, we would walk on the road until the sun rose. We walked fast for forty minutes. Suddenly it was daylight and we could hear in the distance the sound of a wagon coming along the tracks. We hid in the bush.

"Good-by, Jean. Thanks and good luck. God bless you and your family." I insisted he take the five hundred francs. In parting, he explained how, if the Cuic-Cuic business didn't work out, I could locate his village, make a detour around it and find myself on the path where I'd first met him. He used it twice a week, so we'd be bound to meet. I shook hands with my black friend and he hurried off down the road.

Van Hue said, "Let's go." We pushed into the bush. He picked out the direction immediately and we moved with good speed. The bush was not very thick; he was able to separate the branches and liana without having to cut them with his machete.

CUIC-CUIC

In less than three hours we found ourselves facing a mud pond. There were water lilies in bloom and large green leaves stuck to the mud. We followed along the edge of the bank.

"Be careful you don't slip. You'll never be able to climb out," Van Hue warned me, having just seen me stumble.

"You go ahead. I'll follow you and be more careful."

A tiny island sat in the sea of mud about a hundred and fifty yards from shore. Smoke was rising from the middle of it. It must be the charcoal pits. I spotted a crocodile in the quicksand—submerged except for its eyes. What on earth could it find to eat in that goo?

We had walked about three-quarters of a mile around the edge of the pond when Van Hue stopped and started to sing at the top of his lungs in Chinese. A man came to the edge of the island. He was small and wearing only shorts. The two Chinese talked at great length, and I was beginning to get impatient when Van Hue said, "Come this way."

I followed him and we retraced our steps.

"It's all right. That was a friend of Cuic-Cuic. Cuic-Cuic's gone hunting, but he should be back soon. We'll wait for him here."

We sat down. Cuic-Cuic arrived in less than an hour. He was a dried-up little guy with the yellow skin of an Annamite, shiny, almost black teeth and frank, knowing eyes.

"You a friend of my brother Chang?"

"Yes."

"Good. You can go, Van Hue."

"Thanks," Van Hue said.

"Here, take this hen partridge."

"Thank you, no." He shook my hand and left.

Cuic-Cuic drew me to where a pig was waiting. We both followed the pig, literally in his footsteps.

"Very careful, Papillon. One false step and you're sucked in. In case of accident, we can't help each other for then we both die. The path is never the same because the quicksand moves. But the pig always finds a way. Once I had to wait two whole days before we could cross."

The black pig sniffed around and was soon off across the quicksand. Cuic-Cuic talked to it in Chinese. I was mystified by this small animal that obeyed him like a dog. My eyes bugged out as the pig crossed to the other side without ever sinking more than an inch or two.

Cuic-Cuic set off after him, saying, "Place your feet in my steps. We have to be quick because the pig's traces disappear almost immediately." We crossed without difficulty. The quicksand never reached above my ankles, and then only at the very end.

The pig made two big detours which made the walk two hundred yards. I was pouring sweat. I wasn't just scared; I was terrified.

During the first part of the crossing I wondered if it was going to be my fate to die like Sylvain. I saw the poor bastard again at that last moment, but although the body was his, his face seemed to have my features. That walk was purgatory. I won't forget it soon.

"Give me your hand." And the little guy, all skin and bones, helped me up the bank.

"Well, my friend, I don't think any manhunt's going to use that path."

"No, we don't have to worry about that."

We walked toward the middle of the little island. The smell of carbon gas grabbed me by the throat. I coughed. It was the smoke from two burning charcoal pits. No problem with mosquitoes here. A little woodman's hut made of leaves stood protected from the wind and veiled in smoke. Standing in front of the door was the little Indochinese we had seen before we met Cuic-Cuic.

"Hi, Mouché."

"Talk French to him. He's a friend of my brother."

The tiny Chinese looked me over from head to foot. Satisfied with what he saw, he held out his hand and gave me a toothless smile.

"Come in. Sit down."

The hut was clean and entirely kitchen. Something was cooking on the fire in a great big pot. There was a single bed made of branches standing over three feet above the ground.

"Help me make something for him to sleep on tonight."

"All right, Cuic-Cuic."

In less than a half hour my bed was made. The two men set the table and we had a marvelous soup, then some meat and onions with white rice.

Cuic-Cuic's friend was the one who sold his charcoal. He didn't live on the island, so by the time night fell, Cuic-Cuic and I were alone.

"It's true I stole the camp chief's ducks. That's why I'm on *cavale*."

We were sitting opposite each other, and from time to time the flames from the little fire lit up our faces. We were feeling each other out, each trying to get to know and understand the other.

Cuic-Cuic's face was barely yellow at all and most of that was sunburn. His brilliant black, slanted eyes looked right through me as we talked. He smoked long cigars he made himself from leaves of black tobacco.

I smoked cigarettes I rolled with the rice paper he provided.

"I left on *cavale* because the chief who owned the ducks wanted to kill me. That was three months ago. What's too bad is that I gambled away all the money I made selling the ducks, plus what I've earned from the charcoal."

"Where do you play?"

"In the bush. There's a game every night with the Chinese from Inini and the liberated prisoners from Cascade."

"You've decided you want to go by sea?"

"It's all I think about. When I sell my next lot of charcoal, I'm going to buy a boat and find a *mec* who knows how to sail it and wants to go with me. I'll have enough charcoal to sell in three weeks. Maybe you and I could buy the boat and leave together, since you say you know how to sail."

"I have money, Cuic-Cuic. We don't need to wait for you to sell the charcoal."

"That's fine. There's a good launch for sale for fifteen hundred francs. The man who wants to sell it is a black who cuts wood here."

"Good. Have you seen it?"

"Yes."

"Can I get a look at it?"

"I'll go see Chocolat—that's what I call him—tomorrow. Tell me about your *cavale*, Papillon. I thought no one could escape from Diable. Why didn't my brother Chang leave with you?"

I described the *cavale*, the wave Lisette and Sylvain's death.

"I can see why Chang didn't want to go with you. You took a big chance. You were damn lucky to get here alive. I'm glad you made it."

We talked a little longer, but since Cuic-Cuic wanted to see Chocolat at daybreak, we went to sleep early, leaving a big branch on the fire to keep it going through the night. The smoke made me cough and choke, but there was one advantage: not a single mosquito.

Stretched out on my pallet under the warm blanket, I closed my eyes. But I couldn't sleep. I was too excited. The *cavale* was working! If the boat was any good, we'd be off to sea in eight days. Cuic-Cuic was a dried-up little guy, but he was obviously strong and tough. He seemed loyal and direct with his friends, although he was probably cruel toward his enemies. Asiatic faces are hard to read: they tell you nothing. But his eyes spoke well for him.

I finally fell asleep and dreamed of a sundrenched sea, my boat joyfully taking the waves toward freedom.

"You want coffee or tea?"

"What do you drink?"

"Tea."

"Then I'll have tea."

The day had barely begun; the fire was still going, and water was boiling in the pot. Somewhere a rooster crowed. No birds here. The smoke must drive them away. The black pig lay on Cuic-Cuic's bed. He was still asleep, the lazy beast. Cakes made of rice flour were browning over the coals. My new pal gave me some sweetened tea, then cut a rice cake in half, spread it with margarine and handed it to me. We ate well. I got away with three rice cakes.

"I'm off now. You come with me as far as the pond. If you hear anyone call or whistle, don't answer. You're in no danger; nobody can get here. But if you show yourself on the edge of the island, you can be shot."

The pig responded to its master's orders and got up. He had something to eat and drink, then we all went outside. The pig made straight for the quicksand. He went down the bank a good distance from where we'd been yesterday, went in about ten yards, then turned around and came back. He didn't care for that spot. It took him three more tries before he found one he liked. Cuic-Cuic followed immediately.

Cuic-Cuic wouldn't be back until evening. I ate the soup he had left on the fire, then collected eight eggs in the henhouse and, using three, made an omelet with some of the margarine. The wind had changed direction and the smoke from the two pits was blowing away. In the afternoon it rained and, well protected, I lay down on my bed of branches.

During the morning I had made a tour of the island. There was quite a large clearing almost in the center. From the felled trees and the sawed wood, I gathered this was where Cuic-Cuic got the wood for his charcoal. There was also a big hole in the white clay, which must be what he used to cover the wood so it burned without making a flame. The chickens pecked around in the clearing. A big rat scurried under my feet and, a few yards farther on, I came across a dead snake at least six feet long. It must have just been killed by the rat.

My day alone on the little island produced a series of discoveries. I found a family of anteaters—a mother and three babies. They had reduced an ant hill to a state of panic. A dozen tiny monkeys jumped from tree to tree in the clearing. At the sight of me a group of marmosets screamed loud enough to wake the dead.

Cuic-Cuic returned. "I couldn't find Chocolat or the boat. He must have gone to Cascade for supplies. That's where his house is. Did you eat well?"

"Yes."

"Still hungry?"

"No."

"I brought you two packages of cheap soldiers' tobacco. It was all there was."

"Thanks. They're all the same to me. When Chocolat goes, how long does he stay in the village?"

"Two or three days. But I'll check tomorrow and every day after that. I have no idea when he left."

It poured rain the next day, but that didn't discourage Cuic-Cuic. He left stark naked, his clothes wrapped in oilcloth under his arm. I didn't go with him. "No use your getting wet," he said.

Finally the rain stopped. The sun came out, and I figured from its position it must be between ten and eleven. One of the two charcoal pits had caved in under the weight of the rain. I went over to examine the disaster. The fire wasn't completely out: smoke still rose from the damp heap. Suddenly I rubbed my eyes at the unexpected sight before me: five shoes were sticking out of the pit. Each shoe was connected to a leg. Conclusion: there were three men slowly cooking in the charcoal pit. Do I need to describe my first reaction? A shiver ran down my spine. Bending over, I pushed a bit of the charcoal aside and discovered the sixth foot.

Cuic-Cuic was a thorough *mec*, all right. He had bumped them off, then laid them in a row and turned them to ashes. I was so shaken that I backed away and headed for the clearing and some sun. I needed warmth. Even in the suffocating heat, I was suddenly shivering and desperate for the good sun of the tropics.

You may think that sweat would have been more natural after such a discovery, but an hour passed before the beads of perspiration started to roll down my forehead. The more I thought about it, the more I realized it was a miracle I was still alive. After all, I had told him I had a good deal of money in my *plan*. Was he waiting to stuff me into a third pit?

I remembered how Chang had told me that Cuic-Cuic had been condemned for piracy and murder aboard a junk. When his group pillaged a boat, they killed everybody, for "political" reasons, they said. So these *mecs* had been killed, one after the other. And I was a prisoner here. A difficult position to be in.

To be blunt about it, I could kill Cuic-Cuic and give him his turn in the pit and no one would ever know. But the pig wouldn't obey me; that hunk of tame pork didn't even speak French. So I'd have no way of getting off the island. The Chinese might obey me if I pulled a gun on him, but once he got me off the island, I'd have to kill him. I could throw him into the quicksand and he'd disappear. But why hadn't he done that to the *mecs* in the pit? After all, the quicksand would have been much simpler. I didn't give a damn for the guards, but if his Chinese friends found out, there'd be a manhunt, and with their knowledge of the bush it would be no picnic to have them on my heels.

Cuic-Cuic had only a single-barreled shotgun that had to be loaded from the muzzle. He kept it with him all the time, even when he was cooking. He slept with it and even carried it with him when he went outdoors to do his business. I must keep my knife open all the time, but I had to get some sleep somehow. Christ! Some partner I'd chosen for my *cavale*!

I couldn't eat the whole day. I still hadn't made up my mind what to do when I heard singing. It was Cuic-Cuic on his way home. I watched him from behind a tree. He was balancing a bundle on top of his head, and I showed myself only when he'd almost reached the bank. Smiling, he handed me the package wrapped in a flour bag, clambered up the bank to my side and headed for the hut. I followed.

"Good news, Papillon. Chocolat is back. He still has the boat. He says it can carry over a thousand pounds without sinking. What you have there are the flour bags for making the sail and jib. That's the first installment. We'll bring the rest tomorrow, when you go to see if you approve of the boat."

Cuic-Cuic told me all this without looking back. We were walking single file—the pig first, then him, then me. It crossed my mind that he wasn't ready to stuff me into the pit if he was suggesting I look at the boat and he was already starting to collect supplies for the *cavale*. He'd even bought the flour sacks . . .

"Look at that, will you! The pit's collapsed. It must have been the rain. With that downpour I'm not surprised."

He didn't go over to the pit but went straight into the hut. I couldn't think what to say or do. To pretend I hadn't noticed anything would be ridiculous. It would be damned funny if I'd spent the whole day on the island and hadn't once gone to look at the pit. It wasn't more than twenty-five yards from the hut.

"You let the fire go out?"

"I'm afraid I wasn't paying attention."

"You didn't eat anything?"

"No, I wasn't hungry."

"You feel sick?"

"No."

"Then why didn't you have any of the soup?"

"Cuic-Cuic, sit down. I want to talk to you."

"Let me light the fire first."

"No. I want to talk to you right away, while there's still light."

"What's the matter?"

"Well, it's the charcoal pit. When it caved in, it uncovered three men you were cooking in it. I want an explanation."

"So that's why you've been acting so strange!" He looked me straight in the eye without a hint of embarrassment. "It upset you?

I understand. It's only natural. I suppose I'm lucky you didn't knife me in the back. Papillon, those three guys were part of a manhunt. About ten days ago I sold a load of charcoal to Chocolat. The Chinese you saw the first day helped me get the bags off the island. It's a complicated business: you take a rope over two hundred yards long and pull the row of bags over the quicksand. Well, between here and the small stream where Chocolat keeps his boat we'd left a number of footprints. Also some of the bags were torn and dropped pieces of charcoal along the way. That's when the first man hunter started sniffing around. I could tell someone was in the bush from the cries of the animals. I saw him without him seeing me. I crossed on the side opposite, made a big semicircle and came up behind him. It was all very easy. He was dead without ever seeing who'd done it. I had noticed before that corpses rise to the surface of the quicksand after a few days, so I carried him and put him in the pit."

"What about the others?"

"That happened three days before you came. It was a very dark and quiet night, which is very unusual in the bush. Those two had been on the edge of the pond since nightfall. The wind blew the smoke their way and one of them broke into a fit of coughing. That's how I knew they were there. Before daybreak I crossed the quicksand on the side opposite from where I'd heard the cough. I cut the first man's throat. He didn't have time to make a sound. The other one was armed with a hunting rifle, but he was so busy watching my island he didn't hear a thing. I got him with a single shot but it didn't kill him so I had to finish him off with my knife. Papillon, those are the three *mecs* you saw in the pit. Two of them were Arabs and the other a Frenchman. It was no cinch carrying them across the quicksand, I can tell you. I had to make two trips."

"And that's really what happened?"

"Papillon, I swear it."

"Why didn't you dump them in the quicksand?"

"I told you, the quicksand gives up its dead. Sometimes a big doe falls in, and a week later she's floating on the surface. It makes a terrible stink until the carrion-eaters have done their work. But that takes a long time and the noise and swooping of the birds attracts attention. Papillon, I swear you have nothing to fear from me. Look, will it make you feel better if I give you my shotgun?"

I had a powerful urge to say yes, but I controlled it and said in as natural a voice as possible, "No, Cuic-Cuic. I'm here because I feel you're my friend. But you have to start the fire up and finish cooking the *mecs* tomorrow. Who knows who might come by after we're gone? I don't want to be accused of three murders, even after I've gone."

"Yes, I'll do it tomorrow. But don't worry, nobody'll ever set foot on this island. They just can't make it over the quicksand."

"What about a rubber raft?"

"I never thought of that."

"If they happened to send some police to have a look around the island, they could do it easily with a raft. That's why we have to get moving as fast as possible."

"Right. We'll start the pit up tomorrow. It won't be hard because it's not really out. All it needs is two ventilation holes."

"Good night, Cuic-Chic."

"Good night, Papillon. Sleep well, you can trust me. I mean it."

I pulled the blanket up to my chin, taking comfort from its warmth. I lit a cigarette. In ten minutes Cuic-Cuic was snoring, his pig breathing heavily beside him. The fire had died down, but the wood glowed when the breeze blew through the hut; it gave me a feeling of peace and calm. I savored the moment and fell asleep. But one thought preyed at the back of my mind: either I would wake up tomorrow and all would be well between the Chinese and me, or he was one hell of an actor. In the latter case I would never see the sun again, for I had too much on him and it would make him uneasy.

The specialist in wholesale murder woke me up, handed me a mug of coffee as if nothing had happened, and wished me good morning with a big, cordial smile. The sun was already up.

"Come, have some coffee and a rice cake. The margarine's already on it."

I had my breakfast, then washed outside with water from a barrel that was always full.

"Give me a hand, Papillon?"

"Sure," I said, not asking what for.

We pulled the half-cooked corpses by the feet. I didn't mention it, but I noticed that all three had been disemboweled. The kindly Chinese must have been rummaging around to see if they had any *plans*. Had they really been hunting Cuic-Cuic? Couldn't they just as easily have been hunting butterflies or deer? Did he kill them out of self-defense or to rob them? Enough of that. They were back in the pit, well covered by layers of wood and clay. Cuic-Cuic made two ventilation holes and the pit was once again doing double duty—making charcoal and reducing three corpses to cinders.

"Let's go, Papillon."

The pig found us a passage in no time. We crossed the quicksand in tight single file. With the first step the awful dread came back to me. Was Sylvain's fate going to be mine? Dripping cold sweat, I plunged in after Cuic-Cuic, following his exact footprints. One thing, anyway—if he got through, I would too.

After a two-hour march we arrived where Chocolat was cutting wood.

"Hello, Mouché."

"Hello, Cuic-Cuic."

"How are things?"

"O.K."

"Show my friend the boat."

It was a very strong boat, a kind of launch for carrying freight. Heavy but sturdy. I dug my knife in everywhere. It never went in deeper than a quarter of an inch. The bottom was sound too. Clearly the boat was made of first-class wood.

"How much will you sell it for?"

"Twenty-five hundred francs."

"I'll give you two thousand."

Sold.

"It needs a keel. I'll pay you another five hundred if you'll add a keel, rudder and mast. The keel must be of hardwood, also the rudder. I want the mast to be ten feet high of a light, flexible wood. When can you have it ready?"

"In eight days."

"Here are two thousand-franc bills and a five-hundred. I'm going to cut them in two and give you the other half when you deliver the boat. You keep the three halves at your house. O.K.?"

"O.K."

"I'll need some permanganate, a barrel of water, cigarettes and matches, and enough food to last four men a month—flour, oil, coffee and sugar. I'll pay for the supplies separately. I want the whole business delivered on the Kourou River."

"Mouché, I can't go with you to the mouth of the river."

"I didn't ask you to. I only said to deliver the boat to the river. We don't want it in this creek."

"Here, take these flour bags with the rope, needles and thread."

We got back to our hideout well before nightfall, but the pig was so tired Cuic-Cuic had to carry him on his shoulders.

I was alone again the next day, sewing the sail, when I suddenly heard voices. I walked toward the quicksand and, well hidden, I watched what was going on on the other side. There were Cuic-Cuic and Van Hue arguing fiercely, throwing their arms about. I gathered that Van Hue wanted to come to the island and Cuic-Cuic didn't want him to. They both had their machetes out. Van Hue was the more excited. Just so long as he didn't kill Cuic-Cuic! I decided to show myself. I gave a whistle and they turned toward me.

"What's going on, Cuic-Cuic?"

Van Hue called out, "I want to talk to you, Papillon, and Cuic-Cuic won't let me."

After another ten minutes of discussion in Chinese they arrived in the wake of the pig. We sat down in the hut, mugs of tea in our hands, and I waited for them to start talking.

"Here's the problem," Cuic-Cuic said. "He wants to go on our *cavale*. I explained that it was not my affair, that you were paying for it and in full charge, but he wouldn't believe it."

"Papillon," the other man said, "he's just got to take me with him."

"Why?"

"He cut off my arm two years ago in a gambling fight and then he made me swear I wouldn't kill him. I agreed on one condition: he would have to feed me the rest of his life, or as long as I demanded it. If he goes off now, I'll never see him again. So either he lets you go alone or he takes me with him."

"That's a weird one! Look, you can come along. The boat's big enough and very strong—we could take even more people. It's okay with me if it's okay with Cuic-Cuic."

"Thanks," Van Hue said.

"What do you say, Cuic-Cuic?"

"O.K., if that's the way you want it."

"One very important thing. Can you leave the camp without being reported missing and reach the river before night?"

"No trouble at all. I can leave any time after three in the afternoon and get to the river in less than two hours."

"Can you find the place at night, Cuic-Cuic, so we can get your pal on board without losing too much time?"

"Sure, that's no problem."

"Be here a week from now and we'll tell you when we're leaving."

Van Hue shook my hand warmly and left in a state of bliss. I watched them say good-by to each other on the opposite bank. They touched hands before separating. So all was well.

When Cuic-Cuic was back in the hut, I said, "That's an unusual arrangement you made with your pal—agreeing to feed him the rest of his life. Why did you cut off his arm?"

"It was a fight over the deal."

"Wouldn't you have done better to kill him?"

"No. He's a very close friend. When I was called before the tribunal, he defended me all the way. He said he attacked me first and I'd acted in self-defense. I agreed to the pact of my own free will and I intend to stick to it. I didn't dare tell you about it because you were paying for the whole *cavale*."

"Let's not discuss it any more. If God wills you to be free again someday, you can do what you think best then."

"I intend to stick by my word."

"What do you plan to do when you're free?"

"I want to have a restaurant. I'm a good cook and Van Hue specializes in chow mein."

Chocolat was as good as his word. Five days later all was ready. We went to look at the boat in a pouring rain. Everything was shipshape. The mast, rudder and keel were installed and of first-class material. The boat was tied up in a bend of the river with the barrel of water and all the supplies. All that remained was to get word to Van Hue. Chocolat took it on himself to go to the camp and alert him. To avoid the danger of having to pick him up from the riverbank, he would bring him directly to our hiding place.

The mouth of the Kourou was marked by two beacons. If it rained, we could safely drift down the middle of the river without running the risk of hoisting sail. Chocolat gave us some black paint and a brush. We were to paint a big K and the number 21 on the sail. This designation belonged to a fishing boat that sometimes went out at night. If anyone happened to see us raising our sail as we hit the sea, they'd think we were the fishing boat.

Departure was scheduled for seven o'clock—one hour after nightfall. Cuic-Cuic assured me that he'd be able to find the path to the hiding place. We'd leave the island at five in order to have one hour of daylight for the march.

We returned to our hut in high spirits. Cuic-Cuic walked in front of me, carrying the pig on his shoulders. He never stopped talking.

"I'm leaving the *bagne*. Thanks to you and my brother, I'm going to be free at last. Maybe if the French ever leave Indochina, I'll even be able to return to my own country."

He seemed to trust me, and the fact that I liked the boat made him as happy as a bird. I felt pretty good too. I was spending my last night on the little island—my last night, I hoped, in Guiana.

If I could get to the open sea, I'd be free. No question about that. The only danger then would be shipwreck. The war had been good for one thing: since it had begun, no convict had been returned to the country he'd escaped from. Of course, if we messed up the *cavale* and were caught, we'd be sentenced to death. I thought of Sylvain. He would have been here with me if he hadn't pulled that half-assed stunt. I fell asleep composing a cable, "Prosecutor Pradel: I've finally definitely escaped the hellhole you sent me to. It took nine years . . ."

The sun was quite high when Cuic-Cuic woke me. We had tea and rice cakes. There were tin cans all over the place. Then I noticed two wicker cages.

"What are you doing with those?"

"They're for my chickens. We can eat them on the *cavale*."

"You're out of your mind, Cuic-Cuic! We're not taking any chickens with us."

"But I want to."

"Are you crazy? You realize what'll happen at daybreak? Your chickens and roosters will be crowing and clucking like mad."

"I won't leave without my chickens."

"All right then. Cook them now and pack them in oil. That'll help preserve them. We'll eat them our first three days out."

He was finally convinced and went off in search of his hens. But the shrieks of the first four he caught must have been a warning to the others. They disappeared into the brush and he wasn't able to catch any more. It's always been a mystery to me how animals smell out danger.

Loaded down like pack mules, we crossed the quicksand behind the pig. Cuic-Cuic begged me to let the pig go with us.

"You swear he won't make a sound?"

"I swear it. He shuts up when I tell him to. Even the couple of times we were chased by a tiger, his hair stood straight up with fear, but he didn't make a sound."

Cuic-Cuic convinced me, so I agreed to take his cherished friend. It was night by the time we reached the place where the boat was hidden. Chocolat was there with Van Hue. With two flashlights I checked to make sure that everything was in order. Nothing missing. The sail rings were around the mast and the jib was in place, ready to be hoisted. I had Cuic-Cuic try the maneuver two or three times. He got it right away. I paid off the black—he'd done a remarkably thorough job. He was so trusting he'd brought gummed tape and the other halves of the bills and asked me to stick them together. It never occurred to him I might take off with all the money. Those who trust others are trustworthy themselves. Chocolat was a good guy. He had seen how convicts were treated, and he felt no guilt about helping three men escape that hell.

"Good-by, Chocolat. Good luck to you and your family."

"Thank you. Thank you very much."

ELEVENTH NOTEBOOK

GOODBYE TO THE *BAGNE*

THE *CAVALE* WITH THE CHINESE

I WAS THE LAST ONE into the boat. Chocolat gave it a shove, and we moved off into the river. We had oars instead of paddles, one for Cuic-Cuic up front, the other for me in the stern.

It was raining. Each of us had a painted flour sack for a slicker.

The current was fast and full of eddies, but in spite of that we made it to the middle in less than an hour. With the help of the ebb tide we passed the beacons three hours later. I knew the sea must be near because the lights were at the mouth of the river. We hoisted sail and were out of the Kourou in a flash. The wind took us on the beam with such force that I had to let out the sail. We hit the sea with a bang, passing through the narrows like an arrow, and were soon far offshore. Twenty-five miles ahead, the lighthouse on Royale gave us our position.

Thirteen days before I had been standing on the far side of that lighthouse, on Diable. For all that our exit to the sea had gone undetected and Grande Terre was soon far behind us, it seemed to bring little joy to my Chinese buddies. Unlike me, these Celestials keep their feelings to themselves. Once we were on the open sea, Cuic-Cuic said in a mild tone of voice, "That was a good start." Van Hue added, "Yes. We made it with little trouble."

"Cuic-Cuic, I'm thirsty. Pour me a shot of rum."

They served me, then had a good slug themselves.

I didn't have a compass, but during my first *cavale* I had learned to navigate by the sun, moon, stars and wind. So, without hesitation, I took a bearing on Polaris and headed straight out to sea. The boat behaved well—it took each wave smoothly with almost no roll. The wind was strong, and by morning we were a long way from the coast and the Iles du Salut. I was tempted to backtrack to Diable to get a good look at it from the sea, but it would have been taking too much of a chance.

For six days we had rough weather but no rain or storms. A strong wind kept us heading in a westerly direction. Cuic-Cuic and Hue were first-rate companions: they never complained, not about the weather, the sun, or the cold at night. The only drawback was that neither would take the tiller to give me a few hours' rest. Three or four times a day they cooked. We had eaten all the hens and roosters. One day I said to Cuic as a joke, "When do we eat the pig?"

He almost had a fit.

"That animal is my friend. Before you kill it, you have to kill me."

My friends were busy all the time. There was always hot tea ready, and they did everything before you had to tell them. They even gave up smoking so I could have all the tobacco.

We had now been gone seven days. I was on the point of collapse. The sun was so hot that even the Chinese were cooked like a pair of lobsters. I just had to get some sleep. I made the tiller fast and left only a small bit of sail up. The boat would go wherever the wind pushed us. I slept like the dead for four hours.

I was awakened by a sudden thump, harder than usual, that almost made me jump out of my skin. I wet my face and in the process made the pleasant discovery that I had been shaved while I slept. Cuic-Cuic had done it and I hadn't felt a thing. And he had oiled my face into the bargain.

Since last night I'd been heading west by southwest, for I thought I had gone too far north. This was because, in addition to being very steady, the boat had the advantage of resisting drift. I hadn't realized this when I made my calculations, so we got somewhat off course.

Suddenly, up in the sky, I saw a dirigible, the first I'd ever seen. It didn't seem to be coming in our direction and it was too far away to estimate its size. The reflection of the sun on the aluminum was so brilliant it hurt to look at it. Now it seemed to be changing its course and coming straight for us. It was growing bigger and bigger, and in less than twenty minutes it was right over us. Cuic and his pal were so impressed by the machine that they kept up an endless babble in Chinese.

"For Christ's sake, talk French so I can understand you!"

"It's an English sausage," said Cuic.

"No, it's not exactly a sausage. It's a dirigible."

Now we could make out every detail. It was losing altitude, turning and turning above us in ever tightening circles. Signal flags were let down. But since we didn't know the first thing about flag language, we couldn't reply. The dirigible wouldn't give up though, and came even closer, so close we could see the people in the cabin. Then they headed straight for land, and less than an hour later a plane appeared and made several passes overhead.

The wind suddenly picked up, and the sea began to get rough.

But the horizon was clear on all sides so there was no danger of rain.

"Look!" said Van Hue.

"Where?"

"Over there. That dot between us and where land should be. That black dot is a boat."

"You sure?"

"I not only know it's a boat, I can also tell you it's some kind of torpedo boat."

"How do you know that?"

"Because there's no smoke coming from it."

In point of fact, only an hour later it was all too clear that it was a warship and it was coming straight for us. It was getting bigger every minute, moving with extraordinary speed. If it came too close, it would be very dangerous in this heavy sea. With its wake going contrary to the waves, it could easily sink us.

It was a pocket torpedo boat. As it came nearer, we could read *Tarpon* on its side, and a British flag hung from the bow. After making a semicircle, the boat came up slowly from behind, keeping carefully abreast of us. The crew was on deck, in the blue of the British Navy.

From the bridge an officer shouted through a megaphone in English, "Stop! Stop, you!"

"Cuic, let down the sails!"

We had the mainsail, spinnaker and jib down in less than two minutes. Only the waves kept us moving now and we were starting to slip sideways. This would be dangerous if we kept it up for long, especially with these high waves. A boat without some form of propulsion—whether motor or sail—won't respond to the tiller.

I cupped my hands and shouted, "Captain, you speak French?"

Another officer took the megaphone. "Yes, Captain, I under-stand French."

"What you want us to do?"

"Bring your boat alongside."

"No, it's too dangerous. We'll crack up."

"We're a warship on patrol. You must obey."

"I don't give a damn who you are. We're not at war with any-body."

"Aren't you survivors of a torpedoed ship?"

"No, we're escaped prisoners from a French *bagne*."

"What *bagne*? What's a *bagne*?"

"A prison, a penitentiary. We're convicts. Hard labor."

"Ah! Yes, now I understand. From Cayenne?"

"Yes, Cayenne."

"Where you heading?"

"British Honduras."

"It can't be done. You must head south-southwest and make for Georgetown. That's an order. You must obey it."

"O.K." I told Cuic to hoist sail and head out in the direction indicated.

We heard a motor behind us. It was a launch that had cast off from the bigger ship and was catching up with us. A sailor with a rifle slung over his shoulder stood in the bow. The launch came up on our starboard and literally grazed us without stopping or ask-ing us to stop. With one leap the sailor was in our boat. Then the launch turned back and rejoined the torpedo boat.

"Good afternoon," the sailor said in English.

He came and sat down beside me and put his hand on the tiller, pointing it a little more to the south. I watched him carefully. He was very good with the boat, no doubt about that. However, I stayed right next to him. You never knew. . . .

"Cigarettes?"

He took out three packs of English cigarettes and gave each of us one.

"My word," Cuic said, "they must have given him the three packs just as he leapt off. After all, you don't go around with three packs in your pockets."

I laughed, then turned my attention back to the Englishman, who was clearly a better sailor than I. I was free to let my mind wander. This time the *cavale* was really a success. I was free. A feeling of warmth crept through me and I realized my eyes were wet with tears.

Before the war ended, I'd have time to become established and win people's respect, wherever I ended up. The only difficulty was that, with the war on, I might not be able to choose where I wanted to live. But that made little difference. No matter where I settled, I would win the respect and confidence of both the ordinary people and the authorities. My way of life would have to be, would be, beyond reproach.

My victory gave me such an extraordinary feeling of security that it was all I could think of. At last, Papillon, you've won. The nine years are behind you and you've won. Thank you, God. You could have done it a little sooner, but Your ways are mysterious. I'm not really complaining because it's thanks to Your help that I'm still young, healthy and free.

My mind was roaming over the two years of French prisons and nine years of *bagne* when I felt a nudge on my arm. The sailor said, "Land."

At four o'clock we passed a blacked-out lighthouse and entered a big river—the Demerara. The launch reappeared. The sailor turned the tiller over to me and posted himself in the bow of the boat. A heavy rope was thrown to him from the launch and he tied it to the forward bench. He lowered the sails himself and, towed very gently by the launch, we sailed twelve miles up the yellow river, the torpedo boat two hundred yards behind. There was a bend in the river and there, spread out in front of us, was a large city. "Georgetown," announced the British sailor. There were freighters, warships and motorboats everywhere, and gun turrets bristled on either side of the water. There were whole arsenals on the navy ships, as well as on land.

We knew a war was on, yet during the years since it had started we in the *bagne* had been completely untouched by it. But Georgetown was on a 100 percent war footing. It gave me a funny feeling to be in an armed city. We drew up to a military pier and the torpedo boat came alongside. Cuic and his pig, Hue carrying a small bundle, and I, empty-handed, climbed up onto the quay.

TWELFTH NOTEBOOK

CAVALE FROM GEORGETOWN

EIGHT DAYS LATER, AFTER A few formalities necessitated by the war, we were free. We went to live with three escaped French convicts who had established themselves in the Hindu quarter of Georgetown and sold fresh vegetables to American sailors in port. I did some professional tattooing on the side. After various stints as restaurant keeper, dealer in butterflies and operator of a striptease joint up in a bauxite mining town—all of which got me and my Chinese partners into trouble with the police—I decided I'd had enough of British Guiana. Cuic-Cuic and Van Hue stayed behind.

Without proper authorization—the war made this a serious offense—and naturally with no passports, five of us, all liberated or escaped cons, set out to sea in a sturdy boat and headed north. We ran into a terrible typhoon and lost everything, the top half of our mast, sail, tiller and all our supplies. All that remained were a small paddle and the clothes on our backs. We used the paddle as a rudder; then we stripped to our undershirts and, with the help of a small roll of wire that had survived the storm, we made a sail out of our pants, jackets and shirts, and attached it to what was left of the mast.

The trade winds picked up and I used them to head due south. I didn't care where we landed, even if it meant going back to British Guiana. The sentence that awaited us there would be welcome after what we'd gone through. My comrades had done themselves proud during and after the storm—which was hardly the word for it—better cataclysm, deluge, cyclone.

We had been out six days—the last two in a dead calm—when we sighted land, or so I thought. I headed for it immediately but decided to say nothing until I was sure. Suddenly there were birds overhead; I must be right. My friends woke up at the sound of their cries. They had been lying in the bottom of the boat, stupefied by the sun and fatigue, their arms across their faces to protect them from the rays.

"Where do you think we are, Papi?" said Chapar.

"Frankly, I don't know. If that piece of land isn't an island, if it's a bay, then it could be the tip of British Guiana—the part that extends to the Orinoco and divides it from Venezuela. But if there's a big space between the land on the right and on the left, then it's not a peninsula but Trinidad. The left side would be Venezuela; that would mean we were in the Gulf of Paria."

I seemed to remember this from the nautical maps I'd studied some time ago. If it was Trinidad on the right and Venezuela on the left, which should we choose? Our fate hung on this decision. With a good fresh wind in our sail, it wouldn't be too difficult to make the coast. For the moment we were heading between the two. Trinidad would mean the same "roast-beefs," the same government as British Guiana.

"They're sure to treat us well," said Guittou.

"Maybe, but what will they do to us for leaving British territory in time of war without proper authorization?"

"What about Venezuela?"

"There's no way of knowing," said Deplanque. "When President Gomez was in power, they made the cons work in road gangs under terrible conditions, then turned them over to France."

"The war may have changed all that."

"But from what I heard in Georgetown, they're neutral."

"Are you sure?"

"Positive."

"Then it's dangerous for us."

We could make out lights on both sides. Then we heard a foghorn—three blasts in a row. Signal lights showed on the right. The moon came out directly in front of our bow. Immediately ahead were two enormous pointed rocks, rising very black out of the sea. They must be the reason for the foghorn.

"Look, floating buoys! There's a whole line of them. Why don't we tie up to one and wait here for daylight? Let down the sail, Chapar."

He dropped the remnants of pants and shirts I had dignified with the name of "sail" and, braking with the paddle, I turned toward one of the "buoys." Luckily a length of rope hanging from the bow had escaped the typhoon's fury. There—we were tied up. Not exactly to the buoy itself, for the strange contraption had nothing you could tie anything to, but to the chain that connected it with the next buoy. It seemed to be a cable marking the channel. We closed our ears to the persistent foghorn and lay down in the bottom of the boat, covered by the sail to protect us from the wind. I felt a gentle warmth creep through my body and fell into a deep sleep.

I awoke to a clear day. The sun was just rising, the sea was fairly heavy, and its blue-green color indicated that the bottom was coral.

"What we going to do? Are we going to land? I'm famished and dying of thirst."

It was the first complaint in all these days of forced fasting—today being the seventh.

"We're so near we might as well land." It was Chapar talking.

From my bench I could clearly see the broken coastline behind the two big rocks. It must be Trinidad to the right and Venezuela to the left. There was no doubt about it: we were in the Gulf of Paria, and the only reason the water wasn't yellow with the silt from the Orinoco was that we were in the middle of the channel to the sea.

"O.K. What do we do? You guys are going to have to decide. It's too big a decision for one man. On the right, we've got the British island of Trinidad; on the left, Venezuela. One thing is certain—given the condition of our boat and our physical condition, we should get to shore as soon as possible. Two of you are liberated cons: Guittou and Corbière. The rest of us—Chapar, Deplanque and I— are in real danger. So actually the three of us should decide. What do you say?"

"It would make more sense to go to Trinidad. Venezuela's an unknown quantity."

"I don't think we'll have to make a decision. It looks like that launch is going to make it for us," Deplanque said.

Sure enough, a launch was heading straight at us. It stopped fifty yards off and a man picked up a megaphone. I could see that the flag wasn't British: lots of stars, very beautiful. I'd never seen it before in my life. It had to be Venezuelan. (Later that flag was to be "my flag," the flag of my new country—to me, the most moving symbol because there, wrapped up in a piece of cloth, were all the noblest qualities of a great people, my people.)

"Who are you?" the man with the megaphone shouted in Spanish.

"We're French."

"Are you crazy?"

"Why do you ask that?"

"Because you're tied up to a string of mines!"

"Is that why you don't come closer?"

"Yes. Get out of there fast."

It took Chapar just three seconds to untie the knot. Unbelievable! We had tied ourselves to a chain of floating mines! It was a miracle we hadn't been blown to bits. The launch took us in tow and the crew passed us some coffee, hot sweetened milk and cigarettes.

"Go to Venezuela. You'll be treated well. We can't tow you all the way because we just got an S O S to pick up someone who's been badly hurt at the Barimas lighthouse. Don't go to Trinidad. Nine chances out of ten you'll strike a mine and then . . ."

After a "Good-by, good luck," the launch moved off, leaving us two quarts of milk. We hoisted sail. At ten o'clock, my stomach almost back in shape from the infusion of coffee and milk, a cigarette between my lips, heedless of all danger, I beached the boat on a stretch of fine sand. At least fifty people were standing waiting to see what on earth could be arriving in this strange vessel with its broken mast and a sail made of shirts and pants.

THIRTEENTH NOTEBOOK

VENEZUELA

THE FISHERMEN OF IRAPA

I DISCOVERED A WORLD, A people, a civilization totally unknown to me. Those first minutes on Venezuelan soil were so moving, it would take a talent far greater than mine to describe the warm welcome we received from these generous people. The men were both blacks and whites, though most of them were the tan of a white man who's been in the sun a few days. Almost all wore their pants rolled up to the knees.

"You poor people! You really are in sad shape . . . !" one of the men said.

The fishing village where we had landed was called Irapa—it was located in the state of Sucre. The young women were all pretty, on the small side but very gracious and hospitable; the middle-aged and old women immediately turned into nurses and substitute mothers for us.

They hung five woolen hammocks in a shed next to one of the

houses, furnished it with a table and chairs, then coated us with cocoa butter from head to foot, not missing an inch of raw flesh. These good people of the coast knew we needed sleep and that we should be fed only in very small amounts.

Almost asleep in our comfortable hammocks, we were fed tidbits by our volunteer nurses—like young birds being fed by their mother. I was so exhausted that what little strength I had gave way completely the moment I hit the hammock. With the layers of cocoa butter coating my raw sores, I literally melted away. I slept, ate, drank, without being fully aware of what was going on.

My empty stomach rejected the first spoonfuls of tapioca. And I wasn't the only one. All of us vomited most of the food the women tried to spoon into our mouths.

The people of Irapa were very poor, but there wasn't one who didn't try to help. Thanks to their care and our youth, we were almost back to normal in three days. We spent long hours talking to the people as we sat in the pleasant shade of our palm-leaved shed. They couldn't afford to clothe us all at once, so they formed little groups: one took care of Guittou, another of Deplanque, and so on. About ten people took care of me.

For the first few days we wore anything and everything, but whatever it was, it was always spotlessly clean. Later, whenever they could manage it, they bought us a new shirt, or pants, a belt, or a pair of slippers. Among the women who took care of me were two very young girls—Indians mixed with Spanish or Portuguese blood. One was called Tibisay, the other Nenita. They bought me a shirt, pants and a pair of slippers they called *aspargate*. They had leather soles and the part that covered the foot was made of cloth. The toes were left bare and the material looped around the heel.

"We don't need to ask where you come from. We know from your tattoos you're prisoners escaped from the French *bagne*."

That was amazing. They knew we were convicts, they knew

about the prisons we'd been in from newspapers and magazines, yet these people thought it perfectly natural to come to our rescue and help us. To clothe someone when you're well off, or to feed a hungry stranger when it doesn't deprive you or your family of anything, is already something. But to cut a corn or tapioca cake in two and share with a stranger a meal that is already too meager for your own people—not only a stranger but a fugitive from justice— that is truly admirable.

Then, one morning, all the villagers were silent. They seemed upset and worried. What was going on? Tibisay and Nenita watched me as I shaved for the first time in two weeks. In the eight days we had been with these warm-hearted people, a thin skin had begun to form over my burns and I thought I could risk it. Because of my beard, the girls had had no idea how old I was. When they saw me clean shaven, they were thrilled and told me in their naïve way that they found me young. Although I was thirty-five, I still managed to look twenty-eight or thirty. But something was bothering them. I could feel it in my bones.

"What's going on? Tell me, Tibisay, what is it?"

"We're expecting the authorities from Güiria any minute. We don't have any police here, but somehow their police found out about you. They're on their way."

A tall handsome black woman came over to me, along with a young man with the beautifully proportioned body of an athlete. The woman was called La Negrita, the affectionate name for colored women used all over Venezuela, where there is absolutely no discrimination, either racial or religious. She said to me, "Señor Enrique, the police are on their way. I don't know whether they mean good or ill. Why don't you hide in the mountains for a while? My brother can show you the way to a small house where no one can possibly find you. Between Tibisay, Nenita and me, we can bring you the news and something to eat every day."

I was so touched that I reached for her hand to kiss it, but she pulled it back and, in the purest way, kissed me on the cheek.

Then a group of horsemen came thundering in like an express train. Each had a machete hanging from his left side like a sword, a belt full of ammunition and an enormous revolver in a holster hanging from the right hip. They leapt to the ground, and a big, bronze skinned man with the Mongol features and hooded eyes of an Indian came up to us. He was about forty years old and wore an enormous straw hat.

"Good day. I'm the chief of police."

"Good day, sir."

"Why didn't you tell us you had five escaped prisoners from French Guiana? I hear they've been here eight days."

"We were waiting till they were well enough to walk and their burns were healed."

"Well, we're taking them back to Güiria. A truck is coming for them."

"Would you care for some coffee?"

"Yes, thanks."

We sat down in a circle and everybody had some coffee. I looked at the chief of police and the rest of his men. They didn't look mean. They gave the impression of obeying orders they didn't necessarily go along with.

"You escaped from Diable?"

"No, we came from Georgetown in British Guiana."

"Why didn't you stay there?"

"It's too hard earning a living there."

He said with a smile, "You thought it would be better here than with the English?"

"Yes. Besides, we're Latins like you."

A group of seven or eight men came up to our circle. At their head was a man of about fifty, white-haired, almost six feet tall, with a light chocolate-colored skin. His huge black eyes betokened a rare intelligence and spirit. His right hand was resting on the handle of his machete. "Chief, what are you going to do with these men?"

"I'm taking them to the prison in Güiria."

"Why can't you let them live with us? Each family will take one."

"Can't. I have orders from the governor."

"But they've done nothing wrong in Venezuela."

"I know. But they're dangerous men or they wouldn't have been condemned to the French *bagne*. They must have committed some serious crimes. Besides, they escaped with no identification and their own police will certainly claim them when they learn they're in Venezuela."

"We would like to keep them with us."

"Impossible. Governor's orders."

"Anything's possible. What does the governor know about people like these? No man is ruined forever. No matter what he's done, there comes a moment in his life when he can be saved, when he can be made into someone good and useful to the community. What do the rest of you say?"

Like a chorus, they said, "Yes. Leave them to us. We'll help them make a new life. Eight days have been enough to show us they're good men."

The chief of police replied, "Men more civilized than us locked them up in dungeons so they couldn't go on doing harm."

"What do you call civilized, chief?" I asked. "You think because the French have elevators, airplanes and a train that runs underground it proves they are more civilized than these people who took us in and nursed us? In my opinion, these people here have a more humane civilization, more generous souls and greater understanding because they live close to nature and without the benefits of a technological civilization. What they lack in the way of progress they make up for in a Christian charity that puts the so-called civilized nations to shame. I'll take an illiterate from this hamlet any day over a graduate of the Sorbonne in Paris—especially if he's like the prosecutor who condemned me to the *bagne*. The first is a man, the second has forgotten how to be one."

"I get your point. All the same, I'm only an instrument. And here's the truck anyway. Please, try to have the right attitude—it will make things a lot easier."

Each group of women embraced her particular charge. Tibisay, Nenita and La Negrita wept as they kissed me good-by. Each man in turn shook hands with us to show how he suffered to see us go to prison.

"Farewell, you good people of Irapa. If I'm ever free again, I'll try to help others the way you—the first people I met in Venezuela—helped me." I was to meet many more like them in later years.

THE *BAGNE* AT EL DORADO

Two hours later we arrived at Güiria, a big village with a port and the pretensions of a city. The chief of police turned us over personally to the district police commissioner. We weren't too badly treated at the police station, but we had to submit to an interrogation by a dim-witted official who wouldn't accept the fact that we had come from British Guiana and that we had been free men there. In addition, he asked us to explain why we had arrived in Venezuela in such a sorry condition after what had been really a very short trip. Then he accused us of trying to make a fool of him with our story of the typhoon.

"You tell me that two huge banana trees keeled over in that tornado, a freighter carrying bauxite went down with everyone on

board, and you—in a fifteen-foot tub wide open to the elements—
came through? Who'll believe you? Not even a senile old beggar in
the marketplace would fall for that one. You're lying."

"Why don't you get in touch with Georgetown?"

"I don't want to get involved with the English."

God knows what kind of report that mulish, pretentious boob
sent off to his superiors. In any event, we were awakened one
morning at five o'clock, put in chains and loaded into a truck.
With ten policemen to guard us, we headed for Ciudad Bolívar, the
capital of the state of Bolívar. The dirt roads made the trip an
agony. Police and prisoners alike, we rattled and shook like a sack
of nuts on the truck floor; it was worse than a toboggan. The trip
lasted five days. We slept in the truck every night, and every morning we started off again on this wild journey toward an unknown
destination. We were all in very poor shape when we finally
arrived in the village of El Dorado.

What was this El Dorado? First, it represented a dream of the
Spanish conquistadores; they had noticed that the Indians from
this region had gold and were therefore convinced that there must
be a mountain of gold or, at the very least, half gold, half earth.
Actually El Dorado was a village on a river full of piranhas—a car-
nivorous fish that devours man or beast in a few hours—and electric fish, the *tembladores*, that electrocute their prey as they swim
around him, then suck the victim as he decomposes. In the middle
of the river was an island and, on the island, a real concentration
camp. This was the Venezuelan *bagne*.

This hard-labor camp was the most inhuman I'd ever seen. It
was a compound about five hundred feet square, surrounded by
barbed wire and with no shelter of any kind. Nearly four hundred
men slept under the sky, exposed to all weathers. Here and there
there were a few a small shelters roofed with zinc.

Without asking us a single question, without giving us any reason for what they were doing, they locked us into the *bagne* at El Dorado at three in the afternoon. We were dead from fatigue after the exhausting trip chained in the truck. At three-thirty—they hadn't even asked us our names—two of us were given shovels and the other three pickaxes. Five soldiers surrounded us, rifles and bullwhips in hand, and a corporal ordered us to the work area under pain of being whipped. We got the point—they were out to demonstrate their authority. It would be very dangerous to disobey them now. Later on, perhaps.

When we reached the work area, we were told to dig a trench along the side of the road that was being built through the virgin forest. We obeyed without a word and went to work with what strength we had, never looking up. But this didn't prevent us from hearing how the guards cursed and flayed the other prisoners. Not one of us was touched. I was convinced that we'd been put to work the moment we arrived to impress upon us our status as prisoners.

After work, covered with dust and sweat, we were admitted back into the prisoners' camp. Still no formalities.

"The five Frenchies, this way." It was our corporal. He was a half-breed, six feet four inches tall. He carried a bullwhip and was in charge of discipline inside the camp.

We were shown where to hang our hammocks near the entrance to the camp. It was in the open, although we did have a zinc roof to keep out the sun and rain.

The majority of the prisoners were Colombians; the rest were Venezuelans. None of the disciplinary camps in the French *bagne* could compare to the horrors of this place. A mule would have died from the treatment they gave the prisoners, yet everybody seemed to be in good health. The reason for this was that the food was plentiful and good.

We held a council of war. We decided that if one of us was hit by a soldier, the best thing to do would be to stop work and lie on the ground. No matter how badly they beat us, we would not get up. Surely a superior officer would turn up one of these days, and somebody would tell us why we were in this *bagne* when we had committed no crime. Our two liberated cons—Guittou and Corbière—considered asking to be returned to France. Then we decided to call Negro Blanco, the corporal, over. I was chosen to do the talking. Guittou went to get him. The cutthroat arrived, his bullwhip in hand, and we gathered around him.

"What do you want?"

I spoke up. "We want to tell you something. We don't intend ever to break a single rule of this *bagne*, and you'll never have a reason to strike us. But we have noticed that you often hit people for no reason whatsoever. So we called you here to tell you that the day you strike any one of us, you're a dead man. Understand?"

"Yes," said Negro Blanco.

"One last piece of advice."

"Yes," he said in a low voice.

"If you have to repeat what I just told you, see that it's to an officer, not a soldier."

"O.K." He went off.

This happened on a Sunday when the prisoners didn't have to work.

An officer came to see us soon afterward. "What's your name?"

"Papillon."

"You're the leader of the Frenchmen?"

"There are five of us and we're all leaders."

"Why were you the one who spoke to the corporal?"

"Because I speak better Spanish."

He was only a captain in the national guard, not the warden of the prison. There were two officers above him, he said, but they were away. Since our arrival he'd been in charge. The other two would be coming back Tuesday.

"In speaking for your group, you threatened to kill the corporal if he struck any of you. Is that right?"

"Yes, and I meant it. But I want to point out that I also told him that at no time would we do anything that justified corporal punishment. Captain, do you know we haven't been convicted by any court, that we've committed no crime in Venezuela?"

"I don't know anything about that. You men arrived at the camp without papers and with only a note from the commissioner in the village: 'Put these men to work as soon as they arrive.' "

"All right then, Captain, be fair. While you're waiting for your superiors to arrive, tell your soldiers we're not to be treated the same as the other prisoners. To repeat, we cannot be treated as convicts for we've committed no offense of any kind in Venezuela."

"All right, I'll deliver the order. I just hope you're not trying to put something over on me."

During the afternoon I took time out to study the prisoners. First, I was amazed to see how healthy they were. Second, I got the impression they were so used to being beaten that when Sunday came, and it was easy to avoid confrontations, they took a masochistic pleasure in provoking their tormentors. They insisted on doing things that were forbidden: they played with dice, they screwed in the toilets, they stole from their friends, they made obscene remarks to the women who came from the village with candy and cigarettes for the prisoners. These women also did some bartering, exchanging woven baskets or small sculptures for money and cigarettes. Some of the prisoners took what the women offered through the barbed wire, then ran off without paying up and disappeared into the crowd. It was obvious that the unfair and unreasonable corporal punishment had provoked a reign of terror throughout the camp which was without benefit to society, law, or order, and in no way corrected the unfortunate inmates.

Even so, the Réclusion at Saint-Joseph was much worse. There it was the silence. Here the fear was short-lived; you could talk at night and when you weren't working, as on Sundays, and there was the rich and abundant food. It meant a man could easily get through his sentence, which was never more than five years in any case.

We spent Sunday smoking and drinking coffee as we talked among ourselves. Some Colombians tried to approach us, but we told them gently but firmly to go away. We were determined to be considered different from the other prisoners. Otherwise we were in for it.

The next day we ate a huge breakfast and filed off to work with the others. We were lined up in two rows facing each other: one row consisted of fifty prisoners, the other of fifty soldiers. One soldier to each prisoner. Between the two rows lay fifty tools: shovels, pickaxes and hatchets. The two rows looked at each other, the prisoners in a state of terror, the soldiers nervous and sadistic.

The sergeant called out a name and a tool. The poor bugger grabbed it, flung it over his shoulder and ran off to start work as the sergeant called out "Number X," meaning a soldier. The soldier fell in behind the poor *mec* and beat him with his whip. This scene was repeated twice a day. It didn't look like men going off to work; it looked like mule drivers thrashing their beasts.

We were scared shitless as we waited our turn. But with us it was different.

"The five Frenchies, this way! You younger ones, pick up those pickaxes; the old men, take these two spades."

We set off toward the work area at a good clip, with four soldiers and a corporal to guard us. This day was worse than the first. Men who had been singled out for special abuse were at the end of their rope and were pleading on their knees for the beating to stop. In the afternoon the prisoners were ordered to gather some scattered pieces of wood from fires that hadn't quite gone out in order to make one big pile. Others were to clean up behind them. The idea was that, instead of a hundred sticks smoldering here and there, there was to be one big fire in the middle of the field. Each soldier whipped his prisoner to make him move faster as he picked up the wood and ran with it to the pile. This devilish relay race had already pushed some of the *mecs* over the brink of sanity and in their hurry they were picking up wood that was still burning. Their hands were on fire, they were walking over the hot coals in their bare feet. This demon dance lasted three hours. Luckily for us, none of us were ordered to take part, for as we were digging, we had decided—in clipped sentences, barely raising our heads—that we would leap on our five soldiers and the corporal, disarm them and shoot into the band of savages on the field.

Tuesday we didn't work but were summoned before the two officers. They were astonished that we should be at El Dorado without documents and without a tribunal having sent us there. They promised to ask the head warden for an explanation the next day.

It didn't take long. The two officers were strict and unnecessarily repressive, but they were correct; they demanded that the head warden come and explain the situation in person.

He was now standing before us with his brother-in-law and the two officers. "I am the warden of the penal colony at El Dorado. You asked to speak with me. What do you want?"

"First, we want to know what tribunal condemned us to this camp? How long is our sentence and what was our crime? We arrived in Irapa by sea. We have committed no offense. So what are we doing here? How do you justify making us work?"

"First of all, we're at war. We must know exactly who you are."

"That may be, but it doesn't justify being locked up in your *bagne*."

"You escaped from French justice. We have to find out if France wants you back."

"Again, that may be. But I repeat, why do you treat us as if we were serving a sentence?"

"For the moment you're here under the vagrancy laws while we proceed to document your case."

This discussion would have gone on forever if one of the officers hadn't cut through the garbage. "Warden, in all honesty, we can't treat these men the way we treat the other prisoners. I suggest that while we wait for word from Caracas, we find some other way of keeping them busy."

"These are dangerous men. They threatened to kill the corporal if he hit them. Isn't that true?"

"Not only did we threaten him, sir, we threatened to kill anybody who took it into their heads to hit any one of us."

"What if it was a soldier?"

"Same thing. We've done nothing to deserve this treatment. Maybe our laws and penal systems are worse than yours, but to be beaten like an animal, that's too much."

The warden turned toward the officers with a look of triumph. "See how dangerous these men are!"

The older of the two officers hesitated for a second. Then, to everybody's astonishment, he said, "These French fugitives are right. There's nothing in Venezuela that justifies their being made to serve a sentence or being subjected to the regulations of this colony. I agree with them there. Warden, either you find them some kind of work away from the other prisoners, or they don't work at all. If they're in with everybody else, sooner or later some soldier is bound to beat them."

"We'll see about that. Leave them in the camp for now. I'll tell you what to do in the morning." Then the warden and his brother-in-law left.

I thanked the officers. They gave us cigarettes and promised that at the evening report they would instruct the officers and soldiers not to strike us under any pretext.

We'd now been here eight days. We had stopped working. Yesterday was Sunday and a terrible thing happened. The Colombians drew lots to see who was to kill Negro Blanco. A man of about thirty lost. He was given an iron spoon, the handle of which had been sharpened on the cement into a pointed, double-edged lance. He stuck bravely by his pact and stabbed Negro Blanco three times near the heart. The half-breed was carried off to the hospital and his assassin was bound to a stake in the middle of the camp. The soldiers went berserk; they searched everybody for weapons and beat the prisoners mercilessly. I wasn't fast enough taking off my pants and one of the frenzied soldiers whipped me on my rear. Corbière picked up a bench and raised it over the man's head. Another soldier pierced his arm with his bayonet, and at the same moment I flattened my attacker with a kick in the belly. I had already picked up his rifle when a loud voice reached us:

"Stop! Don't touch the Frenchies! Frenchie, put down that rifle!" It was Captain Flores, the man who had received us the day we arrived.

He intervened just as I was about to shoot into the melee. If he hadn't, we might have killed a couple of soldiers, but we certainly would have lost our own lives, stupidly, in the far reaches of Venezuela at the other end of the world in a *bagne* where we had no business being.

Thanks to the captain's forceful intervention, the soldiers left us and vented their lust for carnage elsewhere. That was when we had to witness the ghastliest spectacle I'd ever seen.

The poor devil who was bound to the stake in the middle of the camp was systematically whipped by three men at a time, corporals as well as privates. It lasted from five in the afternoon to the next morning at six, meaning sunrise. It takes a long time to kill a man with a whip. They stopped briefly three times to ask him who his accomplices were, who had given him the spoon and who had sharpened it. The man said nothing, even when they promised to end the ordeal if he talked. He lost consciousness several times. They brought him to by throwing buckets of water on him. The worst came at four in the morning. The men whipping him noticed that he wasn't reacting; the contractions of the muscles had stopped.

An officer asked, "Is he dead?"

"We can't tell."

"Well, untie him and put him on all fours."

Propped up by four men, he was more or less on all fours. Then one of the executioners let go a snap of the whip between the man's buttocks that must have reached up and around his genitals. That masterly stroke finally tore a cry of pain from him.

"Keep it up," the officer said. "He isn't dead yet."

He was whipped until sunrise. This bastinado worthy of the Middle Ages was enough to kill a horse, but not this man. They left off the flogging for an hour, and then, watered down with several bucketfuls of water, he was able to get to his feet with the help of some soldiers.

For a moment he managed to stand all by himself. An orderly arrived with a glass in his hand.

"Drink this," an officer ordered. "It'll revive you."

The man hesitated, then drank the stuff in one gulp. One minute later he had collapsed for all time. In his final agony one sentence escaped his lips, "You idiot, they've poisoned you."

Not one prisoner, us included, moved so much as his little finger. We were terrorized to a man. For the second time in my life I wanted to die. Then my attention became riveted to the rifle a soldier near me was holding carelessly. All that held me back was the thought that I would probably be killed before I had time to work the damn breech and shoot.

A month later Negro Blanco was all well again and once more the terror of the camp. But it was in the cards that he would die at El Dorado. One night one of the soldiers on duty aimed his gun at him as he was passing by.

"Down on your knees," the soldier ordered.

Negro Blanco obeyed.

"Say your prayers. You're about to die."

He let him say a short prayer and shot him three times. The prisoners said he'd done it because he couldn't stand the savage way the brute beat up the prisoners. Others claimed that Negro Blanco had squealed on the soldier to his superiors, saying that he had known him in Caracas before he began his military service and that he was a thief. He must have been buried not far from the con who had tried to kill Negro Blanco in the first place. The poor devil was probably a thief, too, but a man of very rare courage.

These events delayed a quick decision on our case. None of the prisoners worked for two weeks. Corbière's bayonet cut was expertly treated by a doctor in the village. For the moment we were held in respect. Chapar left us yesterday to become the warden's cook. Le Guittou and Corbière were freed, for our reports finally arrived from France. They had finished serving their sentences. I'd been using an Italian name. Now the report came through with my real name, my fingerprints and my life sentence, also the report that Deplanque had twenty years, as did Chapar. Proudly sticking out his chest, the warden shared with us the news from France: "You may have done nothing wrong in Venezuela, but we're going to keep you here a little longer before we give you your freedom. You'll have to work and behave yourselves. This will be an observation period."

The officers had complained to me several times about how hard it was to get fresh vegetables in the village. The colony had an area under cultivation but no vegetable garden. They grew rice, corn and black beans and that was all. I agreed to plant a kitchen garden if they provided the seeds. They agreed.

The good thing about this was that it got us out of camp. Two new cons had arrived—they'd been arrested in Ciudad Bolívar— and they joined Deplanque and me in the venture. Toto was from Paris and the other was a Corsican. We had two sturdy little houses built for us out of wood and palm leaves; Deplanque and I moved into one, our new friends into the other.

Toto and I made some high, sloping frames and set their legs in cans of gasoline to prevent the ants from reaching the seed. In no time we had healthy little plants of tomatoes, eggplants, melons and green beans. When they were large enough to resist the ants, we transplanted them. For the tomatoes, we dug a trench around each plant which was always filled with water. That kept the plants moist and discouraged the parasites that flourished in the virgin forest.

"Heh, look at this!" Toto said. "See how it sparkles!"

"Wash it, *mec*."

Then he handed it to me. It was a small crystal as big as a chickpea. Once it was washed, it sparkled even more, especially where the matrix was cracked, for it was still covered with a hard gray crust.

"Could it be a diamond?"

"Shut your trap, Toto. If it's a diamond, you don't want to broadcast it. Maybe we've stumbled on a diamond mine. Let's wait until tonight and meanwhile keep it hidden."

I gave mathematics lessons in the evenings to a corporal who was preparing to become an officer. (Today that corporal is Colonel Francisco Bolagno Utrera, and during our twenty-five-year friendship he has proved himself a man of great nobility and integrity.)

I asked him, "Francisco, what is this? Is it a piece of rock crystal?"

He examined it closely. "No, it's a diamond. Hide it and don't let anybody see it. Where did you find it?"

"Under my tomato plants."

"That's strange. You must have brought it up with the river water you use on the plants. Maybe your pail scrapes the bottom and comes up with a little sand?"

"It's possible."

"That must be it. You brought your diamond up from the Rio Caroní. Why don't you see if you didn't bring up more of them? But be careful. You never find just one precious stone. If you find one, there have to be others."

Toto went to work. He had never worked so hard in his life.

Our two pals—to whom we had said nothing—remarked, "What are you knocking yourself out for, Toto? You're going to kill yourself bringing up all those pails from the river. And why do you always bring up so much sand?"

"That's to lighten the soil, *mec*. If you mix it with sand, the water filters through better."

In spite of the teasing, Toto went on doggedly with his buckets. One day, during one of his trips, he fell flat on his face in front of where we were sitting in the shade. He spilled the bucket, and there in the sand was a diamond as big as two chick-peas. We wouldn't have noticed it except that the matrix was cracked. Toto made the mistake of grabbing it too fast.

"Hey!" Deplanque said. "That looks like a diamond! The soldiers told me there were diamonds and gold in the river."

"That's why I've been carrying all those buckets. I'm not as stupid as you think!" Toto was glad he could finally explain his labors.

To wind up the story of the diamonds, by the end of six months Toto had between seven and eight carats and I had a dozen, plus about thirty small ones in the "commercial" category, in mining terms. One day I found one of over six carats. I had it cut in Caracas later on and it produced a stone of nearly four carats which I had made into a ring. I still have it and wear it day and night. Deplanque also collected a few. I still had my *plan* so I put my stones in it. The others made *plans* out of the tips of cattle horns and kept their little treasures in those.

None of the soldiers knew anything about this except my friend the corporal. The tomatoes and all the rest grew tall and the officers paid us promptly for all the vegetables we brought to their mess.

We were relatively free. We worked without guards and slept in our little houses. We never went near the camp. We were respected and well treated. This didn't keep us from pressing the warden every chance we got to give us our complete freedom. He always answered, "Soon." Yet we'd been here eight months and nothing was happening. So I began to talk *cavale*. Toto wanted no part of it. Nor the others. I wanted to study the river, so I bought myself some fishing equipment. I sold the fish in addition to the vegetables, particularly the famous piranhas, weighing about two and half pounds each, with teeth like a shark's and equally fearsome.

There was a curious guy in the camp. His torso was completely covered with tattoos. On his neck was written "Screw the Coiffeur." His face was all twisted up, and his fat tongue hung out slobbering from his mouth. It was clear he had suffered a stroke. Where, no one knew. He was already there when we arrived. Where did he come from? The one sure thing was that he was an escaped *bagnard*. Tattooed on his chest was "Bat d'Af," which was the nickname of the French punishment brigade in Africa. No question about it: that and his "Screw the Coiffeur" made it clear he'd been a con.

Everybody called him Picolino. He was very well treated, got his food regularly three times a day, plus cigarettes. His intense blue eyes were full of life and sometimes even expressed happiness. When his eyes lighted on someone he loved, they glistened with joy. He understood everything you said to him, but he couldn't speak. Nor could he write, for his right arm was paralyzed and his left hand was missing the thumb and two fingers. This poor wreck spent hours hanging onto the barbed wire, waiting for me to come by on my way to the officers' mess with my vegetables. Every morning I stopped to talk to Picolino. He would lean on the barbed wire and look at me with those lively blue eyes in his dead body. I'd make a few pleasantries and he'd bob his head or blink his eyes to let me know he understood. For a moment his paralyzed face lighted up and his eyes gleamed with all the things he wished he could tell me. . . . I always brought him a few tidbits—a tomato, a lettuce or cucumber salad already dressed, or a small melon, or a fish cooked over the coals. He wasn't hungry because he ate so well, but it was a change from the regular diet. A few cigarettes rounded off my small offerings. These brief visits with Picolino became a habit, to such an extent that soldiers and prisoners referred to him as "Papillon's son."

FREEDOM

An extraordinary thing happened. I found the Venezuelans so appealing I decided to join my fate to theirs. No, I wouldn't go on a *cavale*. I would accept my unwarranted position as a prisoner in the hope that I would someday be one of them. It may seem paradoxical. The savage way they treated their prisoners was hardly likely to make me want to live with them, yet I came to understand why both prisoners and soldiers found the punishment normal. If a soldier did something wrong, he got a whipping too. And, a few days later, the same soldier would be talking to whoever had flogged him as if nothing had happened.

This barbarous system was the product of the dictator Gomez and had outlived him. There is still a civilian official who punishes the people under him with lashings of the bullwhip.

My liberation came in the wake of a revolution. A coup d'état, half military, half civilian, unseated General Angarita Medina, the president of the republic and one of the greatest liberals in Venezuela's history. He was such a good democrat that he didn't even try to resist the coup d'état. They say that he refused to let Venezuelans kill each other to keep him in power. I cannot believe that that great democratic soldier knew what was being perpetrated at El Dorado.

One month after the revolution all the officers were transferred. There was an inquiry into the death of the con who had stabbed Negro Blanco. The warden and his brother-in-law disappeared and were replaced by a former lawyer-diplomat.

"Papillon, I'm setting you free tomorrow, but I wish you'd take poor old Picolino with you. He has no identity card, but I'll make him one. Here's yours. It's all in order and has your right name.

Now these are the conditions: you must live in the country for a year before you move into the city. It will be a sort of parole so we can see how you're faring and what you're doing with yourself. If at the end of the year the district leader gives you a certificate of good conduct—as I believe he will—then your confinement is at an end. I think Caracas would be an ideal city for you. In any event, you're now legally authorized to live in this country. Your past is of no concern to us. It's up to you to show that you deserve the opportunity to become a respectable person. I hope you'll be my fellow citizen before five years are out. God go with you! And thanks for taking care of Picolino. I can give him his freedom only if someone states in writing that he'll take charge of him. Maybe a hospital can do something for him. Let's hope so."

I was to be set free with Picolino the next morning at seven. I felt a great warmth in my heart. I was done forever with the road of the condemned. It was October 18, 1945. I'd been waiting fourteen years for this day.

I withdrew into my little house. I made my excuses to my friends; I needed to be alone. The emotion I felt was too vast and too beautiful to expose to others. I turned my identity card over and over in my hand: my picture was in the left-hand corner and above it the number 1728629, and the date. In the middle, my last name, and under that, my first name. On the back was the date of my birth: November 16, 1906. Everything was in order—it was even signed and stamped by the Director of the Identification Service. My category in Venezuela: "resident." That was really something, that word *resident*. It meant I was domiciled in Venezuela. My heart was thumping. I wanted to get down on my knees to pray and thank God. "But, Papi, you don't know how to pray, and you've never been baptized. What God do you propose to pray to when you don't belong to any religion? The God of the Catholics? Of the Protestants? The Jews? The Mohammedans?" Whichever I chose, I would have to make up a prayer from scratch because I'd never known any prayer from start to finish. But what did it matter which God I prayed to? Whenever I'd called on Him or cursed Him in the past, hadn't I always thought of Him as the God that belonged to the baby Jesus in his manger with the donkey and the cows standing around? Maybe my subconscious still held a grudge against the good sisters in Colombia. So why didn't I close my mind to everything but the one and only sublime Bishop of Curaçao, Monsignor Irénée de Bruyne, and, further back still, the good father at the Conciergerie?

For all that I was innocent of the murder for which one public prosecutor, a few cops and twelve cheesehead jurymen had condemned me to hard labor for life, the fact is that I had been a bum. It was because I had been a bum and an adventurer that they had found it so easy to graft on their tissue of lies. I grant you, opening other people's safes is not a commendable profession, and society has the right and duty to protect itself from the likes of me. If I had been pitched down the road of the condemned, I have to be honest and admit that I had been a permanent candidate for the *bagne*. True, my punishment wasn't worthy of the French people, and if society needed to protect itself, it didn't have to sink so low—but that's beside the point. I can't erase my past with a swipe of the sponge. I must rehabilitate myself in my own eyes first, then in the eyes of others.

The great majority of Frenchmen will not admit that a man with my past can become a good man. That's the difference between the Venezuelan people and the French. You remember that poor fisherman in Irapa who tried to explain to the chief of police that no man is ever lost for good, that he must be given a chance to become an honest man? Those almost illiterate fishermen lost in the Gulf of Paria in the vast estuary of the Orinoco have a humane philosophy that many of my countrymen could envy. We have too much technological progress, life is too hectic, and our society has only one goal: to invent still more technological marvels to make life even easier and better. The craving for every new scientific discovery breeds a hunger for greater comfort and the constant struggle to achieve it. All that kills the soul, kills compassion, understanding, nobility. It leaves no time for caring what happens to other people, least of all criminals. Even the officials in Venezuela's remote areas are better for they're also concerned with public peace. It gives them many headaches, but they seem to believe that bringing about a man's salvation is worth the effort. I find that magnificent.

Yes, by God, I'd do everything in my power to become honest and stay that way. The one difficulty was that I'd never worked at anything, I didn't know how to do anything. But I wouldn't care what I did to earn a living. It might not be easy, but I'd manage somehow. I was sure of it. Tomorrow I'd be like other men.

Should I let my father know I was free? He'd had no word from me for years. I wondered where he was. Probably the only news he'd had about me was when the police looked him up each time I made a *cavale*. No, I mustn't hurry that one. I had no right to open a wound that the years might almost have healed. I'd write him when I was established, when I had a steady job, when my problems were behind me and I could say to him, "Father, your son is finally free and an honest man. Here's where I'm living, this is what I'm doing. You can hold your head up now. That's why I'm writing to say that I love you and will always think of you with deep respect."

It's not all that easy to step out of the chains you've been dragging around for fourteen years. They tell you you're free, they turn their backs on you, you're no longer being watched. It's that simple. Yet you still wonder. . . . You don't make over a life the way you sew on a button. And if today, twenty-three years later, I'm a married man with a daughter, living happily in Caracas as a Venezuelan citizen, I have to confess to many more adventures between then and now, some of them successful, some failures, but always as a free man and a good citizen. Maybe some day I'll write them down, along with other interesting stories I didn't have room for in this book.